D1
FOUNDATIONS

A Biblical Tour of Our Past, Present & Future

{RICK PETERMAN}

Publishing

> *This is a tool*
>
> *that God can use*
>
> *to give us a fresh*
>
> *exiting look at*
>
> *the Bible*

deepfoundations.org
Above is the new website & below is the original website.
revelationillumination.com
You are welcome to like Deep Foundations on Facebook.
facebook.com/deepfoundations.org
You are also welcome to view my teaching videos on YouTube.
The videos are early attempts to share some of the highlights found in this book but are not nearly as informative as this book.
youtube.com/user/RickeyPeterman
On a more personal level there are also activity videos at:
Youtube.com/Rickey Peterman Activities
&
facebook.com/RickeyPeterman

Table of Contents

General Information

Regarding the Author

Special Thanks

Introduction

Section 1 - Identification

Section 2 - Illustration

Section 3 - Application

Section 4 - Transformation

Section 5 - Illumination

General Information

The photograph: on the cover was taken by the author. This sunrise appeared on Christmas morning 2010. The perspective is from a lifeguard stand on Fort Lauderdale's Beach in Florida. It was a celebration of the conclusion of the rough draft of Revelation Illumination, which was the first edition of this book.

Section 1 – Identification: This section may not be as interesting as some following sections but it contains vital keys to help you understand how things work.

Section 2 – Illustration: This section will be very interesting to those who enjoy history. The main focus is the life and times of Jesus Christ.

Section 3 – Application: This section will help you find personal fulfillment and victory.

Section 4 – Transformation: This section will be very interesting to those who enjoy prophecy and want to envision our destiny.

Section 5 – Illumination: This section contains some final clarifying notes to help you understand the Bible and walk in wisdom.

Keys to get the most out of this book: All the scripture verses are from the King James translation of the Holy Bible, unless otherwise noted. For many of us the King James Bible is hard to read. Some old English words are odd and the spelling is sometimes different. For instance the word privately is spelled privily in Mathew 1:19, Mathew 2:7 and in twelve other verses throughout the King James Bible. That was fine in 1611 when the first edition of King James became available because Webster did not complete his dictionary until 1828. Therefore, there was no standard to verify the correct spelling of a word. Every legitimate translation of the Bible has it's strong and week points. Don't get hung up on a word or section in this book that doesn't make sense to you. Read on and consider what God clearly reveals to you. On the longer Bible passages concentrate on the key words, which are often underlined. Ask God to illuminate the main themes without struggling over distracting details. After you have seen the big picture, then go back and reread everything in order. Look closer at the details and see how all the Biblical references fit together to revel a portrait of transforming truth. I highly recommend highlighting things you want to remember and find again. You also may want to look up the verses in your favorite translation and note the ones you want to easily find again in your own Bibles. You will be amazed at the new insights and applications God will share with you. People have told me after reading the original edition of this book (which was called Revelation Illumination) that they seen something new every time they read it. This book contains the original and additional information as well as a better presentation. Originally, I was only going to use a Bible verse one time because I had so many to use. I thought it might emphasize that the Bible has much to say about many subjects. I decided to remove that self-imposed limitation because many verses have more than one message contained in them and some verses should be repeated for emphases. I don't mean to overuse capitalization, but to distinguish references to God I have capitalized all words referring to God. I have also capitalist words referring to the Holy Bible such as the "Word of God." Most do not capitalize earth but I did to distinguish between earth as references to dirt or ground and Earth the name of our planet. I also capitalized Heaven and Hell as names of specific places where people will spend eternity and not just a state of mind. Excessive capitalization may be a little harder to read but I hope you will pause and consider what is being stated. It is my hope and prayer that you do not let any prejudice or textual style blind you to the important realities presented in this book. You could look at this book like a three way conversation. There are God's Words, my commentary and your thoughts and prayers. I encourage you to talk to God and ask Him to clarify His Word to you (John 14:26). God's written Word is set apart with bold print. The many Bible verses presented in this book will do at least one of four things. They will introduce subjects, verify commentary, elaborate on the facts or conclude many of the topics.

Demons are real. They do not want you to read or understand the things contained in this book. They will attempt to distract you. They will try to promote shallow thinking and short attention spans that lead to distortions. It will take an effort on your part to focus on the many powerful truths reveled in this book and see beyond the cloud of confusion that has blinded most of our world. Ask God to show you things from the Bible that you have never seen before (John 16:12-13).

Regarding the Author

I was born September 3 1956 and given the name Rickey Lee Peterman. My parents named me after Little Ricky on the "I Love Lucy" show. I grew up in the countryside, about 25 miles northeast of Grand Rapids Michigan. If you were to tell any of my friends or teachers that I would one day write a book, they would probably laugh out loud, because I am dyslexic. That's why for many years I've been a tradesman working in my little auto body shop in Fort Lauderdale. I moved my body shop to its final location in 1985. That was the year I met Marsha. In February 1987 Marsha and I purchased our house and had our wedding on Valentines Day in the back yard on the dock. Work slowed down in 1999, so I let my last employee go and started working by my self with my wife Marsha doing the books. At the end of that year I found a neglected Corvette Stingray in tall weeds behind a warehouse and acquired it for $1500.^{00}. As you can imagine it needed a lot of work. I basically resurrected it from the dead. During the slow times at my shop, I was quite content rebuilding and upgrading my 1970 Vette into a trophy winning show car, which hit the road in 2011. At the same time I was finishing the car for its first car show, I was finishing the rough draft of my first book called *Revelation Illumination*. Like the car, I continued to make improvements to the book for the next several years. I'm not a professional writer. In fact, my clerical skills are probably one the weakest areas of my life. I thank God for my wife Marsha and spell-check. I also thank God for Kate Donohue who in 2012 took the time to read early transcripts and point out typos as well as teaching me some writing principals. The book still had typos and sections I wanted to improve, but near the end of 2012 I printed an initial 2500 hardcover copies anyway and I started distributing them. In 2014 I did a YouTube video series on the book called *Deep Foundations*. Deep Foundations would become the new name of the final edition of the book. I continued to work on the book almost daily and was exited about how God's Word was unfolding. In 2016 I sold my body shop and prepared to publish this life-changing book called *Deep Foundations*. When I began this project many years ago, I knew nothing about the business of writing or publishing a book. However, there was absolutely no doubt in my mind that God wanted to change that because in the end it's not about the messenger, it's about the message. (1 Corinthians 1:27)

Special Thanks & Gratitude

To Jesus Christ:

I thank God for providing the grace and opportunity to partner with Him to present this book to you. It was during a morning prayer walk, the Spirit of Christ provided the name Deep Foundations. The Holy Spirit of God also provided the inspirational insights to His Word and the encouragement to get through the many discouraging times. I also want to thank Jesus for His prayers to the Father on my behalf (John 17:20).

To My Wife Marsha:

For all her help and patience, especially in 2007/2008 converting my hand printing into type and introducing me to Microsoft Word.

To Kate Donohue:

For donating 10 months in 2011/2012 to go over grammar and discussing the written clarity of the forerunner of this book, which was called Revelation Illumination.

To Friends and Family:

I appreciate everyone that helping me to find typos and places to improve clarification. You may also contact me on Facebook if you find a typo or have a question.

Introduction

Have you ever thought about the big picture of life regarding origins, conflicts, and destiny? Can we truly understand the complexities of the Word of God? This book brings into harmony the Biblical truths and practical applications in order to dispel dangerous deceptions and distortions. The things revealed in Deep Foundations may shake things up a bit (Ezekiel 37:7). However I pray it helps unify the body of Christ in Biblical truth (John 17:17-21). The body of Christ is a Biblical reference that identifies the church. Satan attempts to divide and misguide the body of Christ by promoting religious traditions, misconceptions and heresies above God's Word. Metaphorically speaking, the church is like a massive fleet of ships (James 3:4-5). God desires that every ship adjust their rudder (words) to point at truth and find hidden treasures. If any find themselves off course and in a fog then the first step is to compare the setting of their rudder (words) with God's compass (the Bible). Even if everything seems to be smooth sailing, we should continue the check the compass because a little deviation over a long period of time results in a big unpleasant course correction later. If we consistently adjust our words to be in harmony with God's Word we will find true success. Knowing and speaking the truth in love is the goal of this book. By connecting the dots of truth and pulling back the veil of mystery and confusion in this extraordinary puzzle we call life, the portrait of reality is revealed. The reality is that you can understand God's treasure map and discover your purpose and potential to fulfill your destiny. Revealed are opportunities to realize and apply transforming information essential to making wise decisions. You will be empowered with keys to unlock your personal success and endless treasures. I think you will find this book enlightening, empowering, thought provoking, and well documented in the authority of Scripture. Each chapter contains unique gems not often seen in public. Many of the truths revealed in the coming pages are the result of many questions I had years ago. Finding there were no common or consistent answers to them, I went to our Creator, the source of truth. In God's Word I have found many amazing and consistent insights that have stood the test of time. Over the years, I have found these answers and insights have not only given me peace of mind, but have also enabled me to see many miraculous things. I have also included a few recent revelations to help you have an unshakable faith in the Bible.

Back cover

I believe the information contained in this book will be interesting, relevant, and useful to at least four types of people.

To the Skeptic:

The honest doubter can see how the Bible has logical and reasonable answers to the problems in our world. It reveals the causes and effects we see all around us, as well as the reasonable conclusions, we often don't see in time. (Galatians 6:7)

To the Truth Seeker:

You may be looking at all the different religions of the world with their isolated and disconnected ideas that promote contradictions. It is important to know how to test them to find out if they have true lasting treasure or are just an illusion that temporarily makes you feel good. (John 8:32)

To the Believer:

It gives a foundation for our belief, connecting the facts between the origins of Genesis 1 to the destiny of Revelation 22. By examining the details and illustrating the sequences of events, we can see and understand how redemption works, as well as the many benefits available to us. (Luke 6:48)

To the Spiritual Leader:

It encourages and challenges us with truth, exposing the Deceivers' strategy. It gives Biblical insight to the mysteries and questions of life. It helps us to envision our future rewards, reflect on our present position, and take a closer look at our past traditions and assumptions in the light of our ultimate authority, the Word of God. (2 Timothy 2:7)

Section 1

Identification

CHAPTER 1

RECEIVING TRUTH OR BLINDING DECEPTIONS

2 Timothy 2:15

15. **<u>Study</u> to shew thyself approved unto God, a workman that needeth not to be ashamed, <u>rightly dividing the Word of Truth</u>.**

The verse above states that there are right ways to "divide," put together, and interpret the Word of Truth. If Biblical truth is put together incorrectly or misapplied, it is no longer Biblical truth bringing light and life, but rather deception bringing darkness and confusion. The Bible is like a jigsaw puzzle. You can sometimes get the wrong piece to fit, but the pattern will be incorrect. The picture will be distorted, confusing, and misleading. I am not saying you need to understand the whole Bible to see what a verse is saying, because nobody but God understands every detail of the Bible. What I am saying is many times people compartmentalize truth. Many people also segment their life into spiritual and secular. Worst of all, many people believe things that have no foundation in the truth. These things lead to inconsistencies and false assumptions. Everyone needs to start somewhere to gain an understanding of the Bible. It is better for you to understand the Bible's basic themes now rather than latter, when it is too late to apply the benefit of what the Bible offers. The way most people begin a jigsaw puzzle is with the border outline. It's usually best to start your Biblical journey with a basic foundation or outline. Then as you fill in the details the big picture becomes clearer and you will realize the wisdom of God. God will help you to see new things in His Word when you are ready.

John 16:12

12. **<u>I have yet many things to say unto you</u>, but ye cannot bear them now.**

1

A part of spiritual growth is gaining a deeper understanding of the Bible and how to properly apply it to our life and circumstances. God will not contradict His Word. God will use His Scriptures to speak to us.

Psalm 19:8

8. **The statutes of the LORD are right, <u>rejoicing the heart</u>: the commandment of the LORD is pure, <u>enlightening the eyes</u>.**

Notice the "commandment of the LORD" is singular; so what is the commandment?

John 15:12

12. **This is <u>My commandment</u>, That ye <u>love</u> one another, as <u>I have loved you</u>.**

How much dose God love us?

John 3:16

16. **For <u>God so loved the world, that he gave His only begotten Son</u>, that <u>whosoever</u> believeth in Him should not perish, but have everlasting life.**

God's love was so strong that He was able to make the hard but necessary choices for the good of others. This is a foundation that even a child can understand. It is a foundation we can build on. We can connect all Biblical truths to this foundation either directly or indirectly (1Corinthians 3:11-14). Even if you know the Bible from cover to cover, it is good to make sure all the pieces are connected properly and you see the entire picture in the right light. "Selah" is a Biblical word used in the Psalms and Habakkuk. One definition is, "to pause and think about that." Because of the unique layout of this book I will often use *Selah* instead of dividing subjects into paragraphs. *Selah* (pause and think about that). The first word in the first verse of the first

2

chapter of this book is study. "Study" is not a bad word. It means you take time to think, <u>be consistent, and stay connected to the foundation of truth revealed in God's Word</u>. This is where meditation comes in. Meditation does for the mind what exercise does for the body. Meditating on the Bible is important and life changing because it strengthens, renews, and sharpens the mind. In order to grasp some truths, we must take time to refocus and organize our thoughts before we can see all the ramifications of the information. *Selah*. This book may be challenging for some to read, but like mental exercise it will strengthen your understanding of the Bible. Speed-reading is fine to get the context of the subjects and see the big picture, but then go back and look at the details. You can also skip ahead to read any chapter because each one addresses different subjects. However every chapter contains keys to better understand the following chapters. This book contains many scriptures and is a tool to get deeper into the Bible. The Bible is the true foundation. Bible study is the key to spiritual growth. Whether you spend time on one verse or one book of the Bible, try to picture what is being said and consider the meaning behind each word. Remember the principle and consider how you can apply it to your life. Look for God's voice to you in His Word. The Bible is a big complex book. If you don't know where to start, you might want to begin with the powerful truths in the Gospel of John of the New Testament. Take the time to ponder and pray about what it is God is saying to you. *Selah*. I remember as a boy seeing books that only had dots with numbers next to them. They didn't make much sense until I connected the dots. The dots were points of change, and once connected in order, the picture was obvious. In that same way, let's connect the points of Biblical truth in order, so that we can see the powerful pictures hidden in Genesis 1 through Revelation 22.

2 Timothy 3:16-17

16. **All Scripture is given by inspiration of God**, and is **profitable** for **doctrine**, for **reproof**, for **correction**, for **instruction in righteousness**:

17. **That the man of God may be perfect, thoroughly furnished unto all good works**.

The Bible is like a treasure map containing God's personal instruction and direction for life. God is the Author. He used a variety of different godly men as instruments, just as an author might use different pens or fonts, each having its own color or style. Nonetheless, the message comes from the author, not the instrument. *Selah.* All God's Word is true, but not necessarily all translations of His Word (more on that later). First, let's look at 2Timothy 3:16 and define the four important benefits mentioned there.

Doctrine: is the foundation or basis of our belief. True Biblical doctrine must include all of what the Bible says on a subject.

Reproof: is a strong discipline that calls us to repent from sin.

Correction: is course correction; an adjustment to refocus and refine our motives, actions, words and goals.

Instruction in Righteousness: is the key to abundant life. It is the blueprint for right living, which brings peace and fulfillment. It shows us how we overcome evil by doing good.

Notice that 2Timothy 3:17 ends with "good works." "Good works" are the result of knowing and doing what the Bible says. That is when we are furnished with rewards and abilities, both here and in Heaven. If we have no idea what the Bible says and think we are hearing God, it may actually be Satan, the angel of light, trying to deceive. We always need to test the spirits to see the source of the information. The tool for this test is God's Word, the Bible.

1 John 4:1

1. **Beloved, believe not every spirit, but try the spirits whether they are of God: because many false prophets are gone out into the world.**

Those preaching or believing in a false gospel will not be blessed by God in the end. The gospel is God's plan for salvation. It tells us how to receive eternal life, which qualifies us for Heaven. The Apostle Paul affirmed the importance of the Biblical gospel.

Galatians 1:8-9

8. **But though we, or an angel from Heaven, preach any other gospel unto you than that which we have preached unto you, let him be accursed.**

9. **As we said before, so say I now again, if any man preach any other gospel unto you than that ye have received, let him be accursed.**

After the risen Christ appeared to Paul on the road to Damascus, Paul quit following the man-made theology and traditions of his time. Jesus began revealing to him God's plan for his life. Paul was to be an instrument to record God's Word in the Holy Bible, which is now completed.

Galatians 1:11-12

11. **But I certify you, brethren, that the gospel which was preached of me is not after man.**

12. **For I neither received it of man, neither was I taught it, but by the revelation of Jesus Christ.**

Many honest skeptics have examined the Bible and discovered how true and life changing it is. One of them even wrote a best selling book regarding the Bible called *"Evidence that Demands a Verdict"* by Josh McDowell. Another one, who was an atheist from Yale University named Lee Strobel, set out to disprove the Bible. After thoroughly examining the facts, he became a Christian apologist. His findings lead him to write *"The Case for Christ"* and *"The Case for a Creator"* as well as many other books. This book assumes you already know or may consider that the Holy Bible is true. The fact is, God's Word is not only true, unique and historic; it is also eternal.

Luke 21:33, Mark 13:31

33. **Heaven and Earth shall <u>pass away</u>: but My Words shall <u>not pass away</u>.**

The Earth as we know it will pass away, as pointed out in Chapter 17 of this book; but the book for life, the Holy Bible, will never change or go away. In the end, only the distortions and counterfeits will be disintegrated, leaving the pure, true, Word inspired and authored by God. In the end God will properly connect every Biblical point and resolve every misconception. Then we will see the multidimensional Word of God like never before. For now we can believe God and trust God's Word for eternal life or later wished we did.

1 Peter 1:23-25

23. **Being born again, not of corruptible seed, but of <u>incorruptible</u>, by the <u>Word of God, which liveth and abideth for ever</u>**

24. **For all flesh is as grass, and all the glory of man as the flower of grass. The grass withereth, and the flower thereof falleth away:**

25. **But the <u>Word of the Lord endureth for ever. And this is the</u> <u>Word which by the gospel is preached unto you.</u>**

Is the Holy Bible less true if it contradicts many or any of our popular beliefs? Are we deceived if we believe a lie? *Selah.*

Exodus 23:30

30. **By little and little I will drive them out from before thee until thou be increased and inherit the land.**

In 1977, God used this passage to show me that being set free from deception and bondage is a process. I must not get impatient or discouraged, but rather allow God's Word to drive out every deception.

John 8:32

32. **And ye shall know the truth and the truth shall make you free.**

Start with securing the foundation of truth. Know what you believe and why. You build a strong wall against the deceiver with one solid block of truth at a time. If you find an impostor crumbling, pull it out and replace it with strong truth for that area. The integrity of the wall will be strengthened, and it will stand firm against the test of time and any storms that may come along. This is illustrated in the parable about a house built on a rock instead of on shifting sand (Matthew 7:24-27). *Selah.* The truth is like food for the soul.

Proverbs 24:13-14

13. **My son, eat thou honey, because it is good; and the honeycomb, which is sweet to thy taste:**

14. **So shall <u>knowledge of wisdom</u> be unto thy soul: when thou hast found it, then there shall be a reward and thy expectations shall not be cut off.**

Proverbs 25:16
16. **Hast thou found <u>honey</u>? Eat so much as is sufficient for thee, lest thou be filled therewith and vomit it.**

If you don't want to lose or forget the information (honey), the information needs to become revelation. To receive personal revelation, you need to start with wisdom, grow in knowledge, and remember to pace yourself, because digestion takes time. Digestion time is prayerful meditation time. Then insight will become a part of your perception. In a sense, a light turns on in your head, and you see things a little differently. Wisdom comes from God opening our eyes to the proper application of truth.

James 1:5-8
5. **<u>If any of you lack wisdom let him ask of God</u>, that giveth to all men liberally, and upbraideth not: and it shall be given him.**

6. **But let him <u>ask in faith</u> nothing wavering. For he that waverth is like a wave of the sea driven with the wind and tossed.**

7. **For let not that man think that he shall receive anything of the Lord.**

8. **A double minded man is unstable in all his ways.**

Ask God to open your eyes to focus on truth. Then walk in the truth by seeking and speaking the truth. It is wise to build your life on a solid and stable foundation of truth.

Ephesians 4:14-15

14. That we henceforth be no more children, tossed to and fro, and carried about with every wind of doctrine, by the sleight of men, and cunning craftiness, whereby they lie in wait to deceive;

15. But <u>speaking the truth in love</u>, may grow up into Him in all things, which is the head, even Christ:

It is important to speak the truth but it is more important to speak the truth with love. We should monitor what come out of our mouth. Is it helpful and true or prideful and deceitful?

Proverbs 21:23

23. Who so keepeth his mouth and his tongue keepeth his soul from troubles.

The Bible has much to say about our words and the power they have to affect our lives. Satan uses unbridled words to spread his destruction (James 3:2-8). Evil words will never create a godly atmosphere. Releasing evil words is similar to setting a wildfire. They have the power to bring about uncontrollable destruction. It is dangerous to talk like a fool because those words come from our old nature. When our old nature is magnified and empowered by our words, our vision suffers and blindness begins. Once the hazy fog of darkness has set in, we start living our lives based on feelings and assumptions instead of faith and truth. When you have foresight and see clearly, you don't need to touch or feel something to know that it is real and true. You don't have to act like a blind person feeling their way around, because you can clearly see the path you need to follow. We are to live by faith in God not feelings. *Selah.* In Luke 8:22-25, Jesus told the disciples to take Him to the other side of the lake (Sea of Galilee). After it got dark (Mark 4:35) and a storm came upon them, the disciples misplaced their faith, focusing on their changed circumstances. Their words reflected their lack of faith in God's Word, which is the foundation of truth (they were going to the other side). The result recorded in Luke 8:25 was Jesus asking them, "Where is your faith?" Is our faith rooted in God and His Word or in something else? Although the disciples' words where fearful, at least they turned to Jesus for help. It is wise to know where or who to turn to in trouble. It is also wise to have faith in the Truth, not upon our feelings or changing circumstances. Feelings are important, and they can happen. However, feelings are not the engine on our train of success. They are the caboose.

Romans 1:17

^{17.} **For therein is the righteousness of God revealed from faith to faith: as it is written, the <u>just shall live by faith</u>.**

Faith is complete trust in God and His Word. Faith in God's Word is the key. If we get onboard the train empowered by this faith, everything else will fall in line eventually, including our feelings. *Selah.* The facts are; God's Word is essential, true, powerful, and eternal. So, what does the Devil do about it? He surrounds the diamond of God's Word with cheap glass and plastic. Then he attempts to draw our attention to his alternatives as a good replacement for the precious rock of Truth. However, it does not matter how nice the glass looks or how much plastic you possess. It all proves to be valueless junk when tested by fire (1Corinthians 3:13-15).

2 Corinthians 11:14-15

^{14.} **And no marvel; for <u>Satan himself is transformed into an angel of light</u>.**

15. **Therefore it is no great thing if his ministers also be transformed as the ministers of righteousness; whose end shall be according to their works.**

We do not need to examine the many counterfeits of Satan, but rather remember his deceptive strategy. It's his main tool of destruction.

2 Peter 2:1-2 *(with a clarifying word)*

1. **But there were <u>false prophets</u> also among the people, even as there shall be <u>false teachers</u> among you, who privily (*privately*) shall bring in <u>damnable heresies</u>, even <u>denying the Lord that bought them</u> and bring upon themselves <u>swift destruction</u>**

2. **And many shall follow their pernicious ways; by reason of whom <u>the way of truth shall be evil spoken of</u>.**

With a casual reading of 2Peter 2:1, you might assume that "swift" destruction means soon, almost immediate. Then you might look around at all the false teachers deceiving for years and say, "I don't see it, the Bible does not fit my reality." However, with a closer look at the Word of God, it becomes very evident how patient God is, giving men time to repent (as we will see in Chapter 6). Therefore, "swift" does not necessarily mean soon. It does mean that after judgment finally comes, all the bad fruit will quickly and suddenly be separated and cast into Hell Fire. There is no halfway point. For example, read Psalms 73 and 37. From the perspective of eternity, our time is short, and judgment day will be here soon enough. *Selah.* There are many religions teaching different ideas regarding life after death and how to improve it. The most dangerous of all deceptions are the false teachings that rise to the level of "damnable heresies." These are the heresies that destroy our lives and condemn us to Hell. They deny how and when the Bible says we receive redemption, which is the key to our ultimate salvation. They deny that Jesus Christ is the only Redeemer and the only way for us to get to Heaven (as explained in chapter 11). For example, they may say that Jesus was a good teacher, but that the key to Heaven is joining their religious group, not receiving Christ as your personal Savior. They may preach that you will go to Heaven if you radically sacrifice your life as a suicide bomber or martyr. Or they may say you don't have to do anything at all, because everyone is going to Heaven. All these poor deceived people will be shocked at the judgment seat of God, when they try to cash in their man-made plastic belief systems. Then judgment fire will melt away the deceptions, leaving them no value and no savior. Even atheists will see the foolishness of having a creation without a Creator and that their evolution leads from life to death. These are referred to as "damnable heresies" that will eventually "bring upon themselves swift destruction," because they are "denying the Lord that bought them." Jesus died on the cross to pay for the sins of the whole world. Some misunderstand this and believe that this means the whole world will be saved (all inclusive). However the Bible is clear that this refers to the fact that anyone can be saved (non exclusive). This is obvious if you read John 3:16 and the verses following it to get the context for who will be saved.

John 3:16-17

16. For God so loved the world, that He gave His only begotten Son, that <u>whosoever</u> believeth in Him should not perish, but have everlasting life.

17. For God sent not His Son into the world to condemn the world; but that the world through Him might be saved.

With His death, Jesus bought everyone back from destruction. Even though the payment was enough for all mankind to be saved, many will not receive salvation, but will continue "denying the Lord that bought them." Their destiny will be the same place as Satan, forever missing their life with Jesus.

John 3:18-19

18. **He that believeth on Him is not condemned: but he that believeth not is condemned already,** because he hath not believed in the name of the only begotten Son of God.

19. **And this is the condemnation, that <u>light is come into the world, and men loved darkness</u> rather then light, because their deeds were evil.**

If you feel wrapped up in confusion and deceptive darkness, then do what Lazarus did in John 11:40-44. Even though he had been dead four days, Lazarus heard Jesus' words, moved toward Him, got into the light, and allowed Jesus' friends to help him get free from the bondage of corruption. Jesus wants us to come to Him as we are, in spite of our bondages and hang-ups so He can start the process of setting us free. Once you are free, don't go back and try on the corrupting grave clothes of the past. They still have the power to bind and blind you, even after you are alive in Christ.

Galatians 5:1

1. **Stand fast therefore in the liberty wherewith Christ hath made us free, and <u>be not entangled again</u> with the yoke of bondage.**

Now let's look at something less dangerous, but still very important, if we desire to walk with freedom in the light of Truth.

2 Peter 1:20-21

20. **Knowing this first that <u>no</u> prophecy of the <u>Scriptures is of any private interpretation.</u>**

21. For the prophecy came not in old time by the will of man: but holy men of God spoke as <u>they were moved by the Holy Ghost</u>.

Many Scriptures have more than one meaning or application. For instance, there is a surface truth, and with meditation on the passage, you may see deeper truths or multiple applications and principles. These new insights do not contradict the Biblical theme but instead they are in harmony with the complete Bible and add fullness to the symphony of truth. However, if the interpretation contradicts the Biblical theme, it must be rejected in order to see the truth. All Scripture is God's Word, but not necessarily all translations. Most translations contain the truth in general, but on some details some translators have misunderstood or misinterpreted the original text, giving the appearance of contradictions. In that case, the mistranslations are just plain wrong and bring darkness and confusion. For example, many people believe Israel was in Egypt 430 years because they misread or have a poor translation of Exodus 12:40. The Scriptures clearly reveal Israel was not in Egypt 430 years. To say Israel was in Egypt 430 years contradicts Galatians 3:17-18, in which all translations record that it was 430 years between Abraham and Moses. In Exodus 12:40, the NIV and most modern translations state "the length of time the Israelite people lived in Egypt was 430 years." The 430 years cannot apply to this statement and also the time between Abraham and Moses. One statement is incorrect. Some Bibles contain a footnote on this verse "Egypt and Canaan." If Canaan were included in the text it would be still be misleading unless you realized the seed of Israel was in Abraham. In reality Exodus 12:40 is a reference to Israel's patriarch Abraham living a short time in Egypt and then entering into covenant with God in Canaan (Galatians 3:18). Then 430 years latter Moses introduced the Passover resulting in the exodus to Mount Sinai where God gave Moses the Levitical Law.

In chapter 6 of this book, we will see compelling information about why this makes a big difference regarding prophecy and knowing how long a prophetic generation is. In preparation for that, let's take a little time now to study Exodus 12:40 and see what is actually being said. The plainly written phrase, "length of time" is misleading because it is a rare translation of the Hebrew word בָשׁוֹמ, which is spelled mosab or mowshab, depending on which concordance you look it up in. If you open an *NIV Concordance* to word number 4632 you would see that "mosab" is found 43 times in the Old Testament, but only once is it translated into the three words "length of time." The other 42 times, the word "mosab" was translated as places where lived, settlements, dwellings, etc. None of these 42 times had anything to do with chronological time. This is confusing because the word seems to be about camping, but the context calls for a timeframe. Therefore what is a good translation of this word mosab? There are different methods to translating the Bible. Some use the approach of reassembling the sentence thought for thought. Others use the context but translate the Bible word for word. Not to go into detail on the different styles of translating the Bible, but if you look closely at the NIV and the King James you may notice that the sentence structure is often a little different. In Exodus 12:40 the emphasis is clear in the NIV but wrong, whereas the King James translation can be read with the correct emphasis. Both translations focus on Egypt but their perspective on timing is different. The King James, the New King James, the Webster's translation and the Modern English Version are a few Bibles that properly translated this Hebrew word mowshab in this sentence. Rather than "length of time," these versions use the word "sojourning." Sojourning is an old English word that means to rest or stay temporarily in the midst of a journey. That is exactly what Abraham and Israel was doing in Egypt. They were temporarily staying in Egypt in the midst of their journey of becoming a nation in the Promised Land. The Israelites knew this journey began with Abraham and the promise given to him by God. That is why they call it the Promised Land. Many years later after leaving Egypt, during the annual Feast of First Fruits, Israel was to remember the important points of their humble beginnings. They were to remember the journey to become a nation in the Promised Land, by reciting the following phrase:

Deuteronomy 26:5-9

5. **And thou shalt speak and say before the Lord thy God, <u>a Syrian ready to perish was my father, and he went down into Egypt, and sojourned there with a few,</u> and became there a nation, great, mighty, and populous:**

6. **And the Egyptians evil entreated us, and afflicted us, and laid upon us hard bondage:**

7. **And when we cried unto the Lord God of our fathers, the Lord heard our voice, and looked on our affliction, and our labour, and our oppression:**

8. **And <u>the Lord brought us forth out of Egypt with a mighty hand,</u> and with an outstretched arm, and with great terribleness, and with signs, and with wonders:**

9. **And <u>He hath brought us into this place, and hath given us this land,</u> even a land that floweth with milk and honey.**

Notice that there is an obvious gap between verses 8 and 9. There is no mention of the 40 years spent wandering around in the wilderness. I would like to use this passage to point out several important things. First, I believe there is a less obvious gap earlier in this statement. Verse 5 may seem to apply to Jacob going to Egypt, but Jacob and Joseph were called Hebrews, not Syrians.

The 430 years did not start with Jacob going to Egypt. We will see conclusively in Chapter 6 of this book that the 430 years started long before Jacob. It started with the covenant promise given to Abraham, the father of the Jewish Nation. When we get to Chapter 6, we will also see why this is important for us today. Returning to verse 5, we see that the "father" was called a Syrian. Abraham did live in Syria before going into the Promised Land. There was a famine the year Abraham entered the Promised Land, (Genesis 12:10) so he kept going south and "sojourned" in Egypt for a short time before making his home in the Promised Land. Most Israelites refer to Abraham, not Jacob, as their father. Here are a few examples.

Acts 7:2
2. **And he said, men, brethren, and fathers, hearken; the God of glory appeared unto <u>our father Abraham</u>, when he was in Mesopotamia, before he dwelt in Charran,**

Luke 1:73
73. **The oath which He sware to <u>our father Abraham</u>,**

Romans 4:12
12. **And the father of circumcision to them who are not of the circumcision only, but who also walk in the steps of that faith of <u>our father Abraham</u>, which he had being yet uncircumcised.**

Luke 13:16
16. **And ought not this woman, being a <u>daughter of Abraham</u>, whom Satan hath bound, lo, these eighteen years, be loosed from this bond on the Sabbath day?**

Deuteronomy 26:5 addresses the origin of the Nation of Israel. What is not obvious is the gap in time and information. It begins with Father Abraham going to Egypt, but then jumps to Israel's population multiplication. Such gaps are not uncommon in the Bible. The Bible is a big book. It is full of the Truth we need, but many times there are gaps of information. This does not mean there are errors. The Apostle John addresses one of the main purposes of the Bible.

1 John 5:13

13. **These things have I written** unto you that believe on the name of the Son of God; that <u>ye may know that ye have eternal life</u>, and that ye may believe on the name of the Son of God.

The Apostle John also addresses the gaps in the information as well.

John 21:24-25

24. **This is the disciple which <u>testifieth of these things</u>, and <u>wrote these things</u>: and we know that his testimony is true.**

25. **And <u>there are also many other things</u> which Jesus did, the which, if they should be written every one, I suppose that even the world itself could not contain the books that should be written. Amen.**

Some may say John exaggerated to make the point, but the point he makes is true. There was a lot that John did not record, and there was much more that Jesus did when John was not present to see. For instance, there is not a full report on what Jesus was doing at the angelic rebellion when Satan took one-third of the angels with him to corruption. Jesus was present at creation and sometimes showed up in the Old Testament, but only a few sentences are given to us for all those centuries. The point is that Jesus is God. Although we have only a short glimpse at His life in the Bible, it is all we need. We must be careful and not be quick to say the Bible has errors or exaggerations. If we begin with that mindset, we will often miss the Truth. *Selah.* I read translations like the NIV as a commentary and to get the flow of the story. By reading a variety of translations I sometimes notice things I might miss in the King James Version. In some places the wording in the KJV can be difficult to understand. However, I have found it to be a more accurate translation. Therefore, I believe the KJV is a better study Bible. Although the best Bible is the one you can read and understand. *Selah.* When a word is italicized in the KJV, it is the translators' way of telling you the word was added by them to help clarify the text. In Exodus 12:40, the word "was" is added, not translated. The sojourn was 430 years at that point and would continue another 40 years in the wilderness. The children of Israel did not claim possession or control of the wilderness at that time, even though it was actually part of the land promised to Abraham.

Genesis 15:18

18. **In the same day the Lord made a covenant with Abram, saying, unto thy seed have I given this land, from the river of Egypt unto the great river, the river Euphrates:**

Instead of causing confusion and blindness, the correct translation brings harmony and illumination to God's Revelation. *Selah.* Sometimes it is not corrupted manuscripts or misinterpretations that lead to confusion, but rather our own traditions and popular beliefs. For example, if Jesus were put in the tomb on Good Friday night and rose before sunrise Sunday morning, it would contradict Jesus' own words when He said that He would be in the grave three days and three nights (Matthew 12:40). This is a mathematical contradiction. We must disbelieve one – our choice. The Biblical point of view is explained in Chapter 9. There you will see all four gospels confirm that Jesus was exactly three days and three nights in the tomb. All four gospels agree that Jesus was put in the tomb at the end of Preparation Day. According to the Bible, Preparation Day was the day to get all the leaven (which represented sin) out of the house and sacrifice the Passover Lamb. On Preparation Day it took many priests all afternoon to sacrifice the thousands of lambs to prepare for the Passover meal for the nation of Israel. Jesus was put in the tomb at the end of Preparation Day, which was Wednesday that year. Thursday was the High Sabbath of Passover. Friday was the Holly Feast of Unleavened Bread. Saturday was the weekly Sabbath. Sunday was Resurrection day and a sheaf of first fruits was offered as a wave offering (Acts 26:23, Mathew 27:52-53). We miss a lot of insightful symbolism with our misguided popular traditions. These inconsistencies also fuel skepticism towage Christianity and the Bible. We should always trust and preach the Bible even when it is not popular. *Selah.* These kinds of doctrinal differences do not rise to the level of missing our redemption and therefore should not be a point of contention. Just because someone does not agree on some of these less dangerous areas is no reason to not treat them like a brother or sister. Love, fellowship, and respect for one another will bring more light than trying to prove a point to the point of division and contention. Always keep the fruit of the Spirit the focus of importance, even above the gifts of the Spirit. We must avoid pride and live our lives as examples of love and wisdom. We must always be sensitive to each other's journey of faith. If someone is going the right direction, we should encourage him or her to keep going, not criticize where they are right now.

Proverbs 27:17

17. **Iron sharpeneth iron; so a man sharpeneth the countenance of his friend.**

We should be "sharpening," encouraging, and helping each other so we can defeat the Deceiver, not doing Satan's work for him by backstabbing or wounding each other. We should be willing to let God use others to sharpen us because we can all use some improvement. Look for the good. Do not make a habit of, as the old saying goes, "throwing the baby out with the bath water." Regarding the concealed or less obvious truths in the Bible, some may say, "I don't care about that" or "It does not matter." Maybe they are working on another area of the puzzle, or they may not realize the value of the details to the big picture. The question is; do you want to go deeper into God's Word? Do you want to walk in the light of truth and see where you are and what God is doing? *Selah.* In war, a general sees the big picture and the little details a little differently than a new recruit. Now is a time of spiritual war. Later all the lights will be on and we will see clearly all the hidden mysteries of this life. I do not want to believe or fight for a lie, only find out I was wrong. In the end, God will show all of us what is true and how it fits His pattern. I decide now to walk in that light, no matter how small or how life changing it may be. Don't get me wrong; I still have my own dark human nature. I am not perfect yet, but at least I can hopefully see where I am missing the mark or that God will show me soon afterward. My ongoing prayer is for God to correct me quickly when I am wrong. He has faithfully shown me many times were I misspoke, misunderstood, or acted badly. It is my desire to stand corrected.

CHAPTER 2

ORIGINS & DEFINITIONS

Genesis 2:7

7. **And the Lord God formed man of the dust of the ground, and breathed into his nostrils the breath of life; and <u>man became a living soul.</u>**

The primary thing we want to see here is that "man became a living soul." The soul is who you are. You will see that throughout the Bible, the soul is a reference to the individual person and souls are referring to people. There is a current misunderstanding being commonly taught that the soul is only the mind, will, and emotions. That philosophy can sometimes be illustrative of the interactions between the conscious (they call soul) and subconscious (they call spirit). However, it is not a Biblical definition of the soul. That description is like saying I am a brain, belly and heart, but in reality I am much more than that. Please bear with me for a few sentences while I attempt to describe the shortcomings of this inadequate definition. To begin with, this may be a little hard to distinguish but the soul has a unique ability to bear fruit. It gives personality to the fruit of the Spirit. The fruit of the Spirit is not a product of our intellectual ability or our willpower or our passionate moods, (mind, will and emotions) although they may give their consent. Like the mind, will and emotions; reproduction is another system of the soul, but it is not a definition of the soul. The soul has a special capacity to bear good fruit though its connection to the Spirit of Christ.

John 15:5

5. **I am the vine, ye are the branches: He that abideth in me, and I in him, the same <u>bringeth forth much fruit: for without me ye can do nothing</u>.**

The second point is that Holy Spirit and our human nature both have their own a mind, will, and emotions. Animals have their own distinct mind, will and emotions. Our soul has a mind, will, and emotions; but saying that is all our soul is, promotes a misconception of who we are and how we were created. It also lacks clarification because it doesn't distinguish our soul's mind, will, and emotions from our spirit, which has its own mind, will, and emotions, as we will see.

Hebrews 4:12

12. **For the Word of God is quick and powerful, and sharper than any two edged sword, piercing even to the <u>dividing of the soul and spirit</u>, and of the joints and marrow, and is a discerner of the thoughts and intents of the heart.**

For proper diagnosis, we need proper definitions and an understanding of how the systems work. *Selah.* In this chapter we will go deep into God's Word to uncover insights to the trinity. Because of the common misconceptions, the first thing truth seekers need to do is set aside superficial ideas of human configuration and the current popular concepts about God, in order to understand what is being said in this chapter. You won't get the true perspective of this book unless you read it from cover to cover. I suggest you prayerfully read it a second time in the light of the whole picture. One chapter builds the foundation for the next one, but you can jump ahead and read chapters in any order that interest you. Each chapter focuses on a different Biblical truth. The main focus of this chapter is how we can understand the trinity. Even if you don't agree with the definitions or illustrations in this chapter, at least keep them in the back of your mind. Then see if God doesn't bring them forward to show how they fit the pattern of the Bible. Understanding the puzzle of the trinity solves many mysteries of life. Don't let predetermined thoughts confuse you with presumptions that lead to distortions.

Proverbs 18:13

13. **He that answereth a matter before he heareth it, it is folly and shame unto him.**

It is important for truth seekers to see the correct and consistent definition of a word in order to get the true impact of it. If the Deceiver (Satan) can simply change the meaning of a word, then he can darken the illuminating power of that word and hide or distort the true picture the word is trying to reveal. *Selah.* For example I currently see the Deceiver redefining words like Hell, calling it only the "grave" and eternal as "ages of ages" (an unspecific but limited period of time). If you use these inadequate definitions consistently throughout the Bible you will clearly see that some sentences become senseless. The clarity of others becomes distorted or diluted. One of the Devil's oldest tricks is to redefine God's Word with his distorted, diluted, perversion of it. *Selah.* In this and the next chapter we will look at a couple of words that are a little harder to define but when properly understood, they will open up insights to life that are priceless. Even if these first few chapters seem confusing or irrelevant, I encourage you to keep reading. I strongly believe that God will show you amazing Biblical truths before it is too late to benefit from them. So, let's investigate this section by taking a fresh look at how it all started and establish some key and consistent definitions to clear up the confusion about our soul and spirit.

Genesis 1:26-27

26. **And God said; let <u>Us</u> make man in Our image, after <u>Our likeness</u>: and <u>let them</u> have dominion over the fish of the sea, and over the fowl of the air, and over the cattle, and over all the**

Earth, and over every creeping thing that creepeth upon the Earth.

27. So <u>God created man in His own image</u>, in the image of God created He him; male and female created He them.

Often when the Bible uses the word man it is gender neutral. "Man" is often short for mankind. In verse 27, male and female are in the category or family of man (mankind).

Genesis 5:2 (NKJV)
2. He created them male and female, and blessed them and <u>called them Mankind</u> in the day they were created.

Mankind was created in God's image and likeness. Notice that "man" is multiple (male and female) and that God is multiple because God said, "Let Us." There are not many kinds of Gods. There is one God, Creator of all things, with three individuals in that category.

1 John 5:7
7. For there are <u>three</u> that bear record in Heaven, the <u>Father</u>, the <u>Word</u>, and the <u>Holy Ghost</u>: and <u>these Three are One</u>.

Don't let a religious spirit tell you it is taboo to try to understand God. While it is true that God is far above our limited ability to figure Him out. That doesn't mean that we can't understand and know what God shows us about Himself. In the preceding Scripture, God reveals that He has three parts and that they are connected to make one God. The "Father" is Jehovah, and the third person is referred to as the Holy Ghost or Holy Spirit; but who or what is the "Word?"

John 1:14

^{14.} **And the <u>Word was made flesh,</u> and dwelt among us, (and we beheld His glory, the glory as of the only begotten of the Father,) <u>full of grace</u> and truth.**

The "Word" is a reference to "Yeshua, Jesus Christ" the "Son of God," who is full of grace. Let me give you a little side note about grace that might be helpful to understanding this verse. Some define "grace" as undeserved favor or with the acronym <u>G</u>od's <u>R</u>iches <u>A</u>t <u>C</u>hrist's <u>E</u>xpense. This can be said about us, but not about Christ. This definition does not work in the preceding verse, because it is more of a description of mercy than of grace. Grace simply means empowering favor and has nothing to do with whether it is earned or not. I would like to offer my opinion of a better way to understand grace. First consider that grace is the root word of graceful. I see grace as it is used in the New Testament to be the application of God given power and ability to act and think properly with perfect timing. By applying God's grace we receive blessings and increased favor with God. God loves everyone, but favors those that draw close to Him. You could say that a life "full of grace" is a graceful life. The opposite of a graceful life is a clumsy, stumbling, aimless, foolish life. *Selah.* The grace of God was upon Jesus (Luke 2:40). Jesus is full of grace (John 1:14). Jesus can give us grace and wisdom for success if we ask for them in faith (James 1:5, Hebrews 4:16). The grace of God can rest upon us to empower us (2Corinthians 12:9). We are saved by grace, which is choosing to act upon what God has enabled us to do, which is to receive His Son (Ephesians 2:8-9). It is not good to start conflicts and divisions over the definitions or applications of grace. Instead consider what it means to live a life "full of grace" (power and ability to act and think properly with perfect timing) as Jesus did. *Selah.* Lets get back to the main subject, the Trinity. The Father, Son, and Holy Spirit revealed their individuality at Jesus' baptism.

Luke 3:21-22

^{21.} **Now when all the people were baptized, it came to pass, that <u>Jesus also being baptized</u>, and praying the heaven was opened,**

^{22.} **And the <u>Holy Ghost descended</u> in a bodily shape like a dove upon Him and a <u>voice came from heaven, which said, Thou are My beloved Son</u>; in Thee I am well pleased.**

Every member of the Trinity has a voice. God can speak your language. In the previous verse the Father is speaking. All the red letters in the Bible are words that Jesus has spoken. In Acts 13:2 and Hebrews 3:7 the Holy Spirit spoke to people. There are times when God is silent but God has not lost His voice. If you never hear God then the problem may be that you lack ears to hear God (Acts 28:27, Matthew 13:15). For example, if you want to hear a certain radio station, you need to tune it in. In the same way, if you want to hear God personally speak to you, then you should tune into God's Word. If you haven't heard God for a long time, it may be because your old nature is drowning out God's voice or distracting you from following what God has said. *Selah.* Lets look again at how the Holy Bible clearly reveals the diversity of the trinity of both God and man. Man is created in the image of God according to Genesis 1:26-27. Therefore, man is not just body and soul or body and spirit. Mankind also has three parts:

1. The Body

2. The Spirit, or more specifically the Human Nature

3. The Soul

The human nature and soul are both spirit kind. They are twins but not identical. They are kind of like Esau and Jacob. The first twin, the "human nature," is masculine (we are not talking about males and females). What I am saying is that in the Bible the man carries the authority and identity. This is what distinguishes the masculine human nature as the identity of the species and the authority given to it. The nature has many titles and names we will get into later. The "soul" is feminine. It has the ability to bear fruit. <u>The "soul" is the person you are, and the "nature" is the species you are.</u> This is an important understanding if you want to truly understand Bible. It is the key to knowing how salvation works. Let me say it again; according to the Bible, the "soul" is the person you are. You and me are both individual souls. The "nature" is the species we are. We are human because we have a human nature. These identifications are consistent, distinctive, and vital, as we will see later. *Selah.* Let's look at some sequences and applications illustrated at creation that reveal more insights into the trinity.

Genesis 2:7

7. And the Lord God <u>formed man</u> of the dust of the ground, and breathed into his nostrils the <u>breath of life</u>: and man <u>became a living soul</u>.

The body was formed out of the dust of the earth. Then God breathed the "breath of life" into it. Breath or wind is one of the definitions of the Hebrew word for spirit. Once the first twin (the living spirit) was in the body, then the second twin (the soul) appeared, and Adam became a person. *Selah.* There is another interesting sequence. First God created the earth. Second, out of the earth He brought forth man (masculine). Third, out of man, He brought forth woman (feminine). In this sequence of creation, we see how the trinity is connected, yet distinctive and distinguishable. *Selah.*

Romans 1:20

20. **For the <u>invisible things</u> of Him from the creation of the world are <u>clearly seen,</u> being understood by the things that are made, <u>even His eternal power and Godhead:</u> so that they are without excuse:**

I believe that God gave us a picture of the "Godhead" Trinity at our creation. Let's see how God is represented in the creation of Adam's body, spirit, and soul. In this sequence, the body would represent the Father. This is not to say that the Father is physical. John 4:24 plainly reveals that He is spirit. In this illustration I am referring to the functions of the body more than the substance or structure of the body. To illustrate how Adam's body (more than his spirit or soul), represents the Father in the Godhead (Trinity of God), consider how the Father embodies all of creation. For instance, there is nothing outside of the spirit body of the Father. With this in mind, we can see a more vivid picture of what is being said in Revelation 3:16. In a sense, all of creation described in Genesis 1 would be like micro cells in the stomach of the Father. The following statements are extremely important to remember, if you want to understand what is going on in our world. We are not created as a part of God as some believe, no more than the contents of our stomach are part of our body; but rather the body will give the contents boundaries and can influence them. The physical world is not a manifestation of God. It is a creation of God. God sustains the environment for His creation to continue, but creation was designed with the ability to function independently of God within its given parameters. God created the laws of nature and the cycles of life. God created the law of sowing and reaping. These things were designed to function without God micromanaging their every move. For example, God dose not micromanage Satan, but God dose manage and restrict Satan to operate in a Sovereignly designed environment (Job 1:8-19). God can also overrule the laws of nature, which Jesus often demonstrated. God has the ability to established higher superseding laws and principals. It is God's choice when to introduce a new law or creation. It was God's choice to create you at this time (Esther 4:14). *Selah.*

Acts 17:26-28

26. And hath made of one blood all nations of men for to dwell on all the face of the Earth, and <u>hath determined the times before appointed, and the bounds of their habitation</u>;

27. <u>That they should seek the Lord</u>, if haply they might feel after Him, and find Him, though He be not far from every one of us:

28. For <u>in Him we live</u>, and move, and have our being; as certain also of your own poets have said, for we are also His offspring.

We are God's offspring in that we are created in God's image. However, we are not naturally or automatically His children. Figuratively speaking, from our perspective in the stomach full of good and evil, we cannot imagine the full impact of our destiny (Deuteronomy 28:13). We have two roads before us. Symbolically speaking, we will either travel the narrow road (through the blood) that leads to eternal abundant life or we will be swept along the wide road (the waste track) that leads to destruction, with the final destination being Hell Fire. Similar to the colon, Hell Fire is the container of waste and corruption.

Matthew 7:13-14

13. Enter ye in at the strait gate: for <u>wide is the gate, and broad is the way, that leadeth to destruction</u>, and many there be which go in thereat:

14. Because strait is the gate, and narrow is the way, which leadeth unto life, and few there be that find it.

The head and the brain activity would be the throne area of the body. The Bible gives us only a glimpse of Heaven's Capital City and the Throne of God, where the identity of the Father is concentrated and making decisions for the body. *Selah.* This illustration of the Father God is like a very crude sketched-out blueprint of an enormous magnificent temple. Do not read too much into all of this, because the details regarding God are far beyond our understanding. This illustration can give us some perspective by showing that everything has a place, but it falls far short of the reality of the vast, complex, omnipresent Spirit of God the Father. *Selah.* Using this perspective we can better understand Revelation 3:15-16. This verse is revealing that near the end, there will only be hot Spirit filled churches or cold dead religious churches. The lukewarm, ½ hearted, hypocritical church attitude will have no place at the end. The Biblical phrase is uncomfortably graphic; "I will spew thee out of my mouth." The sickening lukewarm attitude will be vomited out of the body, which is out of existence, because there is nothing outside of the Father.

Psalm 139:7-8

7. Whither shall I go from Thy Spirit? Or whither shall I flee from Thy presence?

8. If I ascend up into <u>Heaven, Thou art there</u>: if I make my bed in <u>Hell, behold Thou are there</u>.

The Father is omnipresent. That means He is everywhere. To say God is everywhere except Hell is to say God is not omnipresent. The Father is present, even when He is not personally connected to the ongoing activity. Latter we will get into how Hell is different than anywhere else in the anatomy of God. For now just remember the Father is omnipresent. He is at the same time in multiple dimensions of Heaven, Earth, and even in Hell.

Jeremiah 23:24

24. **Can any hide himself in secret places that I shall not see him? Saith the Lord. Do not <u>I fill Heaven and Earth</u>? Saith the Lord.**

There is no place we can go where the Father is not already there.

Psalm 139:11-12

11. **If I say, Surely the darkness shall cover me; even the night shall be light about me.**

12. **Yea, the darkness hideth not from Thee; but the night shineth as the day: the darkness and the light are both alike to Thee.**

The Father can see all the hidden things. Even things we are completely unaware of.

Proverbs 15:3

3. **The eyes of the Lord are in <u>every place,</u> beholding the evil and the good.**

The Father sees and knows everything. He does not hide himself from evil. He sees all, and at some point, He will take action.

Ezekiel 11:5

5. **And the Spirit of the Lord fell upon me, and said unto me, speak; thus saith the Lord; thus have ye said, O house of Israel: for <u>I know the things that come into your mind, every one of them</u>.**

The Father not only knows what we are thinking, He also knows where the thought came from. *Selah.* In the other illustration of creation (the Earth, Adam, and Eve), the Father would be like the Earth, the foundation and source material for Adam. Adam's body would be a special accumulation of earth material and, because Eve was taken out of Adam's side, she too would be connected to the original source material. *Selah*. Using the Earth, Adam, and Eve sequence let's look at how Adam represents the Holy Spirit of God. The first thing we see is that Adam can come and go. He is not omnipresent. For instance, if I'm not born again and want to be part of God's family, I must first ask the Holy Spirit (of Jesus) into my heart (more on that later). The point is that the Holy Spirit cannot come into a place where He already is. In the Old Testament, the Holy Spirit would come to empower some people and could leave them (Psalm 51:11). Many people know the Holy Spirit descended on Jesus at His baptism. In Chapter 8 of this book, we will see that the Holy Spirit left Jesus just before He died and then came back to raise Jesus from the dead. Therefore, the Holy Spirit is not omnipresent, because He has the ability to "come upon you" (Acts 1:8). *Selah*. Although the Holy Spirit is often invisible, He can appear in a "bodily shape" as He did at Jesus' baptism. The Holy Spirit's shape can also change and multiply into separate bodies. For instance, in Luke 3:22 He looks like a dove; and in Acts 2:2-4 the Holy Spirit appears as multiple tongues of fire. I believe it is the Holy Spirit taking on the shape of God's glory and presence in the giant of Exodus 33:18-23. In the Bible, when we see two visible appearances of God in the same place, it is probably Jesus and the Holy Spirit of God (John 1:18). Like the Father, the Holy Spirit can be in numerous places. He can be in different locations at the same time. However, there are places where the Holy Spirit is not present; therefore He has the ability to arrive and depart. *Selah*. The one place you will never see the Holy Spirit is in the eternal Lake of Fire. The first identifying word of the Holy Spirit is "Holy." The Bible says the Trinity of God is "Holy, Holy, Holy" (Isaiah 6:3, Revelation 4:8). Holiness is the main attribute of the

33

Divine Nature of God. The best single word that identifies God and things pertaining to God is Holy. Corruption and rebellion greaves the Holy Spirit to the point He either turns away from it or burns the sin away (Exodus 33:3-5).

Deuteronomy 22:14

14. For the LORD thy God walketh in the midst of thy camp, <u>to deliver thee</u>, and to give up thine enemies before thee; therefore shall thy camp <u>be holy: that He see no unclean thing in thee, and turn away from thee</u>.

The Holy Spirit understands we are sinners and fall short of perfection but He looks at our efforts and focuses on our deliverance. He looks at our heart and empowers us, so that we can be delivered from our enemy Satan. The Holy Spirit will never break His union with a Christian because of the New Testament Covenant that Jesus established. However our fellowship with Him can diminish or be enhanced. These things will be thoroughly explained in section 3 of this book. For now remember and consistently apply these two distinguishing classifications. God the Father is omnipresent which means He sees all and cannot turn and go away. On the other hand the Holy Spirit can and dose turn away from corruption and rebellion, unless He is going to purify the situation. People's statements that God is too holy to look on sin and the Biblical references of God being a consuming fire (Hebrews 12:29, Deuteronomy 4:24) are references to Holy Spirit of God. The Holy Spirit can turn away from corruption or burn away corruption but He will not participate in corruption. *Selah.* Besides His ability to visibly appear, draw closer, and disappear, we can distinguish that, like Adam, the Holy Spirit is masculine, because the "nature" is defined as masculine (which will become clear by the time you finish Chapter 15). As illustrated at Adam's creation of his body, spirit-nature and soul, the spirit represents the Holy Spirit. The Holy Spirit is the Divine Nature of God, carrying with Him power, identity, and authority.

Acts 1:8

8. But ye shall receive <u>power, after that the Holy Ghost is come</u> upon you: and ye shall be witnesses unto Me both in Jerusalem, and in all Judea and in Samaria, and unto the uttermost part of the Earth.

Since the Holy Ghost is the Divine Nature or God Nature, then who is the Soul of God? God has a Soul.

Leviticus 26:11-12

11. And I will set my tabernacle among you: and <u>My Soul</u> shall not abhor you.

12. And <u>I will walk among you, and will be your God</u>, and ye shall be my people.

The New International Version and other modern Bibles use the word "I" instead of the less understood but more specific phrase "My Soul." The Hebrew word for soul is nephesh. We first see this Hebrew word in Genesis 2:7 where the King James Bible translates nephesh to soul. It is then repeated many times in the Bible referring to both created souls and God's Soul (nephesh). Many Bibles regularly translate nephesh to soul in references to God and people. However the King James Bible is the most consistent in their translation of the word nephesh to soul. This consistency gives us greater opportunity to understand the word and what it represents.

Isaiah 42:1

[1.] Behold My servant whom I uphold; Mine elect in whom <u>My Soul</u> delighteth; I have put <u>My Spirit</u> upon him: He shall bring forth judgment to the Gentiles.

In Isaiah the Father God refers to Christ the God-man and acknowledges both God's Spirit and God's Soul. Like the Holy Spirit, God's Soul (Jesus the Son of God), is different from the Father in that He is not omnipresent. He came to Earth, He left Earth, and He is coming back to Earth again.

Acts 1:9-11

[9.] And when He had spoken these things, while they beheld, He was taken up; and a cloud received Him out of their sight.

[10.] And while they looked stedfastly toward heaven as He went up, behold, two men stood by them in white apparel;

[11.] Which also said, ye men of Galilee, why stand ye gazing up into heaven? <u>This same Jesus</u>, which is taken up from you into heaven, <u>shall so come</u> in like manner <u>as ye have seen Him go into heaven</u>.

To truly understand the Bible we need to be consistent in our definitions and applications of the Word. The statement that Jesus is coming again would not make sense or be true if Jesus were omnipresent. Therefore, not being at a certain place and time means that He has limited first-hand knowledge of that place or time.

Matthew 24:36

[36.] But of that day and hour knoweth no man, no, not the angels of Heaven, but <u>My Father only</u>.

To be clear, Jesus has unlimited access to knowledge because He is always connected to the Father. *Selah.* For example, I saw a news program featuring a young military man serving overseas. His desire was to be with his wife for the birth of their first child. Arrangements were made whereby the young soldier was able to see, talk with, and comfort his wife through labor. He was also one of the first to see and talk to his newly delivered child even though, in reality, he never left his post on the other side of the planet. Nevertheless, at that very moment, he was virtually in that delivery room with all the emotions of the expansion of his family, because of his connection to the Internet. Likewise, Jesus is virtually with us because of His connection to the Father.

Matthew 18:20
20. **For where two or three are gathered together in My name, there am I in the midst of them.**

On the other hand, Jesus can physically experience personal confirmation and fresh tangible knowledge.

Psalm 53:2
2. **God looked down from Heaven upon the children of men, <u>to see if</u> there were any that did understand, that did seek God.**

Genesis 18:20-21
20. **And <u>the Lord said</u>, because the cry of Sodom and Gomorrah is great, and because their sin is very grievous;**

21. **<u>I will go down now, and see</u> whether they have done altogether according to the cry of it, <u>which is come unto Me</u>; and if not, I will know.**

This is one reason God can experience different fresh emotions (John 11:35). Jesus the Son of God stated:

John 14:28

28. Ye have heard how I said unto you, I go away, and come again unto you. If ye loved Me, ye would rejoice, because I said, I go unto the Father: for <u>my Father is greater than I.</u>

Jesus was leaving Earth and going to where the Father is concentrated and making decisions for the body, to the Throne Room in the Capital City of Heaven. He was about to take His place at the right side of the seat of power and send us God's empowering Spirit. When Jesus says that the Father is greater, He means that the Father is omnipresent, carrying with that special first-hand knowledge, not that the Son is less of a God.

John 1:1

1. In the beginning was the Word, and the Word was with God, and the <u>Word was God.</u>

During creation, Eve was taken out of Adam who was taken out of the Earth.

Genesis 2:21-23

21. And the Lord God caused a deep sleep to fall on Adam, and he slept; and He took one of his ribs, and closed up the flesh in its place.

22. Then the rib which the Lord God had taken from man He made into a woman, and He brought her to the man.

23. And Adam said: "this is now bone of my bones and flesh of my flesh; she shall be called woman, because <u>she was taken out of man.</u>"

Indirectly Eve had the same physical origin and source material as Adam (from the Earth).

Genesis 3:19

19. **In the sweat of thy face shalt thou eat bread, till thou return unto the ground; for out of it wast thou taken: for <u>dust thou art, and unto dust shalt thou return</u>.**

Psalm 104:29

29. **Thou hidest thy face, they are troubled: thou takest away their breath, <u>they die, and return to their dust</u>.**

Ecclesiastes 12:7

7. **Then shall the <u>dust return to the earth as it was</u>: and the spirit shall return unto God who gave it.**

If I simply took a sheet of 100-year-old paper and tore off a corner, then took that corner and tore off a small part, then I would have three pieces of paper. They would be different sizes and shapes but they are all still paper. They are all still 100 years old. Although both Adam and Eve had a common link to the Earth, all three had different identities. Jesus is from God and is God with a distinguishable identity. Notice that with the progression from the Father to the Holy Spirit and then to the Son, there is a diminishing degree of omnipresence. *Selah.* Water, ice, and steam is a good analogy of the Trinity, because all three are H_2O, but exist in different forms. This is relatively easy to see, but what is hard for me to understand is that God had no beginning. He always was and is the great "I AM." "I AM" as opposed to I began. This is somewhat like seeing a circle stamped on a paper, because the two dimensional circle has no beginning or ending. In God's multidimensional case, nothing is outside of the endless sphere of God. This is mind-boggling from our linear viewpoint, but we can see and understand to some degree the Trinity of God by His Revelation. *Selah.* To keep things in perspective regarding God's Soul. Eve symbolizes God's Soul (Jesus) because Eve has a special ability to bear fruit. This is similar to calling Christians the "bride of Christ" even though many of us are men. Even so, we are called to produce the fruit of the Spirit. *Selah*. Besides the soul's ability to bear fruit, the soul also represents the person or personality of the body.

John 14:9
9. **Jesus saith unto him, have I been so long time with you, and yet hast thou not known Me, Philip? <u>He that hath seen Me hath seen the Father;</u> and how sayest thou then, shew us the Father?**

Jesus is the Soul of God revealing the Father, but Jesus was not a feminine man. Jesus was a warrior on a mission to defeat Satan and set the captives free. Everywhere Jesus went as a man, He was in charge under the authority of the Godhead. Even at His mock trial and the painful birth of our salvation on the cross, He was in complete control with God's authority. Jesus revealed to Peter that He could call legions of angels to his aid.

Matthew 26:53
53. **<u>Thinkest thou that I cannot now pray to My Father,</u> and He shall presently give Me more than twelve legions of angels?**

Jesus had the authority to command the angel army, but He also had power to change the situation of the crucifixion all by Himself.

John 18:6-8
6. **<u>As soon then as He had said unto them, I am He, they went backward, and fell to the ground.</u>**

7. **Then asked He them again, whom seek ye? And they said, Jesus of Nazareth.**

8. **Jesus answered, I have told you that I am He: if therefore ye seek Me, <u>let these go their way:</u>**

Even though Peter had just violently cut off Malchus' ear (Matthew 26:51, Mark 14:47) which Jesus healed (Luke 22:50-51) they still let Peter and the others go at Jesus' request. Jesus was in charge of Heaven and Earth and yet He laid His life down for us, his bride (John 10:18).

Ephesians 5:25, 32

25. **Husbands, love your wives, even as Christ also loved the church, and gave Himself for it;**

32. **This is a great mystery: but I speak concerning Christ and the church.**

The "church" is a body of people (males and females) who bear the fruit of Christ. It is not a building. *Selah.* In creation, God reveals to us a glimpse of His creative power and a shadow of the Godhead Trinity. We are created in God's image as a trinity, consisting of a body, a spirit, and a soul. To properly understand the trinity of mankind, we must first understand the many ways the Bible uses the word "spirit." The best and most consistent definition of the word spirit is simply an unseen motivator. This definition works every place the word is used. Therefore, to understand what the word spirit refers to, we must read the context to determine the classification of the unseen motivator. Here are a few examples where the word spirit does not refer to our human nature.

Proverbs 18:14

14. **The spirit of a man will sustain his infirmity; but a wounded spirit who can bear?**

Here the unseen motivator is determination or feelings of depression.

Proverbs 16:18

18. Pride goeth before destruction, and an <u>haughty spirit</u> before a fall.

In Proverbs 16:18 the unseen motivator is an overinflated ego.

Galatians 6:1

1. Brethren, if a man be overtaken in a fault, ye which are spiritual, restore such a one in the <u>spirit of meekness;</u> considering thyself, lest thou also be tempted.

Here the unseen motivator is a humble attitude. By the way, "meekness" is not weakness. Meekness means to have our power under the control of the master. It's like a powerful wild high-spirited horse that has been trained to trust the rider to choose the direction and speed to go, by a simple gesture of the reins. *Selah.*

Joshua 5:1

1. And it came to pass, when all the kings of the Amorites, which were on the side of Jordan westward, and all the kings of the Canaanites, which were by the sea, heard that the Lord had dried up the waters of Jordan from before the children of Israel, until we were passed over, that their <u>heart melted</u>, neither was there <u>spirit</u> in them <u>any more</u>, because of the children of Israel.

These kings did not fall down dead. They simply lost the motivation to fight. Here the word "heart" is like the word "spirit." It refers to their motivating affections, and thinking not to a physical heart. Chapter 4 will define the heart according to the Bible. You will see its importance and how it fits the trinity of man. This chapter will continue to focus on the word spirit. You will find there are many places in the Bible the word "spirit" has nothing to do with our human nature as it relates to the soul.

Isaiah 11:2

2. And the <u>Spirit of the Lord</u> shall rest upon him the <u>spirit of wisdom</u> and understanding, the <u>spirit of counsel</u> and might, the <u>spirit of knowledge</u> and of the fear of the Lord:

"Spirit of the Lord" is normally the Holy Ghost. We see the Spirit of the Lord empowering the spirit of prophesy in 1Samuel 10:6. The spirit of wisdom, understanding, counsel, might, knowledge, producing the fear of the Lord (which is the beginning of wisdom, Proverbs 9:10) are the unseen motivating attributes that the Holy Ghost will manifest in and through Christ. For instance, we can't see the unseen motivating spirit of wisdom; but like the wind, we can see its influence. *Selah.* The word spirit is not necessarily referring to God or a ghost or a demon. It can refer to any number of unseen motivators. It can refer to natural phenomena like the wind, or intoxicating drinks that promote changed attitudes. The word is used to refer to God, angels, demons, our own human nature and soul, as well as spiritual gifts and talents. With this in mind, we can better understand what is being said in the following verses.

Revelation 3:1

1. And unto the angel of the church in Sardis write; these things saith He that hath the <u>seven spirits</u> of God, and the seven stars; I know they works, that thou hast a name that thou livest, and art dead.

Much of Revelation is symbolic language, written in code. The Bible is the definer and interpreter of that code.

Revelation 4:5

5. And out of the throne proceeded lightings and thunderings and voices: and there were seven lamps of fire burning before the throne which are the <u>seven spirits of God</u>.

The Bible plainly reveals that God is a Trinity. Therefore, there cannot be seven Gods.

Revelation 5:6

6. **And I beheld and lo in the midst of the throne and of the four, beasts, and in the midst of the elders, stood a Lamb as if it had been slain, having seven horns and seven eyes, which are the <u>seven spirits</u> of God <u>sent forth into all the Earth</u>.**

Revelation 5:6 is the third and final time the seven spirits of God are mentioned, and they are sent forth to the Earth. So, what are those seven unseen motivators of God? I believe they are the seven motivating gifts supplied by the Holy Ghost to the body of Christ, the church.

Romans 12:4-8

4. **For us we have many members in one body, and all members have not the same office:**

5. **So we being many, are one body in Christ, and every one members one of another.**

6. **Have then gifts differing according to the grace that is given to us whether (1)<u>Prophecy</u> let us prophecy according to the proportion of faith;**

7. **Or (2)<u>Ministry</u>, let us wait on our ministering; or he that (3)<u>Teacheth</u> on teaching;**

8. **Or he that (4)<u>Exhorteth</u> on exhortation: he that (5)<u>Giveth</u> let him do it with simplicity; he that (6)<u>Ruleth</u> with diligence; he that showeth (7)<u>Mercy</u>, with cheerfulness.**

The first-mentioned motivating gift to the church is the prophet. This is not a fortuneteller. The office of the prophet is sort of a quality control department. Prophets are often seen correcting or speaking out from God's point of view. The spirit of mercy is more like a first-aid department reaching out with love and compassion to the broken. Every gift has its positive and negative points. For instance the prophet has to guard against the spirit of criticism and becoming judgmental instead of walking in love (Revelation 2:1-5). The compassionate (gift of mercy) has to be careful not to condone sin, but instead strive for sanctified purity (1Corinthians 5:1-8). These gifts balance each other out so correction is done in love and restoration involves discipleship. All seven of these gifts motivating the church are important for a well-balanced representation of the body of Christ. *Selah.* I hope this wasn't too confusing. The main thing to remember is that "spirit" is used to represent many different kinds of unseen motivators, and some may not necessarily be living. In the next chapter, we will look at one application of the word "spirit" as it refers to our human nature and how it affects our destiny.

Hebrews 4:12

12. **For the Word of God is quick and powerful, and sharper than any two edged sword, piercing even to the <u>dividing of the soul and spirit</u>, and of the joints and marrow, and is a discerner of the thoughts and intents of the heart.**

CHAPTER 3

THE FALL

Genesis 2:15-17

15. And the Lord God took the man, and put him into the Garden of Eden to dress it and to keep it.

16. And the Lord God commanded the man, saying, of every tree of the garden thou mayest freely eat:

17. But of the tree of <u>knowledge of good and evil</u>, thou shalt not eat of it: for <u>in the day</u> that thou eatest thereof thou shalt <u>surely die</u>.

Everything God created was perfect, at least in the beginning. Adam and Eve were perfect, but they were young and naive. God did not make them puppets, although that would have been simpler. God is Sovereign, which means nobody rules over God. God determines our boundaries. God establishes the rules within those boundaries. God is ultimately in control of everything. However, God dose not micromanage our every move or circumstance. He made mankind in His image as a trinity with the power to think and choose and build for themselves. *Selah.* This diagram illustrates the trinity of man.

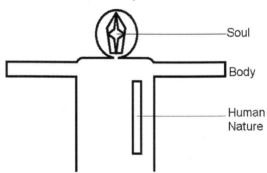

Satan was already corrupted, and his desire was to rule over God's new creation. (Details about Satan's beginning and ending

46

are revealed in chapter 17 of this book.) In order to establish his corrupt world system, Satan needed mankind to serve him. Fueled with deception, Satan has three powerful weapons of mass destruction.

2 John 2:16

16. **For all that is in the world, the <u>lust of the flesh</u>, and the <u>lust of the eyes</u>, and the <u>pride of life</u>, is not of the Father, but is of the world.**

We can see in Genesis 3:1-7 how Satan used these three weapons to seduce Eve. Eve responded to Satan's opening deceitful question by stating that God said she could not even touch the forbidden fruit. God's instruction to Adam was not to consume the forbidden fruit (Genesis 2:17). Adam and his helper Eve was suppose to take care of everything in the garden (Genesis 2:15).

Genesis 3:2-3

2. **And the woman said unto the serpent, we may eat of the fruit of the trees of the garden:**

3. **But of the fruit of the tree which is in the midst of the garden, God hath said, ye shall not eat of it, neither shall ye <u>touch it</u>, lest ye die.**

For victory against the deceptions, distortions and perversions of Satan, we need to know the difference between God's Word and man's added commentary. *Selah.* When Adam and Eve sinned it began a chain reaction resulting in a world full of corruption. Let's look closely at what happened that led to their fall.

Genesis 3:6

6. **And when the women saw that the tree was <u>good for food</u>, and that it was <u>pleasant to the eyes</u>, and a tree to be desired to**

make one wise, she took of the fruit thereof, and did eat, and gave also unto her husband with her: and he did eat.

Notice the trinity of satanic weapons at work – lust of the flesh (good for food), lust of the eyes (pleasant to look at), and pride of life (to make one wise). After considering Satan's lies, Eve tested man's well-intended commentary and touched the fruit. Nothing happened, so she believed Satan, rebelled against God's Word, and consumed the poison. She then spread the poison to her husband, who was supposed to protect her from defilement, not join her.

1 Timothy 2:14

[14.] **And Adam was not deceived, but the woman being deceived was in the transgression.**

Adam was not deceived by the Devil, but he no doubt noticed that Eve didn't fall down dead. In fact, Eve seemed more seductive than ever; so Adam yielded to peer pressure and his love for Eve (which was greater than his love for God), and consumed the forbidden fruit.

Genesis 3:17

[17.] **And unto Adam He said, because thou hast hearkened unto the voice of thy wife, and hast eaten of the tree, of which I commanded thee, saying, thou shalt not eat of it: cursed is the ground for thy sake; in sorrow shalt thou eat of it all the days of thy life;**

Adam chose to follow Eve's example to his own death. It was not the immediate physical death of the body, although sin would take its corrupting toll on the body over time. The death they both experienced immediately was spiritual death. The human nature died that day. It did not evaporate or go to sleep. What happened was that the light went out, and corruption set in.

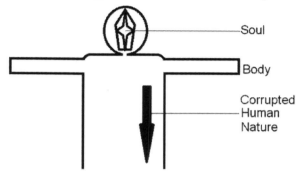

Romans 1:21-22

²¹· **Because that when they knew God they glorified Him not as God, neither were thankful; but became vain in their imaginations, and <u>their foolish heart was darkened;</u>**

²²· **<u>Professing themselves to be wise, they became fools.</u>**

Before we go any further, I would like to point out that Adam was never a baby or an adolescent. The day Adam was created, he received his wife Eve and could fellowship with God. Adam probably looked like a perfect 30-year-old man. If a doctor or scientist examined him, they would say there is no way Adam could be less than a year old. The Bible answers the old question; "What came first the chicken or the egg?" The Bible clearly explains it was the chicken and it was able to bear fruit of its own kind (species). Meaning you may find a variety of chicken eggs but there are no chickens laying snake eggs. *Selah.* Some say the Earth is millions of years old. There are two things I would like to point out regarding the Earth. First, like Adam and Eve, many things were created mature or with age already built in. When Adam looked at Eve, he did not see a baby, but rather a grown woman. Second, even though Adam was created only a few thousand years ago, some believe remnants of the Earth may be much older, because between Genesis 1:1 and Genesis 1:2, the Earth may have been destroyed during Satan's fall. Nevertheless, God took this formless void area, built our three-dimensional planet, and then created all mortal life. Genesis 1:1 begins with God giving us the bottom line – God is the Creator. Then He goes back to fill in a few of the details in Genesis 1:2 through Genesis 2:3. There are six days of creation, and the seventh day is when God rested and enjoyed the fruit of His labor. God begins the daily cycle at night. The Bible does not say how long the darkness lasted until God illuminated the Earth.

Genesis 1:2-5

2. **And the Earth was without form, and void; and <u>darkness</u> was upon the face of the deep. And the Spirit of God moved upon the face of the waters.**

3. **And <u>God said, let there be light</u>: and there was light.**

4. **And God saw the light, that it was good: and God <u>divided the light from the darkness</u>.**

5. **And God called the light <u>day</u>, and the darkness He called <u>night</u>. And the <u>evening and the morning were the first day</u>.**

God called this the first day or day one. It wasn't until the fourth day that He created the lunar day, which began and ended at sunset.

Genesis 1:14-19

14. **And <u>God said, let there be lights in the firmament of the heaven</u> to divide the day from the night; and let them be for signs, and for <u>seasons</u>, and for <u>days</u>, and <u>years</u>:**

15. **And let them be for lights in the firmament of the heaven to give light upon the earth: and it was so.**

16. **And God made two great lights; the greater light to rule the day, and the lesser light to rule the night: he made the stars also.**

17. **And God set them in the firmament of the heaven to give light upon the earth,**

18. **And to rule over the day and over the night, and to divide the light from the darkness: and God saw that it was good.**

19. **And the <u>evening and the morning were the fourth day</u>.**

This resulted in the twenty-four hour day, the seven-day week, and the four seasons per year. Just a note, there is an exception to the 24-hour day. In places like northern Alaska, the daytime could last for months before the night concludes it. I am just pointing out that if God wanted a longer lunar day, it was available to Him. However to be clear, God can create everything out of nothing in a mere moment of time. God can also stop the sun from going down and supernaturally extend the day, which He demonstrated in Joshua 10:12-14. *Selah.* For those who want to know more about this creation, progression, and purpose, God reveals many important relevant details in Genesis 2:4 through Revelation 20. God begins to reveal His next creation in Revelation 21. God will have no problem showing us the complete detailed process when we have the time and ability to comprehend all the complexities of the ecosystems that interact to form this creation. For now God asks us to trust Him that He can do what He said He did. *Selah.* There is evidence across our planet that the earth (which was like a greenhouse because of the water canopy) was destroyed by water during the days of Noah.

Someday the earth will be destroyed again by purifying fire and reformed for the last time. The earth did not suffer major destruction when Adam sinned but it was changed (Genesis 3:17-18). Also Adam and Eve experienced a new powerful emotion – FEAR.

Genesis 3:10

10. **And he said, I heard Thy voice in the garden, and <u>I was afraid</u>, because I was naked: and I hid myself.**

Fear is faith in the negative. It acts like a magnet to attract unwanted circumstances roaming around, seeking a way into your life (1Peter 5:7-10). Fear can open the door to what you reluctantly believe. It can also activate and empower satanic activity. *Selah.* Job was the most righteous man around, but he was not perfect. He was so righteous that he tended to be self-righteous and proud of his abilities and actions, as we see later in the book of Job. The Bible says pride goes before a fall (Proverbs 16:18). God was going to help Job not to be arrogant or self-righteous. God was also going to deliver Job from fear. Job did not fear death, but his fear of losing his health, wealth, and children made him vulnerable to experience satanic activity in these three areas.

Job 3:25

25. **For the thing which <u>I greatly feared</u> is come upon me, and <u>that which I was afraid of is come unto me</u>.**

Just for the record, after Job's season of tribulation, he moved up to the next level of spiritual growth – wise and humble fearlessness – and was then blessed beyond measure. The Bible has many examples of God saying, "Do not fear," or "Fear not." The one exception is "The fear of the Lord."

Proverbs 9:10

^{10.} **The fear of the Lord is the <u>beginning of wisdom</u>: and the knowledge of the Holy is understanding.**

Fear of the Lord opens a door to God. It is a desire to separate ourselves from those things that God disapproves of and will judge.

Proverbs 3:7

^{7.} **Be not wise in thine own eyes: <u>fear the Lord, and depart from evil</u>.**

As we mature as Christians, this fear is replaced by love and respect for who God is and what He has done. For example, as we become closer to Christ, we avoid evil, not out of fear of consequences, but out of love and respect for Christ. We do not want to grieve him. Also as we mature we understanding that evil is bad and God is good. God knows what is best and He is our friend. I don't fear my friends. I desire His loving instruction and correction.

1 John 4:18

^{18.} **There is <u>no fear in love;</u> but perfect love casteth out fear: because fear hath torment. <u>He that feareth is not made perfect in love</u>.**

God knew Adam and Eve's fear was the fruit of their sin. The definition of "sin" comes from an old archery term. The amount of "sin" was the distance by which your arrow missed the target. God wanted Adam and Eve to recognize their sin and confess it. Acknowledging that they had fallen short of perfection, not excuse or blame someone else for their actions. *Selah.* I do not believe Adam and Eve were in the Garden of Eden long, because God told them to multiply (Genesis 1: 28). The man gives the identity to the species. A defiled woman can birth an undefiled child if the father is undefiled. If the seed of Adam were undefiled, then his children would be undefiled. That was definitely not the case.

Genesis 4:8

8. And Cain talked with Abel his brother: and it came to pass, when they were in the field, that Cain <u>rose up against</u> Abel his brother, and <u>slew him</u>.

The first children were fathered by a defiled human (Adam), and therefore inherited from their father a defiled human nature, just like we inherit our fallen human nature from our fathers, unless you are virgin born. In the Bible, we trace our personal sin nature back to Adam, not to Eve even though she sinned first.

Romans 5:12, 14

12. Wherefore, as <u>by one man sin entered into the world, and death by sin</u>; and so death passed upon all men, for that all have sinned:

14. Nevertheless death reigned from Adam to Moses, even over them that had not sinned after the similitude of <u>Adam's transgression</u>, who is the figure of Him that was to come.

The corrupted human nature is the problem in our world today. It started with the first sin that began a cycle of death and corruption.

Romans 1:28-32

28. And even as they did not like to retain God in their knowledge, God gave them over to a reprobate mind, to do those things which are not convenient;

29. **Being filled with all unrighteousness, fornication, wickedness, covetousness, maliciousness; full of envy, murder, debate, deceit, malignity; whisperers,**

30. **Backbiters, haters of God, despiteful, proud, boasters, inventors of evil things, disobedient to parents,**

31. **Without understanding, covenantbreakers, without natural affection, implacable, unmerciful:**

32. **Who knowing the judgment of God, that they which commit such things are worthy of death, <u>not only do the same, but have pleasure in them that do them</u>.**

The sin nature is like a cancer. It cannot be allowed to infect Paradise because it would corrupt it. Cancer is basically rebellious cells. They can grow or be suppressed, but the cure is to remove them completely. Ultimately, that is what needs to be done with the sinful nature. For now we need to learn how to reduce its destructive influence. To do that we will need help. The first step is to recognize that there is a problem, then identify and isolate it. This is not always easy, as we are about to see.

Jeremiah 17:9

9. **The <u>heart is deceitful</u> above all things, and <u>desperately wicked</u>: who can know it?**

The human nature communicates though the unsanctified heart to our soul. This verse points out that the natural heart is infected and corrupted by the fallen human nature. The heart magnifies the fallen nature's deceptive ability because we tend to trust our heart. The heart is a reflection of the nature it is connected to. The next chapter will reveal how the heart is the battlefield and explain how the heart can be regenerated. Here we need to see what causes the heart to be wicked. We need to uncover the source of the deceitful heart. It is the fallen human nature. The human nature may say that you are a good-hearted person, too good to go to Hell. However, like a virus to the soul, the symptoms listed in Romans 1:28-32 will eventually appear, contaminating the environment. The sinful nature has convinced some people that there is no Hell and all roads lead to Heaven. Don't be deceived. The light of truth will prove how destructive those kinds of statements are. The human nature is in complete unity with Satan. Even when it is promoting things that seem to be good, they are the bait to control you and distract you from God. The human nature hides behind many different activities and identities, which we will see in chapter 13. The Bible refers to it by many names and titles.

Romans 8:6-8

6. **For to be carnally minded is death; but to be spiritually minded is life and peace.**

7. **Because the <u>carnal mind</u> is enmity against God: for it is <u>not subject to the law of God, neither indeed can be</u>.**

8. **So then they that are in <u>the flesh cannot please God</u>.**

Here the human nature is called the "carnal mind." It is the producer of carnal thoughts. The fallen nature of carnality is the root of secular humanism. The human nature is also called the "flesh." Some confuse the flesh with our bodies, and sometimes the word can be referring to a body. However, in verse 8 and in many other places, the flesh is another name for our human nature. We know that by the context of the sentence and by comparing other scriptures for harmony. I can please God in my body, and I am encouraged and told how to do so in the Bible. Our body can be the temple of the Holy Spirit, so in our body we can please God. However, we cannot please God in our "flesh."

God is not pleased with us producing the corrupt fruits of the flesh nature listed in Romans 1:28-32. In Romans 8:6-8, we see that the fallen human nature does not submit to God and more importantly, cannot summit to God ("neither indeed can be"). That means that the fallen human nature cannot be redeemed. It is not regenerated. It will never change. It is permanently part of the dark side. In a sense, it is the son of Satan.

John 8:44

44. Ye are <u>of your father the Devil</u>, and the lusts of your father ye will do. He was a murderer from the beginning, and abode not in the truth, because there is no truth in him. When he speaketh a lie, he speaketh of his own: for <u>he is a liar, and the father of it</u>.

The human nature died that day in the Garden of Eden, and its destiny was sealed for eternity. We are all born with this corrupted nature, which we inherit from our human fathers. God speaks to you individually as the soul you are and tells you there is hope – if you come to the Master Physician. He will start by opining up your heart and giving you a new nature (Acts 16:14, 2Peter 1:4).

Ephesians 2:1-3

1. And you hath He quickened, who were dead in trespasses and sins;

2. Wherein in time past ye walked according to the course of this world, according to the prince of the power of the air, <u>the spirit that now worketh in the children of disobedience</u>:

3. Among whom also <u>we all had</u> our conversation in times past in the lusts of <u>our flesh</u>, fulfilling the desires of the flesh and of the mind; and <u>were by nature the children of wrath</u>, even as others.

CHAPTER 4

THE HEART OF THE MATTER

First of all it is important to realize the different definitions the Bible applies to the word heart. This will eliminate some of the confusion. The Bible uses the word heart in a variety of ways. Here are four definitions with corresponding Bible passages.

1) - Center or Foundation:

Exodus 15:8

8. **And with the blast of Thy nostrils the waters were gathered together, the floods stood upright as an heap, and the depths were congealed in the <u>heart of the sea</u>.**

2) - Physical Heart Pump of the body:

2 Kings 9:24

24. **And Jehu drew a bow with his full strength, and smote Jehoram between his arms, and the <u>arrow went out at his heart</u>, and he sunk down in his chariot.**

3) - Source of our Emotions and Feelings:

Proverbs 15:13

13. **A <u>merry heart</u> maketh a cheerful countenance: but by <u>sorrow of the heart</u> the spirit is broken.**

We will see in this chapter the word heart has a fourth definition. It is this fourth definition that is less obvious yet most prominent throughout the Bible.

4) - The Connecting Bridge to the Soul:

Proverbs 27:19

19. **<u>As in water</u> face answereth to face, so the <u>heart of man to man</u>.**

The "heart of man," "answereth" the soul of man. The heart is a reflection of you and your motivating desires. Your heart is also a reflection of the nature it is connected to. Basically the heart is the transmitter of information and the soul is the final decision maker. The heart is a transmitter with many channels. Just as our physical heart receives and pumps out blood, our spiritual heart receives and pumps out information. The heart can be divided and deliver contrary messages at the same time. It would be like a stereo with the right and left channels tuned into two different stations. The soul can be confused by the mixed messages.

James 1:8

8. **A <u>double minded</u> man is <u>unstable</u> in all his ways.**

The soul can tune in, or change the heart station in order to focus on one message at a time.

James 4:8

8. **Draw nigh to God, and He will draw nigh to you. Cleanse your hands, ye sinners; and <u>purify your hearts, ye double minded</u>.**

Many people are confused about the heart and mind. Many think the heart only represents the emotions and that the mind represents the intellect. Actually in the Bible's original languages of Hebrew and Greek the words translated as heart (בֵל and *kapoia*) apply to the thoughts or intentions of an individual more than their emotions. When the Bible says their "Heart was not right" as in Psalm 78:37 or Acts 8:21, God is commenting on their thinking not their emotions. *Selah.* Many things from many sources attempt to get into our heart. Always remember the soul has the final word on what remains in the heart. The heart is a transmitter of information as well as emotions. The heart transfers the emotions and communicates the information that is placed into it. The frequency the heart is transmitting can be changed. It can be tuned in, turned up or distorted with multiple messages. The frequency the heart is transmitting can be changed by the soul to avoid undesirable messages. *Selah.* Many times when people are defining the body, soul and spirit they are actually defining the body, soul and heart. It is this application of the word heart that we will examine in this chapter. The heart is different from our soul and nature. To put it simply, the heart is the driveway to get to the soul. The heart is like a bridge between our soul (the person) and our nature (the species). The heart is also our connection to the Holy Spirit of God. The heart is similar to a fiber-optic cable in the way it can be changed by the color of the light source. The heart can be illuminated to transfer the pure light of revelation from God or darkened by the black light of deception from Satan. Our heart is transformed by the spirit or nature it is actively connected to.

Psalm 51:10

10. **Create in me a clean heart, O God; and renew a right spirit within me.**

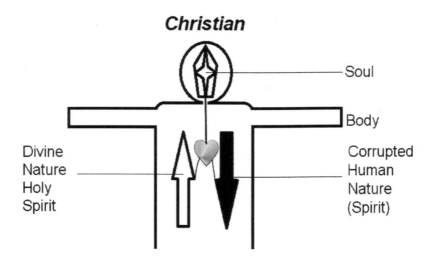

Many people are blind to God because their heart is dark. Many others see a distortion of God or are dedicated to false gods because their corrupted heart has deceived them. In the beginning mankind was created with a pure heart and had the ability to see God in the proper light.

Matthew 5:8

8. **Blessed are the <u>pure in heart</u>: for they shall see God.**

When Adam and Eve were created they had a pure, but naive heart. Naive because they only knew good and had no personal knowledge of evil. We can have a pure heart without being naive (Mathew 10:16). God dose not want His children to be gullible but instead analytical and discerning (Proverbs 13:1). That is known as godly wisdom. We must not permit religious traditions, secular humanism, or anything else, numb our senses or blind us to the truth. Adam and Eve lacked wisdom and disobeyed God. God made it clear to them that the day they sinned they would die. The day they ate of the fruit of "the knowledge of good and evil" they learned evil and they died spiritually. Sin entered their life and they attempted to hide from God. Their heart became polluted because their nature died. The light went out in the human spirit and it became corrupted. This corrupting darkness defiled the species. The dark spirit (nature) brought fearful darkness and corruption to their heart. This corruption was passed on from Adam and Eve to their descendants.

Romans 1:21

21. **Because that, <u>when they knew God</u>, they glorified Him not as God, neither were thankful; but <u>became vain in their imaginations</u>, and their <u>foolish heart was darkened</u>.**

The heart is a reflection of its connection. As descendants of Adam we are all born with a defective heart.

Ephesians 4:18

18. Having the <u>understanding darkened</u>, being alienated from the life of God through the ignorance that is in them, because of the <u>blindness of their heart</u>:

This ignorance of God and blinding deception is the problem in the world today.

Hebrews 3:12

12. Take heed, brethren, lest there be in any of you an <u>evil heart of unbelief</u>, in departing from the living God.

Unbelief needs to be replaced by the knowledge and understanding of the truth. God's truth goes out to everyone but only benefits them that retain it.

Matthew 13:19

19. When any one heareth the Word of the kingdom, and understandeth it not, <u>then cometh the wicked one, and catcheth away that which was sown in his heart</u>.

The Devil is the author of confusion. He wants to cover your eyes so you can't see him robbing you of God's provision. Satan has an active campaign with one main objective – to keep God's Word from taking root in your heart.

Luke 8:12-15

12. Those by the way side are they that hear; <u>then cometh the Devil, and taketh away the Word out of their hearts, lest they should believe and be saved</u>.

^{13.} **They on the rock are they, which, when they hear, receive the Word with joy; and these have <u>no root,</u> which for a while believe, and in time of temptation fall away.**

^{14.} **And that which fell among thorns are they, which, when they have heard, go forth, and are <u>choked with cares and riches and pleasures of this life,</u> and bring no fruit to perfection.**

^{15.} **But that on the good ground are they, which in an <u>honest and good heart,</u> having heard the Word, <u>keep it,</u> and bring forth fruit <u>with patience.</u>**

The truth is that we have a wise creator. He is referred to as God. God has a purpose for his creation. God is able to communicate in numerous ways to his creation. God also has the ability to preserve and fulfill His Word. If you want to know God, you need to open your eyes up to the truth about creation and honor the Word of God.

Hebrews 11:6

^{6.} **But <u>without faith it is impossible to please Him</u>: for he that cometh to God <u>must believe that He is,</u> and that He is a rewarder of them that diligently seek Him.**

We need to seek God where He reveals Himself. God reveals Himself in the Word of God. In John 1:1-14 Jesus is called the illuminating Word. We see God in the proper light when we see how Jesus reflects the Father. *Selah.* The first step in being set free of blinding deceptions is fixing our heart. Our heart can be fixed but it first needs to be willing to receive correction and instruction. We need to open our heart up to the light of Biblical truth.

Ephesians 1:18 (NAS)

18. I pray that the <u>eyes of your heart may be enlightened,</u> so that you will know what is the hope of His calling, what are the riches of the glory of His inheritance in the saints,

Many versions of the Bible translate this verse using the word "heart" instead of "understanding" which is the word used in the King James Version. Understanding begins by the light of God entering our heart and revealing truth to our soul. At that point we have a choice. We can shut our eyes to it and remain in darkness or open our eyes and examine how to apply it. We should start this process by asking the Holy Ghost to help us to see clearly what is being said.

John 14:26

26. But the Comforter, which is <u>the Holy Ghost, whom the Father will send in My name, He shall teach you</u> all things, and bring all things to your remembrance, whatsoever I have said unto you.

Jesus sends His Spirit (the Holy Ghost) to every heart to reveal God's love and deliverance for us.

Acts 15:8-9

8. And God, which knoweth the hearts, bare them witness, <u>giving them the Holy Ghost,</u> even as he did unto us;

9. And put no difference between us and them, <u>purifying their hearts by faith</u>.

This starts with seeing the light of truth, and then we can take the next step and ask the Author of truth to come into our heart. Then God will begin purifying our heart of deception and corruption. Our connection to the light of God removes the blinding satanic darkness.

Psalm 108:1

1. O God, my heart is fixed; I will sing and give praise, even with my glory.

This is a process that takes time, but if you remain faithful there is an increasing joy and wisdom in knowing you are destined for personal glory.

Psalm 86:11

11. Teach me Thy way, O LORD; I will walk in Thy truth: unite my heart to fear Thy name.

To fear God's name means we do not take it in vain (without thought). Instead we respect it and consider it Holy. *Selah.* We should also strive to realize that God's Word contains power and authority. We have a choice to respect and receive the light of truth from God's Word or reject it. All who reject God's Word remain in darkness. God says we are either allies or rebels against Him.

Luke 11:23

23. He that is not with Me is against Me: and he that gathereth not with Me scattereth.

All who rebel against God are deceived about their activity and its corrupting results. We can be deceived even after we know the truth.

Deuteronomy 11:16

16. Take heed to yourselves, that your heart be not deceived, and ye turn aside, and serve other gods, and worship them;

All deception leads to some degree of darkness. We are all learning and growing in the truth. We only need to focus on one thing at a time. We should focus on what God is shining His spot light on.

Psalm 119:105

105. Thy <u>Word is a lamp</u> unto my feet, and a <u>light unto my path</u>.

If we ignore God and move away from the direction God's light is pointing, we will find ourselves in darkness. This darkness will infect our heart. It will first divide our heart with a mixture of confusion and deception. This can happen in even the most religious environments.

Matthew 16:6

6. Then Jesus said unto them, <u>Take heed and beware of the leaven</u> of the Pharisees and of the Sadducees.

The Sadducees were promoting false religious teachings. The Pharisees were into extremes. Both were out of balance with the truth of God's Word and promoted hypocritical and inconsistent doctrines.

Luke 12:1(b)

1(b). ... He began to say unto His disciples <u>first of all, Beware ye of the leaven of the Pharisees,</u> which is <u>hypocrisy</u>.

Matthew 16:12

12. Then understood they how that He bade them not beware of the leaven of bread, but of the <u>doctrine of the Pharisees and of the Sadducees</u>.

God was using leaven to illustrate the effect a little sin can have on the entire life. Jesus also addressed worldliness with the same warning of its ability to grow and influence the entire life.

Mark 8:15

15. And He charged them, saying, <u>Take heed, beware</u> of the leaven of the Pharisees, and of the <u>leaven of Herod</u>.

The leaven of Herod represents the secular rebellion against God and His Word. You may recall that Herod the Great tried to kill baby Jesus and Herod Antipas beheaded John the Baptist. Herod Antipas also mocked Jesus and sent Him back to Pilate to be crucified. Jesus was using leaven to illustrate the distorting effect sin has on the heart. He was also illustrating that both religious and secular "leaven" distorts the truth. That is why the Lord's Supper uses unleavened bread to represent Jesus. The bread that represents Jesus' body is not puffed up, nor is the fruit of the vine that represents Jesus' blood fermented with yeast. 1Corinthians 5:6-8 calls us to become unleavened like Jesus. *Selah.* All of us make mistakes and experience shadows of confusion and mystery. However, if we are attempting to hit the target, God will sharpen our focus. Remember, the definition of sin is missing the target. If we willfully reject and turn away from the target revealed in God's Word, it has a powerful compounding effect on our heart.

Galatians 5:9

9. A <u>little leaven</u> leaveneth the <u>whole lump</u>.

It may not be noticeable at first but sin will continue to promote a growing deception and corruption unless it is removed. When God points out a mistake, He empowers us with grace to correct it. Jesus enables us to be renewed and free of deception. If we are in harmony with God's Word it will purify our heart and unite us with God.

John 14:6

6. <u>Jesus saith</u> unto him, <u>I am</u> the way, <u>the Truth</u>, and the life: <u>no man cometh unto the Father, but by me</u>.

The truth leads us to God. If we mix truth with the leaven of the Sadducees (false doctrines), or the leaven of the Pharisees (unbiblical extremes and traditions), or the leaven of Herod (secular wickedness) it will lead to a divided heart. A divided heart is the first step to deception and corruption.

1 Corinthians 5:6

6. Your glorying is not good. Know ye not that <u>a little leaven leaveneth the whole lump</u>?

God considers the heart that treasures His Word a good heart. A good heart makes time for Bible study and prayer. To have a good heart we must guard it from becoming compartmentalized or puffed up with the things of this world. We must not let anything crowd out our time with God.

Ephesians 4:27

27. Neither <u>give</u> place to the devil.

Give no place for the Devil to work though you. We remove demonic strongholds by uprooting the lust of the flesh early before it grows into sinful actions that we will eventually regret.

James 1:15

15. Then when <u>lust hath conceived</u>, it bringeth forth sin: and sin, when it is finished, bringeth forth death.

If corruption takes over a pure heart it will make a good person evil. Sin in the heart will lead to inconsistent speech and evil actions. Evil actions empower the satanic forces of death to bring darkness to the environment. The spiritual environment affects the direction of a family as well as a nation. God encourages his people to let their light shine in this dark world. The light of God starts in our heart, comes through our actions and illuminates our environment with good things.

Matthew 12:35

35. A **good man** out of the **good treasure of the heart** bringeth forth good things: and an **evil man** out of the **evil treasure** bringeth forth **evil things.**

Satan will attempt to hide the light of truth about God with a fog of deception and corruption. Satan's desire is to first corrupt the heart then the person and ultimately the world.

Isaiah 32:6

6. For the **vile person will speak villany,** and **his heart will work iniquity,** to **practise hypocrisy,** and to **utter error against the LORD,** to make empty the soul of the hungry, and he will cause the drink of the thirsty to fail.

We can treasure God's Word or neglect it. If we neglect or reject God then we open our heart up to Satan. *Selah.* Satan attempted to contaminate the first church with deceptive donations.

Acts 5:3-4

3. But Peter said, Ananias, why hath **Satan filled thine heart to lie** to the Holy Ghost, and to keep back part of the price of the land?

4. Whiles it remained, was it not thine own? and after it was sold, was it not in thine own power? why hast thou **conceived this thing in thine heart?** thou hast not lied unto men, but unto God.

Satan first planted deception in the heart. Once that was accomplished and the person was corrupted then Satan used that person to deceive the church. By the grace of God, Peter exposed the deception. The result was that the church grew in power and respect. *Selah.* Satan is always planting deceptive evil weed seeds. Every day we need to uproot what Satan plants in our heart or it will choke out the fruit of the Holy Spirit. Satan especially desires to defile those following Jesus and turn them into betrayers.

John 13:2

2. **And supper being ended, the <u>Devil having now put into the heart</u> of Judas Iscariot, Simon's son, to betray him;**

Judas was an opportunist. Judas was not a believer. He was a follower for his own personal gain. Judas was the treasurer and a thief. John reveals Judas' hypocritical heart in his gospel. All four "he" references in John 12:6 refer to Judas.

John 12:6 (NIV)

6. **He did not say this because he cared about the poor but because <u>he was a thief</u>; as keeper of the money bag, he used to <u>help himself</u> to what was put into it.**

We also see Satan's influence on Peter who was a true believer and follower of Jesus. It is found in Mark 8:33 leading to Mark 14:30 resulting in Mark 14:72. We need to pray for our leaders to have the "breast plate of rightness" to protect their hearts from satanic attacks. Satan desperately desires to destroy Christian leaders. Therefore we should pray that our leaders' hearts remain true to God. *Selah.* Our biggest problem is the sabotaging nature inside not the demonic activity outside. Satan's favorite tool to plant evil seed in our heart is the old nature, which the Bible often calls the "Old Man." If corrupting seed is allowed to take root in the heart, the heart will become corrupted. It will then feed corrupted information to the soul. Remember, the heart is like a fiber-optic bridge to the soul. It looks and acts like the source it is plugged into. A dark heart is a heart that has "become one" with the dark spirit. The black light of deception will come from the dark spirit through the heart and attempt to defile the soul. The Bible has much to say about a heart that has been corrupted by the dark spirit and how it affects the culture.

Matthew 15:18-19

18. But those things which proceed out of the mouth come forth from <u>the heart</u>; and they <u>defile the man</u>.

19. For <u>out of the heart proceed evil thoughts</u>, murders, adulteries, fornications, thefts, false witness, blasphemies:

Mark 7:21

21. For from within, <u>out of the heart</u> of men, <u>proceed evil</u> thoughts, adulteries, fornications, murders,

Even a mature Christian has to continually monitor their heart. If the heart is left unguarded, then the "Old Man" can plant landmines and set us up to explode when Satan pushes our buttons.

Jeremiah 17:9

9. The heart is <u>deceitful</u> above all things, and <u>desperately wicked</u>: who can know it?

If we cannot trust our own heart, then what can we trust? We can trust Jesus. Jesus gives us His Divine Nature to guide us. The Holy Spirit will never leave a Christian but a Christian can brake fellowship with Him and have their heart darkened. If this happens to a Christian, their heart will feed their soul deceptive information, which promotes corruption. We see the fruit of this activity in the life of Christian backsliders and disgraced leaders.

Our biggest heart problem is our connection to our fallen human nature. This corrupted spirit will always resist the Holy Spirit of God.

Acts 7:51

51. Ye <u>stiffnecked and uncircumcised in heart</u> and ears, ye do always <u>resist the Holy Ghost</u>: as your fathers did, so do ye.

The uncircumcised heart is the natural heart that is controlled by the carnal human nature. *Selah.* What is the biggest difference between a corrupted nature and a corrupted heart? The heart can be regenerated but the nature's degeneration is irreversible. The Bible often calls the human nature the "flesh." Do not confuse this "flesh" with the body. A Christian's body is the temple of the Holy Spirit (1Corinthians 6:19). God revealed to me that the reason He used the term "flesh" to describe the old nature is because it is a reference to circumcision. The flesh needed to be cut away for a man to be in the Abrahamic covenant. God often uses the physical to illustrate spiritual truths. The physical circumcision of the flesh is a cymbal not a qualification for the circumcision of the heart. The "flesh" (corrupted nature) needs to be circumcised (removed) from the heart for us to enter the perfect environment of Heaven. When you understand how the "flesh" nature works you will understand the reason why the "flesh" is not allowed in Heaven. The "flesh" works the same way a virus infects a cell. Once the virus is attached to the cell it will penetrate the cell. The virus will either enter the cell itself or inject the cell with instructions. Either way the virus (sinful nature) reproduces itself in the cell (the heart). After the virus multiplies itself, it takes over the cell. It then uses the cell to spread its destructive influence. *Selah.* The heart can be set free from the sickening virus of sin. There is an antivirus for the heart. The heart can be regenerated. The heart needs to be regenerated for the soul to be saved. What dose it mean to be regenerated? In Latin the word is regeneratio, which means, "being born again." The secular definition is to be formed or created again or restored to a better, higher, or more worthy state. Physical regeneration replaces a lost or injured body part by new growth of tissue. It is like a lizard re-growing its tail or a crab reconstructing a lost claw. This does not apply to all cells, just as regeneration does not apply to the human nature. The heart is different from the nature because the heart can be regenerated, the nature cannot. According to the Bible regeneration happens when the Spirit of God enters the heart and illuminates the soul. This is set in motion by repentance. The soul can repent. Repentance is simply turning from one activity or direction and going the other way. For the soul to repent means the soul turns from self-centeredness and self-righteousness to God. If the soul turns to God, God will help us to focus on truth and better relationships. God will illuminate the heart so we can see clearly to pull the plug of the deceptive virus of sin. Until we are perfected in Heaven this is done by faith and repentance instead of removal. Repentance is turning from the "flesh" to the Spirit of God. If we turn to God then God's grace will empower us to cut off our connection to sin. It is not automatic. It is a matter of choice. Circumcision is a physical illustration of the spiritual answer to our heart problem. The Bible often refers to the circumcision of the heart. That term refers to the cutting off the flesh nature from producing fruit in our heart. We do this by focusing on our connection to God. We are all born with an uncircumcised heart. All of us have the same infection of corruption. There needs to be an intentional disconnect from the deceptive information of the sinful nature to stop the corruption that is polluting our nation (Jeremiah 4:1-4). God encourages us and empowers us but won't make the decision for us. God allows us to make the decision to have a circumcise heart.

Deuteronomy 10:16

16. **Circumcise therefore the foreskin of <u>your heart</u>, and <u>be no more stiffnecked</u>.**

A stiff-necked person is someone that resists turning their eyes to God. They are set in their ways and resist the Holy Spirit's attempt to redirect them. I have heard it said that we cannot resist God. That statement is unbiblical. God wants His children to be wise yet many spend their life in foolish carnality (1Corinthians 3:3). God is not willing that anyone parish (2Peter 3:9) yet many parish. God would not say, "be no more stiff-necked" if we could not stubbornly resist God. For love to truly be love it needs to have a choice to love or not. It also needs a choice as to what degree to demonstrate love. *Selah.* In this life the heart is the battleground. Both good and evil are fighting for control. Evil uses the fog of deception and good uses the light of truth. Our heart is the key to our destiny. To be free of bondage and deception we need to circumcise our heart. We need to cut off the attitude of rebellion against God and His Word. We do this by learning from our mistakes and daily focusing on who God is and His love for us. *Selah.* I don't mean to belabor the point but in conclusion let's review what it means to have a circumcised heart and why that is a good thing. First we need to realize that to become a child of God we need to have the Nature of God. The human nature is corrupted and will never stop sinning. We are born with the nature of sinful man. We are born-again into the family of God by receiving a new nature. This new nature the Bible calls the Divine Nature. We receive the Divine Nature by receiving the Holy Spirit of Jesus into our heart. We do not deserve and cannot earn the Divine Nature. The Divine Nature is a gift from God. It is because of our connection with the Divine Nature that we know God intimately. If you know God personally, He will never say to you the most fearful words God could decree – "Depart from Me."

Matthew 7:22-23

22. Many will say to Me in that day, Lord, Lord, have we not prophesied in Thy name? and in Thy name have cast out devils? and in Thy name done many wonderful works?

23. And then will I profess unto them, <u>I never knew you: depart from Me</u>, ye that work iniquity.

There is only one place where we can actually depart from God. It is a place of disconnection and isolation, which the Bible calls the Lake of Fire. This fire is eternal; it will never be quenched. You will never see Jesus or the Holy Spirit in the Lake of Fire. It is a place God created for devils.

Matthew 25:41

41. Then shall He say also unto them on the left hand, <u>Depart from Me</u>, ye cursed, <u>into everlasting fire</u>, <u>prepared for the Devil and his angels</u>:

The Lake of Fire is completely void of God's influence except for His confinement. This place is the antithesis of God. It is anti-God and anti-Christ. It is completely void of all God's attributes. The result is instead of love and life there is torment and hopelessness.

Revelation 20:14-15

14. And death and hell were cast into the <u>lake of fire. This is the second death</u>.

^{15.} **And whosoever was not found written in the book of life was cast into the lake of fire.**

There are many references and warnings about Hell and the eternal Lake of Fire. Don't let Satan deceive you into thinking there is no such place, or that the Bible doesn't warn us about it. Jesus repeatedly said it is better to suffer amputation or blindness than to end up in Hell Fire (Mark 9:43-48, Mathew 5:29-30, Mathew 18:8-9). As mortals, we have a fallen human nature, which is destine to be quarantined in the Lake of Fire. However as Christians we also have God's Divine Nature, which is destine for eternity in Heaven. The Divine Nature enables our heart and soul to be purified and perfected. This process is explained in chapters 11 through 15 of this book. The bottom line is we need this purification from corruption to qualify for the standard in Heaven, which is perfection. We cannot achieve perfection on our own. That is why we need to ask God into our life and allow God to wash away all the filth that was planted in out heart.

Jeremiah 24:7

^{7.} **And <u>I will give them an heart to know me</u>, that I am the LORD: and <u>they shall be my people</u>, and I will be their God: for they shall return unto me <u>with their whole heart</u>.**

In Heaven our whole heart, soul and body will become completely perfected. We will retain our unique individuality, but our flaws will be removed. The "flesh" will be removed. Eternal life begins with a new heart. A new heart starts here and now by turning from rebellion to connecting with God. The main fruit of this connection is love. If we turn to God, and get to know Him, He will fill our heart with love and light. God will dispel the darkness and one by one tear down the walls of satanic deception and depression. Removing the satanic worldview is not only good for us and our country, but it allows us to leave a Godly heritage to our descendants.

Deuteronomy 30:6

6. **And the LORD thy God will circumcise thine heart, and the heart of thy seed, <u>to love the LORD thy God with all thine heart</u>, and <u>with all thy soul</u>, that thou mayest live.**

Like it or not, we are involved in the ultimate battle of good verses evil. The battlefield of the heart is ground zero. With God's help we can stop the old nature's demonic influence over us. This is a continuing process of applying faith and repentance. If we do our part God will do His part.

Proverbs 3:5-6

5. **<u>Trust in the LORD</u> with all thine heart; and lean not unto thine own understanding.**

6. **In all thy ways <u>acknowledge Him</u>, and <u>He shall direct thy paths</u>.**

While we are in our natural body our battle is to keep our connection to God flowing through our heart. That is why the Bible often repeats the need to pray.

1 Timothy 5:17

17. **Pray without ceasing.**

This is not saying to become a monk and commit all our time to formal prayer. Instead it is practicing the presents of God in our daily life. It is like walking with a friend. Sometimes your quiet, but if a thought comes to mind you share it and discuss it. God wants us to casually and spontaneously pray about everything. If we have unbroken fellowship with God then we can receive God's (*rhema*) Word to guide and direct us. A timely word from

God may come audibly though TV, radio or people, although most of the time His Spirit speaks with a "still small voice" in our heart (1Kings 19:11-13). God is so close that we can hear Him whisper to us if we turn down the distractions. Maintaining companionship with God, results in victory over Satan. The Bible refers to this battle in 1Timothy 6:12 as the "good fight of faith." Satan uses distracting and deceptive noise to drown out God's voice. Satan also uses corruption to build walls in our heart to separate us from God. Satan compartmentalizes our heart to have strongholds from which he uses to control us. Satan was very successful in taking over the hearts of mankind before Noah's flood.

Genesis 6:5

5. **And GOD saw that the wickedness of man was great in the earth, and that every imagination of the <u>thoughts of his heart was only evil continually</u>.**

Satan's desire is to rob God from enjoying His creation. Satan does this by deceiving mankind into thinking evil is good.

Galatians 6:7

7. **Be not deceived; God is not mocked: for <u>whatsoever a man soweth, that shall he also reap</u>.**

We will be held accountable for what we allow to take root in our heart. Things rooted in our heart are revealed by our spontaneous actions and speaking.

Luke 6:45

45. **A good man out of the good treasure of his heart bringeth forth that which is good; and an evil man out of the evil treasure of his heart bringeth forth that which is evil: for <u>of the abundance of the heart his mouth speaketh</u>.**

The problem is in this life we tend to have both of these hearts speaking to us and through us.

Psalm 12:2

2. **They speak vanity every one with his neighbour: with flattering lips and <u>with a double heart do they speak</u>.**

If we allow sin to take root in our heart, it will divide our heart and separate us from connecting to God. Sin will produce corruption in our life and reduce our rewards in Heaven.

2 Chronicles 12:14

14. **And he did evil, because he prepared not his heart to seek the LORD.**

No one in Heaven will have an evil heart. There will be no attraction to evil in Heaven. The pollution of the "flesh" (corrupt human nature) will not be allowed in Heaven. These sinful motivations and activities will be removed (circumcised) from all God's children. *Selah.* God comes to every individual and offers him or her a new start with a new heart.

Jeremiah 32:39

39. **And I will give them <u>one heart</u>, and <u>one way</u>, that they may fear me for ever, <u>for the good of them</u>, and of their children after them:**

"One heart" means that in Heaven our heart is not divided between two natures. "One way," is the reason why it is not divided. Our heart is not divided because it has one connection to one nature, the Divine Nature of God. Our connection to the sinful nature will be severed and permanently removed from us. This is what the term circumcision of the heart is referring to. This is first done by faith, which leads to the ultimate circumcision of the heart at the judgment seat of Christ (which is described in chapter 15). By faith we can keep our heart from the old nature's deadly intoxication and contamination.

Proverbs 4:23

23. **Keep thy heart with all diligence; for out of it are the issues of life.**

Keeping our heart clean involves regular sweeping away the naturally accumulating dirt. The ultimate purification is the circumcision of the heart. By removing the old nature, God removes our heart connection to sin.

Ezekiel 37:23

23. **Neither shall they defile themselves any more with their idols, nor with their detestable things, nor with any of their transgressions: but I will save them out of all their dwellingplaces, wherein they have sinned, and will cleanse them: so shall they be my people, and I will be their God.**

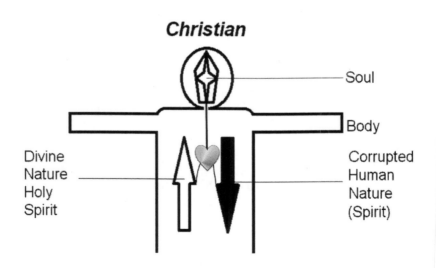

Section 2

Illustration

CHAPTER 5

THE LAST ADAM – THE GOD-MAN

Hebrews 2:14-18

14. For-as-much then as the children are partakers of flesh and blood, He also Himself likewise took part of the same that through death He might destroy him that had the power of death, that is the Devil;

15. And deliver them who through fear of death were all their lifetime subject to bondage.

16. For verily <u>He took not on Him the nature of angels but He took on Him the seed of Abraham.</u>

17. Wherefore in all things it behoved Him <u>to be made like unto His brethren,</u> that He might be a merciful and faithful high priest in things pertaining to God, to make reconciliation for the sins of the people.

The Son of God was made flesh. He inherited His mortal body that could feel pain from His human mother, the Virgin Mary. Jesus not only took on a human body, He also became part of humanity ("like His brethren"). He joined the human race, because "He took on Him" a human nature. This nature was not the "nature of angels," but rather a pure human nature like the one with which Adam was originally created. Jesus did not inherit a corrupt human nature from a corrupt father, because He did not have a corrupted father. He was virgin born. The Holy Spirit was His actual father.

Isaiah 7:14

14. Therefore the Lord Himself shall give you a sign; behold, a <u>virgin shall conceive</u>, and bear a son, and shall call his name Immanuel.

There are two Hebrew words that are put together to produce the name (or title) Immanuel. The definitions of the words are "God" and "with us." "God-with-us," reveals a description and exclusive identity of Jesus Christ. He is a combination of 100% Soul of God with 100% nature of man. God identified with us by becoming one of us, (human). Then He walked among us to help us.

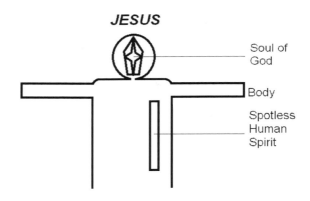

JESUS

1 Corinthians 15:45

45. **And so it is written, <u>the first man Adam</u> was made a living soul; <u>the Last Adam</u> was made a quickening Spirit.**

In the Bible, the "Last Adam" is referring to Jesus. One reason is because Adam and Jesus are the only men to begin this life with a perfect spotless human nature. This is why it was so important for Jesus to be virgin born. *Selah.* He was and is truly unique. He is the Messiah, the God-man. He had a human nature, giving Him the identity of man; and He is the Soul (personality) of God who had no beginning. Jesus the God-man also had a natural body, which is referred to as the seed of woman (Genesis 3:15).

1 Corinthians 15:22

22. **For as in Adam all die even so in Christ shall all be made alive.**

Another reason Christ is seen as the last Adam is because from Him will come a new race of descendants, not physically born, but born again of the Spirit.

1 Corinthians 15:47-49

47. **The first man is of the earth, earthy; <u>the second man is the Lord from Heaven</u>.**

48. **As is the earthy, such are they also that are earthy: and as is the heavenly, such are they also that are heavenly.**

49. **And <u>as we have borne the image of the earthy, we shall also bear the image of the heavenly.</u>**

1 Corinthians 15:53-54

53. **For <u>this corruptible must put on incorruption, and this mortal must put on immortality</u>.**

54. **So when this corruptible shall have put on incorruption, and this mortal shall have put on immortality, then shall be brought to pass the saying that is written, death is swallowed up in victory.**

These verses refer to all those who are born again into the family of Jesus Christ. *Selah.* Let's set aside our traditions for a moment and examine the life and times of Jesus Christ according to the Bible. We begin in the sixth month on the Jewish calendar (Aug. 15 to Sep. 12 of 6 BC). This is just before the Feast of Tabernacles.

Luke 1:26-35

26. **And in the sixth month the angel Gabriel was sent from God unto a city of Galilee, named Nazareth,**

27. **To a virgin espoused to a man whose name was Joseph, of the house of David; and the virgin's name was Mary.**

28. And the angel came in unto her, and said, hail, thou that art highly favoured, the Lord is with thee: blessed art thou among women.

29. And when she saw him, she was troubled at his saying, and cast in her mind what manner of salutation this should be.

30. And the angel said unto her, fear not, Mary: for thou hast found favour with God.

31. And, behold, <u>thou shalt conceive</u> in thy womb, and bring forth a son, and shalt call his name Jesus.

32. He shall be great, and shall be called the Son of the Highest: and the Lord God shall give unto Him the throne of his father David:

33. And He shall reign over the house of Jacob for ever; and of His kingdom there shall be no end.

34. Then said Mary unto the angel, how shall this be, seeing I know not a man?

35. And the angel answered and said unto her, <u>the Holy Ghost shall</u> come upon thee, and the <u>power of the Highest shall</u> overshadow thee: <u>therefore</u> also that holy thing which shall be born of thee <u>shall be called the Son of God.</u>

God fathered the human being that would be conceived latter that year. The Angel directed Mary to go to Elisabeth's home (Luke 1:36-37). Mary probably traveled with family heading south for the Tabernacle Feast. When Mary entered Elisabeth's home, God's presence was magnified and Elisabeth was filled with the Holy Ghost (Luke 1: 15, 41). Elisabeth then confirmed to Mary that she would be the mother of the Messiah (Luke 1:42-43).

Luke 1:45

45. **And <u>blessed is she that believed</u>: for there <u>shall be</u> a performance of those things which were told her from the Lord.**

Elisabeth's words "shall be" and things shared at the end of this chapter indicate the conception had not happened yet. Since there was no evidence that Mary was pregnant, she had to walk and talk by faith for a few months. Mary and Elisabeth may have learned from Zacharias who was unable to speak words of doubt (Luke 1:18-20). *Selah.* Jesus is God's only begotten son, He is the Son of God. The rest of God's children would be adopted. Jesus' Soul was and is God and had no beginning. His human nature and new identity began the day when the Virgin Mary conceived a baby from the Holy Spirit. She knew it would not be easy. Who would believe her? Would her future husband even believe her?

Matthew 1:18-25

18. **Now the birth of Jesus Christ was on this wise: when as his mother Mary was espoused to Joseph, before they came together, she was found <u>with child of the Holy Ghost.</u>**

19. **Then Joseph her husband, being a just man, and not willing to make her a public example, was minded to put her away privily.**

20. **But while he thought on these things, behold, the angel of the Lord appeared unto him in a dream, saying, Joseph, thou son of David, fear not to take unto thee Mary thy wife: for that which is <u>conceived in her is of the Holy Ghost.</u>**

21. **And she shall bring forth a son, and thou shalt call his name Jesus: for He shall save His people from their sins.**

22. **Now all this was done, that it might <u>be fulfilled</u> which was spoken of the Lord by the prophet, saying,**

23. Behold, <u>a virgin shall be with child</u>, and shall bring forth a son, and they shall call his name Emmanuel, which being interpreted is, God with us.

24. Then Joseph being raised from sleep did as the angel of the Lord had bidden him, and took unto him his wife:

25. And <u>knew her not till she had brought forth her firstborn son</u>: and he called his name Jesus.

Joseph and Mary got married, but Mary remained a virgin until after Jesus was born to avoid any chance of contamination from a fallen human father.

Luke 2:1-2 (NKJV)

1. And it came to pass in those days that a decree went out from Caesar Augustus that all the world should be registered.

2. This census <u>first took place</u> while Quirinius was governing Syria.

You may not be aware of it but there is some controversy over Luke's timing for the trip to Bethlehem. Therefore, incase it ever comes up; I would like to offer a couple of brief thoughts.

First, the census: To say, a census for taxing "first took place" indicates there were others later. Rome issued multiple censuses to have an accurate count of Rome's growing taxable population and citizenship. *Selah.* Many critics of the Bible have been silenced with recent archeological finds. Yet many details of ancient history will never be unearthed. Therefore a lot of historical speculation is based on assumptions instead of having all the facts. Luke was aware of this early census as well as the later census in 6AD, which appears to be referred to by the historian Josephus. Lets not forget Josephus was born after these events and published his observations nearly 100 years after the birth of Christ. Josephus was just a man doing his best to preserve and explain history as he saw it. He did not know or record everything. Luke is considered to be one of two secretaries that God used to record the main events regarding the conception and birth of Christ. If there is ever a conflict between historians or scientists and God's Word, eventually God's Word will be proven true and all that stand against it proven false. That is not to say we should not study the truth and attempt to explain the confusion away for the sake of the deceived. In doing so we will become a light of truth (Matthew 5:14-16) that grows stronger in our ability to understand and explain the Bible. We will find that the Bible not only can be trusted but it also has all the answers we need to make wise decisions. Remember, all the darkness needs to do to prevail is hide the light.

<u>Second, Quirinius governing</u>: The Greek word Luke used for governor (KJV) or governing (NKJV) had more to do with leadership than politicks. Strong's definition of this Greek word hegemoneuo (G2230) is "to be leader, to lead the way, to rule, command." Apparently Quirinius was a ruling officer, governing the military over Syria between 12 and 2 BC, which would be the time of Jesus' birth. As a military leader Quirinius may well have been in charger of overseeing a census in and around Syria.

Just considering these two observations can explain away most of the controversy over Luke's timing. Satan loves to sidetrack people with half-truths and distorted details to create doubt and confusion (Genesis 3:1-5). Don't fall for Satan's traps and miss the point God wants you to know. More important than the timing, is that this undeniable event Luke is referring to in this second chapter of his gospel would change the world. God was about to fulfill many prophecies starting with Jesus' birthplace.

Luke 2:4-5

4. **And Joseph also <u>went up from Galilee, out of the city of Nazareth,</u> into Judaea, unto the City of David, which is called <u>Bethlehem;</u> because he was of the house and lineage of David:**

5. **To be taxed with Mary his espoused wife, being great with child.**

Jesus fulfilled every prophecy regarding His first coming, even the city of His birth (Micah 5:2). From Nazareth, Mary and Joseph went 70 miles south to Bethlehem. This was about a 95 to 125 mile journey depending on the path they took. They went up in elevation. It didn't matter which direction you came from, you would have to go "up" to Jerusalem. Bethlehem is five miles south of Jerusalem. The little town of Bethlehem was crowded when they arrived. Many people were travailing because of the census (Luke 2:3). This also may have been a time when many Jews gathered in and around Jerusalem for a special Jewish feast. Because of the influx of people the only shelter Joseph could find was some sort of a cave or shed that was used as a stable.

Luke 2:7-11

7. **And she brought forth her firstborn son, and wrapped him in swaddling clothes, and laid him in a manger; because there was no room for them in the inn.**

8. **And there were in the same country shepherds abiding in the field, keeping watch over their flock by night.**

9. **And, lo, the angel of the Lord came upon them, and the <u>glory of the Lord shone round about them</u>: and they were sore afraid.**

10. **And the angel said unto them, fear not: for, behold, I bring you good tidings of great joy, which shall be to all people.**

^{11.} **For unto you is born this day in the city of David a Saviour, which is Christ the Lord.**

"Glory" is often associated with light or a spotlight. The light "shone round about them," so the shepherds could not miss it, even though many did. The night sky lit up the area around the shepherds, and then came the celebrated birth announcement.

Luke 2:13-15

^{13.} **And <u>suddenly</u> there was with the angel <u>a multitude of the heavenly host</u> praising God, and saying,**

^{14.} **Glory to God in the highest, and on Earth peace, good will toward men.**

^{15.} **And it came to pass, <u>as the angels were gone away from them into heaven,</u> the shepherds said one to another, let us now go even unto Bethlehem, and see this thing which is come to pass, which the Lord hath made known unto us.**

Notice that the night sky was lit up with "multitude of the heavenly host." The shepherds would see them lighting up the night, and then they vanished away into the heavens. Then the shepherds went to see Jesus.

Luke 2:20-22

^{20.} **And the shepherds returned, glorifying and praising God for all the things that they had heard and seen, as it was told unto them.**

^{21.} **And <u>when eight days were accomplished</u> for the circumcising of the child, his name was called Jesus, which was so named of the angel before he was conceived in the womb.**

22. And <u>when the days of her purification according to the law of Moses were accomplished, they brought him to Jerusalem</u>, to present him to the Lord;

The Lord guided Moses in writing the first five books of the Bible. The Jews of Jesus' time were well acquainted with the Law of Moses. It was a guide for Jesus' parents. On the eighth day, Jesus was circumcised in Bethlehem in accordance with the law. By looking at the Law of Moses we can see that the family remained in Bethlehem a little over a month.

Leviticus 12:1-4

1. And the <u>Lord spake unto Moses, saying,</u>

2. Speak unto the children of Israel, saying, if a woman have conceived seed, and born a man child: then she shall be unclean seven days; according to the days of the separation for her infirmity shall she be unclean.

3. And in the <u>eighth day</u> the flesh of his foreskin shall be <u>circumcised.</u>

4. And <u>she shall then continue</u> in the blood of her purifying <u>three and thirty days;</u> she shall touch no hallowed thing, <u>nor come into the sanctuary, until the days of her purifying be fulfilled.</u>

Leviticus 12:6-8

6. And <u>when the days of her purifying are fulfilled</u>, for a son, or for a daughter, she shall bring a lamb of the first year for a burnt offering, and a young pigeon, or a turtledove, for a sin <u>offering, unto the door of the tabernacle of the congregation, unto the priest:</u>

7. Who shall offer it before the LORD, and make an atonement for her; and she shall be cleansed from the issue of her blood. This is the law for her that hath born a male or a female.

8. And <u>if she be not able to bring a lamb, then she shall bring two turtles, or two young pigeons</u>; the one for the burnt offering, and the other for a sin offering: and the priest shall make an atonement for her, and she shall be clean.

When Jesus was about 40 days old, Mary and Joseph went north to Jerusalem to fulfill their duty according to the law. They went to the temple in Jerusalem to offer their sacrifice.

Luke 2:24

24. And to <u>offer a sacrifice according to that which is said in the law of the Lord</u>, a pair of turtledoves, or two young pigeons.

They stayed in the area just long enough to fulfill the law and make an offering of two birds.

Luke 2:39

39. And when they had performed all things according to the law of the Lord, <u>they returned unto Galilee to their own city Nazareth</u>.

By the time Jesus was three months old, He was home in Nazareth in the house Joseph had built before marrying Mary. Joseph was a carpenter. It was Jewish tradition that, between the proposal and the wedding, the man would build a special place for his wife. I'm sure Joseph was excited about building their home and anticipating the day when Mary would join him there. After the bridal chamber (called the "huppah") was finished, the father of the groom would set the wedding date. I believe there is an exciting spiritual picture behind this tradition. If you search "Jewish Bridegroom" or "Jewish Wedding Traditions in Bible

Times," you will find many interesting details that parallel our salvation. The key elements are that Jesus came to Earth to initiate a way for us to join His family (the engagement covenant). Now He is in Heaven preparing our eternal home there (John 14:2-3). At the Father's command, Jesus will return to bring His bride (the redeemed) home for the wedding (Revelation 19:7). *Selah.*

Let's look again at the Nativity, Jesus' birth. Where were the wise men? Well, they were far away to the east. That night they were at home looking at the starry sky. A bright light suddenly appeared on the horizon in the direction of Jerusalem. Just a note about the "star in the east;" the Greek word translated as "east" is anatole. This word actually means a rising of light, which is usually in the east (Genesis 1:14-19) except in this case. This rising light probably looked like a bright shooting star except that it wasn't moving from the western horizon. I think it is obvious this star was the same angel, joined by the heavenly host, that the shepherds saw light up the sky. While the wise men thought about what this could mean, the light abruptly shot off into heaven. They were amazed and curious. They needed to know what it meant. They sought to solve the mystery and finally discovered the answer in the prophesies of the Bible.

Isaiah 11:1

1. **And there <u>shall come forth a rod</u> out of the stem of Jesse, and a branch <u>shall grow</u> out of his roots:**

Was there a rod of light introducing the birth of Jesus Christ? Yes. Who is Jesse? He was King David's father, a descendent of Jacob whose name was changed to Israel. This is another, although indirect reference that the Messiah will come from Jesse and David's hometown of Bethlehem. The previous verse Isaiah 11:1 and the following verse Numbers 24:17 refer to the bloodline of

Mary, as well as that of Jesus the Messiah. I believe they are also describing the events surrounding Jesus' birth. I'm referring to the appearance of a rod or scepter of light that grew larger as more angels appeared in the night sky above the shepherds. This was the special light in the night referred to as a "star" that the wise men seen. It guided them to Jesus from far away in the east.

Numbers 24:17a

17a. **I shall see Him, but not now: I shall behold Him, but not nigh: <u>there shall come a star</u> out of Jacob, and a <u>scepter shall rise out of Israel</u>, ...**

The wise men decided to go see this special King and prepared gifts and provisions for their journey to Jerusalem. After they finally arrived in Jerusalem, they met with the evil King Herod. Herod was having serious health problems, both mental and physical. He was considered a madman by many and was jealous and insecure about retaining his throne. Before the wise men arrived, Herod had gone as far as killing members of his own family to protect his position and power. News of a new King no doubt alarmed Herod.

Matthew 2:7

7. **Then Herod, when he had privily called the wise men, enquired of them diligently <u>what time the star appeared</u>.**

After diligently seeking all the information he could find from the wise men and the Holy Scriptures, Herod discovered that the child had been born in the village of Bethlehem two years earlier.

Micah 5:2

2. **But thou, <u>Bethlehem Ephratah</u>, though thou be little among the thousands of Judah, yet out of thee shall He come forth**

unto Me that <u>is to be Ruler</u> in Israel; whose goings forth have been from of old, from everlasting.

Hoping the new King was still in Bethlehem, Herod sent the wise men to find Him.

Matthew 2:8-12

[8.] And <u>he sent</u> them to Bethlehem, and said, go and search diligently for the young child; and when ye have found Him, bring me word again, that I may come and worship Him also.

[9.] When they had heard the king, they departed; and, lo, <u>the star, which they saw in the east, went before them, till it came and stood over where the young child was.</u>

[10.] <u>When they saw the star, they rejoiced</u> with exceeding great joy.

[11.] And when they were come into the <u>house,</u> they saw the <u>young child</u> with Mary his mother, and fell down, and worshipped Him: and when they had opened their treasures, they presented unto Him gifts; gold, and frankincense, and myrrh.

[12.] And being warned of God in a dream that they should not return to Herod, they departed into their own country another way.

The wise men headed south to Bethlehem Ephrata; but after they left Jerusalem, they saw that familiar star and became excited and rejoiced. This was no ordinary star. They recognized it as the same star they saw when they were in the east (the one shepherds saw in the night sky). They also noticed that the star (angelic rod of light standing on the horizon) was moving around to the north. It led the wise men all the way to Nazareth and stood on the roof of the very house where Jesus was living. After presenting their gifts they spent time talking with the "young child" Jesus, who was in his terrific two's (because Jesus never had the terrible two's). Then the wise men returned home rejoicing because they experienced the presence and directional leading of God.

Matthew 2:16-18

16. Then Herod, when he saw that he was mocked of the wise men, was exceeding wroth, and sent forth, and <u>slew all the children that were in Bethlehem, and in all the coasts thereof, from two years old and under, according to the time which he had diligently enquired of the wise men</u>.

17. Then was fulfilled that which was spoken by Jeremy the prophet, saying,

18. In <u>Rama</u> was there a voice heard, lamentation, and weeping, and great mourning, Rachel weeping for her children, and would not be comforted, because they are not.

After discovering that the wise men did not follow his instructions, Herod went on a furious warpath. The wise men had told him that the angelic birth star had first appeared two years earlier, so Herod ordered the killing of all the children "from two years old and under." He not only killed those children five miles to the south in Bethlehem, but also the children all around the area "coasts thereof." This included Samuel's hometown (1Samuel 25:1) of Ramah (Jeremiah 31:15), which was five miles north of Jerusalem. God kept Jesus out of Herod's reach. God also provided provisions for the next trip Jesus' family would take, through the generous gifts of the seekers of God, "the wise men."

Matthew 2:13-15

¹³· **And when they were departed, behold, the angel of the Lord appeareth to Joseph in a dream, saying, arise, and take the young child and his mother, and flee into Egypt, and be thou there until I bring thee word: for <u>Herod will seek the young child to destroy him</u>.**

¹⁴· **When he arose, he took the young child and his mother by night, and departed into Egypt:**

¹⁵· **And was there until the death of Herod: that it might be fulfilled which was spoken of the Lord by the prophet, saying, out of Egypt have I called my Son.**

How could Herod find Jesus all the way up in Nazareth? The answer is simple – the recent census. Herod would start killing all the young children in the family line of David. He would also inquire about where the wise men and their entourage had traveled. Therefore, after the wise men departed, Joseph did not hesitate to follow God's instruction. He quickly left with Mary and Jesus at night so no one would even know which direction they headed.

Matthew 2:19-20

¹⁹· **But when Herod was dead, behold, an angel of the Lord appeareth in a dream to Joseph in Egypt,**

²⁰· **Saying, arise, and take the young child and his mother, and go into the land of Israel: for they are dead which sought the young child's life.**

There seems to be some confusion about the year Herod the Great died. Historians state that he died after an eclipse of the moon, but before the Passover. From Jerusalem, you could witness an eclipse in years 1 and 4 BC. The popular, but most unlikely year of Herod's death is 4 BC. In the 1966 *Journal of the Theological Studies,* W. E. Filmer shows the historical reasons why many mistakenly assume Herod died in 4 BC. He also provides substantial historical evidence to show Herod's death would have been shortly after the lunar eclipse seen on January 9 in 1 BC. The confusion comes from some common mistakes, as well as Satan surrounding the truth with anti-facts and decoys. This is common for the deceiver and is to be expected. *Selah.* For example, let's look for a few minutes at how the deceiver promotes the theory of evolution as a fact of history. Evolution is not science. It cannot be tested or proven. It is a theory based on a fairytale. I'm familiar with the historical anti-facts presented by evolutionists. If you believe them, you have more faith than I have. There are more than just missing links. There are crafted deceptions commonly known to be hoaxes, and yet are still taught as facts in many schools. In addition to the missing links and frauds, the theory is totally illogical. Its claims are way beyond God's provisions for adaptation or variation within a species. It claims that complex functional systems, both matter and spirit, came from chaos and a random sequence of coincidences over a long period of time. The theory of evolution is similar to believing that a large junkyard existed in the middle of nowhere, and then it suddenly blew up. The explosion ("Big Bang") caused the dust and junk to miraculously become a fueled-up Learjet taxiing down a runway, destined for a small tropical island. Then, suddenly out of the dust there appeared in a temperature-controlled cockpit, a live highly skilled pilot with his loving wife beside him, as well as their pets. If you look into it, and think about it, you could not believe such foolishness unless you were completely blinded by deception. Those who choose to believe in evolution are either ignorant of the facts about life and the complexities of our world or refuse to open their eyes to the truth. Most evolutionists refuse to believe in God the creator; therefore it leaves them no alternative except to believe the impossibilities of evolution. The magnitude of this deception has influenced our society by promoting the notion that it doesn't matter how you win, just win, even if you have to cheat, steal and kill to win. They call this the survival of the fittest. Evolution denies that there will be a Judgment Day where everyone will be held accountable for his or her actions. Crime skyrockets because criminals believe they will not be caught and held accountable. Evolution has even confused a few Christians who were brainwashed in secular schools and thought God used evolution. To believe this they have to completely reject the first few chapters of the Bible. You cannot truly believe both evolution and the Bible. *Selah.* Deception separates us from reality. It blinds us to the truth. Satan continually promotes his lies and decoys that stand against God's Word from Genesis through the New Testament. Satan cannot hide the historical evidence of Jesus' birth and miraculous life, which has changed the world. Neither can he deny Jesus' death on the cross, and empty tomb, although he would like to. Therefore, he surrounds these truths with his confusing decoys and hopes that at least one of three things will happen.

First: Satan desires to hurt God by steeling what Jesus paid a high price for – you.

Satan would like us to spend our lives chasing his decoys (either deceptions or distractions), overlooking the reality of the matter, resulting in us becoming eternally lost and separated from God's love.

Second: Satan desires to hurt God by contaminating Gods house.

If Satan can't stop us from becoming a Christian, then he tries to cause divisions by getting us to "major on the minors," like the Pharisees. This can lead to promoting distortions and can stir up anger, pride, and unbalanced priorities.

<u>Third</u>: Satan desires to hurt God by slandering God's reputation in order to make God's children distrust Him.

Most of all, Satan wants us to doubt the accuracy of God's Word the Bible by claiming that scientists or historians can disprove the Bible, thereby weakening our faith and trust in God's Word.

In defense of the accuracy of the Bible, I would like to offer my view on the years of Jesus' birth and death, a view that fits both secular history and the Bible. Even if you discount the Bible as being God's Word, you should be aware of the fact that men who were alive during Jesus' time originally recorded the New Testament. Luke talked to many eyewitnesses before writing the Gospel of Luke and Acts. Most of the New Testament writers personally talked with Jesus after His resurrection. Many of them willingly laid down their lives as martyrs rather than deny the truth, as they knew it. What we have to do is decide if we will please God by seeking out and living by the truth.

3 John 1:4

^{4.} **I have no greater joy than to hear that My children <u>walk in truth</u>.**

You will find that valuable truth is usually surrounded (and thus outnumbered) by Satan's clutter and distortions.

2 Timothy 4:3-4

^{3.} **For the time will come when they will not endure sound doctrine; but after their own lusts shall they heap to themselves teachers, having itching ears;**

4. **And <u>they shall turn away their ears from the truth, and shall be turned unto fables</u>.**

We should fact-test all information before making it an important part of our life. The problem is that some things are hard to verify. That is were reasoning and wisdom comes in. Consider how the information links up with what I know to be true. When it comes to spiritual things we should ask ourselves a couple of questions. Are we going to trust God to preserve His Word? Are we going to accept the Bible as our foundational rock of truth upon which to build? If we take God at His Word even when we don't yet really understand it, God will start revealing Himself to us; and the truth will become evident. *Selah.* From the secular point of view, there is evidence that the Passover (14th day of Nisan) occurred on Thursday in the year 30 AD. There are some who calculate this 14th day to be on Wednesday, and others claim it was Friday. Because days were added to every decade to keep pace with the spring and fall equinoxes and other factors, such as there are several different calendars, it is difficult to be precise about the exact day of the week the Jewish priests were using for Passover 2,000 years ago. It is not hard to get an approximate date for events in ancient history. Although to be precise we should also consider how the date fits the patterns of known historical events. There are historians, scientists, Jewish scholars, and others who verify that the 14th day of Nisan in the year 30 was on a Thursday. There is an article posted online that is worth reading, called *"The Crucifixion Date,"* written by M. Orden for *Truth Magazine.* Although I believe that their final conclusion is based on a false assumption (which will be addressed in Chapter 9), I believe the following excerpt to be true regarding the day of Passover in year 30:

A reconstructed dating table, which appeared in *Christianity Today* (March 29, 1974), the results of a computer analysis, corresponds identically with the findings of Humphreys and Waddington. These tables show that the only year between 27 and 34 AD that the 14 Nisan fell on Thursday was in the year 30.

There is a popular belief that Jesus was born after BC to begin AD (there is no year 0) and was crucified in 33 AD. If that were true, Jesus would have been born after Herod died. On the other hand, Jesus' crucifixion in year 30 AD fits nicely with both the secular and Biblical truths, and is in harmony with some generational patterns revealed at the end of chapter 6. If the crucifixion was in 30 AD and Jesus was 33 years old, then depending on how you reckon one's age (whether you are in your first year or have already had your first birthday) and depending on which month Jesus was born, His birth would be no later than year 3 BC and no earlier than year 5 BC. As a result, there is plenty of time for Jesus to be more than two years old in Egypt when Herod died at the beginning of year 1. I cannot say for sure. However, imagine if Jesus' birth were in September of 5 BC. He would then be just over 3 years and 3 months old when Herod died, if Herod died in January of 1 BC as the historical evidence suggests. In August of 26 AD, Jesus would be almost 30 years old when He went to John the Baptist. People would be crowding around and enjoying the warm August weather when Jesus came out of the crowd to be baptized.

Luke 3:21-23

[21.] **Now when all the people were baptized, it came to pass, that Jesus also being baptized, and praying, the Heaven was opened,**

^{22.} **And the Holy Ghost descended in a bodily shape like a dove upon Him, and a voice came from Heaven, which said, thou art my beloved Son; in thee I am well pleased.**

^{23.} **And Jesus himself <u>began</u> to be <u>about thirty years of age</u>, being (as was supposed) the son of Joseph, which was the son of Heli,**

From His baptism, Jesus went to the wilderness and spent the rest of August and September fasting before going into full-time ministry. Jesus spent His 30th birthday fasting and praying. Jesus began his powerful public ministry after He turned 30 years old. People flocked to Him, calling Him "Master," "Rabbi," and "Teacher." Jesus selected His closest disciples and spent the next three-and-a-half years teaching them. He would turn 33 in September of 29 AD; and in the following Passover six months later, He would die for them in 30 AD. This is one scenario that fits both the secular and Biblical facts, but we can't verify its truth at this time. *Selah.* Another scenario that nicely fits Jesus' life and actions is the timing and significance of the Jewish holidays (John 5:39). I'm not an expert on history or the Jewish holidays. I still have much to learn, but I am familiar with the generally accepted facts and some interesting applications. For instance, it is possible that Jesus, the "Light of the World," was conceived in 6 BC during Hanukah, which is called the "Festival of Lights." By the way, there are a variety of ways to spell Hanukah, so please don't get confused or critical of my leaving out the extra letters. Many add an extra K, some add an extra N or put a C in front of the H, but no matter how you spell it, Hanukah was a special celebration of a purified temple. The Messiah (Old Testament) and Christ (New Testament) are titles that refer to God dwelling with us in a purified human body.

Hebrews 10:5

5. **Wherefore when He cometh into the world, He saith, Sacrifice and offering thou wouldest not, but <u>a body hast thou prepared Me</u>:**

God picked a very special time to begin development of the Messiah's body in the Virgin Mary.

Galatians 4:4

4. **But when the <u>fulness of the time was come</u>, God sent forth his Son, <u>made of a woman</u>, made under the law,**

The 8 days of Hanukah in 2016 started on the night of Christmas Eve and ended on New Years Day 2017. Christ is truly the most precious gift, and we should celebrate the conception of Christ. If conceived during Hanukah, then Jesus, the "Prince of Peace," could have been born during Yom Kippur, which celebrates peace on Earth and reconciliation with God (Luke 2:14). This was the time to prepare a small shelter called a "sukkah" for the coming Feast of Tabernacles, a joyful celebration. We know that Jesus died as the sacrificial spotless lamb at the same time the Passover lambs were being killed (Exodus 12:6). The Hebrew word for evening in Exodus 12:6 is plural; "between the two evenings." This was the time between the evening sacrifice (2:30-3:30 pm) and sundown. In addition to Jesus' connection to the week of Passover, the hour Jesus was crucified was significant in the Jewish daily sacrificial system (Exodus 29:38-39). At the beginning of the day, a morning sacrificial lamb was tied to the altar. This was the same time Jesus was bound and delivered to Pilot who bound Jesus to a wiping post before crucifying Him (Mark 15:1). Jesus was put on the cross at the same time the morning daily sacrificial lamb was put on the altar (Mark 15:25). Jesus died at the same time as the daily evening sacrifice was normally killed and put on the altar (Luke 23:44-46). Jesus arose at the beginning of the "Feast of First Fruits," followed later that Sunday by other resurrections, probably around the time of the Wave Offering (Matthew 27:52-53). Then 50 days later, He sent the Holy Spirit during the Feast of Pentecost (Shavuot). Maybe Jesus will come back during the Feast of Trumpets on the 48-hour day of Rosh Hashanah (referred to as "the day that no one knows"). I cannot prove this, but it becomes more fascinating if you understand the reason for the season and ceremony. One day we will clearly see how the entire Bible is pointing to Jesus our savior (John 5:39) and the reason why we need Him. Even now with God's help we can clearly see how the pieces fit together to reveal the facts of life and eternity. *Selah.* There are many things in the Bible a child could and should understand. The Bible is multidimensional. It has a simple message which is found in John 3:16-19 and at the same time it is the deepest most complex book ever written. The Bible revels ancient history, and the causes and effects of our present dilemmas. It predicts future events with 100% accuracy. The most powerful and unique person in the Bible is the Messiah Jesus Christ. In order to identify with us He became a vulnerable little baby in a poor Jewish family. As prophesied He was born in Bethlehem and then was prophesied over, at Jerusalem (Luke 2:25-38). After His second birthday He was visited by magi in Nazareth and was sought after by the king, resulting in Jesus' family sojourning in Egypt. *Selah.* These things are facts but the exact timing of the events is not as clear. In the light of scripture and some credible historical records, I believe the following time-chart represents the best potential timing of Jesus' birth and the events of Jesus' life.

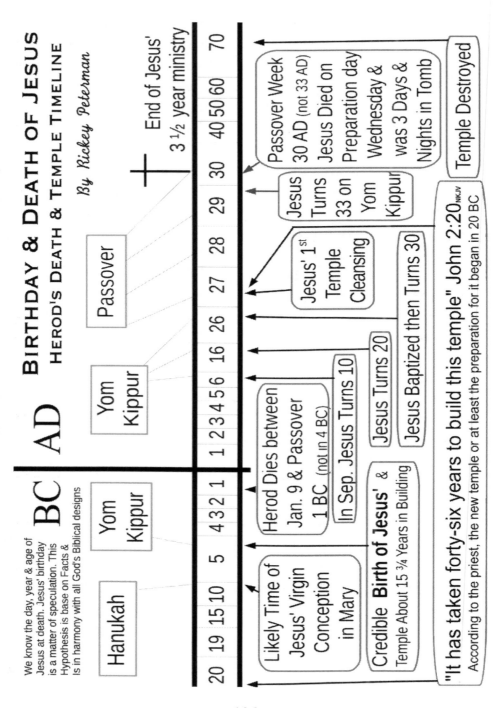

BIRTHDAY & DEATH OF JESUS
HEROD'S DEATH & TEMPLE TIMELINE
By Rickey Peterman

We know the day, year & age of Jesus at death. Jesus' birthday is a matter of speculation. This Hypothesis is base on Facts & is in harmony with all God's Biblical designs

BC | AD

Hanukah

Yom Kippur

Yom Kippur

Passover

Yom Kippur

Passover

End of Jesus' 3 ½ year ministry

20 19 15 10 5 | 4 3 2 1 | 1 2 3 4 5 6 16 26 27 28 29 30 40 50 60 70

Likely Time of Jesus' Virgin Conception in Mary

Herod Dies between Jan. 9 & Passover 1 BC (not in 4 BC)

Credible **Birth of Jesus'** & Temple About 15 ¾ Years in Building

In Sep. Jesus Turns 10

Jesus Turns 20

Jesus Baptized then Turns 30

Jesus' 1st Temple Cleansing

Jesus Turns 33 on Yom Kippur

Passover Week 30 AD (not 33 AD) Jesus Died on Preparation day Wednesday & was 3 Days & Nights in Tomb

Temple Destroyed

"It has taken forty-six years to build this temple" John 2:20 NKJV
According to the priest, the new temple or at least the preparation for it began in 20 BC

106

The timing of these events may be open for discussion. For instance we can lay out a yearly chart and count 46 years from Passover 20 BC to Passover 27 AD. What we don't know is if the priests were counting the 46 years from their approval and the gathering of materials stage or the breaking of ground. Therefore some may see a different year for the beginning of the new temple than others. What we can say for certain is that Jesus' family left Egypt and returned home to Nazareth after Herod's death (Matthew 2:19-20). Jesus grew up in Nazareth as the son of a carpenter.

Luke 2:40

40. **And the child grew, and waxed strong in spirit, filled with wisdom: and the grace of God was upon Him.**

Jesus was full of "wisdom" (knowing how to apply truth properly) and "grace" (having power to act and think properly which gained Him favor).

Luke 2:47, 52

47. **And all that heard Him were astonished at His understanding and answers.**

52. **And Jesus increased in wisdom and stature, and in favour with God and man.**

Jesus did no miracles until He received the Holy Spirit, which was when Jesus was about to be 30 years old. Before His baptism, Jesus' identity (His nature) was human. Everything He did was perfect, but in a natural way. His authority was His humanity, and Jesus was perfect and spotless in His submission to who He was. His personality (Soul) was God eternal, but His identity, authority, and species were human. At conception He took unto

107

Himself a human nature and became a baby boy. As prophesied God's son was born that day in Bethlehem.

Hebrews 2:7

7. **Thou madest Him a little lower than the angels; Thou crownedst Him with glory and honour, and didst set Him over the works of Thy hands:**

Jesus humbled Himself to become a human baby, God's only begotten son, the unique union of Divinity and humanity.

Colossians 1:15

15. **Who is the image of the invisible God, the firstborn of every creature:**

In the Old Testament, the title of "first-born" signified the following:

First: You were specially dedicated unto God.

Second: You were the high priest of the family after the father.

Third: You received a double portion of the inheritance.

Hebrews 2:9

9. **But we see Jesus, who was made a little lower than the angels for the suffering of death, crowned with glory and honour; that He by the grace of God should taste death for every man.**

Colossians 1:18

18. **And He is the head of the body, the church: who is the beginning, the firstborn from the dead; that in all things He might have the preeminence.**

CHAPTER 6

GOD'S SOVEREIGNTY – MAN'S FREEWILL

Can the Sovereign, all-knowing God, the Creator, repent? The word "repent" means to take action in another direction. The word has nothing to do with sin, although it's often correctly associated with sin and the turning away from it. Even so, repentance can also apply to taking a different approach in dealing with something. You can adjust your action according to the moving target. If you didn't adjust and refocus, you would miss the target; and that would be sin as defined earlier. God never sins. His eye is always on the target, and His actions are true. For example, God said He was going to destroy wicked Nineveh.

Jonah 3:5-10

5. So <u>the people of Nineveh believed God</u>, and proclaimed a fast, and put on sackcloth, from the greatest of them even to the least of them.

6. For word came unto the king of Nineveh, and he arose from his throne, and he laid his robe from him, and covered him with sackcloth, and sat in ashes.

7. And he caused it to be proclaimed and published through Nineveh by the decree of the king and his nobles, saying, let neither man nor beast, herd nor flock, taste any thing: let them not feed, nor drink water:

8. But let man and beast be covered with sackcloth, and cry mightily unto God: yea, let them <u>turn every one from his evil way, and from the violence</u> that is in their hands.

9. Who can tell if God will turn and repent, and turn away from His fierce anger, that we perish not?

10. And God saw their works, that <u>they turned</u> from their evil way; and <u>God repented</u> of the evil, that He had said that He would do unto them; and He did it not.

God determined it was time for a change in that area. Change comes in one of two forms – removal or transformation. Nineveh was transformed, because they repented from their evil ways.

1 Corinthians 11:31

31. For if we would judge ourselves, we should not be judged.

Jeremiah 26:13

13. Therefore now amend your ways and your doings, and obey the voice of the Lord your God; and the Lord will repent Him of the evil that He hath pronounced against you.

Wicked Nineveh was destroyed by a revival instead of annihilation. Because they judged themselves and repented, they were no longer wicked Nineveh. They became a community with a new identity and a new outlook on life. They began to respect God. Much later, the city of Nineveh was destroyed, because they fell back into corruption and judgment then fell on them.

Jeremiah 18:8-10

8. <u>If</u> that nation, against whom I have pronounced, turn from their evil, <u>I will repent of the evil</u> that I thought to do unto them.

9. And at what instant I shall speak concerning a nation, and concerning a kingdom, to build and to plant it;

10. <u>If</u> it do evil in my sight, that it obey not my voice, then <u>I will repent of the good</u>, wherewith I said I would benefit them.

God is not looking for revenge against a nation or a people. God's desire is to improve the person, the family, the nation, and the world.

2 Peter 3:9
9. **The Lord is not slack concerning His promise as some men count slackness; but is longsuffering to us-ward, <u>not willing that any should perish</u>, but that all should come to repentance.**

We may see the violence and evil in our world and ask why doesn't God stop it? For one, we are not puppets. We are to learn sowing and reaping. God will give us boundaries, but we are held accountable for our own actions within these boundaries.

Galatians 6:7
7. **Be not deceived; God is not mocked: for <u>whatsoever a man soweth, that shall he also reap.</u>**

God takes no pleasure in anyone's destruction. His desire is that we see the cause and effect, use the knowledge of good and evil, and choose good. He has given us a certain amount of time to decide. The Devil's plan is to blind us to the amount of time we have until it's too late to choose.

Ephesians 5:15-17
15. **See then that ye walk circumspectly, not as fools, but as wise,**

16. **Redeeming the time, because the days are evil.**

17. **Wherefore <u>be ye not unwise, but understanding what the will of the Lord is</u>.**

The Devil has two ditches along God's path for your life. On one side is the ditch of procrastination, "just put it off till tomorrow;" but tomorrow never comes.

2 Corinthians 6:2

2. **For He saith, I have heard thee in a <u>time accepted</u>, and in the day of salvation have I succoured thee: behold, <u>now is the accepted time</u>; behold, <u>now is the day of salvation</u>.**

If the Devil can't get you with procrastination, he will push you to the other extreme and tell you that you don't have enough time. "Live for today, for tomorrow you die," would be his creed. God may want to use you in a mighty way, but if you think the end of the world is upon us, you won't invest the time needed for preparation. *Selah.* In Galatians 1:17-18, it appears that the Pharisee Saul (we know as the Apostle Paul) needed three years with Jesus "the Word" to clarify his message and new direction in life. Moses spent 40 years being prepared in seclusion before God called him at the burning bush to do the impossible (Acts 7:22-36). We read in 1Samuel 16:11 through 18:14 that David knew he was destined to be king, yet waited for God's timing and went back to protecting sheep, out of the limelight. Then, submitting to King Saul, David learned that character is key and the critical importance of following God's Word. Esther spent a year in seclusion and special preparation before meeting her king. Because of her submission to the process, she was able to fulfill her destiny and save her nation (Esther 2:12-17). *Selah.* God did not make a mistake when he picked Saul to be the first king of Israel (1Samuel 10:24). He told the people the negative things about empowering a man as king. Saul proved that God was correct (1Samuel 8:11 through 9:2). Saul looked the part, but his heart wasn't right. He wasn't prepared, so he became corrupted. When Saul was inaugurated as king, he was a humble and dependable man from a prosperous family. Saul was a head taller than most. Saul was a mighty warrior. Saul had a mighty army with the best warriors and generals. David was part of this army, and he was undefeated. Saul was king of the up-and-coming strong nation that was blessed of God. Saul had every material thing he wanted. Saul's every wish was his servants' command. Saul committed suicide because he was not prepared to follow God in his time of success. Ironically, as Saul was dieing from his self-inflicted wound (1Samual 31:4) he had to ask an Amalekite (1Samual 15:18-19) to finish him off (2Samual 1:8-10). Saul is a sad example of a man who had everything, yet was unsatisfied because he lacked character and the meekness to follow God. *Selah.* Some say power corrupts but that is not true, just look at the life of Daniel, Joseph or the most powerful of all Jesus. Power doesn't corrupt it reveals the corruption that is hidden inside. Power gives opportunity for the corruption found in the heart to take action. *Selah.* God's blessings and judgments are conditional. They are based on our actions in response to His Word during our time. Our actions are often based on our preparation or lack thereof for the given situation. God dose not want to judge and condemn us, but He must punish sin and remove evil for the sake of the good and honorable.

Ezekiel 33:11

11. **Say unto them as I live, saith the Lord God, <u>I have no pleasure in the death of the wicked</u>: but that the wicked turn from his way and live: <u>turn ye turn ye from your evil ways</u>; for why will ye die, O house of Israel?**

God doesn't change His mind, but people change their actions. God always wants us to love and respect each other as well as our Creator. That is the target. God doesn't change His mind about this, but He changes His actions and approach to fit the situation. *Selah.* Make no mistake, when time is up, you will love God and respect His creation or you will be eliminated. This sounds harsh but there is a good reason for the severe warning. The reason separation is necessary is similar to a surgeon cutting away cancer so the body can be healthy. The surgeon would not want to remove just part of the cancer if he could get it all, because he knows that the remaining cancer would grow and spread, causing great harm to the body. Even after the surgery, he would recommend additional treatment and monitoring to make sure all the cancer is gone and it doesn't come back. If we cannot walk in love and respect, we will negatively affect our society like a cancer. This is the biggest problem in our world today, but it will not be a problem in Paradise. In Heaven, everyone will naturally love and respect God, love and respect each other, and enjoy taking care of the environment. *Selah.* Loving God is easy. All you have to do is get to know Him, because to know Him is to love Him. If you don't really love God, it's most likely because you don't understand Him or have a misconception regarding His heart, wisdom, and power. *Selah.* Satan (also known as Lucifer) continually tries to distort our perception of God. Lucifer himself misunderstood and underestimated God. He thought he could take God's place. The result was Lucifer's fall into corruption because of his pride.

Isaiah 14:12-15

12. **How art thou fallen from Heaven, O Lucifer, son of the morning! How art thou cut down to the ground, which didst weaken the nations!**

13. **For <u>thou hast said in thine heart</u>, <u>I will ascend</u> into Heaven, <u>I will exalt</u> my throne above the stars of God: <u>I will sit</u> also upon the mount of the congregation, in the sides of the north:**

14. **<u>I will ascend above</u> the heights of the clouds; <u>I will be like the most high</u>.**

15. **Yet thou shalt be brought down to Hell, to the sides of the pit.**

No one, not even top-ranking angels, can replace God's wisdom or power without looking deceived, foolish, and corrupt in the end. *Selah*. God picked Jonah to warn Nineveh, knowing full well that he would run away. It was obvious to those around Jonah that he loved his country Israel (2Kings 14:25), and hated Nineveh the Capital of Assyria. If Jonah went happily to Nineveh and preached their doom, the people of Nineveh probably would have laughed and declared him a crazy fanatic. Then they would have attacked him and probably killed him. Jonah knew God's heart and did not want to give Nineveh any warning or chance to repent.

Jonah 4:2

2. **And he prayed unto the Lord, and said, I pray thee, O Lord, was not this my saying, when I was yet in my country? Therefore I fled before unto tarshish: for I knew that Thou art a gracious God, and merciful, slow to anger, and of great kindness, and repentest Thee of the evil.**

Of his own freewill, Jonah (God's prophet) rebelled against God's direction. However, after the storm, Jonah realized that his life was ruined and he was being consumed by his circumstances. He finally chose of his own freewill to follow God's direction. You would think it's the obvious choice, but many people find themselves in bondage, being consumed, corrupted, and destroyed by their chosen paths in life; and they still resist God's call. However, for those who turn to God of their own freewill, God can use even the worst circumstances to uniquely empower them. Jonah was a changed man after his time in the belly of the great fish. He probably looked different. If I had seen Jonah spit out on the shore from the gaping mouth of a sea monster, I would tell everyone I met. I would also watch closely to see where this unique person was going and what he would do and say. I believe God picked the right man and the best shoreline to empower God's warning, and finally bring revival to a civilization that was on a path to destruction. The Bible does not say why the people of Nineveh believed Jonah, but it does record Jonah's downfall and repentance.

Jonah 2:5-6

5. **The waters compassed me about, even to the soul: the depth closed me round about, the weeds were wrapped about my head.**

6. **<u>I went down</u> to the bottoms of the mountains; the earth with her bars was about me for ever: yet hast <u>Thou brought up my life from corruption</u>, O Lord my God.**

I believe Jonah died that day and was dead three days (Matthew 12:40). In the previous and following verses Jonah acknowledged that his soul departed his body and entered eternity. At that time, Hell contained a place of comfort called Abraham's Bosom where Old Testament saints waited for the Messiah to set them free. In Chapters 11 and 17 of this book there are diagrams and a Biblical explanation of Hell's past, present, and future. In Hell, Jonah was grieved and afflicted himself because of his legacy of rebellion.

Jonah 2:2

2. **And said, I cried by reason of mine affliction unto the LORD, and He heard me; out of the <u>belly of Hell</u> cried I, and Thou heardest my voice.**

Although his body died, his soul was very much alive. As his soul was leaving his body he called out to the Lord.

Jonah 2:7

7. **<u>When my soul fainted within me I remembered the Lord</u>: and <u>my prayer came in unto thee, into Thine Holy Temple</u>.**

Sometimes God has to bring people down in order to lift them up. From Jonah's perspective he had no future. He thought his fate was forever sealed. It looked like he had no hope. However, in reality he had one hope that could change his destiny. *Selah.*

Jonah 2:10

10. And the Lord spake unto the fish, and it vomited out Jonah upon the dry land.

When Jonah hit the ground God revived his body and gave him a command.

Jonah 3:2

2. <u>Arise, go</u> unto Nineveh, that great city, and <u>preach</u> unto it the preaching that I bid thee.

There is some debate about whether it was a fish or whale that swallowed Jonah. In the original language of Matthew 12:40 Jesus called this a "kētos" which is better translated as a great or huge fish with a large gapping mouth. This was no ordinary fish. God especially prepared this fish to be able to swallow Jonah whole.

Jonah 1:17

17. Now <u>the LORD had prepared a great fish to swallow up Jonah</u>. And Jonah was in the belly of the fish three days and three nights.

There are no mistakes or contradictions in God's Word but there are many doors to deeper revelation. *Selah.* Jonah realized he was powerless to save himself or change his circumstances, so he focused on the temple of God.

Jonah 2:4

4. Then I said, I am cast out of Thy sight; yet I will <u>look again toward Thy Holy Temple.</u>

From the belly of this enormous fish, Jonah could not see the holy temple with his natural eyes. He had to look with spiritual eyes and picture it in his mind. Why did Jonah consider the temple of God? The temple was very important, even from the first prayer that was answered regarding it. The Bible recorded King Solomon's prayer of dedication.

1 Kings 8:37-43

37. **If there be in the land famine, if there be pestilence, blasting, mildew, locust, or if there be caterpiller; if their enemy besiege them in the land of their cities; whatsoever plague, whatsoever sickness there be;**

38. **What <u>prayer and supplication soever be made by any man</u>, or by all thy people Israel, which shall know every man the plague of his own heart, and spread forth his hands <u>toward this house</u>:**

39. **Then hear Thou in Heaven Thy dwelling place, and forgive, and do, and give to every man according to his ways, whose heart Thou knowest; (for Thou, even Thou only, knowest the hearts of all the children of men;)**

40. **That they may fear Thee all the days that they live in the land which Thou gavest unto our fathers.**

41. **Moreover concerning a <u>stranger,</u> that is not of Thy people Israel, but cometh out of a <u>far country</u> for Thy name's sake;**

42. **(For they shall hear of Thy great name, and of Thy strong hand, and of Thy stretched out arm;) <u>when he shall come and pray toward this house;</u>**

43. **<u>Hear Thou in Heaven</u> Thy dwelling place, and do according to all that the stranger calleth to Thee for: <u>that all people of the</u>**

<u>Earth</u> may know Thy name, to fear Thee, as do Thy people Israel; and that they may know that this house, which I have builded, is called by Thy name.

The temple was a symbol of God's presence on Earth, a place where prayers were answered and miracles happened, not only for the nation of Israel, but for all people.

1 Kings 9:3

3. And the Lord said unto him <u>I have heard thy prayer</u> and thy supplication, that thou hast made before Me: <u>I have hallowed this house,</u> which thou hast built, to <u>put My name there</u> for ever: and Mine eyes and Mine heart shall be there perpetually.

God answered King Solomon's prayer and blessed the temple with God's presence and power. So, what happened to the temple?

1 Kings 9:6-7

6. <u>But if</u> ye shall at all turn from following Me, ye or your children, and will not keep My commandments and My statutes which I have set before you, but go and serve other gods, and worship them:

7. <u>Then will I cut off</u> Israel out of the land which I have given them; and this house, which I have hallowed for My name, will I cast out of my sight; and Israel shall be a proverb and a byword among all people:

The blessing of God's presence in the temple would last forever, as long as the people didn't reject God. When we reject God and His plans, we are turning to Satan and his plans, whether we realize it or not. God gives us a choice. The temple Solomon built lasted about four centuries. According to historians, war with Babylon destroyed it in 586 BC. The temple was rebuilt 70 years later in 516 BC during the time of Ezra. Then around 20 BC, King Herod announced he would replace this old second temple with a new grand temple. These two temples are referred to as the second temple because there was no gap between the second and third temples. It was this renewed, grand third temple that Jesus entered, at the beginning of his earthly ministry.

John 2:11-16

11. This beginning of miracles did Jesus in Cana of Galilee, and manifested forth His glory; and His disciples believed on Him.

12. After this He went down to Capernaum, He, and His mother, and His brethren, and His disciples: and they continued there not many days.

13. And the Jews' Passover was at hand, and Jesus went up to Jerusalem,

14. And found in the temple those that sold oxen and sheep and doves, and the changers of money sitting:

15. And when He had made a scourge of small cords, He drove them all out of the temple, and the sheep, and the oxen; and poured out the changers' money, and overthrew the tables;

16. And said unto them that sold doves, take these things hence; make not My Father's house an house of merchandise.

These preceding verses describe the first of three times that Jesus would cleanse the temple in this manner. You see, the merchants were shortchanging and taking advantage of the people for profit. Therefore, instead of having a reputation of being a house of prayer and miracles, the temple was a place where people were being ripped off! Well, after this action of cleansing the temple, the temple leaders certainly paid attention to this new representative of God.

John 2:18-21

^{18.} **Then answered the Jews and said unto Him, what sign shewest Thou unto us, seeing that Thou doest these things?**

^{19.} **Jesus answered and said unto them, <u>destroy this temple, and in three days I will raise it up</u>.**

^{20.} **Then said the Jews, forty and six years was this temple in building, and wilt thou rear it up in three days?**

^{21.} **But He spake of the <u>temple of his body</u>.**

The people were looking at the temple building, not realizing that Jesus was referring to Himself, because He was the true Temple of God that the building represented. Jesus is the Temple of God to whom all people can pray. Jesus is the one all people can look to for salvation and see God's presence performing miracles. Nevertheless, God is not done with the temple building. Jesus spoke about what was going to happen to temple building as well as its significance for us.

Matthew 24:1-2

^{1.} **And Jesus went out, and departed from the temple: and His disciples came to Him for to shew Him the buildings of the temple.**

^{2.} **And Jesus said unto them, see ye not all these things? Verily I say unto you, there shall <u>not be left here one stone upon another</u>, that shall not be thrown down.**

Jesus revealed that the temple building was temporary and would be removed after his crucifixion. It was destroyed 40 years later in 70 AD just as He foretold. Jesus also revealed that this destruction was not the end of the temple. It would come back to establish the last generation. *Selah.* Many people have misinterpreted the symbol of the fig tree, believing that it is the nation of Israel. It is not. As we will see, the fig tree is actually a symbol of Israel's temple. References to the fig tree appear many times in the Bible. When we define the fig tree as Israel's temple, the meaning of these passages becomes clear and meaningful. So let's see what Jesus was saying about the fig tree in these various passages and actions. We will start with the conversation that followed Jesus' previous statement about the temple's removal.

Matthew 24:32-34

32. **Now learn a parable of the fig tree; when his branch is yet tender, and putteth forth leaves, ye know that summer is nigh:**

33. **So likewise ye, when ye shall see all these things, know that it is near, even at the doors.**

34. **Verily I say unto you, this generation shall not pass, till all these things be fulfilled.**

Jesus told more than one parable of the fig tree. In this example, He refers to how the fig tree (temple activity) relates to a special season. This is not a yearly season, but rather a generation of time. It is the last generation before Jesus comes back to Earth to establish His kingdom. In another parable, Jesus uses the fig tree to illustrate the end of Passover power in the temple. Passover was a feast to celebrate deliverance from death in the night and being set free from bondage. If you substitute the word "temple" for "fig tree" and substitute "Israel" for "vineyard," the parable makes sense, and the revelation becomes clear.

Luke 13:6-9

6. He spake also this parable; a certain man had a fig tree (temple) **planted in his vineyard** (Israel); **and he came and sought fruit thereon, and found none.**

7. **Then said he unto the dresser of his vineyard** (Israel), **behold, these** three years I come seeking fruit **on this fig tree** (temple), **and find none: cut it down; why cumbereth it the ground?**

8. **And he answering said unto him, lord,** let it alone this year also, **till I shall dig about it, and dung it:**

9. **And if it** (temple) **bear fruit, well: and if not,** then after that thou shalt cut it down.

This parable is talking about the four times Jesus went to the temple for Passover during His three-and-a-half-year earthly ministry. About six months after Jesus was baptized with the Holy Ghost, He went to the temple, and as we read earlier, He cleansed it. At the end of his first year and a half of ministry, He went for the second Passover in the temple. The third Passover was at the end of His second year and a half, and the temple was on probation. At the end of His three-and-a-half-year ministry was His fourth and final Passover at the temple. The "fig tree's" time was up. *Selah.* Let's look at the sequence of events that began Jesus' fourth and last Passover week.

Matthew 21:1-20

1. **And when they drew nigh unto Jerusalem, and were come to Bethphage, unto the Mount of Olives, then sent Jesus two disciples,**

2. **Saying unto them, go into the village over against you, and straightway ye shall find an ass tied, and a colt with her: loose them, and bring them unto Me.**

3. And if any man say ought unto you, ye shall say, the Lord hath need of them; and straightway he will send them.

4. All this was done, that it might be fulfilled which was spoken by the prophet, saying,

5. Tell ye the daughter of Sion, behold, thy King cometh unto thee, meek, and sitting upon an ass, and a colt the foal of an ass.

6. And the disciples went, and did as Jesus commanded them,

7. And brought the ass, and the colt, and put on them their clothes, and they set Him thereon.

8. And a very great multitude spread their garments in the way; others cut down branches from the trees, and strawed them in the way.

9. And the multitudes that went before, and that followed, cried, saying, hosanna to the Son of David: blessed is He that cometh in the name of the Lord; hosanna in the highest.

10. And when He was come into Jerusalem, all the city was moved, saying, who is this?

11. And the multitude said, this is Jesus the prophet of Nazareth of Galilee.

12. And <u>Jesus went into the temple of God, and cast out all them that sold and bought in the temple, and overthrew the tables of the moneychangers, and the seats of them that sold doves,</u>

13. <u>And said unto them, it is written, My house shall be called the house of prayer; but ye have made it a den of thieves.</u>

14. And the blind and the lame came to Him in the temple; and He healed them.

15. And when the chief priests and scribes saw the wonderful things that He did, and the children crying in the temple, and saying, hosanna to the Son of David; they were sore displeased,

16. And said unto Him, hearest Thou what these say? And Jesus saith unto them, yea; have ye never read, out of the mouth of babes and sucklings thou hast perfected praise?

17. And He left them, and <u>went out of the city into Bethany; and he lodged there.</u>

18. <u>Now in the morning as He returned into the city,</u> He hungered.

19. And when He saw a <u>fig tree</u> in the way, He came to it, and found nothing thereon, but leaves only, and said unto it, let <u>no fruit</u> grow on thee henceforward for ever. And <u>presently the fig tree withered away.</u>

20. And when the disciples saw it, <u>they marvelled,</u> saying, <u>how soon is the fig tree withered away!</u>

Here we have the second cleansing of the temple, and the next day, a symbolic lesson with the fig tree. The fig tree's time was up, and after receiving the fatal words, immediately showed signs of death. The disciples probably saw it dropping its leaves as it withered up. Let's back up a little and look at this event from Mark's perspective.

Mark 11:7-19

7. And they brought the colt to Jesus, and cast their garments on him; and He sat upon him.

8. And many spread their garments in the way: and others cut down branches off the trees, and strawed them in the way.

125

9. And they that went before, and they that followed, cried, saying, hosanna; blessed is He that cometh in the name of the Lord:

10. Blessed be the kingdom of our father David, that cometh in the name of the Lord: hosanna in the highest.

11. And <u>Jesus entered into Jerusalem, and into the temple</u>: and when he had looked round about upon all things, and <u>now the eventide was come, He went out unto Bethany with the twelve</u>.

12. <u>And on the morrow</u>, when they were come from Bethany, He was hungry:

13. And seeing a <u>fig tree</u> afar off having leaves, He came, if haply He might find any thing thereon: and when He came to it, <u>He found nothing but leaves</u>; for the time of figs was not yet.

14. And Jesus answered and said unto it, <u>no man eat fruit of thee hereafter for ever</u>. And his disciples heard it.

15. And <u>they come to Jerusalem: and Jesus went into the temple, and began to cast out them that sold and bought in the temple, and overthrew the tables of the moneychangers, and the seats of them that sold doves</u>;

16. And would not suffer that any man should carry any vessel through the temple.

17. And He taught, saying unto them, is it not written, My house shall be <u>called of all nations the house of prayer</u>? But ye have made it a den of thieves.

18. And the scribes and chief priests heard it, and sought how they might destroy Him: for they feared Him, because all the people was astonished at His doctrine.

^{19.} **And when even was come, He went out of the city.**

Here we see the third temple cleansing. The fig tree is right in the middle of the two temple cleansings, no doubt part of the same lesson about the cause and effect of God removing His favor. *Selah.* Jesus and His disciples headed east out of Jerusalem and spent their nights in the Mount of Olives in places like Gethsemane and Bethany.

John 11:18 (NIV)

^{18.} **Now Bethany was less than two miles from Jerusalem,**

Bethany was on the southeastern slope of the Mount of Olives. It would take about an hour to walk to Jerusalem from Bethany. The morning after the fig tree died and the third temple cleansing, Jesus and His disciples were walking back to Jerusalem. The disciples took note of the vanishing rejected fig tree.

Mark 11:20-21

^{20.} **And in the morning, as they passed by, they saw the fig tree dried up from the roots.**

^{21.} **And Peter calling to remembrance saith unto Him, Master, behold, the fig tree which Thou cursedst is withered away.**

The next day the fig tree is a little rotten twig ready to blow away. Peter marveled at how fast the effect of death took hold. Here we have two recordings of the death of the fig tree. First, we see that it was immediately lifeless. Then on the second day, it was in the process of removal. Like the fig tree, the temple had two phases to its demise. The first phase was the removal of spiritual life at Jesus' death.

Matthew 27:50-51

50. Jesus, when He had cried again with a loud voice, <u>yielded up the ghost</u>.

51. And, behold, the <u>veil of the temple was rent in twain from the top to the bottom; and the earth did quake, and the rocks rent;</u>

The thick veil covering the entrance to the Holy of Holy's was ripped open from top to bottom as a sign that (like the fig tree) the temple's time was up. God was removing His blessing. The temple shook and symbolically dropped its leaves (covering). From that time forward things in the temple went mysteriously dark. According to both versions of the Talmud, Jewish scholars living in the first century admitted that for the next forty years the menorah's main temple light (which was referred to as the eternal light) went out every night (John 3:19). This works out to about 14,600 times in a row this ominous sign happened without anyone being able to stop the light from going out. Every year during the Feast of Atonement, lots were cast to choose the atonement sacrifice and the "scapegoat" (Leviticus 16:7-10). The forty years after Jesus' crucifixion the right and left hand results were the same. Also the crimson ribbon removed from the "scapegoat" and tied to the temple door no longer turned white. This indicated their animal sacrifices did not remove or cover their sins (Isaiah 1:18). They also mentioned, during this last forty years the temple doors would miraculously open during the night which they took as a sign of doom because of Zechariah 11:1. Forty is often a transitional number. Forty years after Jesus' crucifixion the temple was burned and entered the second phase of its demise. The temple was destroyed in 70 AD and its valuable gold was plundered. The temple was destroyed just as Jesus predicted (Mark 13:2). *Selah.* Jesus also said it is going to be rebuilt again before He comes back. Lets look at the significance of the temple's return and properly identify the fig tree.

Luke 21:29-32

29. **And He spake to them a parable; behold the <u>fig tree, and all the trees;</u>**

30. **When they now shoot forth, ye see and know of your own selves that summer is now nigh at hand.**

31. **So likewise ye, when ye see these things come to pass, know ye that the kingdom of God is nigh at hand.**

32. **Verily I say unto you, <u>this generation shall not pass away, till</u> all be fulfilled.**

If we believe the fig tree is a nation (Israel), then to be consistent, "all the trees" would be all the nations coming back at the end. We know that the Amalekites and many other nations are not coming back. On the other hand the fig tree, which represents the temple in Israel (the center and core of the Jewish religion) is coming back. All the other trees (religions) with their branches of poison theology are coming back as well. That is why Jesus said "The fig tree, and all the trees." The new age movement is not new. Its roots go all the way back to the tower of Babel. Some form of all the corrupted religions will be present before Jesus comes back again. Christianity will also be here as a lighthouse for the lost, pointing the way into the only safe harbor during this dark stormy time. *Selah*. The mustard seed that grows into a great tree symbolizes the body of Christ. Jesus is the seed and root of Christianity. Jesus refers to Himself as the vine and his followers as the branches.

John 15:5

5. **I am the vine, ye are the branches: He that abideth in me, and**

I in him, the same bringeth forth much fruit: for without me ye can do nothing.

You cannot have true Christianity without being personally connected to Jesus Christ. Jesus compared His kingdom to a mustard seed, not a fig tree or any other religion.

Mark 4:30-32
30. And He said, whereunto shall we liken the kingdom of God? Or with what comparison shall we compare it?

31. It is like a grain of mustard seed, which, when it is sown in the earth, is less than all the seeds that be in the earth:

32. But when it is sown, it groweth up, and <u>becometh greater than all herbs, and shooteth out great branches</u>; so that the fowls of the air may lodge under the shadow of it.

Matthew 13:32
32. Which indeed is the least of all seeds: but when it is grown, it is the greatest among herbs, and <u>becometh a tree</u>, so that the birds of the air come and lodge in the branches thereof.

Christianity looks like a tree (or religion), but is in a different class. "Religion" is rooted in the works and rituals of man attempting to reach their version of God. Christianity is rooted in the relationship between believers and Christ. *Selah.* So, why is the fig tree (the Jewish temple) so important for us today? Let's take another look at how Luke 21 describes the last generation before Christ returns.

Luke 21:27-32
27. And <u>then</u> shall they see the Son of man coming in a cloud with power and great glory.

28. And <u>when</u> these things begin to come to pass, then look up, and lift up your heads; for your redemption draweth nigh.

29. And He spake to them a parable; behold the <u>fig tree</u>, and all the trees;

30. When they now shoot forth, ye see and know of your own selves that summer is now nigh at hand.

31. So likewise ye, when ye see these things come to pass, know ye that the kingdom of God is nigh at hand.

32. Verily I say unto you, <u>this generation shall not pass away, till all be fulfilled</u>.

There are numerous signs of the last days, and they are interesting to discuss. Jesus was discussing some of these signs when He pointed out a particular one, "behold the fig tree" or look at the Jewish temple. Are there signs of life in it, proving that the season has come? Seems to me, the fig tree showing signs of life is a key signal that the last generation has begun. Therefore, if the fig tree, the Jewish temple, has not yet come back (it is common knowledge that it will be back before the end), are we in the last generation yet? I believe that the temple begins the last generation time clock. Before getting into that, I would like to address a popular belief that the Antichrist will build the next Jewish temple. I have looked all through the Bible, including the book of Daniel, and can find no reference to verify that assumption. There are, however, references to the Antichrist setting up shop in the temple and his defiling it. I set up shop and opened my business by making changes to an existing building. I see nothing in the Bible to indicate that the Antichrist won't do the same. *Selah.* So, the question would be, how much time is left after the temple comes back? Would it be a week or seven years or maybe just three and a half years? Will the church be raptured before the last generation starts? How long will the last generation last? There are many who believe and teach that we are almost out of time and that the end is imminent. It's interesting to listen to their perspective on current events. They may be seeing the preparation (birth pains) for the coming big events. It is possible for God to fulfill all the prophecies, including the return of the Jewish temple, the rapture, and have the last generation experience the Great Tribulation leading to Jesus' return during the next ten years. However, we cannot confirm this with any Biblical authority, because as in the time of Nineveh, God desires revival. Therefore, should we be preparing to leave or to lead, and by the grace of God carry out our part in the next great revival? The entire world is due for the next Great Awakening. God is looking at the condition of the harvest (John 4:35, Mathew 9:37-38, Luke 10:1-2, Psalm 94:16, Proverbs 10:5). It seems to me it would be out of character for God to rush through these end time events. For instance, look at the parable in Matthew 25:1-13. There are five wise and the five foolish virgins looking for the Lord's return. One point of the parable is that the Lord returned later than expected. In Mark 4:35-41, Jesus waited to calm the sea until His disciples lost all confidence in their boat and ability and thought they would drown. *Selah.* There will be a time when we only have ten years left. There is a Biblical time limit once the last generation starts. To know the time limit, we need to define the different ways the Bible uses the word "generation." Many believe a generation is 40 years. That would be a transitional generation, represented by the 40 years Israel wandered in the wilderness because of their sin. Another way to use the word would be like taking a three-generational picture. There is a grandson to a grandfather. This refers to lineage not a timetable. Luke 21:32 and Mathew 24:34 are referring to a prophetic generation. It is a statement of prophecy that "this generation **shall not** pass away, till all be fulfilled." The Bible tells us and verifies how long a prophetic generation actually is. It is undisputable once you see it. *Selah.* Right after Jesus pointing out that the last generation was associated with the fig tree (Jewish temple), He talked about Noah.

Matthew 24:37 (NKJV)

37. **"But <u>as the days of Noah</u> were, so also will the coming of the Son of Man be.**

In the days of Noah, evangelism had been failing for an extended period of time. People had a tendency towage evil and were indifference regarding Noah's warning (2Peter 2:5). This is not as much of a specific sign as it is of a general condition. To some degree, spiritual apathy and rebellion is a common description of a large number of people throughout history. Our job as the church is to be faithful in sharing the true for as long as we are here. We don't know when the influence of the church has produced its last convert to Christ. *Selah.* I believe there is a more specific and deeper revelation hidden "in the days of Noah." Jesus was not predicting the day or hour but He was giving us a specific time frame or season for His return. During the days of Noah, the Bible clearly reveals the length of a prophetic generation.

Genesis 6:3

3. **And the Lord said, My Spirit shall not always strive with man, for that he also is flesh: yet his days <u>shall be</u> an hundred and twenty years.**

This is a prophetic statement that man's days shall be 120 years. This gives us the number, but not the proof that it applies to a prophetic generation. For that, we begin with 75-year old

Abraham at the end of a very busy year (more about that later). Abraham was cutting the covenant of promise with God, and at the conclusion, God made a prophetic statement to Abraham.

Genesis 15:16

16. But in the <u>fourth generation they shall</u> come hither again: for the iniquity of the Amorites is not yet full.

God makes a prophetic statement to Abraham that in the fourth (120-year prophetic) generation; Abraham's future children (who came to be known as Israel) would be in the Promised Land. Beginning with that covenant statement, the fourth prophetic generation would be from years 360 to 480. For God's Word to be true, and it is, Israel would have to be in the Promised Land before the end of the fourth generation (120 x 4 = 480 years).

Exodus 12:40-41

40. Now the sojourning of the children of Israel, who dwelt in Egypt, was <u>four hundred and thirty years</u>.

41. And it came to pass at the end of the <u>four hundred and thirty years, even the selfsame day</u> it came to pass, that all the hosts of the Lord went out from the land of Egypt.

It was "the end of" exactly 430 years to the day, the "selfsame day," between Abraham's covenant of promise and Israel coming out of Egypt. There are exactly 430 years between Abraham's covenant and the first Passover. The Passover was a part of fulfilling the covenant of promise.

Genesis 15:14

14. And also that nation, whom they shall serve, <u>I will judge: and afterward shell they come out with great substance</u>.

The day Abraham agreed in covenant with God became the day of celebrating deliverance, which we call the Passover. Abraham made the covenant sacrifice on the afternoon of Passover, Nisan 14 (Genesis 15:9-11). The next Jewish day begins at sundown. At the beginning of Nisan 15, which is the "Feast of Unleavened Bread," God confirmed His covenant with Abraham (Genesis 15:12-18). (I will explain the 400 years later in this chapter). Some assume that Israel was in Egypt the entire 430 years. Some believe that the Jewish people were slaves in Egypt 430 years. Both these statements would contradict God's Word. Whenever we contradict God's Word, it will lead to confusion and blind us from the Revelation God has given to us.

Galatians 3:17-18

[17.] **And this I say, that <u>the covenant,</u> that was confirmed before of God in Christ, <u>the law, which was four hundred and thirty years after,</u> cannot disannul, that it should make the promise of none effect.**

[18.] **For if the inheritance be of the law, it is no more of promise: but <u>God gave it to Abraham by promise</u>.**

Here God's Word refers to the 430 years between covenant of promise given to Abraham (Genesis 15:18) and the law given to Moses on Mount Sinai shortly after Passover (Exodus 19:1-7). Israel was in Egypt only half of the 430 years. According to the timetable in the Bible, Israel was in Egypt about 215 years, as clearly seen in the time chart at the end of this chapter. More than half of these years were a blessing, because Joseph, second to Pharaoh, provided for their every need with the best of Egypt. During the last half of Israel's stay in Egypt, a new Pharaoh (who knew not Joseph) arrived. As a result, Israel experienced bondage and persecution because this new king feared that Israel might join an insurrection, or somehow aid in his defeat.

Exodus 1:6-11

6. And <u>Joseph died, and all his brethren</u>, and all that generation.

7. And the children of Israel were fruitful, and increased abundantly, and <u>multiplied</u>, and waxed exceeding mighty; and <u>the land was filled with them</u>.

8. Now <u>there arose up a new king over Egypt, which knew not Joseph</u>.

9. And he said unto his people, behold, the people of the children of Israel are more and mightier than we:

10. Come on, let us deal wisely with them; lest they multiply, and it come to pass, that, when there falleth out any war, they join also unto our enemies, and fight against us, and so get them up out of the land.

11. Therefore they did set over them taskmasters to afflict them with their burdens. And they built for Pharaoh treasure cities, Pithom and Raamses.

Why are these details so important? Once you see the true portrait and pattern the Word is painting, it not only sheds light on when the last generation starts and how long it could last, it also provides one of the best illustrations of God's sovereignty and man's freewill working together. *Selah.* The Prophetic Generational Time Chart at the end of this chapter makes this easier to see. The top line is the first 120-year generation. It begins with the promise given to Abraham and includes a few highlights. The Bible is clear that Abraham (formerly called Abram) received the promise that preceded the covenant at age 75.

Genesis 12:1-5

1. **Now the Lord had said unto Abram, get thee out of thy country, and from thy kindred, and from thy father's house, unto a land that I will shew thee:**

2. **And I will make of thee a great nation, and I will bless thee, and make thy name great; and thou shalt be a blessing:**

3. **And I will bless them that bless thee, and curse him that curseth thee: and in thee shall all families of the Earth be blessed.**

4. **So Abram departed, as the Lord had spoken unto him; and Lot went with him: and <u>Abram was seventy and five years old when he departed out of Haran.</u>**

5. **And Abram took Sarai his wife, and Lot his brother's son, and all their substance that they had gathered, and the souls that they had gotten in Haran; and they <u>went forth to go into the land of Canaan;</u> and into the land of Canaan they came.**

Nothing more is said about Abraham's age or time in the Promised Land until 10 years later. Some may believe it was towards middle of this decade that Abraham and God made the covenant in Genesis 15. I believe Abraham was still 75 when he made that covenant because Galatians 3:17 refers to it and the timing fits the Biblical pattern. The only reason for confusion is that a lot happened between the call and the covenant. As is so often the case, satanic activity increases before a big God event. *Selah.* I would like to offer my personal opinion as to the timing of the events of Abraham's first year and following decade in the Promised Land. I believe you will see this is possible, logical, Biblical and insightful. Abraham's covenant year has many parallels to the year Isaac was born, which we will look at as well.

Abraham's covenant year begins back in Haran; Abraham turned 75 and God called him south to the Promised Land. He traveled about 30 to 40 days. During his time in the Promised Land, Abraham made offerings (Genesis 12:6-8) and God confirmed that this was the land He had promised.

Genesis 12:9-10

⁹· **And Abram journeyed, going on still toward the south.**

¹⁰· **And <u>there was a famine in the land: and Abram went down into Egypt to sojourn there</u>; for the famine was grievious in the land.**

Abraham kept traveling and exploring because there was a famine. Probably a couple of months had gone by and Abraham was in Egypt and his wife was about to become part of Pharaoh's harem. However, before Pharaoh could sleep with her, a great calamity occurred. These supernatural plagues delivered Sarah back to Abraham, and the truth came out (Genesis 12:14-20). Abraham and Sarah were able to keep the cattle and servants they were given (one of which was Ishmael's mother Hagar), but had to leave the country. Maybe four or five months had passed since they started their pilgrimage, and they were back at Bethel with more cattle and people, but still not much food (Genesis 13:1-7). Abraham gave his nephew Lot his choice of land (Genesis 13:8-9). Lot chose the green land of Jordan where there was plenty of water in spite of the famine, as well as great cities to enjoy (Genesis 13:10-12). After parting from Lot, Abraham went the other way to Hebron (Genesis 13:14-18). Lot thought he had chosen the best land for himself, but didn't realize he was arriving just in time for a war (Genesis 14:8-12). Sodom lost the war again, and because they had not paid their servitude from their loss 14 years earlier, Sodom was plundered. Lot and his family were taken captive. It may have been five or six months since Abraham had seen Lot, but once again he came to Lot's rescue. With a bold and wise strategy, Abraham did what the evil kings could not. He delivered Lot, the rest of the captives, and the booty back to Sodom (Genesis 14:13-17). It was a very busy year, but Abraham still found time for God (Genesis 12:1, Genesis 12:7, Genesis 12:8, Genesis 13:4, Genesis 13:14-18, Genesis 14:20 and Genesis 15:1-18). I believe the 75th year of Abraham's life began with the call and the promise, became a roller coaster ride of emotions and events, ending up with the all important day when God would make a special covenant with Abraham to confirm the promise (Genesis 15:1-8, Genesis 15:18). *Selah.* After that, things simmered down for a while. Years went by until Sarah no longer believed she would have a child and shared her doubts with Abraham. After all, it had been almost a decade since God made the covenant with Abraham about his children (Genesis 16:1-3). Abraham turned 85, and time was running out – or so they thought. This was a different kind of test. Instead of the earlier intense activity, God seemed silent, and Abraham and Sarah had to wait and wait and wait some more. Many people fail this test of patiently trusting God's Word. They give up hope or they rush ahead of God. Abraham and Sarah decided to take things into their own hands. They applied the carnal works of the flesh and the commonly accepted practices of their day to satisfy their desire for a legacy. Consequently, by the time Abraham was 86, the fruit of their misunderstanding of God's timetable arrived.

Genesis 16:16

16. **And <u>Abram was fourscore and six years old</u>, when Hagar bare Ishmael to Abram.**

Ishmael was born when Abraham was 86 years old. Ishmael was 14 years old when the promise of the covenant arrived, which was Sarah's child Isaac. A year earlier when Abraham was 99,

God revealed that the time of the promised birth had come (Genesis 17:1-17). Shortly after they obeyed God's Word regarding the covenant, God revealed that Isaac would be born in 9 months (Genesis 18:1-14). It was another year of intense activity, similar to their first year in the Promised Land. It was a mirror reflection of the year when Abraham was 75. This time instead of ending with a covenant, it started with a covenant (Genesis 17:2). This time instead of Sodom being plundered it was destroyed (Genesis 19:1-29). Also once again Sarah needed to be rescued by God from another foreign king (Genesis 20:2-18). During this eventful year (Genesis 17:1- 21:5), Abraham turned 100 and saw God's promise fulfilled when Isaac was born.

Genesis 21:5

5. And **Abraham was an hundred years old**, when his son Isaac was born unto him.

Just as a farmer needs to recognize whether it is seedtime, growth-time, or harvest-time, we also need to discern the season we are in. Abraham's life is an example of what happens if we misunderstand God's timing and follow our fleshly desires. The results are short-lived happiness followed by frustration, grief and depression. Everyone makes mistakes, but we can still enjoy God's blessings if we realign ourselves with God's Word (Genesis 17:23). To some degree we experience all three activities (sowing, growing, and reaping) at once, but often one will seem to dominate our circumstances. Different projects may be in different seasons of their maturity. They begin with the seed, which is the initial idea, activity or act of obedience. Then comes the opportunity for growth and development. We seem to be going in circles trying to find our way. It can seem like we are spending a lot of time going nowhere. There is a lot of effort without much accomplishment. It is dark and discouraging but if we look to God we will see the light of His Word pointing out our next step (Psalm 119:105). As the prophet Jeremiah experienced, we may be in the center of God's will and find our activities seem fruitfulness. This is the time to remember God's previous words to us and meditate on God's Biblical principals. This is the time to refine character and establish faithfulness. In order to have a good harvest we must continue to apply the water of God's Word and be parent (Ephesians 5:26-27). Even if we become unfaithful, if we learn from our error and return to applying God's Word we will see a wonderful harvest. This process helped Abraham to become the man of faith that God would refer to as His friend. Israel experienced this pattern as they left the bondage of Egypt and were refined in the wilderness resulting in finally possessing the Promised Land.

Galatians 6:9

9. **And let us not be weary in well doing: for in due season we shall reap, if we faint not.**

Whether our days are full of intense activity or seem boring and God seems quiet; it is wise to follow God's Word and trust God for the results. *Selah*. If you look again at the time chart at the end of this chapter, the middle line shows the four 120-year generations. The 400-year line begins with Isaac's fifth birthday party when Ishmael mistreated Isaac so much that they had to be separated (Genesis 21:8-14). That began an alternating cycle of good and evil for Isaac and his descendants, which were seen as foreigners. As the 400-years was coming to the end, God called Moses at the burning bush to deliver Israel out of bondage (Exodus 3:1-10). *Selah*. Persecution or prosperity could not stop Isaac's descendants from fulfilling their destiny and becoming a strong nation in their promise-land. After much turmoil, they reached their peak as a nation during the time of David and

Solomon and became the strongest, richest nation on Earth. Yet Jerusalem is destine for its greatest glory when Jesus the King of kings comes back. *Selah.* Satan can't change the prophecies of God. The 400 years can be a little confusing, but it clearly illustrates that God was not surprised by the actions of man or Satan. Long before the trouble began, God had the plan and promise of deliverance, even to the exact year the prepared deliverer was to be called into action. The year God picked for Israel's deliverance from Egypt was 430 years after the covenant. This was also 400 years after Isaac was publicly declared as the "firstborn" child of promise (Genesis 17:19) and patriarch to Jesus the Messiah. The time was right and Moses reluctantly but humbly accepted God's timetable and plan to use him as the deliverer. At the Passover and exodus from Egypt, the 400-year and the 430-year prophesies were both fulfilled. *Selah.* In a similar way the very year of Jesus' crucifixion was prophesied using symbolic language (Daniel 9:25-26). The Bible prophesied, in 30 AD the Messiah would be cut off resulting in our deliverance from the bondage of sin. Jesus arrived at the exact right time and place to fulfill every prophecy regarding His first coming as our Savior. Before God created the world, He knew the day that He would redeem the lost.

1 Peter 1:18-21

18. **Forasmuch as ye know that ye were not redeemed with corruptible things, as silver and gold, from your vain conversation received by tradition from your fathers;**

19. **But with the precious blood of Christ, as of a lamb without blemish and without spot:**

20. **Who verily was <u>foreordained before the foundation of the world</u>, but was manifest in these last times for you,**

21. **Who by Him do believe in God, that raised Him up from the dead, and gave Him glory; that your faith and hope might be in God.**

2 Timothy 1:9-10

9. **Who hath saved us, and called us with an holy calling, not according to our works, but according to His own purpose and grace, which was <u>given us in Christ Jesus before the world began,</u>**

10. **But is now made manifest by the appearing of our Saviour Jesus Christ, Who hath abolished death, and hath brought life and immortality to light through the gospel:**

More than a thousand years before Jesus' death, the Bible describes many details of the earth-shaking day that Jesus died (Psalm 22:14-18). The Bible prophesied that Jesus would be crucified hundreds of years before crucifixion was invented. The Bible states Jesus is coming to Earth again as the King of kings and Lord of lords. Just as Jesus' first coming as our Savior was at the perfect prophesied time, His second coming as the Lord of the Earth will be at the perfect time as well. *Selah.* If you look at the bottom line of the time chart at the end of this chapter, you will see it is undisputable how long a prophetic generation is. The Bible reveals there is only one key that will unlock the prophetic timetable regarding the length of the last generation. The bottom line on the time chart begins at 360 (3 x 120 = 360), the end of the third generation and the beginning of the forth and final generation. During this prophetic time, Israel was to be in the Promised Land. It proves that a prophetic generation is 120 years, because the popular numbers of less than a 120-year generation would have expired before God and Moses delivered Israel from Egypt, let alone entered the Promised Land. We see in this time chart based on God's Word that a prophetic generation is not 40, 70, or even 100 years; the 120-year number given to Noah fits perfectly. What's really interesting is that at year 430 (70 years after that prophetic fourth generation started), Israel came out of Egypt and received directions and provisions from God. Around the end of the second year (Exodus 40:17) Israel was at edge of the Promised Land but because of fear (lack of faith in God) they refused to go in. Even though God told them to go and possess the land, they chose of their own freewill to rebel against God's plan (Numbers 14:1-11, Numbers 14:26-35). Some say God is Sovran therefore we can't resist God's will, but both saved and unsaved people rebel against God's will on a regular basis and here is one more example. God is Sovran but God's plan is big enough to allow for people's freewill to choose. The consequence of this rebellion was that they would not enjoy the Promised Land but instead died wandering around in the wilderness. Even if you believe (as I once did) the 40 years started after this rebellion it doesn't change God's timetable. As seen on the chart at the end of this chapter, God still had a few years remaining to fulfill the prophecy before the end of the forth-prophetic generation. The Bible says the wilderness era was 40 years.

Joshua 5:6

6. **For the children of Israel walked <u>forty years in the wilderness,</u> till all the people that were men of war, which came out of Egypt, <u>were consumed, because they obeyed not the voice of the Lord</u>: unto whom the Lord sware that He would not shew them the land, which the Lord sware unto their fathers that He would give us, a land that floweth with milk and honey.**

The children of the Jewish slaves would learn the price of rebellion. After the 40-year wilderness experience had passed (40 years from exiting Egypt - Exodus 16:35) Israel entered the Promised Land. Simply adding 40 to 430 gives us 470. It was the year 470, ten years before the end of the fourth and final 120-year generation. The children of the slaves obeyed God, fulfilling the prophecy and entered their land. They crossed the Jordan River on dry ground because it stopped flowing from the town of Adam (Joshua 3:13-17). Then they saw Jericho miraculously handed to them because God crushed the mighty fortress walls. At the conclusion of the forth-prophetic generation we see the fulfilled prophesy of Genesis 15:16. In this fourth prophetic generation Israel enters and occupies the Promised Land, fulfilling what God promised Abraham. This fulfilled prophecy and the undisputable fact that a Prophetic Generation is a 120-year block of time is clearly seen by examining the Biblical time chart. *Selah*. There are multiple messages in this illustration, but the one I would like to stress is God's sovereignty. God rules, God established the boundaries and gave us time. God often waits for the storm to get severe or the harvest to ripen before He takes action to change the situation. God is in no rush. God is never late. We have a choice. We can choose to rebel against God's plan, then later be held accountable for our choice and suffer the consequences. On the other hand, our souls can choose to follow God's plan and enter our personal Promised Land that God has prepared for us. It is our choice, and we alone are responsible for our choices. We can blame no one else for our decision, not even God. We are not puppets. We are free to choose our destiny. Our soul has a freewill to choose to obey or rebel. At judgment day that will be very clear.

Deuteronomy 30:19

[19.] **I call Heaven and Earth to record this day against you, that I have set before you life and death, blessing and cursing: therefore choose life, that both thou and thy seed may live:**

God wants you to choose life, God enables you to choose life, but He won't force you to choose life. Even if you choose corruption, He can still use you for a different purpose. Please forgive me for my frankness, but the choice is ours whether we end up glorified or as fertilizer.

2 Timothy 2:19-21

19. **Nevertheless the foundation of God standeth sure, having this seal, the Lord knoweth them that are His. And, let every one that nameth the name of Christ depart from iniquity.**

20. **But <u>in a great house there are not only vessels of gold</u> and of silver, but also of wood and of earth; and <u>some to honour,</u> and <u>some to dishonour.</u>**

21. **<u>If a man therefore purge himself from these, he shall be a vessel unto honour,</u> sanctified, and meet for the Master's use, and prepared unto every good work.**

God's grand plan is big enough to include every situation, because God is sovereign. He rules. There is no one greater or even close to God and His wisdom or power. Yet, He has given you and me the choice to participate or rebel. We will choose which direction in life we want to go. God provides the destiny.

Proverbs 16:9

9. **A man's heart deviseth his way: but the Lord directeth his steps.**

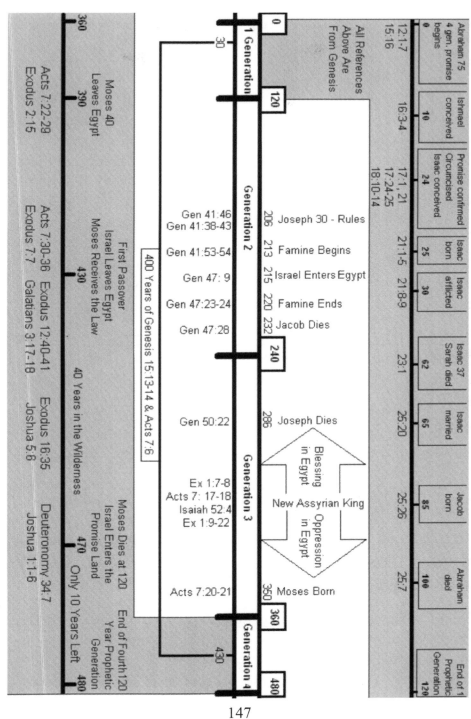

147

CHAPTER 7

POWER FROM ON HIGH

Generally speaking we only read what we are interested in. This and the next chapter may not seem as interesting as chapter 9 or section 4. If you find yourself loosing interest, its okay to jump ahead to see the history and prophesy presented in those arias. You may even want to use your highlighter to help you find, retain and share with friends what God shows you. These next couple of chapters are important in order to see the big picture with all the main pieces in their proper place. Every chapter contains foundational principals to support an unshakable faith that removes mountains of confusion. So lets dive in and digest the important information in these next couple of chapters.

Matthew 3:11, 13-15

11. <u>I indeed baptize you with water unto repentance</u>: but He that cometh after me is mightier than I, whose shoes I am not worthy to bear: <u>He shall baptize you with the Holy Ghost</u>, and with fire:

13. Then cometh Jesus from Galilee to Jordan unto John, to be baptized of him.

14. But John forbad Him, saying, I have need to be baptized of Thee, and comest Thou to me?

15. And Jesus answering said unto him, suffer it to be so now: for thus it becometh us to fulfil all righteousness. Then he suffered Him.

John the Baptist was calling people to take action to demonstrate their repentance. One of the many good deeds John promoted and became famous for was a baptism of repentance. This baptism was an event that the people could look back to as a defining moment of repentance from selfish gain in order to follow God. Remember that the definition of "repentance" is to take action in another direction. When Jesus was about 30 years old, His life dramatically changed. Up to that point, His actions were perfect, but natural. Then Jesus repented from the natural to the supernatural. Jesus was already sinless. He did not need to repent from sin because He never missed the target. At His baptism, a new authority came into His life, and Jesus took action in another direction. This was the beginning of a whole new life for Jesus. This was a defining moment to begin a ministry that would change the world.

Luke 3:21-22

21. Now when all the people were baptized, it came to pass, that Jesus also being baptized, and praying, the heaven was opened,

22. And the <u>Holy Ghost descended in a bodily shape like a dove upon Him,</u> and a voice came from heaven, which said, Thou art My beloved Son; in Thee I am well pleased.

Luke 4:1

1. And <u>Jesus being full of the Holy Ghost</u> returned from Jordan, and was led by the Spirit into the wilderness,

In a way, Jesus had a born-again experience. The Holy Spirit of God came into His body. After that, He had two spirits, the human nature and the Divine Nature, two authorities with different identities and desires.

JESUS

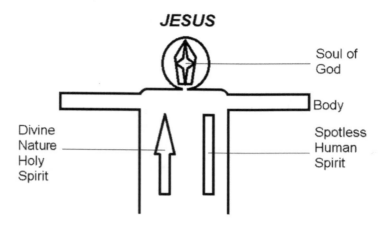

Jesus received the Holy Spirit, giving His Soul a life-changing alternative with a new identity, power, and authority. That is when He began doing miracles.

John 2:11

11. This <u>beginning of miracles</u> did Jesus in Cana of Galilee, and manifested forth <u>His glory</u>; and His disciples believed on Him.

The "beginning of miracles" was a transformation of natural water into abundant fruit of the vine. There are a lot of questions and confusion about this first miracle. Was it an object lesson about the coming new covenant? Was Jesus' first miracle of turning water to wine done to contrast Moses' first miracle of turning water to blood? Was Jesus endorsing alcohol? We can speculate but one thing should be clear about the wine associated with Jesus, especially to alcoholics. Jesus was not providing abundant fermented wine as His first miracle so everyone could celebrate by getting drunk. That would be a sin according to the Bible.

Ephesians 5:18

18. And <u>be not drunk</u> with wine, wherein is excess; but be filled with the Spirit;

We are to be under the influence of the Holy Spirit, not under the influence of alcohol.

Proverbs 20:1

1. **Wine is a mocker, strong drink is raging: and <u>whosoever is deceived thereby is not wise</u>.**

God wants us to be wise, but alcohol tends to make us fools and dull our senses both spiritually and physically. In excess, it can be unhealthy to our bodies.

Isaiah 5:20-22

20. **<u>Woe unto them that call evil good, and good evil; that put darkness for light, and light for darkness</u>; that put bitter for sweet, and sweet for bitter!**

21. **<u>Woe unto them</u> that are wise in their own eyes, and prudent in their own sight!**

22. **<u>Woe unto them that are mighty to drink</u> wine, and men of strength to mingle <u>strong drink</u>:**

In my teenage years, I made some bad choices to explore the dark side. I still loved God, but wanted to do my own thing. At first it was a party; but I soon learned that, one way or another, the Devil eventually burns all his friends. I didn't feel like Satan's friend, but we were certainly spending a lot of time together. I felt like a spaced-out burnout by the time I was 20 and definitely needed help. I can verify the old proverb, "Sin will take you further than you want to go, cost you more than you want to pay, and keep you longer than you want to stay." I thought the only one who could truly understand and help me was Jesus. So I asked Him to sort out and fix my broken confused life. I started spending a lot of time with God and His Word. Psalm 40 became very real to me, especially verse 2. The destruction in my young life started when I wanted to be part of the crowd of people that God looks at and says, "Woe unto them." Jesus loves that crowd and came to Earth to show us all a better way to live. Jesus came to set us free from self-destruction and deception. Jesus desires and enables us to enjoy a constructive and satisfying life. It's the abundant life full of peace, love, and joy, as well as all the fruit of the Holy Spirit. Unlike Satan, Jesus would never encourage me to be a part of the "woe unto them" crowd.

James 1:13

13. **Let no man say when he is tempted, I am tempted of God: for God cannot be tempted with evil, neither tempteth He any man:**

I once heard a homeless alcoholic claim that Jesus' first miracle was turning water into wine, thinking somehow that Jesus condoned having abundant alcohol on hand, thus enabling a time for drunkenness. If that were true, how much wine did Jesus make for this celebration? Was there enough wine for everyone or even anyone to get intoxicated? Would it be considered an excess amount of alcohol? The Bible says how much wine Jesus made.

John 2:6-7

6. **And there were set there <u>six waterpots</u> of stone, after the manner of the purifying of the Jews, containing two or three firkins apiece.**

7. **Jesus saith unto them, fill the waterpots with water. And <u>they filled them up to the brim</u>.**

This was about 162 gallons of wine at three firkins apiece. The party probably started out with alcohol, so Jesus wanted to make sure there were no more spirits left to be confused with His sobering drink, thus His statement in John 2:4 that it was not yet time. After the guests had consumed all the old wine, Jesus provided well over 100 gallons of fresh wine. If this wine were fermented wine, then Jesus would be providing the means and temptation to get drunk for His first miracle, which would certainly not be manifesting His glory. Some may think it was alcohol, because the governor of the feast declared that it was much better than the former wine. In ancient Israel fermented wines were of poor quality and often tasted like vinegar. Preserved grape juice was a better tasting option throughout the year. There was also fresh squeezed from preserved grapes. Josephus mentions the well-preserved ripe fruits in Masada. Also there was a process of boiling down grape-juice to a concentrate that you would just add water to in order to drink. Some may disagree but there is historic evidence that Israel had options of what to drink. Year around they could choose to drink alcohol and many did or they could avoid intoxication and drink nonalcoholic beverages. Nevertheless what Israel was accustomed to drinking has no effect on the new wine Jesus was offering as a gift. Do you think the Creator of good-tasting fruit could put together the perfect blend of various grapes, and if He wanted a little more sparkle and kick, add just a little special supernatural carbonation for the occasion? Don't forget that this was no ordinary drink. It was the result of a miracle. No doubt, Jesus' wine was extremely satisfying, without the side effect of causing the guests to make fools of themselves by indulging in His 162-gallon gift. Some of Jesus' critics called Him a wine bibber and glutton (Matthew 11:19, Luke 7:34). They also called Him a deceiver (Matthew 27:63) and a blasphemer (Matthew 26:65) among other names. They obviously did not know Jesus the King of kings and Prince of Peace very well, since these slanderous statements could not be farther from the truth.

Proverbs 31:4, 6-7

4. It is not for kings, O lemuel, it is <u>not for kings to drink wine; nor for princes strong drink:</u>

6. Give <u>strong drink unto him that is ready to perish,</u> and wine unto those that be of heavy hearts.

7. <u>Let him drink, and forget his poverty, and remember his misery no more.</u>

Fermented wine and strong drinks are painkillers. Like other drugs, alcohol is often misused and abused. It is addicting and dangerous. Wine in the Bible is simply fruit of the vine. Wine can be fermented or unfermented grape juice. They may look the same, but one is a liquid drug while the other is simply fruit juice. New wine is fresh squeezed grapes (Isaiah 65:8 KJV) and usually unfermented. Historians confirm that the people of Jesus' day were free to choose their drink, even when grapes were not in season. We are free to choose our drink, but we should consider how it affects our witness and our judgment.

Romans 14:13

13. Let us not therefore judge one another any more: but judge this rather, that no man put a stumblingblock or an occasion to fall in his brother's way.

Daniel and his three young friends may seem extreme in their decision to reject the king's food and wine but God blessed them and made them wiser for it. Not to be offensive to those that promotes alcohol, but the question I would ask is; why they promote or justify social drinking? Is it just for self-satisfaction, or an escape from the reality and tensions of this life? Or, do they believe Jesus' enemies and believe Jesus participated in and condoned alcoholic intoxication to some degree or as they would say with moderation? If they assume Jesus consumed and promoted alcohol then their perception of Jesus is not in harmony with many Scriptures. I have seen Christian friends that promoted alcohol become deceive about other parts of the Bible. One of them ended up zealously proclaiming and trying to prove that there is no Hell and everyone will go to Heaven, even the Devil. Another one's marriage fell apart because of alcohol. I have been to Christian parties were alcohol was consumed and it looked no different than the drinking parties of my youth.

2 Corinthians 6:17

17. **Wherefore come out from among them, and be ye separate, saith the Lord, and touch not the unclean thing; and I will receive you,**

1 Corinthians 10:31

31. **Whether therefore ye eat, or drink, or whatsoever ye do, do all to the glory of God.**

Jesus does promote a drink that is "to the glory of God." Jesus gave his life to provide this drink, which will truly set us free. It is the drink that we will share with Him at the "Marriage Supper of the Lamb."

Matthew 26:27-29

27. **And He took the cup, and gave thanks, and gave it to them, saying, drink ye all of it;**

28. **For this is My blood of the New Testament, which is shed for many for the remission of sins.**

29. **But I say unto you, I will not drink henceforth of this <u>fruit of the vine</u>, until that day when I drink it new with you in my Father's kingdom.**

To remove the confusion, every accurate translation of the Bible does not use the word wine in referring to the Lord's Supper, but instead uses the phrase "fruit of the vine." Jesus was able to share with his disciples, unleavened bread and the pure uncontaminated "fruit of the vine" even though it was not the season for grapes. Grapes and figs have the same harvest season. The Bible tells us in Mark 11:13 that the week that Jesus introduced the Lord's Supper was before fig (or grape) season. *Selah.* At the wedding feast in Cana Jesus blessed the servants' obedience in collecting natural water by turned their efforts into His abundant "fruit of the vine" for all to enjoy. This was the first of many miracles performed by Jesus. Let's move on and look at what empowered Jesus' to perform these miracles. It's clear from the Bible that Jesus Christ did no miracles before He was baptized, which is when the Holy Ghost entered Him.

Acts 10:37-38

37. That word, I say, ye know, which was published throughout all Judaea, and began from Galilee, <u>after the baptism</u> which John preached;

38. How <u>God anointed Jesus of Nazareth with the Holy Ghost and with power: who went about doing good, and healing all that were oppressed of the Devil</u>; for God was with Him.

After Jesus received the Holy Ghost, He became one with the Holy Ghost. Everything He did was in obedience to this new higher authority. His Soul was completely submitted to this new identity. Jesus was a perfect reflection of the Triune God.

John 8:28

28. Then said Jesus unto them, when ye have lifted up the Son of man, then shall ye know that I am He, and that I <u>do nothing</u>

of myself; but as my Father hath taught Me, I speak these things.

The people at that time and place recognized Jehovah or "the Father" as a reference to God the Creator and not some foreign false god or idol. Jesus referred to the Father in Him, just as many Christians refer to Jesus in us. To say Jesus dwells in us is good and Biblical but He actually dwells in us by the power of His Holy Spirit. The Holy Spirit comes to us and indwells us who respond to God's Word.

1 John 3:23-24

23. **And this is His commandment, That we should believe on the name of His Son Jesus Christ, and love one another, as He gave us commandment.**

24. **And he that keepeth His commandments dwelleth in Him, and He in him. And hereby we know that He abideth in us, by the Spirit which He hath given us.**

Many of Jesus' references regarding the Father and our statements that "Jesus is in us" are actually referring to the Holy Spirit of the Father. It is the Spirit that Jesus sends to us in His name. The Holy Spirit is one with God the Creator and Savior. The Father was always in Jesus because the Father is omnipresent. The new miracle-working direction came to Jesus when the Holy Spirit came into His body, giving Him supernatural authority, and empowered Jesus to start doing miracles.

Luke 4:14

14. **And Jesus returned in the power of the Spirit into Galilee: and there went out a fame of Him through all the region round about.**

The Holy Spirit of God initiated everything Jesus did and said. In obedience to the Father, Jesus denied His human nature and obeyed His Divine Nature.

John 14:10-12

10. **Believest thou not that I am in the Father, and the Father in me? The words that I speak unto you I speak <u>not of myself</u>: but the Father <u>that dwelleth in Me, He doeth the works</u>.**

11. **Believe Me that I am in the Father, and the Father in Me: or else believe Me for the very works' sake.**

12. **Verily, verily, I say unto you, he that believeth on Me, the works that I do shall he do also; and <u>greater works than these</u> shall he do; because I go unto my Father.**

Jesus was about to do the greatest work of paying for our redemption. No one else could do that. Jesus completed that work and took His place in Heaven where the Father is concentrated and continually manifesting His Glory. Then Jesus sent His empowering Spirit to us. The "greater works" He refers to is the multiplication of the Great Commission.

Luke 19:10

10. **For the Son of man is come <u>to seek and to save that which was lost</u>.**

Matthew 4:19

19. **And He saith unto them, <u>follow Me</u>, and I will make you fishers of men.**

The day Jesus rose from the dead, He commissioned His followers to expand what He had begun.

John 20:19-22

19. Then the same day at evening, being the first day of the week, when the doors were shut where the disciples were assembled for fear of the Jews, came Jesus and stood in the midst, and saith unto them, peace be unto you.

20. And when He had so said, He shewed unto them His hands and His side. Then were the disciples glad, when they saw the Lord.

21. Then said Jesus to them again, peace be unto you: <u>as my Father hath sent Me, even so send I you.</u>

22. And when He had said this, He breathed on them, and saith unto them, <u>receive ye the Holy Ghost</u>:

The disciples received the Holy Ghost on Resurrection Sunday as the first fruit of their salvation. The Holy Spirit helps us see the truth. The Holy Spirit enabled the disciples to go deeper into God's Word and see God's grand plan. Luke recorded more of what Jesus said at that time and mentions Jesus opening their understanding (by breathing the Holy Ghost into them).

Luke 24:44-49

44. And He said unto them, These are the words which I spake unto you, while I was yet with you, that <u>all things must be fulfilled</u>, which were written in the law of Moses, and in the prophets, and in the psalms, concerning Me.

45. Then <u>opened He their understanding, that they might understand the scriptures,</u>

46. And said unto them, Thus it is written, and thus it behoved Christ to suffer, and to rise from the dead the third day:

^{47.} **And that repentance and remission of sins should be preached in His name among all nations, beginning at Jerusalem.**

^{48.} **And ye are witnesses of these things.**

^{49.} **And, behold, I send the promise of my Father <u>upon you</u>: but tarry ye in the city of Jerusalem, until <u>ye be endued with power from on high</u>.**

The disciples first received the Holy Spirit from Jesus (John 20:22) and they began to properly "understand the scriptures" (Luke 24:45). Then fifty days later on the Feast of Pentecost they were anointed with the Holy Spirit's power to fulfill their part of the Great Commission (Acts 1:1-11, Acts 2:1-11).

Matthew 28:18-20

^{18.} **And Jesus came and spake unto them, saying, <u>all power is given unto Me in Heaven and in Earth</u>.**

^{19.} **<u>Go ye therefore, and teach all nations, baptizing them</u> in the name of the Father, and of the Son, and of the Holy Ghost:**

^{20.} **Teaching them to observe all things whatsoever I have commanded you: and, lo, I am with you alway, even unto the end of the world. Amen.**

The same Holy Spirit that empowered Jesus to do miracles would now become available to empower His church. It started on the day of Pentecost, the beginning of the Church Age. Jesus commissioned His followers to teach and baptize. The teaching part is simply learning the truth and sharing it with others. *Selah.* Jesus also told them to baptize. The significance of baptism may seem a little confusing, because different religions have different points of view and emphases on the subject. The Bible acknowledges there is more than one type of baptism. Otherwise, there would be no need for a doctrine regarding baptisms (Hebrews 6:2). Remember, what is intended by the word "baptism" needs to be consistent with other established Biblical doctrines. Baptism does not necessarily involve being submerged in water, although I believe that is what Jesus was referring to in Matthew 28:19. Baptism can refer to a transforming event we go through which has nothing to do with water. For example, Jesus endured a baptism of suffering the day He was beaten and crucified.

Luke 12:50

50. **But I have a baptism to be baptized with; and how am I straitened till it be accomplished!**

John the Baptist had already baptized Jesus in water three and a half years earlier. Jesus was not referring to water baptism in this verse. John's baptism was called a baptism of repentance but Jesus was about to go through a baptism of suffering. Baptism can also be a transitional event, like when God made a temporary path for Israel to be saved by crossing the Red Sea on dry ground (Exodus 14:1-31, Exodus 15:1-22). They were in the Sea, but they were not in the water, nor did they get wet. After Israel crossed the Sea, the walls of water that were miraculously frozen came crashing down, crushing and drowning the entire pursuing enemy. Israel was free of their enemy repossessing them and they were able to move forward toward the Promised Land. Moses was God's point man to develop this new nation.

1 Corinthians 10:1-2

1. **Moreover, brethren, I would not that ye should be ignorant, how that all our fathers were under the cloud, and all passed through the sea;**

161

2. And were all <u>baptized unto Moses in the cloud and in the sea;</u>

Israel was "baptized unto Moses" being their leader, resulting in the "Law of Moses" and the "Old Covenant." The Law of Moses is the standard throughout most of the Old Testament. It is mentioned in the New Testament and is acknowledged that it cannot save or justify us.

Acts 13:39

39. And by Him all that believe are justified from all things, from which ye <u>could not be justified</u> by the <u>law of Moses</u>.

The Law of Moses could not justify us because we broke the law. Therefore, God was about to do a new thing and introduce a New Covenant that would bless the whole world. *Selah.* The New Covenant depended upon the sacrifice blood of Jesus the "Lamb of God" to wash away past, present and future sins.

Ephesians 1:7

7. In whom <u>we have redemption through His blood, the forgiveness of sins</u>, according to the riches of His grace;

Galatians 3:26-27

26. For ye are all the <u>children of God by faith in Christ Jesus</u>.

27. For as many of you as have been <u>baptized into Christ have put on Christ</u>.

We do not physically "put on Christ." We will see the baptism mentioned here is a spiritual baptism not a physical baptism. No one is "baptized into Christ," with, or by water. Only the Holy Spirit can place us into Christ's body and Christ into our hearts. Some assume water baptism is required for salvation. If you believe this, I hope you are teachable. I hope you will consider the following Scriptures as well as the explanations of the verses

162

used to support that assumption. Many people in the book of Acts were water baptized, but we will see there is no requirement to get physically wet to become "children of God." Verse 26 of the previous passage states we are "children of God by faith in Christ Jesus." This means that after you are a believer then you become a receiver of the Holy Ghost. Sometimes believing and receiving are combined into one word or referred to as faith. Saving faith is more than head knowledge. Simplifying this process into one word is fine, but you should recognize there is the spiritual progression of believing God's Word and receiving God's Spirit. This may take years or moments depending on the individual. The question is; who or what are you putting your faith in for your eternal destiny? If you are putting your faith in water baptism or good works for salvation, then you need to remove at least some of your faith away from Christ as your savior and receiving His Spirit for salvation (Romans 10:2-13). As long as you receive Jesus' Holy Spirit in your heart you will go to Heaven, even if you believe that you need to add your religious traditions and good works to help Jesus save you. After we get to Heaven Jesus will point out the truth.

Isaiah 64:6

6. **But we are all as an unclean thing, and all our righteousnesses are as filthy rags; and we all do fade as a leaf; and our iniquities, like the wind, have taken us away.**

Isaiah 1:18

18. **Come now, and let us reason together, saith the LORD: though your sins be as scarlet, they shall be as white as snow; though they be red like crimson, they shall be as wool.**

On judgment day we will be glad if we can properly answer the following question.

Colossians 1:13-14

13. **Who hath delivered us from the power of darkness, and hath translated us into the kingdom of His dear Son:**

14. **In whom we have redemption through His blood, even the forgiveness of sins:**

Our deliverance from Hell is based on faith in what Christ has done for us, and receiving Jesus' gift of the Holy Spirit. We cannot earn the Holy Spirit with our good works or rituals. Salvation is a matter of the heart's connection to the Holy Spirit. *Selah.* At the birth of the church the first Jewish Christians received the powerful Holy Ghost as a seal of completion concerning their personal salvation as well as a deposit for the future transformation.

Ephesians 1:12-13

12. **That we should be to the praise of His glory, who first trusted in Christ.**

13. **In whom ye also trusted, after that ye heard the word of truth, the gospel of your salvation: in whom also after that ye believed, ye were sealed with that Holy Spirit of promise,**

Notice there in no mention of needing to be water baptized or do any good works for salvation. Only believe and receive the Holy Spirit who "sealed" us as God's redeemed. There is a baptism mentioned elsewhere but it is a Spirit baptism not water baptism.

1 Corinthians 12:13

13. **For by one Spirit are we all baptized into one body, whether we be Jews or Gentiles, whether we be bond or free; and have been all made to drink into one Spirit.**

Christianity began when people turned away from the old idea of redemption based on works. They trusted in Christ's payment for there sins. Then they received the Holy Spirit who immersed them into the family of God, which is often referred to as the body of Christ or the church. Don't be confused by the literal and figurative statements in the Bible. The Holy Spirit supplies the wisdom to understand the difference between the spiritual and the physical. For instance, if we read John 6:47-63 we see Jesus is making a spiritual statement. The crowd took it literally and missed the point. Jesus' followers were never suppose to physically eat Jesus' body or drank his blood. That would be an abomination according to the Bible. It is also wrong to think Jesus was saying just partake of the Lord's Supper and be saved. The Lord's Supper is a symbol to remember how Jesus paid for our salvation. Like water baptism it was to be done after we are born-again into God's family. *Selah.* We don't need to guess what kind of baptism, what kind of wine, or what kind of spirit the Bible is referring to in a scripture verse. The Holy Spirit enables us to see how the Bible defines itself.

Isaiah 28:9-10

9. **Whom shall He teach knowledge? and whom shall He make to understand doctrine? Them that are weaned from the milk, and drawn from the breasts.**

10. **For precept must be upon precept, precept upon precept; line upon line, <u>line upon line; here a little, and there a little</u>:**

John 16:12-15

12. **I have yet many things to say unto you, but ye cannot bear them now.**

13. **Howbeit when He, the <u>Spirit of truth</u>, is come, <u>He will guide you into all truth</u>: for He shall not speak of himself; but**

whatsoever He shall hear, that shall He speak: and He will shew you things to come.

14. **He shall glorify Me: for He shall receive of Mine, and shall shew it unto you.**

15. **All things that the Father hath are Mine: therefore said I, that He shall take of Mine, and shall shewit unto you.**

There are some important keys the Holy Spirit will apply when you study the Bible. The first one is to determine if the information is literal or a parable or a parallel. If it is a parable or parallel then look for the principals or point of the story. God often uses familiar things to show us the hidden spiritual truths. Foundational trues that are often repeated in the Bible help us to interpret puzzling verses and their implications. If a statement is not in harmony with the majority of scripture then first read the context. Consider the time, people and purpose of the information. If the verse still seems contrary then maybe a word is misinterpreted or misapplied. For instance, by examining all the scriptures on salvation, it will become obvious that water baptism is not the solution to the sin problem. That is what John the Baptist was pointing out in Matthew 3:11. Water baptism is important, and early Christians did so as an act of repentance, obedience, and allegiance to God. It was a way of committing themselves to be a part of Christ's local church. There is nothing wrong with water baptism unless it replaces the true salvation experience. I can be baptized in water and reject the Holy Spirit and end up in Hell. On the other hand I can receive the Holy Spirit without ever being baptized in water and enter Heaven as my everlasting home. I do not need to be circumcised or water baptized to come under the provisions of the New Covenant. After I put my faith in the Gospel of Christ and receive the powerful Holy Ghost, I am "born again" (John 3:3). Once I am born again I will always be a part of the family of God. This will be clearly explained and illustrated in chapter 11. *Selah*. An excerpt from Peter's sermon at Pentecost has confused many people because it seems to make water baptism a qualification for salvation.

Acts 2:38

38. **Then Peter said unto them, repent, and be baptized every one of you in the name of Jesus Christ for the remission of sins, and ye shall receive the gift of the Holy Ghost.**

Taken at face value, it appears to say (repent) turn from your current sins, and (be baptized) in water to wash away your past sins. Then you can qualify to receive the Holy Ghost. In doing so you will save yourselves, which is implied in verse 40. Is that interpretation in harmony with the Bible or just a false assumption? Taken out of context this verse is confusing, but let me offer an explanation that is in harmony with the Bible. Let's look reasonably at the three key phrases that confuse people. They are [1]repent, [2]be baptized and [3]the gift of the Holy Ghost. First let's look at the complete context of this verse. Peter said [1]repent. Repent from what? What they were to repent of is mentioned leading up to this statement.

Acts 2:36-37

36. **Therefore let all the house of Israel know assuredly, that God hath made that same Jesus, whom ye have crucified, both Lord and Christ.**

37. **Now when they heard this, they were pricked in their heart, and said unto Peter and to the rest of the apostles, Men and brethren, what shall we do?**

Peter answered their question by saying repent. [1]Repent in Peter's response stands for receiving salvation. We turn (repent) from rejecting Jesus and trusting in our good works to earn us Heaven. We turn (repent) to Jesus being our savior. The Apostle Paul verified this by making it his central message and biggest conflict with his pears.

Acts 20:21

[21.] **Testifying both to the Jews, and also to the Greeks, repentance toward God, and faith toward our Lord Jesus Christ.**

"Repentance toward God" means we turn to God and accept His Word regarding salvation. God's plan of redemption is to recognize that Jesus Christ's crucifixion paid for our sins, past and present and even our future sins. Realize every sin can be forgiven except one. There is only one sin Jesus' death on the cross did not cover. That sin is the rejection of Jesus' free gift of eternal life. We have to recognize who Jesus is and personally receive the free gift of His Spirit for our salvation. After we are saved we have the opportunity to be properly water [2]baptized and dedicate ourselves to Jesus and His local church. In baptism we identify with Jesus' death, burial and resurrection. We go down under the water as a symbol of us burying our old rebellious ways of the past. We rise out of the water with a clean conscience and new commitment to be more like Christ. Philip the evangelist was asked directly about the qualification for water baptism.

Acts 8:36-38

[36.] **And as they went on their way, they came unto a certain water: and the eunuch said, See, here is water; what doth hinder me to be baptized?**

37. And Philip said, <u>If thou believest</u> with all thine heart, thou mayest. And he answered and said, I believe that Jesus Christ is the Son of God.

38. And he commanded the chariot to stand still: and they went down both into the water, both Philip and the eunuch; and he baptized him.

Water baptism is a symbol that we have chosen to identify with Christ, join His family, and live as His disciple. Joining God's family begins with asking Jesus to be the Savior of our soul. After that we can ask Jesus to be the Lord of our life. We can ask Jesus to be our Lord and Savior at the same time. Although the Biblical reality is that Jesus is first our Savior. Then He enables us to have victory over sin by making Him Lord of our daily decisions and actions. *Selah.* [3]The gift of the Holy Ghost that Peter mentioned in his sermon is spiritual power. Peter received the Holy Spirit on Resurrection Day (John 20:22), fifty days latter he was empowered by the Holy Ghost on Pentecost. On Resurrection day Jesus gave the disciples the Holy Spirit but told them to wait for the gift of supernatural empowerment.

Acts 1:4-5
4. And, being assembled together with them, commanded them that they should not depart from Jerusalem, but <u>wait for the promise</u> of the Father, which, saith He, ye have heard of Me.

5. For John truly baptized with water; but ye shall be <u>baptized with the Holy Ghost</u> <u>not many days hence.</u>

Acts 1:8
8. But <u>ye shall receive power, after that the Holy Ghost is come upon you: and ye shall be witnesses</u> unto Me both in

Jerusalem, and in all Judea, and in Samaria, and unto the uttermost parts of the Earth.

On the Feast of Pentecost they were engulfed "baptized with the Holy Spirit" which resulted in a special anointing of power for evangelism. *Selah.* I am still learning about all the ramifications of this experience but I would like to offer one observation. To be born-again is a permanent event. Once we are born-again we have eternal life and will never be unborn (John 10:28). Normally we are only baptized in water once but you can do it again if you desire. The Holy Spirit's anointing of empowerment or baptism of the Spirit seems to be different. It has an initial experience but then needs to be maintained or renewed. The Holy Spirit can surround us in God's awesome presence and power but to consistently walk in that anointing is the challenge. For example The Holy Spirit anointed Peter to speak regarding the birth of the church and thousands were saved. Yet later Peter was not walking in the anointing of the Holy Spirit. Instead, he allowed his flesh to take control and ended up being rebuked by Paul (Galatians 2:11-16). This is why we should not follow a misdirected preacher but instead walk in truth and pray God would bring illumination and correction. Remember, no one but Jesus is perfect. If a church has a Biblical foundation we should support the leadership. Samuel became a friend of God and example of how we should treat misguided spiritual leaders. He did not join in their deceptions or corruptions nor did he rebel, but instead served them in grace and truth. He spoke the truth from God to them and prayed for them. *Selah.* It is a choice to learn the plan of God and enter into harmony with it. After we are part of the family of God ("in Christ Jesus") we are destine for Heaven; but to walk in the power of the Spirit is optional. We need to continually choose to turn from the flesh nature to the

Divine Nature. This enables us to act "walk" in the power of the Holy Spirit.

Galatians 5:25

25. **If we live in the Spirit, <u>let us also</u> walk in the Spirit.**

If we walk in the Spirit we will save ourselves from being caught up in the traps and bondages of this world's ungodly lifestyles.

Romans 8:1

1. **There is therefore now <u>no condemnation</u> to them which are in Christ Jesus, <u>who walk not after the flesh, but after the Spirit.</u>**

Paul had to confront and condemn some of the lifestyles and actions of the Corinthian church. They considered themselves spiritually mature but was actually deceived and in need of correction. At Pentecost Peter warned the people to free themselves from ungodly lifestyles.

Acts 2:40

40. **And <u>with many other words</u> did he testify and exhort, saying, Save yourselves from this untoward generation.**

On the Feast of Pentecost the Church Age began. Some call it the dispensation of grace (Ephesians 3:2-6 KJV), which is the same as saying the age of favor because of the Holy Spirit. No longer were animal sacrifices necessary. Many Jews accepted Jesus' sacrifice for their sins to be sufficient. They were then individually identified and water baptized into the first local church.

Acts 2:41

41. **Then they that gladly received his word were baptized: and the same day there were added <u>unto them</u> about three thousand souls.**

171

About 3000 people were baptized into the first local church. As active members, they started to spread the Good News in order to fulfill the Great Commission. Water baptism is basically a demonstration of a repentant heart. Christians came to recognize it as a testimony of turning away from the old ways to a new redeemed lifestyle. It is the Holy Spirit that gives us the power to correctly live this new lifestyle. The Holy Spirit came into people that had participated in John's baptism of repentance as well as those that had not experience water baptism. The New Testament reveals that receiving salvation through the Holy Spirit came first, then we are empowered to repent and live the resurrected lifestyle symbolized by water baptism. The Apostle Paul (who was first known as Saul) was an example of this progression. He was a religious zealot (Acts 9:1-2). Then he met Jesus on the road to Damascus (Acts 9:3-5). Paul changed his mind and believed Jesus (Acts 9:6-12). After Paul believed, then he received his eternal partner, the Holy Spirit (Acts 9:17), and his eyes were opened. Then he was baptized in water (Acts 9:18) and began preaching the Good News and expanding God's church (Acts 9:20-22). *Selah.* The proper perspective on baptism can be confusing so I will address it a little more in the last chapter of this book. As we conclude this chapter I hope you recognize the important transforming power of the Holy Spirit. He empowered Jesus to do miracles. He enabled Jesus' disciples to understand the Scriptures. The book of Acts starts with the Holy Spirit initiating the Church Age with power from on high. The Holy Ghost is still empowering individuals today to share God's love and experience the presents of God. *Selah.* After Jesus was glorified by being resurrected from the dead the Holy Spirit empowered His disciples to change their world. The Holy Spirit would sustain them during persecution and the many difficulties Satan would use in an attempt to defeat them. Their legacy is still changing our world today, in spite of all the evil Satan is injecting into this world. Now all believers in Jesus are empowered by this same Holy Spirit and called to light up this dark world.

Matthew 5:16

16. **Let your light so shine before men, <u>that they may see</u> your good works, and glorify your Father which is in Heaven.**

In order to see evangelism and transformation we need to allow the Holy Ghost to flow through us into our environment. Jesus referred to the Holy Spirit as living water because He has the power to give life, quench our desire for fulfillment and cleanse us from the worldly filth.

John 7:38-39

38. **He that believeth on Me, <u>as the scripture hath said</u>, out of his belly shall flow rivers of living water.**

39. **(But this spake He of the Spirit, which <u>they that believe on Him</u> should receive: for the Holy Ghost was not yet given; because that Jesus was not yet glorified.)**

CHAPTER 8

HOW WAS JESUS TEMPTED?

Hebrews 2:18 (NKJV)

18. For in that He Himself has suffered, being tempted, He is able to aid those who are tempted.

Temptation is not sin, but submitting to it is. Jesus struggled against temptation. His temptation in the Garden of Gethsemane was more than most of us will ever experience.

Luke 22:41-44

41. And He was withdrawn from them about a stone's cast, and kneeled down, and prayed,

42. Saying, Father, if thou be willing, remove this cup from Me: nevertheless <u>not My will, but Thine, be done.</u>

43. And there appeared an angel unto Him from Heaven, strengthening Him.

44. And being in an <u>agony</u> He prayed more earnestly: and His <u>sweat</u> was as it were great drops of <u>blood</u> falling down to the ground.

Jesus' last night in the Garden of Gethsemane was no doubt His toughest battle against temptation. He was stressed to the point of sweating blood. I have never experienced that degree of temptation, and I doubt you have either. This was not the kind of temptation that can be walked away from. Mater of fact, that was the temptation; just walk away and do nothing. Jesus didn't yield to temptation, but instead emerged the victor. Jesus is the sinless spotless Lamb of God. He had a pure human nature. That nature was designed for life and wanted to live. Jesus' human nature knew what was about to happen and wanted no part of it. The diagram below helps us to see that Jesus had both a soul and a human nature. He also received the Divine Nature at His baptism. Jesus' Soul was experiencing conflict between His two natures. The source of this internal turmoil Jesus was experiencing that night is the same internal conflict that we experience. The struggle is to turn from the human nature "not my will" and submit to God's plan. The day had come that Jesus would be severely beaten, whipped mercilessly and then endure the excruciating pain of crucifixion (Isaiah 53:2-12). After that He would be defiled with our sins, which would end His mortal life. Through prayer Jesus was able to look past the bloody conflict before Him and focus on the Glory of God. Jesus was not tempted to do evil but instead He was tempted not to do good.

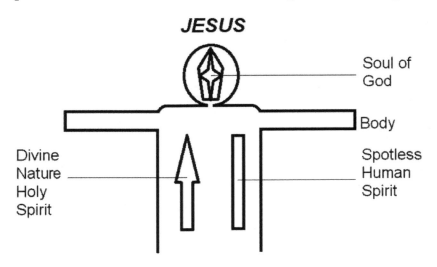

Soul of God

Body

Divine Nature Holy Spirit

Spotless Human Spirit

James 1:13-15

13. Let no man say when he is tempted, I am tempted of God: for God cannot be tempted with evil, neither tempteth He any man:

14. But every man is tempted, when he is drawn away of his own lust, and enticed.

^{15.} **Then when lust hath conceived, it bringeth forth sin: and sin, when it is finished, bringeth forth death.**

Jesus was not tempted by corruption or vile thoughts or actions. That would be like trying to tempt me to eat cockroaches. Even the thought of it is repulsive to me, and there is no way I could ever be tempted to do that. In the same way, Jesus never was tempted by or attracted to evil.

Hebrews 4:14-15

^{14.} **Seeing then that we have a great High Priest, that is passed into the Heavens, Jesus the Son of God, let us hold fast our profession.**

^{15.} **For we have not an High Priest which cannot be touched with the feeling of our infirmities; but was in <u>all points tempted like as we are, yet without sin</u>.**

Jesus was tempted at all the same points (or sources) that we are, but not with the same activities. We all have different temptations. For example, an alcoholic might feel a strong urge to take a drink followed by a stronger urge to take another drink. For me, that is not a temptation. It is just a choice. Nevertheless, I can relate, because long ago I was addicted to cigarettes. I quit many times before I finally won the victory over that strong temptation. Jesus can relate because He was tempted in the Garden of Gethsemane. This temptation was putting an extreme amount of pressure on Him. He was in "agony" and sweating blood to resist it. He stayed in prayer until the temptation finally passed and He had won the victory. Where did this temptation come from? It came from the same place many of our temptations come from – our human nature. In chapter 14, I will go into detail on how to have victory over this type of temptation. Jesus' human nature wanted to live. That is not bad unless a higher authority wants to go in another direction. We are to obey every authority except when a higher authority says otherwise. If that happens, it would be a sin to obey the lesser authority.

Acts 4:19

19. **But Peter and John answered and said unto them, whether it be right in the sight of God to <u>hearken unto you more than unto God, judge ye</u>.**

After Jesus prayed through His temptation and received victory over His human nature, He could go through the impending excruciating pain with a noble attitude. He could properly finish the job He came to do.

Philippians 2:5-8

5. <u>**let this mind be in you, which was also in Christ Jesus:**</u>

6. **Who, being in the form of God, thought it not robbery to be equal with God:**

7. **But made Himself of no reputation, and took upon Him the form of a servant, and <u>was made in the likeness of men</u>:**

8. **And being found in fashion as a man, <u>He humbled Himself, and became obedient</u> unto death, even the death of the cross.**

Jesus was not only tempted by His human nature as we are. He was also tempted by the Devil himself, just as Eve was tempted. The Devil and his demonic forces often attack in-order to test the strength of our decision to follow God. The Devil tested Jesus right after His baptism.

Luke 4:1-4

1. **And Jesus being full of the Holy Ghost returned from Jordan, and was led by the Spirit into the wilderness,**

2. **Being forty days tempted** of the Devil. And in those days He did eat nothing: and when they were ended, He afterward hungered.

3. And the <u>Devil said unto Him, if</u> Thou be the Son of God, command this stone that it be made bread.

4. And <u>Jesus answered him, saying, it is written</u>, that man shall not live by bread alone, but by every Word of God.

The Devil didn't start tempting Jesus after 40 days. He tried to wear Jesus down throughout the 40 days. After Jesus had been "forty days tempted," the Devil showed up and suggested that Jesus should follow his method to feed His flesh. This was probably around dinnertime. If Jesus had given into temptation and performed this miracle, it would be listed as the first miracle in Jesus' ministry, done at Satan's direction for the purpose of self-satisfaction. That would definitely not be a good way to begin a ministry. Jesus had the power (Matthew 15:33-38), but would not allow the Devil to direct Him on how to use it. So, the Devil came back with another approach.

Luke 4:5-8

5. And the Devil, taking Him up into an high mountain, <u>shewed unto Him</u> all the kingdoms of the world in a moment of time.

6. And the Devil said unto Him, all this power will I give Thee, and the glory of them: for <u>that is delivered unto me; and to whomsoever I will I give it</u>.

7. If Thou therefore wilt worship me, all shall be Thine.

8. And Jesus answered and <u>said unto him, get thee behind Me, Satan: for it is written</u>, thou shalt worship the Lord thy God, and Him only shalt thou serve.

Notice that the Devil "showed" Jesus the kingdoms of the world. That is because the Devil knows that many of his most destructive temptations begin at the eye gate, and then enters the heart as an idea or desire to have what the Devil has shown us (Job 31:1).

Matthew 6:22-23

22. The light of the body is the eye: if therefore thine eye be single, thy whole body shall be full of light.

23. But if thine eye be evil, thy whole body <u>shall be</u> full of darkness. If therefore the light that is in thee be darkness, how great is that darkness!

The Devil knew that Jesus wanted the people of the world come to Him. Therefore, the Devil tried to make a deal with Jesus. Some musicians and executives have taken the Devil up on this deal, but not Jesus. The Devil has three weapons of temptation that he uses in a variety of ways.

1 John 2:16

16. For all that is in the world, the <u>lust of the flesh</u>, and the <u>lust of the eyes</u>, and the <u>pride of life</u>, is not of the Father, but is of the world.

Even after 40 days without food, Satan could not trick Jesus into acting out of fear for His health, or to satisfy his natural appetite by taking Satan's suggestion for food. Satan then applied his next weapon, the "lust of the eyes" for people and the things of this world. Jesus preferred solitude rather than accepting Satan's offer of power and popularity. Because the first two temptations didn't work, the Devil pulled out his third and most deceptive categorical temptation – "pride."

Luke 4:9-13

9. And he brought Him to Jerusalem, and set Him on a pinnacle of the temple, and said unto Him, if thou be the Son of God, cast Thyself down from hence:

10. For it is written, He shall give His angels charge over Thee, to keep Thee:

11. And in their hands they shall bear Thee up, lest at any time Thou dash Thy foot against a stone.

12. And Jesus answering said unto him, it is said, thou shalt not tempt the Lord thy God.

13. And when the Devil had ended all the temptation, he departed from him for a season.

Since Jesus was consistently using the Bible, the Devil tried to seductively misuse the Bible to lure Jesus into sin. He tried to get Jesus to misapply the Bible. In an effort to promote self-righteousness and pride, the Devil stated that Jesus could get away with anything because He was too important to fall or become disabled. Nevertheless, Jesus knew the Bible and the proper application of it, so the Devil could not fool Him by this distortion. Jesus knew the danger of pride and humbly refused to allow it to be associated with His actions (Philippians 2:5-8).

Proverbs 16:18

18. Pride goeth before destruction, and a haughty spirit before a fall.

The Biblical references to pride causing a fall are not talking about the power of gravity. Instead, they are references to the power of pride and its ability to cause us to fall from a position of righteousness. This is what happened to Satan. Pride entered

Satan's heart and he fell from a position of being a highly respected and powerful good angel. Satan became the father of lies and corruption that we call the Devil. Pride is the first sin, which resulted in Heaven being divided and Earth being corrupted.

1 Corinthians 10:12-13

12. **Wherefore let him that thinketh he standeth take heed lest he fall.**

13. **There hath <u>no temptation taken you but such as is common to man</u>: but God is faithful, who will not suffer you to be tempted above that ye are able; but will with the temptation also make a way to escape, that ye may be able to bear it.**

Being proud of our status in life, what we know, our abilities, or our sense of importance can blind us to the truth. Arrogance can make us think we can get away with foolish things that will hurt us and hurt our mission in life. Pride is a lot like bad breath. Without consistent maintenance, it can creep up on us without our realization. The odor of arrogance is offensive to God as well as to others. More than being right or wrong God is looking at whether we are proud or humble (Luke 18:9-14). *Selah.* Pride comes in when we become self-absorbed. Pride can come in two forms – optimistic boasting or pessimistic degrading that results in false humility. Both forms of pride are unbalanced and undesirable extremes. The one form of pride focuses on self-exaltation the other focuses on self-abasement. They both magnify their-self. They are not to be confused with self-respect, which produces good moral character. *Selah.* The antidote to pride is to focus on others.

Philippians 2:3-4

^{3.} **Let nothing be done through strife or vainglory; but in lowliness of mind let each esteem other better than themselves.**

^{4.} **Look not every man on his own things, but every man also on the things of others.**

The Devil's temptations for Jesus failed to cause Jesus to fall into sin. Therefore, the Devil left to regroup for another series of temptations. We see the next temptation series in Matthew. Hoping Jesus may have reconsidered his advice, Satan came back in the morning. The Bible indicates this series of temptations started in the morning after 40 days and 40 nights were completed.

Matthew 4:1-4

^{1.} **Then was Jesus led up of the Spirit into the wilderness to be tempted of the Devil.**

^{2.} **And when He had fasted forty days and forty nights, He was afterward an hungred.**

^{3.} **And when the tempter came to Him, he said, if Thou be the Son of God, command that these stones be made bread.**

^{4.} **But He answered and said, it is written, man shall not live by bread alone, but by every word that proceedeth out of the mouth of God.**

Although it is a different time, it is same temptation and same response. Again, Jesus did not yield. Therefore, Satan changed his approach. Notice how the order of the second and third temptations is reversed. Satan used the same temptations on Eve and on Jesus that he uses on us, but he shuffles and mixes them together. *Selah.* The first letter in the words Warning, Warfare and Weapons is W. The W can help us men recognize and remember the top three strong satanic temptations that was used on all the fallen religious leaders. Just remember Wealth, Wine and Women. Ladies please don't be offended. To be gender neutral Women in this line up stands for any improper sexual relationship. This is associated with the lust of the eyes. Wine represents drug and alcohol abuse, lust of the flesh. Wealth represents stealing or the improper use of power, the pride of life. It doesn't matter which form the temptation or deception takes, yielding to it always leads to some degree of bondage, disappointment, or confusion. All twisting of God's Word is the bait for a fall.

Matthew 4:5-7

5. **Then the Devil taketh Him up into the holy city, and setteth Him on a pinnacle of the temple,**

6. **And saith unto Him, if Thou be the Son of God, cast Thyself down: for <u>it is written,</u> He shall give His angels charge concerning thee: and in their hands they shall bear Thee up, lest at any time Thou dash Thy foot against a stone.**

7. **Jesus <u>said unto him, it is written again,</u> thou shalt not tempt the Lord thy God.**

As Jesus demonstrated, the best defense against satanic Biblical distortions is to know, understand, and wisely speak God's written Word. Speak it consistently and appropriately.

Matthew 4:8-11

8. **Again, the Devil taketh Him up into an exceeding high mountain, and sheweth Him all the kingdoms of the world, and the glory of them;**

9. And saith unto Him, all these things will I give Thee, if Thou wilt fall down and worship me

10. **Then saith Jesus unto him, get thee hence, Satan**: for it is written, thou shalt worship the Lord thy God, and Him only shalt thou serve.

11. Then the **Devil leaveth Him**, and, behold, **angels came** and ministered unto Him.

Now Jesus would take charge of the situation and command Satan to leave, "get thee hence." Jesus was ready to move on, replacing the fallen angel Satan with God's guardian angels.

James 4:7

7. **Submit yourselves therefore to God**. **Resist the Devil**, and he will flee from you.

We also have power over the demonic spirits by first submitting to God. Then properly applying Christ's identity (name) and authority with faith and wisdom to our lives and actions. The progressively increasing light of God will drive away the darkness.

Luke 10:17-20

17. And the seventy returned again with joy, saying, Lord, **even the devils are subject unto us through Thy name**.

18. And He said unto them, I beheld Satan as lightning fall from Heaven.

19. Behold, I give unto you power to tread on serpents and scorpions, and over all the power of the enemy: and nothing shall by any means hurt you.

20. **Notwithstanding in this <u>rejoice not, that the spirits are subject unto you; but rather rejoice, because your names are written in Heaven</u>.**

Jesus was tempted by conflict with His human nature, from Satan himself, and from peer pressure. Sometimes a group of people will reject you or even persecute you if you don't join them. It gets even worse if you oppose them, revealing their errors and standing up for what is right and true. Jesus experienced all of this, as well as the strongest peer pressure, which comes from those closest to us.

Mark 8:31-33

31. **And He began to teach them, that the Son of man must <u>suffer many things, and be rejected</u> of the elders, and of the chief priests, and scribes, and be killed, and <u>after three days</u> rise again.**

32. **And He spake that saying openly. And <u>Peter took Him, and began to rebuke Him</u>.**

33. **But <u>when He had turned about and looked on his disciples</u>, He rebuked Peter, saying, get thee behind Me, Satan: for thou savourest not the things that be of God, but the things that be of men.**

Satan couldn't trip Jesus up directly, so he tried the indirect approach. Satan deceived a close friend (Peter), who strongly encouraged Jesus to take the easy way out. Knowing and seeing that Satan had set the trap, Jesus exposed it. All the disciples could see the conflict between Jesus' spoken words and His best friend's well-meaning, but deceptive advice. Jesus would follow God's plan even if no one else would understand or go with Him.

CHAPTER 9

TIME OF CRUCIFIXION

Of all the important events that have occurred throughout history, one is dramatically significant to us. More than anything else, this event is the door to our glorious destiny. I am referring to the crucifixion and resurrection of Christ. How we perceive this event is the basis of our redemption. God's church is built upon this foundational rock. Yet Satan has planted confusion around this very root of our salvation, the core to our conversion experience. Satan uses the same deceptive approach on the church that he used on Eve. He starts with "Hath God said," followed by an accusation that God's Word is wrong; "shall not," followed by his alternate conclusion, that you will be god and make your own rules. Just as Eve had a choice to believe God's Word or the tempting alternative, we also have a choice. What is that choice? The choice is your answer to this all-important question. Do you believe Jesus? To be more specific; do you believe His personally spoken words? Do you believe that Jesus knew what He was talking about and how to say it? On the other hand, do you believe and promote the traditions of man over God's Word? Many have fallen into a common trap of discounting God's Word and promoting the popular deceptions of Satan. For example, Jesus' statement regarding the time between his burial and resurrection is plainly recorded in the Bible.

Matthew 12:40 (NKJV)

40. **"For as Jonah was <u>three days and three nights</u> in the belly of the great fish, so will the Son of Man be <u>three days and three nights</u> in the heart of the earth."**

Jesus made it clear that He would be in the tomb three days and three nights. The Bible reveals that Jesus actually died on

Wednesday, not Friday. I think it would be powerful to focus on what Jesus accomplished on the cross during the Wednesday service before Resurrection Sunday. Maybe we could call it Wonderful Wednesday because of what Jesus did for us that day. Jesus paid the ultimate price to demonstrate God's love for us. If you desire tradition, it is not evil to honor Jesus' crucifixion on Good Friday, no more than it is evil to have a memorial service for someone who died a few days or weeks earlier. It is good to set aside special days to commemorate Jesus' birth, death, and resurrection. The problem and confusion arise when we repeat and promote a lie inspired by Satan. If we believe and promote something that dose not add up and is not based on facts then it is actually a false assumption or a superstition. Faith is not superstitious or void of facts. Mater-of-fact faith is based on understanding the facts.

Romans 10:17

17. So then <u>faith cometh</u> by hearing, and hearing <u>by the Word of God</u>.

Faith is trusting God's Word instead of fairy-tails and traditions of men. Christians should not be deceived by the common misconceptions of our day.

1 Timothy 1:4 (NKJV)

4. <u>nor give heed to fables</u> and endless genealogies, which cause disputes rather than godly edification which is in faith.

Paul wrote this to his son in the faith and warned him and others about straying from the truth of God's Word and twisting it to suit our selfish purposes. He shared some of his testimony of when he zealously promoting his birth heritage and religious philosophy as Saul. This caused him to discount Jesus' words and try to stop what God was doing. He acknowledged he did it in ignorance.

1 Timothy 1:13

13. Who was before a blasphemer, and a persecutor, and injurious: but I obtained mercy, because <u>I did it ignorantly</u> in unbelief.

If we continue to promote deceptions after the truth becomes clear to us, we are no longer blameless because of our ignorance. If we become enlightened to the truth and turn away from it to promote deception, our actions enter the realm of rebellion. It doesn't matter whether it is a large church or an individual. If we become rebellious, it will limit God's power to us. Most people in the world can count to three, so you don't have to be an intellectual to seriously wonder about our Christian math skills (2Peter 1:20). Why should the unsaved believe Jesus if we don't even believe Jesus? We do not need to discount, correct, or change Jesus' plainly spoken words. This is what Peter got into when Satan used him to oppose the Holy Spirit. Peter reprimanded Jesus as He was teaching about His rising from the dead after three complete twenty-four hour days. I know we just looked at this passage in chapter 8, but this time let's look at it from Peter's point of view. In this passage Jesus is teaching the disciples about His resurrection "after three days."

Mark 8:31-33

^{31.} **And He began to teach them, that the Son of man must suffer many things, and be rejected of the elders, and of the chief priests, and scribes, and <u>be killed, and after three days rise again.</u>**

^{32.} **<u>And He spake that saying openly. And Peter took him, and began to rebuke Him.</u>**

33. But when He had turned about and looked on his disciples, He rebuked Peter, saying, get thee behind me, Satan: for thou savourest not the things that be of God, but the things that be of men.

Peter made some false assumptions and began denying Jesus' plainly spoken words regarding His death and resurrection. It led to Peter fighting against God's ultimate plan in the Garden of Gethsemane. After that, Peter completely denied his association with Jesus, resulting in bitter depression, remorse, and brokenness. Let's not be too hard on Peter or any disciples that may be following Saint Peter's leading. Peter experienced God's presence and promoted God's Word more than many others, but Peter needed to repent in this area. He needed to accept Jesus' Word as true and reliable before he could move on in truth and light. *Selah.* Jesus plainly stated that He would be three days and three nights in the tomb. No matter how many ways you look at it, there are not even close to three days and three nights between late Good Friday night and early Easter Sunday morning. Biblically speaking, that would only be one complete day (Saturday). When Jesus used day and night together as He did in Matthew 12:40, it is not a metaphor or vague reference. He was specifically referring to three complete 24-hour days. In 2Corinthians 11:25 the English phrase "a night and a day" was use for a single 24-hour day. The phrase night and day (which we usually refer to as day and night) was translated from one Greek word. That Greek word is nychthemeron (Strong's #G3574). It is defined as one 24-hour day and nothing else. The Greek word Nychthemeron is simply two Greek words night (nyx) and day (hemera) put together into one word (Nychthemeron), which means one 24-hour day. Jesus was in the tomb three days not one day; therefore Jesus used the plural words of days and nights. Jesus plainly stated He would be in the tomb three days as well as three nights. *Selah*. To clear up the confusion and prove to the skeptical world that we can count and add properly, let's put our faith in the Bible's order of events instead of misguided traditions and fables. Once we understand a few facts, God's Word is very clear in proving that Jesus was in the tomb exactly three days and three nights. The first fact we should understand is that the Jewish time clock is different from the Gentile clock. We both have 12-hour clocks, but our Gentile day begins and ends at 12 midnight. The Jewish day ends and begins around sundown as stated in Genesis.

Genesis 1:5, 8, 31

5. **And God called the <u>light day</u>, and <u>the darkness He called night</u>. And the <u>evening and the morning</u> were the first day.**

8. **And God called the firmament Heaven. And the <u>evening and the morning</u> were the second day.**

31. **And God saw every thing that He had made, and, behold, it was very good. And the <u>evening and the morning</u> were the sixth day.**

The Jewish first hour of the day starts in the evening at sunset. The first twelve hours are divided up into four nightly watches (Matthew 14:25). An hourglass (sand timer) marked these four nightly watches. The priest would add or subtract a little sand to keep pace with the season. Sunrise is the beginning of the daytime twelve hours, to which Jesus referred to in John 11:9. The twelve hours are not referring to twelve sixty-minute hours. Instead, they are twelve equal segments of time between sunrise and sunset. This varies depending upon the season. Because exact Jewish time is constantly changing depending on season and location, it is fruitless to argue about a few minutes and miss the point; which is Jesus was 3 days and 3 nights in the tomb. For simplicity and consistency, in this book we will consider sunrise to be 6 am and sunset to be 6 pm. Since the Passover began about two weeks after the Spring Equinox, this timetable is accurate to within several minutes. This would consistency reflect a six-hour difference between Jewish time and the time we normally use. Even today, pinpointing the exact time of an event can be confusing to the casual observer. This is because our time changes across the country and we also use daylight savings time part of the year. In just a few minutes you could gain or loose an hour by crossing into another time zone. The year the Deep Foundations e-book was first published can be an example of this sort of confusion. I say my e-book was first published in 2017. Amazon uses the year 2016. Who is right? Can we both be correct? Yes, because I was at home in Fort Lauderdale when I pushed the publish button. It was about ten minutes after the New Year of 2017 had begun. The Amazon headquarters are in Seattle where it was still 2016. You see what first appears to be a contradiction actually narrows the timeframe in which the event occurred. We will see latter in this chapter that Jesus actually uses a similar scenario to tell us the time of night that He would rise from the dead. *Selah.* To dispel the confusion in order to understand the timing of the four Gospels we need to understand which clock the authors were using to describe the crucifixion. Three of them were using the Jewish clock. Six o'clock would be the beginning of the Jewish first hour, which would be completed at seven o'clock. The beginning of the Jewish third daytime hour would be our 9 am. This is confusing but important, because John's Gospel uses Gentile time, and Matthew, Mark and Luke use Jewish time. That is why there appears to be a conflict in their timing. In reality this proves they did not copy each other but were looking at different clocks. *Selah.* Not only is Jewish time different from Gentile time, the Jewish calendar is also different.

The Jews have more than one calendar, which can lead to a lot of confusion regarding the dating of history and prophecy. The Jewish prophetic calendar has 360 days in it. The (sun) Solar calendar has 365.24 and the (Moon) Lunar calendar has 354.37 days in them. Therefore on Leap years our daily calendar adds an extra day and the Jewish calendar adds an extra month to keep pace with the seasons. On leap years the Jewish calendar doubles the last month resulting in a 13-month year. Jewish calendars have two different New Years per year. They celebrate the civil New Year in their seventh month at Rosh Hashanah, because it is believed that this is the month of Adam's creation. For instance, at Rosh Hashanah, September 2020, the Jewish calendar counts 5,781 years since Adam was created. Just a note, there seems to be some missing years in the Jewish calendar, so it may actually be closer to the year 6,000. *Selah.* God instructed Moses to start the religious calendar in the month of the Passover, which is in March or April, depending upon the year.

Exodus 12:2

2. This month shall be unto you the beginning of months: <u>it shall be the first month of the year</u> to you.

This passage refers to the month of Aviv, which came to be known as Nisan, the month of the Passover. The first event of the year was preparation for the Passover celebration. The Passover celebration would last a week and included the Feast of Unleavened Bread. The Passover celebration started on the 14th day and continued until the 21st day (Exodus 12:18). Before the Passover, there was much preparation, which concluded on the final preparation day, which was the 13th day of Nisan.

Exodus 12:3, 5-7

3. Speak ye unto all the congregation of Israel, saying, in the <u>tenth day of this month they shall take to them every man a</u>

<u>lamb,</u> according to the house of their fathers, a lamb for an house:

5. Your lamb shall be without blemish, a male of the first year: ye shall take it out from the sheep, or from the goats:

6. And ye shall keep it up <u>until the fourteenth day</u> of the same month: and the whole assembly of the congregation of Israel shall kill it in the evening.

7. And they shall take of the blood, and strike it on the two side posts and on the upper door post of the houses, wherein they shall eat it.

This was the actual Passover that the celebration commemorated. Notice that the four days of examination (the 10, 11, 12, 13) correlate with Jesus entering Jerusalem on Palm Sunday. The Lamb of God was then questioned and examined for error. Jesus was examined for four days, from the beginning of the 10th day to the end of the 13th day. This included Palm Sunday and the day He hung on the cross for all to see. All four Gospels declare that Jesus was crucified on Preparation Day. Preparation Day was set aside for removing the leaven, which represented sin. *Selah.* The Jews started calling this final preparation day, the first day of unleavened bread. I suppose it was because there was no leaven left in the house. Preparation Day was also the day for killing the spotless Passover lambs. After Israel built their temple they were instructed to come together at Jerusalem to celebrate Passover. There were a lot of Passover lambs to be slain at the temple. Josephus stated that there were at least 256,500 Passover lambs killed in the temple shortly before it was destroyed in 70 AD. Because this would take many priests several hours to complete they would begin on Preparation Day several hours before sundown.

Luke 22:7

7. Then came the day of unleavened bread, when the Passover must be killed.

As we seen in Exodus 12:6 the lamb was to be inspected "up until the 14th day" of the month, but not including the 14th day. The word evening can refer to the end of the day, which commonly came to be accepted as the time between 3 pm and sunset. It was also a term for the beginning of the new day. Jesus died and was buried between the evenings. The original Passover lambs were to be killed "in the evening," around sunset which was the transition to the new day. The lambs were to be killed in their homes because the temple had not been built yet. After its blood was applied to their door area, the lamb was roasted, which took quite a while.

Exodus 12:8

8. And they shall eat the flesh in <u>that night</u>, <u>roast with fire</u>, and unleavened bread; and with bitter herbs they shall eat it.

They ate the Passover meal during the night at the very beginning of the 14th day of Nisan. The first Passover meal was probably completed by midnight, which is when the death angel passed over the homes that had the blood applied (Exodus 11:4).

Exodus 12:29

29. And it came to pass, that <u>at midnight</u> the Lord smote all the firstborn in the land of Egypt, from the firstborn of Pharaoh that sat on his throne unto the firstborn of the captive that was in the dungeon; and all the firstborn of cattle.

The Passover lamb was killed at the end of preparation-day then the blood was applied to the entrance of their home. The meat was then roasted and consumed before midnight when the actual

Passover occurred. *Selah.* One more thing we need to note. "Sabbath" does not mean Saturday. Sabbath means a day of rest. In the Bible, there are many more Sabbaths than Saturdays. Saturday was a Jewish weekly Sabbath; but there were also High Sabbaths, like the Passover, and other special days. Here are a couple of examples.

Leviticus 23: 24
24. **Speak unto the children of Israel, saying, in the seventh month, in the <u>first day</u> of the month, shall ye have a <u>Sabbath</u>, a memorial of blowing of trumpets, an holy convocation.**

Leviticus 23:32
32. **It shall be unto you a <u>Sabbath of rest</u>, and ye shall afflict your souls: in the <u>ninth day</u> of the month at even, <u>from even unto even, shall ye celebrate your Sabbath</u>.**

The Sabbath began at sundown and ended at the following sundown. We will focus on the High Sabbath of Passover and the events surrounding this special week.

Leviticus 23:4-5
4. **These are the feasts of the Lord, even holy convocations, which ye shall proclaim in their seasons.**

5. **In the <u>fourteenth day of the first month</u> at even is the Lord's Passover.**

The Passover began in the evening, which was the beginning of the 14th day of Nisan. Passover is a High Sabbath that celebrates the deliverance received after the blood of the lamb was properly applied.

Exodus 12:13-14

13. And the blood shall be to you for a token upon the houses where ye are: and <u>when I see the blood</u>, I will <u>pass over you</u>, and the <u>plague shall not be upon you to destroy you</u>, when I smite the land of Egypt.

14. And <u>this day shall be unto you for a memorial;</u> and ye shall keep it a feast to the Lord throughout your generations; ye shall keep it a feast by an ordinance for ever.

A form of Passover is to be celebrated forever as a memorial. The memorial feast was a huge reunion, celebrating the gift of freedom from bondage (Deuteronomy 16:1-7). There were special days in the Passover week.

Numbers 28:16-18

16. And in the <u>fourteenth day</u> of the first month is the <u>Passover</u> of the Lord.

17. And in the <u>fifteenth day</u> of this month is the feast: seven days shall <u>unleavened bread</u> be eaten.

18. In the first day shall be an holy convocation; ye shall do <u>no manner of servile work therein</u>:

The 15th day is a special feast. Many have confused this with the Feast of the Passover Lamb, but the Bible is clear that the Passover was on the 14th day (Numbers 9:1-5). The original Passover was at midnight of the 14th, and the Lamb was to be slain and roasted before midnight. On the night of the 14th, the Lamb was to be the featured entree with a side of bitter herbs and unleavened bread.

Exodus 12:8

8. **And they shall eat the flesh <u>in that night,</u> roast with fire, and unleavened bread; and with bitterherbs they shall eat it.**

All the leftover Passover lamb was to be consumed by fire before morning

Exodus 12:10

10. **And ye shall <u>let nothing of it remain until the morning;</u> and that which remaineth of it until the morning ye shall burn with fire.**

During the original Passover, after the sun arose, Israel gathered their things and the gifts from the Egyptians and left their homes in Goshen.

Exodus 12:35-36

35. **And the children of Israel did according to the word of Moses; and they borrowed of the Egyptians jewels of silver, and jewels of gold, and raiment:**

36. **And the LORD gave the people favour in the sight of the Egyptians, so that they lent unto them such things as they required. And they spoiled the Egyptians.**

More than a million people left their homes in Egypt and assembled at Rameses. There are a variety of ways to spell Rameses (Rameses, Ramses or Raamses). The Bible is clear that this city was built by Israeli slave labor.

Exodus 1:11

11. **Therefore they did set over them taskmasters to afflict them with their burdens. And they built for Pharaoh <u>treasure cities,</u> Pithom and <u>Raamses.</u>**

On the 15th, they organized in Rameses and began their systematic departure from the nation of Egypt. They looked more like a vast army marching out than an unorganized mob.

Numbers 33:3

3. And they <u>departed from Rameses</u> in the first month, on the <u>fifteenth day of the first month;</u> <u>on the morrow after the passover</u> the children of Israel went out with an high hand in the sight of all the Egyptians.

Exodus 12:51

51. And it came to pass <u>the selfsame day,</u> that the LORD did bring the children of Israel out of the land of Egypt by their armies.

Exodus 13:18 (NKJV)

18. So God led the people around by way of the wilderness of the Red Sea. And the children of Israel went up in <u>orderly ranks</u> out of the land of Egypt.

They had no time for preparing lamb because they were traveling. The featured entree for the special feast commemorating their march to freedom was unleavened bread.

Exodus 12:37-39

37. And the children of Israel journeyed from Rameses to Succoth, about six hundred thousand on foot that were men, beside children.

38. And a mixed multitude went up also with them; and flocks, and herds, even very much cattle.

39. And <u>they baked unleavened cakes of the dough which they brought forth out of Egypt,</u> for it was not leavened; because

they were thrust out of Egypt, and could not tarry, neither had they prepared for themselves any victual.

The feast of unleavened bread was to commemorate their departure, which was on the 15th day of Nisan (Numbers 28:17).

Exodus 12:17
17. **And ye shall observe the <u>feast of unleavened bread</u>; for in this selfsame day have <u>I brought your armies out of the land of Egypt: therefore shall ye observe this day</u> in your generations by an ordinance for ever.**

The Passover Feast was on the 14th day of Nisan, which was Thursday (not Wednesday or Friday) the year Jesus was crucified. The 15th was the Holy Feast of Unleavened Bread, which was on Friday that year. *Selah.* We traditionally celebrate Christ's resurrection on Easter. Easter is actually named after the obscure pagan goddess Eostre. She seems to be associated with fertility and the dawn of spring. Symbols of fertility (Easter bunnies and colored eggs) are added to celebrate this holiday. Easter is often on a different week than the Passover, because we celebrate Easter the first Sunday after the full moon following the spring equinox. We normally use this holiday to celebrate the resurrection of Christ. While it's wonderful to set aside a day to celebrate Christ's resurrection, don't let tradition cloud out the truth. Jesus is associated with the Passover lamb, not the goddess Eostre or the Easter bunny. It is a true statement to say, "This Easter we will celebrate Christ resurrection" or on Good Friday say, "Today we honor Christ's death." In contrast, it is a false statement to say, "Good Friday is the day Jesus died." The difference is a subtle one, and yet it is like day and night. One statement is true while the other statement promotes a lie, confusion, and darkness, because Jesus did not die on a Friday. *Selah.* As examined earlier in Numbers 28:17, the Bible states that the Feast of Unleavened Bread began after the Passover, on the 15th day of Nisan. It seems that the Jewish people traditionally began eating unleavened bread on Preparation Day, the day before the Passover. It was referred to as the "first day of unleavened bread" which some might confuse with the Feast of Unleavened Bread. As a matter of fact, the NIV translation even calls this "the first day of the Feast of Unleavened Bread." So like Christ's crucifixion day, there was a Biblical day of the event with symbolic significance and a different traditional day of the event. This can be confusing if you assume that tradition and God's Word are always the same. Once you see the facts and understand them, you can see not only where the confusion comes in, but also how the Bible clearly backs up Christ's Words. Jesus was in the tomb three complete days and three complete nights. *Selah.* Let's look at the order of events leading up to Christ's burial and resurrection. Verses 12 and 14, of the following group of verses are the most confusing in the lineup. They can be hard to reconcile, but let's see how all the rest of the verses support the interpretation and explanation at the end of this passage.

Mark 14:12-17

12. **And the first day of unleavened bread, <u>when they killed the Passover</u>, His disciples said unto Him, where wilt Thou that we go and prepare that Thou mayest eat the Passover?**

13. **And He sendeth forth two of His disciples, and saith unto them, go ye into the city, and there shall meet you a man bearing a pitcher of water: follow him.**

14. **And wheresoever he shall go in, say ye to the goodman of the house, the Master saith, where is the guestchamber, where I shall eat the Passover with My disciples?**

^{15.} **And he will shew you a large upper room furnished and prepared: there make ready for us.**

^{16.} **And His disciples went forth, and came into the city, and found as He had said unto them: and they made ready the Passover.**

^{17.} **And <u>in the evening</u> He cometh with the twelve.**

There are two important points to remember about this passage.

The first point is the day of this event. Verse 12 mentions "the first day of unleavened bread," which was from a Jewish tradition, not Numbers 28:17. The first day of unleavened bread is probably a reference that the last of the leaven had been removed from their houses and they began eating only unleavened bread. It was before the Passover on the day "they killed the Passover" lambs. It was Preparation Day, which occurred on Wednesday that year. I believe this conversation actually started on Tuesday afternoon as they were looking forward to the work to be done on Wednesday (Preparation Day). For example, I could be looking for my ship to come in, and finally I see it on the horizon approaching me. I could rightfully make the general statement, "my ship is here." I can see it, but it's not time to get onboard yet. *Selah.* Many Jews at that time believed the Messiah would come and deliver Israel from the Romans.

Acts 1:6

^{6.} **When they therefore were come together, they asked of Him, saying, Lord, wilt Thou at this time <u>restore again the kingdom to Israel?</u>**

Many Jews at that time believed that their deliverance would be on Passover. This was because Moses delivered Israel from Egypt on Passover and spoke of one that was to come.

Deuteronomy 18:15

15. The LORD thy God will raise up unto thee a <u>Prophet from the midst of thee</u>, of thy brethren, <u>like unto me</u>; unto Him ye shall hearken;

Most of the Jewish people (including John the Baptist, Matthew 11:2-3) made the wrong assumptions about the significance of the Passover and the deliverance Jesus was bringing. The disciples acknowledged this after Jesus' crucifixion.

Luke 24:21

21. But <u>we trusted that it had been He which should have redeemed Israel:</u> and beside all this, to day is the third day since these things were done.

The disciples may have been looking forward to the Passover all year, like I look forward to Christmas. They were probably reflecting on Palm Sunday's triumphal entry and a variety of miracles such as raising Lazarus from the dead. They were full of anticipation and eager to start preparing for the Passover. Then about 6 pm our Tuesday (their Wednesday), they posed the question to Jesus, where do we start? Jesus directed them to a place that was already "prepared," except for a few personal details. Therefore, He only sent two of them to announce their arrival and finish the details. They were probably not gone long. Then the two disciples returned to inform the remaining disciples that everything was ready. Then, "in the evening He came." It was probably shortly after sunset when Jesus and the twelve disciples arrived at the Upper Room. We do not know what time it was, but we do know the day. By the end of this chapter it will become undisputedly clear (if you believe the Bible) that the Lords Supper was on Wednesday, the beginning of Preparation Day, our Tuesday evening. *Selah.*

The second point is the most important. It takes more time to comprehend this information, but it is the key to understanding what happened that week. Jesus was about to introduce a New Covenant represented by a new Passover. The former covenant, which was founded on works of the law, was about to be replaced by the New Covenant, which is eternal. The Old Covenant contains a lot of symbolism to help us understand the New Covenant. For instance the Jewish temple was a forerunner and symbol of Christ's body, where God's power was available to answer prayers.

John 2:19, 21

19. **Jesus answered and said unto them, Destroy <u>this temple</u>, and in three days I will raise it up.**

21. **But he spake of the <u>temple of his body</u>.**

The Passover Lamb was a forerunner and symbol of Christ's spotless pure humanity.

John 1:36

36. **And looking upon Jesus as He walked, he saith, behold <u>the Lamb of God</u>!**

John 1:29

29. **The next day John seeth Jesus coming unto him, and saith, Behold the <u>Lamb of God, which taketh away the sin of the world</u>.**

The perfect Lamb of God was to be sacrificed for our deliverance (1Peter 1:18-19). The Bible is clear that it is the blood of Jesus, "the Lamb of God" that eradicates our sins. We have yet to comprehend the full extent of the sacrifice God made for us (2Corinthians 5:21). For now we know that Jesus died an excruciating death, which initiated our redemption. The new Passover meal (to memorialize the sacrifice and our redemption) would be called the Lord's Supper. *Selah.* Because of its importance, let's examine the Bible's account of the introduction of the New Covenant and why the Old Covenant needed to be replaced. In the book of Hebrews chapters 8 through 10 the Bible goes into detail about replacing the Old Covenant with the New Covenant and the reasons why it was necessary for our redemption. You may want to read it in your favorite translation. Here are some excerpts from the King James Translation. Particularly notice the underlined words to focus on the point of this lengthy passage.

Hebrews 8:1-2

[1.] **Now of the things which we have spoken this is the sum: we have such an High Priest, who is set on the right hand of the throne of the majesty in the Heavens;**

[2.] **A Minister of the sanctuary, and of the <u>true tabernacle, which the Lord pitched, and not man</u>.**

Hebrews 8:5-9

[5.] **Who <u>serve unto the example and shadow of Heavenly things,</u> as Moses was admonished of God when he was about to make the tabernacle: for, see, saith He, that thou make all things according to the pattern <u>shewed to thee in the mount</u>.**

6. But now hath He obtained a more excellent ministry, by how much also He is the mediator of a <u>better covenant,</u> which was established upon <u>better promises.</u>

7. For if that first covenant had been faultless, then should no place have been sought for the second.

8. For finding fault with them, He saith, behold, the days come, saith the Lord, when <u>I will make a New Covenant</u> with the house of Israel and with the house of Judah:

9. <u>Not according to the covenant that I made with their fathers in the day when I took them by the hand to lead them out of the land of Egypt;</u> because they continued not in my covenant, and I regarded them not, saith the Lord.

Hebrews 8:13

13. In that He saith, <u>a New Covenant, He hath made the first old. Now that which decayeth and waxeth old is ready to vanish away.</u>

Hebrews 9:1

1. Then verily the <u>first covenant had also ordinances of divine service, and a worldly sanctuary.</u>

Hebrews 9:9-12

9. <u>Which was a figure for the time</u> then present, in which were offered both gifts and sacrifices, that could not make him that did the service perfect, as pertaining to the conscience;

10. Which stood only in meats and drinks, and divers washings, and carnal ordinances, imposed on them <u>until the time of reformation.</u>

11. But <u>Christ being come an High Priest of good things to come, by a greater and more perfect tabernacle, not made with hands, that is to say, not of this building;</u>

12. Neither by the blood of goats and calves, but <u>by His own blood He entered in once into the holy place, having obtained eternal redemption for us</u>.

Hebrews 9:15

15. And for this cause He is the mediator of the <u>New Testament</u>, that by means of death, for the redemption of the transgressions that were under the first testament, they which are called might receive the promise of eternal inheritance.

Hebrews 9:24

24. For <u>Christ is not entered into the holy places made with hands, which are the figures of the true;</u> but into Heaven itself, now to appear in the presence of God for us:

Hebrews 10:1

1. For the <u>law having a shadow of good things to come, and not the very image of the things, can never with those sacrifices which they offered year by year continually make the comers thereunto perfect</u>.

Hebrews 10:9-10

9. Then said He, lo, I come to do thy will, O God. <u>He taketh away the first, that he may establish the second.</u>

10. <u>By the which will we are sanctified through the offering of the body of Jesus Christ once for all</u>.

Even though the old English may be a little like reading a letter from a lawyer you should read the context that surround the main points. However if you just read what I've underlined in

Hebrews, the message is relatively clear. God's blessing has moved from the Old Covenant based in works of the law to the New Covenant based in faith in what Christ has done. If you read the entire passage in your Bibles you will see a special room mentioned called the Holiest of All or the Holy of Holies or the Most Holy place, depending on your translation. The Holiest of All or the Holy of Holies was the Most Holy Room in the temple. No one could enter or see the room except one person. Once a year, a high priest humbly entered the room on the 10th day of the 7th month (the Day of Atonement). Historians say that he entered with a rope around his ankle so that if he died in the sacred room, others could drag him out without going in. The high priest had one purpose for going in. It was to sprinkle the lifeblood of the sacrifice on the golden mercy seat (Leviticus 16:2-34). This was the atonement offering for that year. It was like a payment of interest until the sin debt could be paid off. There was no provision for full repayment of the sin debt under the Old Covenant. All they could do was to keep making the interest payments, because they had no ability to pay off the principal debt. Christ paid off the debt in full. Jesus spoke the word "Telco" from the cross, meaning paid-in-full, no more debt, and no more interest payments. *Selah*. There was only one way into the Holy of Holies, which was through a very thick curtain referred to as a veil. This is the curtain that supernaturally ripped open from top to bottom when Jesus died. This unveiling revealed that the power of atonement had been transferred from the temple to Christ's death on the cross. *Selah*. We now honor Christ's sacrifice with the Lord's Supper. Although some may call it Communion, it is actually a symbol recognizing the New Covenant provided by Jesus Christ who is our Passover Lamb. The New King James Bible is quite clear regarding our new

Passover (The Last Supper), which is eternal and not bound to any particular day of the year.

1 Corinthians 11:23-26 _(NKJV)

23. **For I received from the Lord that which I also delivered to you: that the Lord Jesus on the same night in which He was betrayed took bread;**

24. **And when He had given thanks, He broke it and said, "take, eat; this is My body which is broken for you; <u>do this in remembrance of Me</u>."**

25. **In the same manner He also took the cup after supper, saying, "this cup is the <u>New Covenant</u> in My blood. This do, <u>as often as you drink it</u>, in remembrance of Me."**

26. **For as often as you eat this bread and drink this cup, you proclaim the Lord's death till He comes.**

Let's take a close look at the wording in John 13 regarding the timing of the Last Supper, which we now call the Lords Supper.

John 13:1-2, 30

1. **Now <u>before the feast of the Passover,</u> when Jesus knew that His hour was come that He should depart out of this world unto the Father, having loved His own which were in the world, He loved them unto the end.**

2. **And <u>supper being ended,</u> the Devil having now put into the heart of Judas Iscariot, Simon's son, to betray Him;**

30. **He then having received the sop went immediately out: and it was night.**

Notice the words; "supper being ended." This was the Last Supper, the same night Judas left to betray Jesus. It is very clear

208

that the Last Supper was "before the Feast of the Passover." The Passover feast was on Thursday. The Last Supper took place on Wednesday Jewish time (Tuesday night Gentile time, somewhere between 6 pm and midnight). At the conclusion of the events of the Upper Room, Jesus and his disciples went to the Garden of Gethsemane. I believe they were there until well after midnight because the disciples couldn't stay awake for even an hour to pray with Jesus.

Mark 14:37-43

37. **And He cometh, and findeth them sleeping, and saith unto Peter, Simon, sleepest thou? <u>Couldest not thou watch one hour?</u>**

38. **Watch ye and pray, lest ye enter into temptation. The spirit truly is ready, but the flesh is weak.**

39. **<u>And again He went away, and prayed,</u> and spake the same words.**

40. **And <u>when He returned, He found them asleep again, (for their eyes were heavy,</u>) neither wist they what to answer Him.**

41. **And <u>He cometh the third time,</u> and saith unto them, sleep on now, and take your rest: it is enough, the hour is come; behold, the Son of man is betrayed into the hands of sinners.**

42. **Rise up, let us go; lo, he that betrayeth Me is at hand.**

43. **And immediately, while He yet spake, cometh Judas, one of the twelve, and with him a great multitude with swords and staves, from the chief priests and the scribes and the elders.**

Jesus was taken from the Garden of Gethsemane to stand before a mock trial arranged by the religious leaders. Then early Wednesday morning, He was sent to Pontius Pilate.

Luke 22:63-67

63. And the men that held Jesus mocked Him, and smote Him.

64. And when they had blindfolded Him, they struck Him on the face, and asked Him, saying, prophesy, who is it that smote Thee?

65. And many other things blasphemously spake they against Him.

66. And <u>as soon as it was day</u>, the elders of the people and the chief priests and the scribes came together, and led Him into their council, saying,

67. Art thou the Christ? Tell us. And He said unto them, if I tell you, ye will not believe:

Mark 15:1

1. And straightway in the <u>morning</u> the chief priests held a consultation with the elders and scribes and the whole council, and bound Jesus, and carried Him away, and delivered Him to Pilate.

John 18:28

28. Then led they Jesus from Caiaphas unto the hall of judgment: and it was <u>early</u>; and they themselves went not into the judgment hall, lest they should be defiled; but <u>that they might eat the Passover</u>.

Notice that Jesus had finished his "New Testament" Passover (the Lord's Supper) many hours earlier, but the religious leaders were still looking forward to their Passover and didn't want to be defiled. The Passover had the following exceptions to being observed on the 14th day of the first month:

Numbers 9:10-11

10. Speak unto the children of Israel, saying, if any man of you or of your posterity shall be <u>unclean by reason of a dead body, or be in a journey afar off</u>, yet he shall keep the Passover unto the Lord.

11. The <u>fourteenth day of the second month at even they shall keep it</u>, and eat it with unleavened bread and bitter herbs.

Thus, the men who removed Jesus from the cross would not be celebrating the Jewish Passover until the following month. For them, it must have been the most wonderful Passover ever. The order of events and how they support Jesus' words recorded in the Bible become very clear if you study the Crucifixion Time Chart at the end of this chapter. *Selah.* It is clear that after the early morning trials and beatings, Jesus was presented before the gathering mob. It was around the first hour of the day, Jewish time (about 6 am Gentile time). Remember John uses the Roman-Gentile clock and the other Gospels use the Jewish time clock.

John 19:14

14. And it was <u>the preparation of the Passover</u>, and about the <u>sixth hour</u>: and he saith unto the Jews, behold your King!

The decision was popular – "Crucify Him!"

Mark 15:25

25. And it was the third hour, and they crucified Him.

Jesus was nailed to the cross at the third hour Jewish time (9 am Gentile time). Jesus was on the cross a total of six hours. Using the Gentile time clock, Jesus was nailed to the cross at 9 am Wednesday. At noon, darkness covered the land until Jesus died at 3 pm Wednesday afternoon. According to Jewish law, a lamb was sacrificed for the daily evening sin offering at around 3

211

o'clock in the afternoon. The Passover lambs were also beginning to be sacrifice around this time in evening. The Bible is clear that preceding the Passover feast was Preparation Day. This was a time of massive sacrifice, removing leaven, personal preparation, and dedication. This year God provided the special Passover Lamb that was to be killed before the Passover meal in order to provide deliverance. This Preparation Day would be unforgettable to all of the witnesses and is still talked about today. It was the day Jesus died.

Mark 15:33-39

33. **And when the sixth hour was come, there was darkness over the whole land until the ninth hour.**

34. **And at the ninth hour Jesus cried with a loud voice, saying, eloi, eloi, lama sabachthani? Which is, being interpreted, my God, my God, why hast Thou forsaken Me?**

35. **And some of them that stood by, when they heard it, said, behold, He calleth Elias.**

36. **And one ran and filled a spunge full of vinegar, and put it on a reed, and gave Him to drink, saying, let alone; let us see whether Elias will come to take Him down.**

37. **And Jesus cried with a loud voice, and gave up the ghost.**

38. **And the veil of the temple was rent in twain from the top to the bottom.**

39. **And when the centurion, which stood over against Him, saw that He so cried out, and gave up the ghost, He said, truly this man was the Son of God.**

The Father God never left or turned his back on Jesus, even while His only begotten Son suffered such agony on the cross. Why? The Father is omnipresent. He cannot leave. The Father can increase or decrease His intensity and activity, but He is always here. Also notice that the next moment after the "My God why hast Thou forsaken Me?" statement, Jesus spoke to the Father, saying "Father, into Thy hands I commend My spirit." Jesus put His perfect human spirit into the Father's hands.

Luke 23:44-46

[44.] **And it was about the sixth hour, and there was a darkness over all the earth until the ninth hour.**

[45.] **And the sun was darkened, and the veil of the temple was rent in the midst.**

[46.] **And <u>when Jesus had cried with a loud voice, He said, Father, into Thy hands I commend My spirit</u>: and having said thus, He gave up the ghost.**

I strongly believe the God who left Jesus before His death was the Holy Spirit, the Divine Nature of God. He would come back later to raise Jesus from the dead.

Romans 8:11

[11.] **But if the Spirit of Him that raised up Jesus from the dead dwell in you, <u>He that raised up Christ from the dead</u> shall also quicken your mortal bodies by <u>His Spirit that dwelleth in you</u>.**

After the Holy Spirit left Jesus, what remained on the cross was the perfect human nature (the species of man) and God's grieving Soul (the divine personality), which together left the sinless body at death. Illustrated on the following pages are the stages Christ went through on the cross.

Mark 15:25

^{25.} **And it was the third hour, and they crucified Him.**

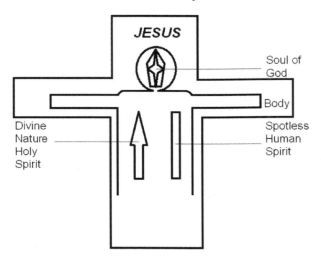

Then about six hours later:

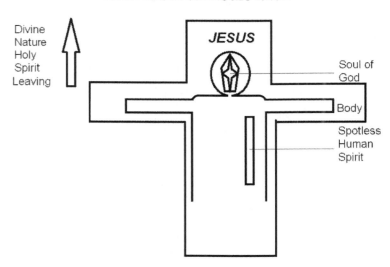

Mark 15:34

^{34.} **And at the ninth hour Jesus cried with a loud voice, saying, eloi, eloi, lama sabachthani? Which is, being interpreted, <u>My God, My God, why hast Thou forsaken Me?</u>**

Time of Crucifixion

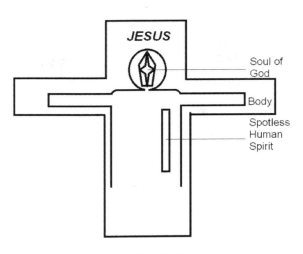

Mark 15:37

37. **And Jesus cried with a loud voice, and gave up the ghost.**

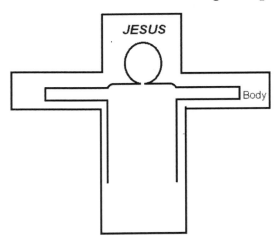

John 19:30-31

30. **When Jesus therefore had received the vinegar, <u>He said, it is finished: and He bowed His head, and gave up the ghost.</u>**

31. **The Jews therefore, because <u>it was the preparation</u>, that the bodies should not remain upon the cross on the Sabbath day, (for <u>that Sabbath day was an high day</u>,) besought Pilate that their legs might be broken, and that they might be taken away.**

In the Bible, this is the only time that vinegar flavored wine touched Jesus' lips. Jesus received the drink fermented with yeast and then He died. I believe the yeast in this desensitizing drink represented our sins. Just before He died, Jesus proclaimed in a loud voice, "It is finished," translated from the word "Teleo," a banking term referring to a debt that was paid off. The debt was finished. It was over. What is the sin debt and what was paid off you might ask.

Romans 6:23

23. **For the <u>wages of sin is death</u>; but the gift of God is eternal life through Jesus Christ our Lord.**

The spotless Lamb of God paid for all the sins of all the people, including everyone in the past, present, and future. This happened on Preparation Day, the day the Passover lamb was killed for the next day's High Sabbath of Passover. Like the Passover example of applying the blood of the lamb to the doorpost, the payment Jesus Christ made for us has to be personally applied for it to count on our behalf. *Selah.* Now we come to the length of time the Bible states Jesus was in the tomb.

Mark 15:42-43

42. **And now when the <u>even was come</u>, because <u>it was the preparation</u>, that is, the day before the Sabbath,**

43. **Joseph of Arimathaea, an honourable counsellor, which also waited for the kingdom of God, came, and went in boldly unto Pilate, and craved the body of Jesus.**

Joseph could see the evening fast approaching, which was the end of the Preparation Day. This would be between 3 and 6 pm Gentile time. The evening offering was around 3 pm. The evening or end of the Jewish day would occur around 6 pm.

Luke 23:52-54

52. This man went unto Pilate, and begged the body of Jesus.

53. And he took it down, and wrapped it in linen, and laid it in a sepulchre that was hewn in stone, wherein never man before was laid.

54. And <u>that day was the preparation, and the Sabbath drew on.</u>

They rushed to wrap the body and get it to the tomb before 6 pm Gentile time, or at least before dark which was almost upon them.

John 19:41-42

41. Now <u>in the place where He was crucified</u> there was a garden; and in the garden a <u>new sepulchre,</u> wherein was never man yet laid.

42. There laid they Jesus therefore because of the Jews' <u>preparation day;</u> for the <u>sepulchre was nigh at hand.</u>

The new sepulcher was nearby, and they had just enough time. Perfect timing, exactly as God would have it. Matthew, Mark, Luke and John all say Jesus was put in the tomb on Preparation Day. If you count the days and nights, it is clear that Jesus was in the tomb exactly three days and three nights, just as Jesus had said. He was placed in the tomb at the end of Preparation Day and then the door was sealed with a roman seal at the beginning of Passover, which was Thursday Jewish time. He was there all night and all day Thursday; all night and all day Friday, the second day; and all night and all day Saturday. After the end of the third night and day Jesus left the tomb, long before sunrise Sunday morning. Mark quoted Jesus telling us the timeframe in which He would leave the tomb.

Mark 8:31

31. And **He began to teach them**, that the Son of man must suffer many things, and be rejected of the elders, and of the chief priests, and scribes, and be killed, and **after three days rise again**.

Jesus' resurrection would be after the conclusion of the third day Jewish time. We just counted the days and seen that the third day was Saturday. Jesus' resurrection would be after sundown Saturday evening. Later Mark quotes Jesus again teaching about His death and resurrection.

Mark 9:31

31. For He taught his disciples, and said unto them, The Son of man is delivered into the hands of men, and they shall kill Him; and after that He is killed, **He shall rise the third day**.

Here Mark quotes Jesus saying He will rise on the third day. This may look to some like a contradiction, but to those who understand the Bible, it is a revelation. Your translation may miss this because many of them say after three days, to agree with Mark 8:31. Nonetheless all translations quote Jesus' statement in John 2:19 as "in three days" not after three days.

John 2:19

19. **Jesus answered and said unto them, Destroy this temple, and in three days I will raise it up.**

Jesus left the tomb after and during the third day. Both of these contrary statements from Jesus are true. Jesus taught that He would leave the tomb on the third day before midnight concluded that Saturday. Jesus left the tomb while it was still the third day – Roman time. "He shall rise the third day." Jesus also taught that He would leave the tomb after the third day – Jewish time. "After three days rise again." If we see the whole picture of what Jesus was saying, we see Jesus revealed that He would leave the tomb on Saturday between sundown and midnight. Although Jesus actually departed the tomb Saturday night Gentile time we can rightfully say Jesus rose from the dead early Sunday Jewish time. *Selah.* After Jesus left the tomb an angel came and rolled back the sealed stone door to reveal Jesus was already gone.

John 20:1

1. **The first day of the week cometh Mary Magdalene early, <u>when it was yet dark,</u> unto the sepulchre, and seeth the stone taken away from the sepulchre.**

Jesus was free to go after 6 pm Saturday. Jesus stated He would leave the tomb before midnight on Saturday. Sunday the discovery was made and everyone was talking about the empty tomb. *Selah.* Lets back up and look at the activity around the tomb during and following those prophetic three days. Fearing that someone might take the body, the religious leaders went to Pilate to request a three-day guard. This was at the beginning of Passover after the close of Preparation Day, probably shortly after 6 pm Wednesday night (Gentile time).

Matthew 27:62-66

62. **Now the next day, that <u>followed the day of the preparation,</u> the chief priests and Pharisees came together unto Pilate,**

63. **Saying, sir, we remember that that deceiver said, while He was yet alive, <u>after three days</u> I will rise again.**

64. **Command therefore that the sepulchre be made sure <u>until the third day, lest His disciples come by night,</u> and steal Him**

away, and say unto the people, He is risen from the dead: so the last error shall be worse than the first.

^{65.} Pilate said unto them, ye have a watch: go your way, <u>make it as sure as ye can</u>.

^{66.} So <u>they went, and made the sepulchre sure, sealing the stone, and setting a watch</u>.

Once they knew the guards were on duty at the tomb, the religious leaders could finally relax and enjoy their Passover, believing the Jesus movement was finished. Then came the end of their weekly Sabbath, Saturday evening 6:00 Gentile time. At the "end of the Sabbath" the three nights and three days were completed. At the "dawn," or in other words, around the beginning of Sunday, "early, when it was yet dark" everything changed. The earth shook, the dead raised up, angels appeared to mankind, and the great gravestone had been rolled away to show everyone that Jesus was already gone. Hallelujah!

Matthew 28:1-15

^{1.} In the <u>end of the Sabbath, as it began to dawn toward the first day of the week,</u> came Mary Magdalene and the other Mary to see the sepulchre.

^{2.} And, behold, there was a great earthquake: for the angel of the lord descended from Heaven, and came and rolled back the stone from the door, and sat upon it.

^{3.} <u>His countenance was like lightning,</u> and his <u>raiment white as snow:</u>

^{4.} And for fear of him the keepers did shake, and became as dead men.

^{5.} And the angel answered and <u>said unto the women, fear not ye: for I know that ye seek Jesus, which was crucified.</u>

^{6.} <u>He is not here: for He is risen, as He said. Come, see the place where the Lord lay.</u>

^{7.} <u>And go quickly, and tell His disciples that He is risen from the dead;</u> and, behold, He goeth before you into Galilee; there shall ye see Him: lo, I have told you.

^{8.} And <u>they departed quickly</u> from the sepulchre with fear and great joy; <u>and did run to bring His disciples word.</u>

^{9.} And as they went to tell His disciples, behold, Jesus met them, saying, all hail. And they came and held Him by the feet, and worshipped Him.

^{10.} <u>Then said Jesus unto them, be not afraid: go tell My brethren</u> that they go into Galilee, and there shall they see Me.

^{11.} Now when they were going, behold, some of the watch came into the city, and shewed unto the chief priests all the things that were done.

^{12.} And when they were assembled with the elders, and had taken counsel, <u>they gave large money unto the soldiers,</u>

^{13.} <u>Saying, say ye,</u> His disciples came by night, and stole Him away while we slept.

^{14.} And if this come to the governor's ears, we will persuade Him, and secure you.

^{15.} So they took the money, and did as they were taught: and this saying is commonly reported among the Jews until this day.

Satan could not change the facts of the death and resurrection of Christ. All he could do is what he always does – tell lies. With a close look, Satan's lie doesn't add up or make sense. Just think about it. Pilate gave the Jewish religious leaders an armed Roman guard to "watch" and overcome any attack or attempt to raid the tomb. These guards had the authority to check inside to verify the contents and then seal the tomb with a Roman seal. The unbroken seal assured that the body remained secure. The clay with a Roman insignia or seal represented the Roman government's authority to execute anyone who broke that seal. The watch was not one or two guards. It was a job performed by the Roman military. A complete Roman guard of numerous soldiers sleeping and not keeping watch is very unlikely, because they would be executed for negligence of their basic duty as recorded in Acts.

Acts 12:19 a

19a. **And when Herod had sought for him, and found him not, he examined the keepers, and commanded <u>they should be put to death</u>...**

These things are easily verified in history and stated in the Bible. *Selah.* I think the Roman guards (which the chief priests asked Pilate for in Matthew 27:62-66) had the primary task of guarding the tomb. Also present as a secondary watch were some of the temple guards whom the chief priest knew and trusted. These secondary guards served as the eyes and ears of the religious leaders. Some of these temple guards may have been with Judas (John 18:3) and were the same ones who escorted Jesus to and from the priest (John18:12-13). It would be these temple guards, "some of the watch," who reported to the priest in Matthew 28:11. Between the Roman government and the Jewish religious leaders, there were no doubt plenty of fresh guards on duty, especially as the notorious third day approached. I believe it was the temple guards who could have been bribed (Matthew 28:12) and spared from the execution that awaited Pilate's Roman army guards. The Roman soldiers failed to secure the tomb area and were accused of sleeping on the job. It is true that the guards passed out (Matthew 28:4) at the appearance of the angel rolling back the stone for the women to see the empty tomb; but who would believe them? I doubt anyone could prevent their execution as an example to other soldiers of the importance of staying alert. I also doubt that the surviving soldiers enjoyed their money very long after promoting the lie inspired by Satan. Someday we will know all the details. *Selah.* Even if you disagree or dismiss the abilities, reputation, or number of soldiers guarding Jesus' tomb, at least consider these three questions. What would motivate the fearful disciples to break open a Roman-sealed tomb with guards around and the earth shaking from an earthquake? Why were the fearful defeated disciples changed into fearless witnesses and martyrs if they had not witnessed the resurrection of Jesus? Would these disciples knowingly die for a lie, or would they simply go back to the lives they had known just a few years earlier?

Acts 4:8-20

8. **Then Peter, filled with the Holy Ghost, said unto them, ye rulers of the people, and elders of Israel,**

9. **If we this day be examined of the good deed done to the impotent man, by what means he is made whole;**

10. **Be it known unto you all, and to all the people of Israel, that <u>by the name of Jesus Christ of Nazareth, whom ye crucified, whom God raised from the dead</u>, even by Him doth this man stand here before you whole.**

11. This is the Stone which was set at nought of you builders, which is become the Head of the corner.

12. Neither is there salvation in any other: for there is none other name under Heaven given among men, whereby we must be saved.

13. Now when <u>they saw the boldness of Peter and John, and perceived that they were unlearned and ignorant men, they marvelled; and they took knowledge of them, that they had been with Jesus</u>.

14. And beholding the man which was healed standing with them, they could say nothing against it.

15. But when they had commanded them to go aside out of the council, they conferred among themselves,

16. Saying, what shall we do to these men? For that indeed a notable miracle hath been done by them is manifest to all them that dwell in Jerusalem; and <u>we cannot deny it</u>.

17. But that it spread no further among the people, let us <u>straitly threaten them</u>, that they speak henceforth to no man in this name.

18. And they called them, and commanded them not to speak at all nor teach in the name of Jesus.

19. But Peter and John answered and said unto them, whether it be right in the sight of God to hearken unto you more than unto God, judge ye.

20. For <u>we cannot but speak the things which we have seen and heard</u>.

CRUCIFIXION TIME LINE

Matthew 12:40
3 Days & 3 Nights

Genesis 1:5,8,13,19,23,31
Night And Then Day

Tuesday	6:00			Mark 14:12-17 Last Supper John 13:1,2&30 Before Passover	**Wednesday-Preparation Day** Jewish Traditional Early Feast of Unleavened Bread
	Midnight	NIGHT		Luke 22:41-44 Garden Temptation	
Wednesday	6:00 —— 12:00 9:00 —— 3:00 Noon —— 6:00 3:00 —— 9:00	D A Y		Mark 15:1 Judgment John 18:28 Early Before Passover John 19:14 Roman Time Mark 15:25 Jewish Time Mark 15:33-39 Total Eclipse Luke 23:44-46 Jesus Died John 19:31 Preparation Day Mark 15:42-43 Preparation Day Luke 23:52-54 Garden Tomb John 19:41-42 Preparation Day	
	6:00	Tomb			
	Midnight	NIGHT-1	DAY-1 Jewish Day & Time	Matthew 27:62-66 Guard at Tomb	**Thursday-Passover** Lev. 23:4,5 High Sabbath Not Saturday Lev. 23:24,32,38,39
Thursday		Roman Day & Time			
	Midnight	NIGHT-2	DAY-2		**Friday-** **Holy Feast** **of** **Unleavened** **Bread** Numbers 28:16-18
Friday					
	Midnight	3			**Saturday-** **Weekly** **Sabbath**
Saturday		3	Tomb		
	Midnight			John 20:1 Jesus' Resurrection	**Sunday-** **Resurrection** **Day**
Sunday					

225

CHAPTER 10

RESURRECTION DAY

John used the Gentile clock to describe the timing of the crucifixion. After the resurrection he focused on the Jewish clock for his account of the events. Although this may be inconsistent, it is not uncommon. John was a Jew and often dealt with Gentiles. We should address people with the language they can understand, but we should also attempt to be consistent to avoid confusing others. *Selah.* Luke used the Jewish clock in his account of the crucifixion, but he quotes others using a Gentile clock regarding Resurrection Day. If he changed someone's account of time to his interpretation of time, it would no longer be an exact quote, but instead it would be a paraphrase. We should keep this in mind when the Bible is quoting what someone said. The Bible contains quotations that are contrary to the theme of the Bible. Sometimes the misleading quotations are subtle and describe the individual's feelings or perceptions. Other times they are clearly in disagreement with God's Word. One obvious example is that the Bible factually quotes Satan speaking lies. These false and misleading statements reveal the true environment and concepts that we may be confronted with in this world. God dose not want us to be naive, but instead wise and have the ability to see the truth in all situations (Mathew 10:16). That is why we must be careful not to take a quotation or anything else in the Bible out of its Biblical context. When we are confronted with confusion, God wants us to trust Him and realize that we may make a mistake, but God makes no mistakes. With these things in mind, let's look at the 4 Gospel accounts describing Resurrection Day and see if we can find a logical sequence of events in order to clear up the confusion and apparent inconsistencies. Actually these differences in the 4 Gospel accounts prove they did not copy or collaborate with each other about how to give their testimony.

Many times when you have 4 witnesses of a big event you may find small inconsistencies because they see and remember things differently. They may describe what stands out to them the most first, then go back and fill in some details in a random order as it occurs to them. Therefore we should examine all the various statements in the context of the bigger picture. In the following pages I have recorded all 4 Gospel's portrayal of Resurrection Day and put them together in a way that shows one possibility of the timing and arrangement of their accounts. There will be places were the same event is repeated in different Gospels. Therefore it will be repeated next to each other in this chapter. There are also a surprising amount of times that the different Gospels fill in a different portion of the events of that day. Therefore these verses from the different Gospels will be lased together in an attempt to understand what it was like for Jesus' followers on Resurrection Day. Some verses can be a little confusing, but I hope after you read this entire chapter you have a better understanding of how the day unfolded according to the Bible. Lets start by looking at Jesus' burial.

Luke 23:52-54

52. This man went unto Pilate, and begged the body of Jesus.

53. And he took it down, and wrapped it in linen, and laid it in a sepulchre that was hewn in stone, wherein never man before was laid.

54. And <u>that day was the preparation</u>, and the sabbath drew on.

This was, not Friday. Jesus did not die on Friday according to the Bible. All 4 Gospels verify Jesus died on Preparation Day, which was the day before the High Sabbath of Passover. Friday was the Holy Feast of Unleavened Bread, not a day the Pharisees would be calling for crucifixions. Do you know why they broke the legs of the two people hanging on crosses next to Jesus? By breaking their legs they would suffocate and die sooner so they could be removed from the crosses before the High Holy Sabbaths began (John 19:30-33). Jesus' legs were not broken because He was already dead, which fulfilled a prophecy (Exodus 12:46, Psalm 34:20). *Selah*. Joseph of Arimathea put Jesus in his tomb at the end of Preparation day. This was Wednesday, the last day to work at getting all the leaven out of the house before the High Sabbath of Passover began. One of the last things done on Preparation Day was killing the Passover lambs and preparing them for the next day's Feast of Passover. The Feast of Passover began after sundown. Jesus was put in the tomb at the end of Preparation Day, which would be between 5:00 and 6:00 pm Wednesday. It was probably the beginning of Passover as they released the huge stone to seal the tomb. This began the three-day time clock.

Luke 23:55-56

^{55.} **And the women also, which came with Him from Galilee, <u>followed after, and beheld the sepulchre</u>, and how His body was laid.**

^{56.} **And they returned, and prepared spices and ointments; and rested the sabbath day according to the commandment.**

The women made plans to get together and return to Jesus' tomb at daybreak Sunday morning to embalm Jesus' body and memorialize His gravesite. They had to wait to do this memorial service until after the Passover (day 1) and the Feast of Unleavened Bread (day 2) and the weekly Sabbath (day 3) had passed. *Selah*. Jesus' resurrection happened after 6:00 pm Saturday but no later than 12:00 midnight. Because of the context of the surrounding events, I believe the Bible indicates Jesus arouse from the dead shortly after 6 pm Saturday. This would be the beginning of the first day of the Jewish week.

Matthew 28:2-4

2. **And, behold, there was a great earthquake: for the angel of the Lord descended from heaven, and came and rolled back the stone from the door, and sat upon it.**

3. **His countenance was like lightning, and his raiment white as snow:**

4. **And for fear of him the keepers did shake, and became as dead men.**

At the sight of these miraculous events the guards passed out. When they revived, they realized Jesus was no longer contained in the tomb and left the seen bewildered.

Mark 16:9

9. **Now when Jesus was risen early the first day of the week, <u>He appeared first to Mary Magdalene</u>, out of whom He had cast seven devils.**

Mary Magdalene often demonstrated her love and gratitude to Jesus for delivering her from the demonic spirits. She couldn't wait to meet with the other women in the morning. She headed for the tomb to mourn as soon as the Jewish Sabbath was over. Remember that this is before daylight savings time. At that time of the year it would get dark around 6:30 pm. It was probably between 6:30 pm and 7:00 pm our Saturday night (but also the beginning of the Jewish first day of the week) when Mary Magdalene first arrived at the tomb.

John 20:1

The first day of the week cometh Mary Magdalene early, when it was yet dark, unto the sepulchre, and seeth the stone taken away from the sepulchre.

Shocked at the sight of the open tomb and missing body, she immediately turned and ran back to Jerusalem to tell Peter and John.

John 20:2-8

2. **Then she runneth, and cometh to Simon Peter, and to the other disciple, whom Jesus loved, and saith unto them, They have taken away the Lord out of the sepulchre, and we know not where they have laid Him.**

3. **Peter therefore went forth, and that other disciple, and came to the sepulchre.**

4. **So they ran both together: and the other disciple did outrun Peter, and came first to the sepulchre.**

5. **And he stooping down, and looking in, saw the linen clothes lying; yet went he not in.**

6. **Then cometh Simon Peter following him, and went into the sepulchre, and seeth the linen clothes lie,**

7. **And the napkin, that was about his head, not lying with the linen clothes, but wrapped together in a place by itself.**

8. **Then went in also that other disciple, which came first to the sepulchre, and he saw, and believed.**

Peter and John left the tomb believing Jesus was gone, but bewildered about why Jesus' body was missing. After Peter and John left, Mary stayed behind near the door of Jesus' tomb.

John 20:11-16

11. **But Mary stood without at the sepulchre weeping: and as she wept, she stooped down, and looked into the sepulchre,**

12. And seeth two angels in white sitting, the one at the head, and the other at the feet, where the body of Jesus had lain.

13. And they say unto her, Woman, why weepest thou? She saith unto them, Because they have taken away my Lord, and I know not where they have laid Him.

14. And when she had thus said, she turned herself back, and saw Jesus standing, and knew not that it was Jesus.

15. Jesus saith unto her, Woman, why weepest thou? whom seekest thou? She, supposing Him to be the gardener, saith unto Him, Sir, if thou have borne Him hence, tell me where thou hast laid Him, and I will take Him away.

16. Jesus saith unto her, Mary. She turned herself, and saith unto Him, Rabboni; which is to say, Master.

It was dark and Mary was blinded by her grief and tears, so Mary could not clearly see who was talking to her. But when Jesus said her name, there was no denying who it was. Nobody knew her or could say her name like Jesus.

John 20:17

17. <u>Jesus saith unto her, Touch Me not; for I am not yet ascended to My Father</u>: but go to My brethren, and say unto them, I ascend unto My Father, and your Father; and to My God, and your God.

Jesus is our High Priest (Hebrews 4:14). He was about to go to Heaven's capital city into the throne room of God and apply His Atonement payment to cancel our debt (Revelation 5:5, 9-10). *Selah.* After Mary had talked with Jesus she could hardly contain herself and rushed to tell the others.

Mark 16:10

10. And she went and told them that had been with Him, as they mourned and wept.

John 20:18

18. Mary Magdalene came and told the disciples that she had seen the Lord, and that He had spoken these things unto her.

Mark 16:11

11. And they, when they had heard that He was alive, and had been seen of her, <u>believed not.</u>

John 20:9

9. For as yet they knew not the scripture, that He must rise again from the dead.

No one believed Mary Magdalene or Jesus' prediction. They did not understand God's Word but instead trusted their perceptions and feelings of loss. This attitude of unbelief permeated the air all night. Initially, only Mary Magdalene believed but as soon as Jesus' mother Mary heard the news, she hoped and wanted to see for herself.

Matthew 28:1

1. In <u>the end of the sabbath, as it began to dawn toward the first day of the week,</u> came Mary Magdalene <u>and the other Mary to see</u> the sepulchre.

This would be shortly after the weekly Sabbath ended and Mary returned from the tomb with the news that she had seen Jesus. This was probably around 8:00 or 9:00 pm Saturday. After telling the disciples that she had seen Jesus, Mary Magdalene headed back to the tomb. This time Jesus' mother Mary accompanied her.

Matthew 28:5-10

5. And the angel answered and said unto the women, Fear not ye: for I know that ye seek Jesus, which was crucified.

6. <u>He is not here: for He is risen, as He said. Come, see the place where the Lord lay</u>.

7. And go quickly, and <u>tell His disciples</u> that He is risen from the dead; and, behold, He goeth before you into Galilee; there shall ye see Him: lo, I have told you.

8. And they departed quickly from the sepulchre with fear and great joy; and did run to bring His disciples word.

9. And as they went to tell His disciples, behold, <u>Jesus met them</u>, saying, All hail. And they came and <u>held Him by the feet</u>, and worshipped Him.

10. Then said Jesus unto them, Be not afraid: <u>go tell My brethren</u> that they go into Galilee, and <u>there shall they see Me</u>.

Notice now the women can touch Jesus because He was back from Heaven where He performed His priestly duty of applying His lifeblood to the Judgment seat for our redemption (Hebrews 8:1-3). After this Mary and Mary returned to Jerusalem to tell Jesus' followers. Even with both ladies conformation that they had seen and talked with Jesus, doubt and confusion persisted. In the confusion the followers of Jesus started heading their separate ways.

John 20:10

10. Then the disciples <u>went away again</u> unto their own home.

It was probably around 8:30 to 9:30 pm Saturday night when some of Jesus' followers started to head their different ways.

Although they were confused, I'm sure they were anxious to tell others about Jesus' missing body. The Bible tells us about Cleopas and Simon as they headed for the village of Emmaus, which was about seven miles from Jerusalem. Jews walked a lot to get from place to place. This was probably around a two-hour walk. Although they hurried back from Emmaus to Jerusalem to give their testimony, they probably arrived back in Jerusalem sometime after midnight. Let's look at how Jesus revealed Himself to these guys according to the Bible.

Mark 16:12

12. **After that He appeared in another form unto two of them, as they walked, and went into the country.**

Luke 24:13-21

13. **And, behold, two of them went that same day to a village called Emmaus, which was from Jerusalem about threescore furlongs.**

14. **And they talked together of all these things which had happened.**

15. **And it came to pass, that, while they communed together and reasoned, Jesus Himself drew near, and went with them.**

16. **But their eyes were holden that they should not know Him.**

17. **And He said unto them, What manner of communications are these that ye have one to another, as ye walk, and are sad?**

18. **And the one of them, whose name was Cleopas, answering said unto Him, Art thou only a stranger in Jerusalem, and hast not known the things which are come to pass there in these days?**

19. And He said unto them, What things? And they said unto Him, Concerning Jesus of Nazareth, which was a prophet mighty in deed and word before God and all the people:

20. And how the chief priests and our rulers delivered Him to be condemned to death, and have crucified Him.

21. But we trusted that it had been He which should have redeemed Israel: and beside all this, <u>to day is the third day since</u> these things were done.

Just a note here: The statement <u>"to day is the third day since"</u> is not a general term, but instead it is a reference to a specific day. The first day since these events would be Thursday. The second day would be Friday and the third day since these events would be Saturday. It was still Saturday the third day. These men were using the Gentile clock, so it would continue to be the third day until midnight. Therefore, if you believe the Bible, this conversation had to happen before 12:01 am Sunday. I believe this conversation happened well before midnight because of the events that followed it. These two men continued to tell Jesus about what they had just gone through.

Luke 24:22-33

22. Yea, and certain women also of our company made us astonished, which were <u>early at the sepulchre;</u>

23. And when they found not His body, they came, saying, that they had also seen a vision of angels, which said that He was alive.

24. And certain of them which were with us went to the sepulchre, and found it even so as the women had said: but Him they saw not.

25. Then He said unto them, O fools, and <u>slow of heart to believe</u> all that the prophets have spoken:

26. Ought not Christ to have suffered these things, <u>and to enter into His glory?</u>

27. And beginning at Moses and all the prophets, <u>He expounded unto them in all the Scriptures the things concerning Himself.</u>

28. And they drew nigh unto the village, whither they went: and He made as though He would have gone further.

29. But they constrained Him, saying, Abide with us: for it is toward evening, and the day is far spent. And He went in to tarry with them.

30. And it came to pass, as He sat at meat with them, He took bread, and blessed it, and brake, and gave to them.

31. And <u>their eyes were opened</u>, and they knew Him; and <u>He vanished out of their sight.</u>

32. And they said one to another, Did not our heart burn within us, while He talked with us by the way, and while He opened to us the Scriptures?

33. And they rose up <u>the same hour, and returned to Jerusalem,</u> and found the eleven gathered together, and them that were with them,

They were exited to tell the others of their encounter with Jesus so they hurried back to Jerusalem and probably made it back in record time.

Luke 24:34-35

34. Saying, <u>The Lord is risen indeed</u>, and hath appeared to Simon.

35. And <u>they told what things were done in the way</u>, and how he was known of them in breaking of bread.

Mark 16:13

13. And they went and told it unto the residue: <u>neither believed they them</u>.

In spite of their doubt about the resurrection the disciples probably continued to gather and come and go from that special upper room. I'm not sure how much sleep the people in that room got that night but eventually morning arrived. In the morning some women arrived with spices to embalm Jesus' body as planned. They gathered with Mary Magdalene while it was still dark and arrived at the tomb around sunrise.

Mark 16:1-2

1. And when the sabbath was past, Mary Magdalene, and Mary the mother of James, and Salome, had bought sweet spices, that they might come and anoint Him.

2. And very early in the morning the first day of the week, they came unto the sepulchre at the rising of the sun.

Salome and Mary are mentioned here, but there were several other women that got together with Mary Magdalene on that morning. They are mentioned in the other Gospels. On the way to the tomb, some of the women raised a logical question.

Mark 16:3

3. And they said among themselves, Who shall roll us away the stone from the door of the sepulchre?

Mary Magdalene and Jesus' mother Mary had the answer, so this was not a discussion they were having. This was a discussion between the other women that accompanied Mary and Mary. This would be Mary's sister (John 19:25), Cleophas' wife Mary (John 19:25), Salome (Mark 16:1), Joanna (Luke 24:10), and the other women that had prepared the burial spices (Luke 23:55-56, Luke 24:1). Why didn't these women know the stone was already rolled away? I don't know. If they asked Mary Magdalene this question, it appears that they did not believe her answer (Mark 16:13) or Mary did not tell them. I'm sure Mary had mixed emotions of excitement about Jesus' resurrection and frustration because nobody believed her (Mark 16:11), so Mary may have wanted to show them instead of tell them. More than likely the women that arrived with the burial spices were like the disciples in that they did not believe what they considered to be unlikely rumors or hallucinations. Remember that Thomas said he would not believe unless he personally touched Jesus' crucifixion wounds (John 20:25-29). He said this after hearing numerous testimonies from many people. Also consider that nobody at that time believed Jesus arose from the dead until they personally experienced a supernatural event. *Selah.* Just as some of us proceed with our plans in spite of changing circumstances, these women proceeded with their plan to go to the tomb Sunday morning with their burial spices.

Luke 24:1-2

1. **Now upon the first day of the week, very early in the morning, they came unto the sepulchre, bringing the spices which they had prepared, and <u>certain others with them</u>.**

2. **And they found the stone rolled away from the sepulchre.**

Notice that by this time Mary Magdalene had been to the tomb at least 4 times. Once by herself, second with Peter and John, then with the other Mary, and now with many other women who were bringing spices for Jesus' body. *Selah.* All 4 Gospels make the discovery of the empty tomb the first point of their account of Resurrection Day. Matthew and John start their accounts on the night of the resurrection. This would be shortly after Jesus arose from the dead. Mark and Luke start their accounts of that day in the morning around sunrise. Then they go back to describe some preceding events that happened before midnight. All 4 gospels declare Jesus arose from the dead on Sunday Jewish time. Because Luke mentions the Gentile timetable in Luke 24:21 we have a better understanding of the timing of the different discoveries of Jesus' resurrection. Jesus also acknowledged the timeframe of His resurrection, which was shared near the end of the previous chapter of this book. Remember Jesus said in multiple locations that He would rise from the grave "on" and "after" the third day. *Selah.* Lets get back to the Gospel's accounts of what happened as the people started to wake up to the truth about the resurrection of Jesus Christ.

Mark 16:4-6

4. **And when they looked, they saw that the stone was rolled away: for it was very great.**

5. **And entering into the sepulchre, they saw a young man sitting on the right side, clothed in a long white garment; and they were affrighted.**

6. **And he saith unto them, Be not affrighted: Ye seek Jesus of Nazareth, which was crucified: He is risen; He is not here: behold the place where they laid Him.**

When the women got to Jesus' tomb, Mary Magdalene probably said to the others that brought the spices, go inside and look for yourself, Jesus is not there.

Luke 24:3-4

3. And they entered in, and found not the body of the Lord Jesus.

4. And it came to pass, as they were much perplexed thereabout, behold, two men stood by them in shining garments:

The angels suddenly appeared in the tomb startling the women. Then the angels addressed the women that brought the spices.

Luke 24:5-8

5. And as they were afraid, and bowed down their faces to the earth, they said unto them, Why seek ye the living among the dead?

6. He is not here, but is risen: <u>remember how He spake unto you when He was yet in Galilee,</u>

7. Saying, The Son of man must be delivered into the hands of sinful men, and be crucified, and the third day rise again.

8. And they remembered His words,

Mark 16:7

7. But go your way, <u>tell His disciples and Peter</u> that He goeth before you into Galilee: there shall ye see Him, <u>as He said unto you</u>.

There was 40 days between Jesus' resurrection and His rapture (Acts 1:9). Jesus may have met with many of His friends in the region of Galilee during this 40-day period (Acts 1:3). Although I think this statement was to be spoken directly to Peter about a specific meeting. I believe Jesus was referring to a particular reunion they would have by the Sea of Galilee. There He would personally restore and commission Peter. Jesus must have been really looking forward to reminiscing with His friends at this last campfire gathering by the Sea of Galilee (John 21:1-19). The Sea of Galilee is also known as the Sea of Tiberias. Jesus told the angels of this upcoming meeting and then one of the angels told Mary and Mary (Mathew 28:7). Then Jesus appeared to Mary and Mary and personally confirmed this special meeting (Mathew 28:10). Now an angel tells several women and reconfirmed the upcoming special breakfast with Jesus. Peter was probably feeling utterly defeated because of his denial of Jesus, so he is mentioned specifically. I believe this message was for specific Galilean disciples but particularly to encourage Peter.

Mark 16:8

8. **And they went out quickly, and fled from the sepulchre; for they trembled and were amazed: neither said they any thing to any man; for they were afraid.**

This time the ladies did not see Jesus but was told to tell the others of Jesus' resurrection. Mark names three of these women, "Mary Magdalene, and Mary the mother of James, and Salome" (Mark 16:1). Then Luke adds to the list Joanna and then reveals that there were "other women that were with them."

Luke 24:9-11

9. **And returned from the sepulchre, and <u>told all these things unto the eleven, and to all the rest.</u>**

10. **It was Mary Magdalene, and Joanna, and Mary the mother of James, <u>and other women that were with them, which told these things unto the apostles.</u>**

11. **And their words seemed to them as idle tales, and <u>they believed them not.</u>**

Nobody believed the women, but since they said that Peter was mentioned by name, he quickly headed to the tomb for the second time, hoping to see the angels or something supernatural.

Luke 24:12

[12.] **Then arose Peter, and ran unto the sepulchre; and stooping down, he beheld the linen clothes laid by themselves, and departed, wondering in himself at that which was come to pass.**

The first time Peter went to the tomb he realized Jesus' body was gone. This time Peter focused on what remained. Peter left the tomb wondering and pondering why the burial clothes remained. He wondered why Jesus' covers where arranged as if the body within them vanished and why the face napkin was move and place so neatly near by (which John mentioned in John 20:7).

John 20:19

[19.] **Then <u>the same day at evening, being the first day of the week,</u> when the doors were shut where the disciples were assembled for fear of the Jews, came Jesus and stood in the midst, and saith unto them, Peace be unto you.**

The disciples were confused about what happened to Jesus' body. They were also in fear of what the religious leader were planning to do to Jesus' followers. They locked the doors and were discussing what they should do. Then Jesus (who left His grave-clothes behind Him) appeared to them wrapped in the garment of righteousness reflecting the glory of God. The disciples though He was a spirit.

Luke 24:36-39

[36.] **And as they thus spake, Jesus Himself stood in the midst of them, and saith unto them, Peace be unto you.**

^{37.} **But they were terrified and affrighted, and supposed that they had seen a spirit.**

^{38.} **And He said unto them, Why are ye troubled? and why do thoughts arise in your hearts?**

^{39.} **Behold My hands and My feet, that it is I Myself: handle Me, and see; for a spirit hath not flesh and bones, as ye see Me have.**

Why does the King James Bible say, "Me have" instead of using the common phrase, I have? I believe God has anointed every letter of His Word (Mathew 5:18, Mathew 24:35, Mark 13:31, Luke 21:33) and will latter arrange it in a cube or square for multidimensional reading. We can agree to disagree, but I also believe it is possible that God has anointed certain translations and will also arrange them to be read in multiple directions, sort of like a crossword puzzle with no empty spaces. If so, then God needed two letters here instead of one. Whether Jesus says Me or I, He is still communicating the same thing, look at Him. God will continue to amaze us even in Heaven. *Selah.* Even though Jesus Himself appeared out of nowhere in this locked upper room, He still had to deal with widespread unbelief.

Mark 16:14

^{14.} **Afterward He appeared unto the eleven as they sat at meat, and upbraided them with their unbelief and hardness of heart, because <u>they believed not them which had seen Him after He was risen.</u>**

Luke 24:40-44

^{40.} **And when He had thus spoken, He shewed them His hands and His feet.**

^{41.} **And <u>while they yet believed not for joy, and wondered,</u> He said unto them, Have ye here any meat?**

42. And they gave Him a piece of a broiled fish, and of an honeycomb.

43. And He took it, and did eat before them.

44. And He said unto them, These are the words which I spake unto you, while I was yet with you, that all things must be fulfilled, which were written in the law of Moses, and in the prophets, and in the psalms, concerning Me.

John 20:20-22

20. And when He had so said, He shewed unto them His hands and His side. Then were the disciples glad, when they saw the Lord.

21. Then said Jesus to them <u>again</u>, Peace be unto you: as my Father hath sent Me, even so send I you.

22. And when He had said this, He breathed on them, and saith unto them, <u>Receive ye the Holy Ghost</u>:

Luke 24:45-48

45. Then opened <u>He their understanding, that they might understand the Scriptures</u>,

46. And said unto them, Thus it is written, and thus it behoved Christ to suffer, and to rise from the dead the third day:

47. And that repentance and remission of sins should be preached in His name among all nations, beginning at Jerusalem.

48. And ye are witnesses of these things.

John 20:23-27

23. Whose soever sins ye remit, they are remitted unto them; and whose soever sins ye retain, they are retained.

24. But Thomas, one of the twelve, called Didymus, was not with them when Jesus came.

25. The other disciples therefore said unto him, We have seen the Lord. But he said unto them, Except I shall see in His hands the print of the nails, and put my finger into the print of the nails, and thrust my hand into His side, <u>I will not believe</u>.

26. And <u>after eight days</u> again His disciples were within, and Thomas with them: <u>then came Jesus, the doors being shut, and stood in the midst</u>, and said, Peace be unto you.

27. Then saith He to Thomas, Reach hither thy finger, and behold My hands; and reach hither thy hand, and thrust it into My side: and <u>be not faithless, but believing</u>.

Jesus knows what we are saying and how we are acting. Even when Jesus dose not seem to be present, He knows if we believe His Word or not. We will either acknowledge His resurrection and Lordship now or at the Great White Throne Judgment. If we do it now (before we die) it is an act of faith, which leads to salvation. If we wait, it will be an affirmation that God provided the path of redemption and we rejected it. If we follow the path of self-righteous rebellion by rejecting Christ it will lead to eternal separation from Christ.

John 20:28-29

28. And Thomas answered and said unto Him, My Lord and my God.

29. Jesus saith unto him, Thomas, because thou hast seen Me, thou hast believed: <u>blessed are they that have not seen, and yet have believed</u>.

Luke 24:49

49. And, behold, <u>I send the promise of my Father upon you</u>: but tarry ye in the city of Jerusalem, until ye be endued with power from on high.

John 20:30

30. And <u>many other signs truly did Jesus</u> in the presence of His disciples, which are not written in this book:

Acts 1:2-3

2. Until the day in which He was taken up, after that He through the Holy Ghost had given commandments unto the apostles whom He had chosen:

3. To whom also He shewed Himself alive after His passion by <u>many infallible proofs, being seen of them forty days</u>, and speaking of the things pertaining to the kingdom of God:

Acts 1:8-11

8. But <u>ye shall receive power, after that the Holy Ghost is come upon you</u>: and ye shall be witnesses unto me both in Jerusalem, and in all Judaea, and in Samaria, and unto the uttermost part of the Earth.

9. And when He had spoken these things, while they beheld, He was taken up; and a cloud received Him out of their sight.

10. And while they looked stedfastly toward heaven as He went up, behold, two men stood by them in white apparel;

11. Which also said, Ye men of Galilee, why stand ye gazing up into heaven? <u>This same Jesus, which is taken up from you into heaven, shall so come in like manner as ye have seen Him go into heaven</u>.

1 Corinthian 15:3-8

3. For I delivered unto you first of all that which I also received, how that <u>Christ died for our sins according to the Scriptures;</u>

4. And that <u>He was buried, and that He rose again the third day according to the Scriptures</u>:

5. And that He was seen of Cephas, then of the twelve:

6. After that, <u>He was seen of above five hundred brethren at once; of whom the greater part remain unto this present</u>, but some are fallen asleep.

7. After that, He was seen of James; then of all the apostles.

8. And last of all He was seen of me also, as of one born out of due time.

John 20:31

31. But these are written, that ye might believe that Jesus is the Christ, the Son of God; and that believing ye might have life through His name.

Mark 16:15

15. And He said unto them, Go ye into all the world, and preach the gospel to every creature.

CHAPTER 11

WHAT HAPPENED TO HELL?

Romans 3:10

10. As it is written, There is <u>none righteous</u>, no, not one:

Romans 3:23

23. For <u>all have sinned</u>, and come short of the glory of God;

All of us that were not born of a virgin have sinned. As sinners we have all fallen short of perfection, so none of us qualify for Heaven. Any and every deviation from the truth is sin. God's Word is the foundation of truth.

1 John 1:10

10. If we say that we have not sinned, we make Him a liar, and His Word is not in us.

Death and corruption are the evidences of sin.

Romans 6:23

23. For the <u>wages of sin is death</u>; but the gift of God is eternal life through Jesus Christ our Lord.

The reason all of us die is because all of us are sinners.

Romans 5:8

8. But God commendeth his love toward us, in that, while we were yet sinners, <u>Christ died for us</u>.

The fruit of sin is death. However, Jesus did not sin. He did not owe the payment for sin. He didn't have to die. He chose to die (John 10:18). Nobody could kill Jesus (Luke 4:28-32). Since He didn't owe a debt for sin, He was free to die for our sins and pay our debt.

Isaiah 53:6-9

6. **All we like sheep have gone astray; we have turned every one to his own way; and the Lord hath laid on Him the iniquity of us all.**

7. He was oppressed, and He was afflicted, yet He opened not His mouth: He is brought as a lamb to the slaughter, and as a sheep before her shearers is dumb, so He openeth not His mouth.

8. He was taken from prison and from judgment: and who shall declare His generation? For He was cut off out of the land of the living: for the transgression of my people was He stricken.

9. And He made His grave with the wicked, and with the rich in His death; because He had done no violence, neither was any deceit in His mouth.

Warning, the following statement may be shocking, but hear me out and you will see how true it is.

Before Jesus' death, everyone went to Hell when they died. The good, the bad, the rich, the poor, the wise, and the foolish all went to Hell. Even King David, a man after the heart of God went to Hell. He spoke of it in Psalm 16.

Psalm 16:10-11

10. For Thou wilt not leave my <u>soul in Hell</u>; neither wilt thou suffer Thine Holy One to see corruption.

11. Thou wilt shew me the path of life: in Thy presence is fulness of joy; at Thy right hand there are pleasures for evermore.

Before Jesus' resurrection from the dead, Hell had at least two parts. On one side, there was flame and torment. On the other side, there was fellowship and comfort; but the souls of the dead were not free to leave. I believe there were three parts to Hell, similar to the layers of an onion.

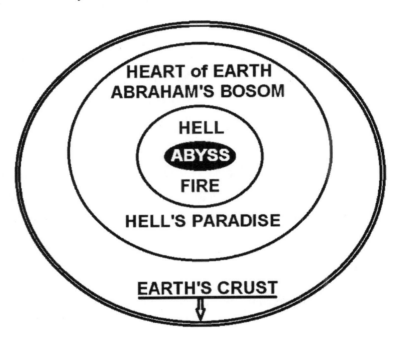

The devils are not in charge of any part of Hell, but instead, an eternity of bondage is their destiny. They are free only at the mercy of God; but if they become too vile and disobedient, their freedom can be further restricted. Jesus often demonstrated His authority over demons.

Matthew 8:28-29

28. **And when He was come to the other side into the country of the Gergesenes, there met Him two possessed with devils, coming out of the tombs, exceeding fierce, so that no man might pass by that way.**

29. **And, behold, they cried out, saying, what have we to do with Thee, Jesus, Thou Son of God? <u>Art Thou come hither to torment us before the time?</u>**

Luke 8:31-32

31. **And they besought Him that He would not command them to go out <u>into the deep</u>.**

32. **And there was there an herd of many swine feeding on the mountain: and they besought Him that He would suffer them to enter into them. And He suffered them.**

The demons know the power and authority of Jesus. They know He has the ability to send them to the Bottomless Pit referred to here as the "deep." There are some fallen angels that have already been sent there. To this day they remain bound in the deep dark Bottomless Pit, awaiting their judgment and destiny in the Lake of Fire.

Jude 6

6. **And the angels which kept not their first estate, but left their own habitation, He hath reserved in <u>everlasting chains under darkness</u> unto the judgment of the great day.**

There is coming a day when the Devil himself will be bound in the deep dark Bottomless Pit. We will see what the Bible has to say about the many events surrounding that time in chapter 16 – "The Devil's Final Destiny." Here we want to identify that there is such a place as "Hell" with the "Bottomless Pit."

Revelation 20:1

1. **And I saw an angel come down from Heaven, having the key of the <u>bottomless pit</u> and a great chain in his hand.**

251

I believe there is an Abyss, black hole or Bottomless Pit at the center of Hell, which leads to another dimension of bondage. This Pit is surrounded by Hell Fire, which is a place of torment. Before Jesus rose from the dead, you could look up from the edge of Hell Fire and see Hell's Paradise where David, Abraham, and the redeemed resided. Jesus referred to this separation in Hell when He spoke of a poor beggar who died in faith and a rich man who thought he had everything.

Luke 16:19-30

19. **There was a certain rich man, which was clothed in purple and fine linen, and fared sumptuously every day:**

20. **And there was a certain beggar named Lazarus, which was laid at his gate, full of sores,**

21. **And desiring to be fed with the crumbs which fell from the rich man's table: moreover the dogs came and licked his sores.**

22. **And it came to pass, that the beggar died, and was carried by the angels <u>into Abraham's bosom</u>: the rich man also died, and was buried;**

23. **And <u>in Hell he lift up his eyes, being in torments</u>, and seeth Abraham afar off, and <u>Lazarus in his bosom</u>.**

24. **And he cried and said, father Abraham, have mercy on me, and send Lazarus, that he may dip the tip of his finger in water, and cool my tongue; for I am tormented in this flame.**

25. **But Abraham said, son, remember that thou in thy lifetime receivedst thy good things, and likewise Lazarus evil things: but now <u>he is comforted, and thou art tormented</u>.**

^{26.} **And beside all this, between us and you <u>there is a great gulf fixed: so that they which would pass from hence to you cannot</u>; neither can they pass to us, that would come from thence.**

^{27.} **Then he said, I pray thee therefore, father, that thou wouldest send him to my father's house:**

^{28.} **For I have five brethren; that he may testify unto them, <u>lest they also come into this place of torment</u>.**

^{29.} **Abraham saith unto him, they have Moses and the prophets; let them hear them.**

^{30.} **And he said, nay, father Abraham: but if one went unto them from the dead, they will repent.**

If you look up the word "bosom" it means a "protective place." Lazarus died and went to Abraham's protective place to camp and wait for his redeemer. This is not a parable (a fictional story that illustrates a truth). Jesus was describing a historical fact to illustrate what He meant when He taught about important priorities and true riches.

Mark 8:36

^{36.} **For what shall it profit a man, if he shall gain the whole world, and lose his own soul?**

True riches are discovered in becoming a friend of the King of kings and having your name known as a resident of Heaven. The poor beggar Lazarus (not to be confused with Martha's brother Lazarus) is a real person with a home in Paradise. I believe Jesus answered the rich man's heart-felt prayer for his brethren "after His resurrection."

Matthew 27:50-53

50. **Jesus, when He had cried again with a loud voice, yielded up the ghost.**

51. **And, behold, the veil of the temple was rent in twain from the top to the bottom; and the earth did quake, and the rocks rent;**

52. **And the <u>graves were opened;</u> and <u>many bodies</u> of the saints which slept <u>arose,</u>**

53. **And <u>came out of the graves after His resurrection, and went into the holy city, and appeared unto many.</u>**

Instead of reflecting defects and corruption like zombies, these saints reflected perfection and glory. They were not revived from the dead, because then they would be mortal and still subject to death. Instead, they were resurrected from the dead as the first fruits. They were physically resurrected to a new dimension of life. A life that is fresh, wonderful and supernatural. It is eternal life. They had died, but they would never die again. The poor beggar Lazarus may have been one of the "many" resurrected saints who went into Jerusalem before going to Heaven. It was probably at the time of the first fruits offering that these saints appeared in Jerusalem. They proclaimed Jesus' power over death and warned the unbelievers that Hell is a reality. There are some that teach there is no Hell, which in Hebrew is defined as the "Singular place of the departed dead." They claim all the words translated as Hell are only graves (which is often plural) and our souls sleep in their graves or evaporate. If that were true then how did Jesus fulfill His promise to the man dying on a cross next to Him? *Selah.* Lets look closely at crucifixion day and consider all the ramifications behind Jesus' dying promise. Before Jesus died, He was crucified between two sinners who were paying for their crimes with their lives. In the agony of crucifixion, one of the sinners saw the light.

Luke 23:39-43

39. **And one of the malefactors which were hanged railed on Him, saying, if Thou be Christ, save Thyself and us.**

40. **But the other answering rebuked him, saying, dost not thou fear God, seeing thou art in the same condemnation?**

41. **And we indeed justly; for we receive the due reward of our deeds: but this man hath done nothing amiss.**

42. **And he said unto Jesus, Lord, remember me when Thou comest into Thy kingdom.**

43. **And Jesus said unto him, verily I say unto thee, to day shalt thou be with Me in paradise.**

Paradise was another name for the good section of Hell. Jesus told one of the sinners that he would be with Jesus in Paradise that day. The other sinner was obviously headed for Hell Fire (Matthew 5:29-30, Matthew 18:8-9, Mark 9:43-48). What made the difference? The one who was redeemed did not get baptized. He couldn't do any good works, because he was being crucified for his bad actions. The difference for that man, and for all mankind, was that he began to "fear God." This does not necessarily mean trembling before God's presence. The fear of God is knowing that God makes the rules, and our destiny is in God's hands (Luke 12:4-5). This man next to Jesus then admitted he was a sinner, saying, "We receive the reward of our deeds." Notice that he did not stop there, but took the life-changing next step. He turned to Jesus and called Him "Lord," recognizing who Jesus was and submitting his life (what was left of it) to Him. The key to his transformation and salvation was when he said, "Remember me." This so-called good thief wanted to have a relationship with Jesus. Christ received him into His kingdom before He died at 3 o'clock on that day. *Selah.* I believe that Jesus took our sins, died as a mortal, and then went first to the torment section of Hell, which is reserved for the containment of corruption. After Jesus paid for our sins, the Father sent the Holy Spirit to Jesus empowering Him to be delivered from Hell (John 10:17-18). When the Holy Spirit rejoined Jesus, He liberated Jesus (Romans 8:11) and enabled Him to preach to the captives.

1 Peter 3:18-19

18. **For Christ also hath once suffered for sins, the just for the unjust, that He might bring us to God, being put to death in the flesh, but <u>quickened by the Spirit</u>:**

19. **<u>By which</u> also <u>He went and preached unto the spirits in prison</u>;**

Before 6 o'clock that day, the redeemed criminal would have his legs broken so that he would suffocate and die. At that point, his soul went to Hell's Paradise, which Jesus referred to as Abraham's Bosom. Jesus was the only one who could cross over the gap between Hell Fire and Paradise. Jesus would be in Hell's Paradise with this man no later than midnight that same day, because Jesus had promised, "Today shalt thou be with Me in Paradise." Jesus arose to the Paradise section of Hell and preached the Good News to those imprisoned and comfortably waiting for their redemption. The Good News was that their sins were paid for, and they would be free to go in three days.

Acts 13:33

33. **God hath fulfilled the same unto us their children, in that He hath <u>raised up Jesus again</u>; as it is also written in the second psalm, thou art my son, this day have I begotten thee.**

The phrases "Raised up Jesus again" and "Raised again," indicates this was not the first time Jesus was raised. Jesus first conquered sin and was raised to the paradise section of Hell to be with the redeemed. Then three days latter Jesus conquered death and was raised from the grave.

Acts 13:34-37

34. **And as concerning that He <u>raised Him up from the dead, now no more to return to corruption</u>, He said on this wise, I will give You the sure mercies of David.**

35. **Wherefore He saith also in another psalm, Thou shalt <u>not suffer Thine Holy One to see corruption</u>.**

36. **For David, after he had served his own generation by the will of God, fell on sleep, and was laid unto his fathers, and saw corruption:**

37. **But He, whom God <u>raised again</u>, saw no corruption.**

Jesus would never again "return to corruption" (Hell Fire) nor would His body "see corruption." It seems that in Jesus' time, it was thought that significant corruption and decay of the body didn't set in until after four days. This may be why they were willing to go to Jesus' dead body shortly after the third day to finish the anointing (Mark 16:1-6) but not willing to open Lazarus's tomb after four days. We see this stated when Jesus arrived at Bethany to revive His friend Lazarus, who had already been dead four days.

John 11:38-44

38. **Jesus therefore again groaning in Himself cometh to the grave. It was a cave, and a stone lay upon it.**

^{39.} Jesus said, take ye away the stone. Martha, the sister of him that was dead, saith unto Him, Lord, <u>by this time he stinketh: for he hath been dead four days</u>.

^{40.} Jesus saith unto her, said I not unto thee, that, if thou wouldest believe, thou shouldest see the glory of God?

^{41.} Then they took away the stone from the place where the dead was laid. And Jesus lifted up His eyes, and said, Father, I thank Thee that Thou hast heard Me.

^{42.} And I knew that Thou hearest Me always: but because of the people which stand by I said it, that they may believe that Thou hast sent Me.

^{43.} And when He thus had spoken, He cried with a loud voice, Lazarus, come forth.

^{44.} And he that was dead came forth, bound hand and foot with graveclothes: and his face was bound about with a napkin. Jesus saith unto them, loose him, and let him go.

Lazarus' body was revived and would latter die again but Jesus' body was resurrected and would never die again. I don't believe Jesus' body had the foul odor of decomposing flesh. I believe it still smelled like expensive perfume, which probably permeated the whole aria (John 12:1-7, Mark 14:1-8). Jesus was truly a sweet smelling savior (Ephesians 5:2). The reason the ladies waited three days to finish anointing the body was because they could not legally go sooner. The first day (Thursday) was the High Sabbath of Passover and the Jews were to do no work. The second day (Friday) was the Holy Feast of Unleavened bread and the Jews were to do no work. The third day (Saturday) was the weekly Sabbath and the Jews were to do no work. *Selah.* Jesus was not in His body when they put it in the tomb at the end of

Preparation Day. The Bible says Jesus' soul was in Hell, but Hell could not contain Him. Jesus suffered and went to Hell to set us free.

Acts 2:26-27, 31-32

26. **Therefore did my heart rejoice, and my tongue was glad; moreover also my flesh shall rest in hope:**

27. **Because Thou wilt not leave my soul in Hell, neither wilt thou suffer Thine Holy One to see corruption.**

31. **He seeing this before spake of the resurrection of Christ, that His Soul was not left in Hell, neither His flesh did see corruption.**

32. **This Jesus hath God raised up, whereof we all are witnesses.**

When Jesus' Soul came out of Hell, it was a glorious eruption of liberation. By opening the way to Heaven, He freed everyone held captive in the Paradise section of Hell. Everything changed that glorious Resurrection Day. The Earth was shaken to its very core. Now there is no Paradise section of Hell. There is no Purgatory. We do not have to wait for Jesus to die for our sins. Now we can go directly to Heaven to be where Jesus is.

2 Corinthians 5:8

8. **We are confident, I say, and willing rather to be absent from the body, and to be present with the Lord.**

Hell has enlarged itself and is now full of hopelessness and continuous torment. There is no relief. Today, sad to say, everyone in Hell is waiting for the last Judgment resulting in a destiny in the Lake of Fire. People who foolishly say they are going to have a party in Hell and encourage their friends to join them will be shocked to discover that their time of celebration will be over, and the endless terrifying nightmare of a Godless world will engulf them.

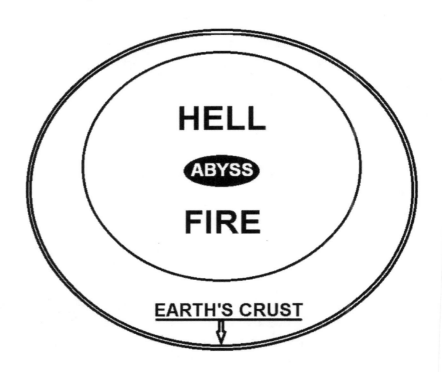

Isaiah 5:14

14. Therefore **Hell hath enlarged herself,** and opened her mouth **without measure:** and their glory, and their multitude, and their pomp, and he that rejoiceth, shall descend into it.

Some may not agree but Hell is a real place according to the Bible. There are many appealing roads to Hell but one road to Heaven. Jesus came to Earth to set free the captives in Hell's Paradise and to offer all mankind the benefits of Heaven as a gift.

Ephesians 4:8-9

8. Wherefore He saith, **when He ascended up** on high, He **led captivity captive,** and gave gifts unto men.

^{9.} **(Now that He ascended, what is it but that He also descended first into the <u>lower parts of the Earth</u>?**

We can thank Jesus for laying down His life in order to pay the penalty for our sins thereby purchasing our freedom.

I Peter 1:18-19

^{18.} **Forasmuch as ye know that ye were not redeemed with corruptible things, as silver and gold, from your vain conversation received by tradition from your fathers;**

^{19.} **But with the precious blood of Christ, as of a <u>Lamb without blemish</u> and without spot:**

1 Corinthians 15:3-8

^{3.} **For I delivered unto you first of all that which I also received, how that <u>Christ died for our sins</u> according to the scriptures;**

^{4.} **And that <u>He was buried, and that He rose again the third day according to the scriptures</u>:**

^{5.} **And that <u>He was seen</u> of Cephas, then of the twelve:**

^{6.} **After that, <u>He was seen of above five hundred brethren at once; of whom the greater part remain unto this present</u>, but some are fallen asleep.**

^{7.} **After that, <u>He was seen</u> of James; then of all the apostles.**

^{8.} **And last of all <u>He was seen</u> of me also, as of one born out of due time.**

I Peter 1:23

^{23.} **Being <u>born again, not of corruptible seed</u>, but of incorruptible, <u>by the Word of God</u>, which liveth and <u>abideth forever</u>.**

261

Section 3

Application

CHAPTER 12

THE KEY TO HEAVEN

Can you get to Heaven if you smoke, abuse drugs and alcohol, or live an immoral lifestyle? Will a proper acting agnostic be allowed into Heaven? If you ask on the street what is the key to unlock Heaven's door, most people would answer that you must be good or obey the Ten Commandments. Nevertheless, what does the Bible say?

John 3:16-17

^{16.} **For God so loved the world, that He gave His only begotten son, that <u>whosoever believeth</u> in Him should <u>not perish</u>, but have <u>everlasting life</u>.**

^{17.} **For God sent not His Son into the world to condemn the world; but that the world through Him might be saved.**

Can a person who dies from smoking, abusing drugs and alcohol, and living an immoral lifestyle possibly go to Heaven? It will become clear in this chapter that the answer is yes. In fact, they may even get to go to Heaven early. What about the agnostic whose life was dedicated to saving the Earth and helping others, then got married and had a loving family who carried on this great work. Even at death, this person cared enough to donate their organs to save others' lives. This good person would surely go to Heaven, right? Sad to say, no agnostic or atheist will go to Heaven. They will have to change to qualify for Heaven. They will have to stop being an agnostic or atheist. The unpardonable sin is unbelief. Unbelief leads to calling God the Holy Spirit unnecessary for personal salvation. To blaspheme the Holy Spirit is saying the Holy Spirit is an irrelevant superstition unworthy of acknowledgment. The unpardonable sin is rejection of God's plan for salvation. If you stop rejecting God's Word and start trusting in what Jesus did, then you will no longer be committing the unpardonable sin and therefore you can be pardoned.

Hebrews 11:6

6. But without faith it is impossible to please Him: for he that cometh to God must believe that He is, and that He is a rewarder of them that diligently seek Him.

Eternal life in Heaven is too important for us to just make assumptions and rationalizations base on people's opinions. It is not wise to develop my own rules and belief system only to find out after it's too late that I was wrong. My personal opinions will be powerless when God informs me about the undeniable truth regarding transformation and salvation. Therefore, to clear up all the confusion about what is required for me to qualify for a home in Heaven, let's look closely at what God's Word has to say about how redemption works.

Romans 3:19-20

19. Now we know that what things soever the law saith, it saith to them who are under the law: that every mouth may be stopped, and all the world may become guilty before God.

20. Therefore <u>by the deeds of the law there shall no flesh be justified</u> in His sight: for <u>by the law is the knowledge of sin</u>.

The Law of Good Works (not just the Ten Commandments) has a purpose. The purpose is not to save us, but to show us that we are not perfect. The Law is the target for perfection. We have to hit the bulls-eye every time to be perfect. The problem is we are often blinded or have a hard time focusing. This is because of our sinful fallen human nature. Therefore, the reality is that we rarely, if ever, hit perfect center. The distance between perfect center and our shot is the amount of sin in our action.

Romans 3:23
23. For **all have sinned, and come short** of the glory of God;

Romans 6:23
23. For the **wages of sin is death**; but the gift of God is eternal life through Jesus Christ our Lord.

The payment or reward for sin is grave clothing. The result of our lack of perfection, or what we earn with our sin, is bondage, corruption and death. The Law shows us we have a problem. *Selah.* If I put all my works together and average my score, it would only take one time missing the target to lower my score below 100% perfect. If I fall short of perfect, then I have sin. Like it or not sin makes me defective. Defective people hurt each other and corrupt the environment. There are no defective people or corruption of any kind in Heaven. There is a designated place that is perfectly able to contain all corruption, thus keeping it from polluting Heaven. It's called the Lake of Fire. Consequently, the target (Law) reveals the problem, but is powerless to solve the problem. The Law can only reveal our score, not replace it with a perfect score.

Acts 13:38-39
38. Be it known unto you therefore, men and brethren, that through this Man is preached unto you the forgiveness of sins:

39. And by Him **all that believe are justified from all things**, from which ye **could not be justified by the law** of Moses.

Ephesians 2:8-9 (*with a clarifying note*)
8. For by grace are ye **saved** through faith; and that (*your salvation is*) **not of yourselves: it is the gift of God**:

9. **Not of works, lest any man should boast**.

The Bible is very clear that my good works cannot justify me. This would be the same as having faith in myself. I have missed the target many times. Salvation is a gift that I cannot earn. I cannot undo my history and have a perfect score. I can't even start now to be perfect because of my fallen human nature. If I think I am good enough to go to Heaven or too good to go to Hell, then it proves that I have misunderstood the devastation of sin and why Jesus had to come and dye for me. Or if I claim that I did some good works to earn the gift of God, then it is no longer a gift. Instead, it would be a payment or reward for my work. It would be a purchase I made, not a gift. To illustrate, let's say I purchased a beautiful house on the beach. It cost me all the money I had at the time. Then, I put your name on the deed and put the deed in the house. I come to you and tell you that I've prepared a place for you and offer you the key. Now you have a choice. You could say I don't believe you, and turn and walk away without ever seeing the place I prepared for you. Then again, you could take the key, reach into your pocket, find a little money and say; I'll pay you for it, and throw your change on the ground before me. Later you could boast about how smart you were and the great bargain you got from me on your glorious mansion. These responses would not only be offensive to the giver, but would also deny the fact that I offered you a free gift of great value.

John 14:2

2. **In My Father's house are many mansions: if it were not so, I would have told you. I go to prepare a place for you.**

The graceful and proper response to the gift offered is to receive it with humble gratitude. So, what is the key to our eternal home in Heaven?

Romans 8:11

11. But <u>if the Spirit</u> of Him that raised up Jesus from the dead <u>dwell in you</u>, He that raised up Christ from the dead shall also quicken your mortal bodies by <u>His Spirit</u> that <u>dwelleth in you</u>.

Receiving the Holy Spirit of Jesus is our key to Heaven. How do we do that?

Romans 10:9-10

9. That if thou shalt <u>confess</u> with thy mouth the <u>Lord Jesus</u>, and shalt <u>believe</u> in thine heart that <u>God hath raised Him</u> from the dead, <u>thou shalt be saved</u>.

10. For with the heart man <u>believeth unto righteousness</u>; and with the mouth <u>confession is made unto salvation</u>.

True belief or saving faith actually has two steps as shown in verse 10.

<u>First</u>: We believe what the Bible says about Jesus. Jesus paid for my sins, and then the Holy Spirit of God raised Jesus from the dead. We understand that the same Holy Spirit of Jesus that raised Him from the dead can live in me and raise me from the dead and prepare me for Heaven.

<u>Second</u>: We act on this belief by asking Jesus into our life and confess that He is our Savior. We are not ashamed because we recognize the all-powerful King of kings and Lord of lords is adopting us into His family. Simply put, we first believe, and then we receive. When we ask Jesus into our heart, it's actually Jesus' Holy Spirit that comes into our heart. He comes in the name of Jesus. The Bible states, what is in our heart will come out our mouth (Matthew 12:34). Our verbal confession is evidence that Jesus' Holy Spirit is in our heart and therefore we are saved. *Selah.* To understand the process, we first have to clearly

recognize the condition into which we are born and the reason we cannot save ourselves.

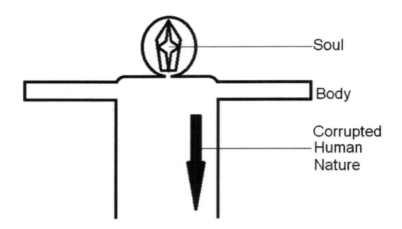

As illustrated in Chapter 3, we are born with a fallen human nature. This human nature is anti-God. If you are familiar with the Calvinistic doctrine of total depravity and being dead in sin, this doctrine applies to our human nature. What is often misunderstood is that this sinful human nature is never redeemed. It is never regenerated. It never changes. It will never stop rejecting God's plan for our life. We all inherited the same type of nature from our father, going all the way back to the first Adam. Its origin goes all the way back to the time when Eve rebelled against God's instruction and trusted the Devil. At that point, she joined the Devil's rebellion against God. She was deceived and didn't realize what she was doing; but nevertheless she was changed, and her nature was corrupted. The Devil was the father of that change.

John 8:41-44

41. **Ye do the deeds of your father. Then said they to Him, we be not born of fornication; we have one father, even God.**

42. Jesus said unto them, if God were your father, ye would love Me: for I proceeded forth and came from God; neither came I of Myself, but He sent Me.

43. Why do ye not understand My speech? Even because ye cannot hear My Word.

44. Ye are of <u>your father the Devil</u>, and the lusts of your father ye will do. He was a murderer from the beginning, and abode not in the truth, because there is no truth in him. When he speaketh a lie, he speaketh of his own: for <u>he is a liar, and the father of it</u>.

The deceptive human nature continually tries to blind us to God. It is never balanced or on target, but instead majors in extremes. It continually distorts God's Word. Jesus made it clear that good works or religion alone cannot fix this problem.

Matthew 23:13, 24-28

13. But woe unto you, scribes and Pharisees, hypocrites! For ye shut up the kingdom of Heaven against men: for ye neither go in yourselves, neither suffer ye them that are entering to go in.

24. Ye blind guides, which strain at a gnat, and swallow a camel.

25. Woe unto you, scribes and Pharisees, hypocrites! For ye make clean the outside of the cup and of the platter, but within they are full of extortion and excess.

26. Thou blind Pharisee, <u>cleanse first that which is within</u> the cup and platter, that the outside of them may be clean also.

27. Woe unto you, scribes and Pharisees, hypocrites! For ye are like unto whited sepulchres, which indeed appear beautiful outward, but are within full of dead men's bones, and of all uncleanness.

28. Even so ye also <u>outwardly appear righteous unto men, but within ye are full of hypocrisy and iniquity</u>.

The soul that is wrapped up in the fallen human nature, will not even hear the unfiltered Word of God.

Romans 7:24

24. O wretched man that I am! Who shall deliver me from the body of this death?

Our old nature cannot and will not be in harmony with God, although there are times when our nature will have less influence on our soul.

Hebrews 4:12

12. For the Word of God is quick, and powerful, and sharper than any twoedged sword, piercing even to the <u>dividing asunder of soul and spirit</u>, and of the joints and marrow, and is a discerner of the thoughts and intents of the heart.

Our nature (human spirit) is totally depraved, but our soul is not totally depraved. Our soul is the eternal part of us that makes us a unique individual. Remember in chapter 2 we learned that the definition of our nature is our species. My nature is human so I am part of the human race. The definition of our soul is an individual or person. I am a soul so I have a unique personality. I am one of a kind. Any soul (person) can be redeemed. The Bible is clear that your soul can be saved and needs to be saved.

Leviticus 17:11

11. For the life of the flesh is in the blood: and I have given it to you upon the altar to make an <u>atonement for your souls</u>: for it is the blood that maketh an <u>atonement for the soul</u>.

1 Peter 1:9

⁹· **Receiving the end of your faith, even the <u>salvation of your</u> <u>souls</u>.**

Jesus shed His perfect sinless blood to make "an atonement for our souls," thus enabling our souls to receive salvation. Salvation is not automatic. God is our redeemer but redemption has two steps. If I wanted to redeem something that had been pawned, the first step is making the payment. Jesus paid a high price for you and me. The second step is taking possession of the purchase. The second step is where we have a choice. Do we want God to take possession of us? Do we want to belong to God as his adopted children? Are we willing to become part of God's family by receiving a new nature? Our soul can choose God. Every soul (person) has an opportunity at some point in their life to choose. You can choose to know your Creator or choose to reject Him. *Selah.* You may ask what about those that died before they were mentally mature enough to make a decision. That is a good question and you will find the answer in Chapter 16 when we look at the last millennium. There are no exceptions. Everyone has at least one opportunity to choose life with his or her creator by receiving the Holy Spirit.

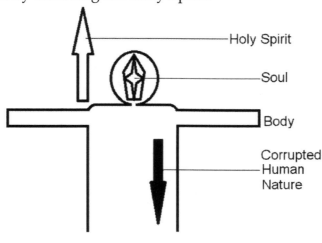

God gives every soul a choice and He encourages you to choose life.

Deuteronomy 30:19

19. I call Heaven and Earth to record this day against you, that <u>I have set before you life and death</u>, blessing and cursing: therefore <u>choose life</u>, that both thou and thy seed may live:

You may ask where is the choice when the name of Jesus is not known. There are still parts of the world where the Bible and the Good News are either banned by religion or unreached by seclusion. That is another good point and the Bible answers it. At some point in time our Creator gives everyone an opportunity to be His friend. It starts with realizing that creation has a Creator then trusting in the light God provides.

Psalm 43:3

3. O send out Thy light and Thy truth: let them lead me; let them bring me unto Thy holy hill, and to Thy tabernacles

Psalm 36:9

9. For with Thee is the fountain of life: in Thy light shall we see light.

The light of God always contrasts our dark environment. The darker the environment the greater this contrast will be.

John 12:35-36

35. Then Jesus said unto them, Yet a little while is the light with you. Walk while ye have the light, lest darkness come upon you: for he that walketh in darkness knoweth not whither he goeth.

36. While ye have light, believe in the light, that ye may be the children of light. These things spake Jesus, and departed, and did hide himself from them.

Without exception the light of the Creator has personally appeared or will appear to every person on Earth in order to give him or her an opportunity to be saved.

Titus 2:11

11. For the grace of God that bringeth salvation hath appeared to all men,

"All men" is a reference to all mankind or every human being. In the end everyone will give an account of what they did after the light of God appeared to them.

John 1:9-12

9. That was the True Light, which lighteth every man that cometh into the world.

10. He was in the world, and the world was made by Him, and the world knew Him not.

11. He came unto His own, and His own received Him not.

12. But as many as received Him, to them gave He power to become the sons of God, even to them that believe on His name:

I have some experience in this area. I am the oldest child and have four brothers and one sister. Before I entered school and before my family went to church, we moved out to a big lake in Michigan called Lincoln Lake. We were sort of like pioneers around 1960, because our well for water was in the front yard with a red hand pump on top of it. One of my earliest memories is sitting in the yard next to the well pump and wondering things like, were did I come from? How did I get here? Where do I go and what happens when I die? I wasn't depressed. I didn't go to church or understand religion. I hadn't heard about Heaven, Hell, or Jesus the Savior. God gave me a little light, He "lighteth every man (all mankind) that cometh into the world." I wanted to know more about eternity.

Ecclesiastes 3:11 (NKJV)

11. He has made everything beautiful in its time. Also <u>He has put eternity in their hearts</u>, except that no one can find out the work that God does from beginning to end.

I wanted to know who the Creator was. After I started school, a young girl asked me if I had received Jesus as my Savior. I didn't know what she was taking about. Why do I need a Savior? Who is Jesus? Even though I didn't understand it, I kept it in mind. Later, my grandparents sent me to a church camp where the cabin counselor told us about Jesus, Heaven, and Hell, and why I needed a Savior. Some of the boys went with the counselor to pray. I wasn't comfortable with that, but I definitely didn't want to go to Hell. That night under the covers I spoke to God praying, please don't let me go to Hell. I later made it public that I had asked Jesus to save me. It all started with a little light that I didn't put out. As the light got brighter, I could see more and more. God is always willing and able to illuminate the truth to anyone who asks, even if He has to send an angel as a missionary to the darkest, most remote place on Earth. Furthermore, there are many reports of miraculous events leading to conversions. The supernatural is seen more often when it lacks the natural (2Corinthians 12:9-10).

Psalm 18:28

28. For Thou wilt light my candle: the Lord my <u>God will enlighten my darkness</u>.

The problem is that most people quench or put out the light, either because of peer pressure or because they are listening to their sinful nature.

Romans 1:19-22

19. Because that which may be known of God is <u>manifest in them</u>; for <u>God hath shewed it unto them</u>.

20. For the <u>invisible things of Him from the creation</u> of the world are clearly seen, being understood by the things that are made, even His eternal power and Godhead; so that <u>they are without excuse</u>:

21. Because that, <u>when they knew God, they glorified Him not as God</u>, neither were thankful; <u>but became vain in their imaginations, and their foolish heart was darkened</u>.

22. Professing themselves to be wise, they became fools,

Every soul will make a choice regarding the light of God. God will not force himself upon anyone. At some point in every life, the Holy Spirit of God comes to every soul (after you are able to understand right and wrong, thus being accountable for the soul's personal sin). Every soul will be held accountable for how it responded to God's light. There are only two choices. You may reject it and put your faith in something inspired by the Devil or receive God and His plan of redemption.

Revelation 3:20

20. **Behold, <u>I stand at the door, and knock</u>: if any man hear My voice, and open the door, I will come in to him, and will sup with him, and he with Me.**

Our soul will be held accountable for the choice it makes about accepting the light of the Holy Spirit in our heart. It's not about saying magic words or walking up front at a church that qualifies us for Heaven. It is not about doing wonderful works or even preaching.

Matthew 7:21-23

21. **Not every one that saith unto Me, Lord, Lord, shall enter into the kingdom of Heaven; but <u>he that doeth the will of My Father which is in Heaven</u>.**

22. **Many will say to Me in that day, Lord, Lord, have we not prophesied in Thy name? And in Thy name have cast out devils? <u>And in Thy name done many wonderful works</u>?**

23. **And then will I profess unto them, <u>I never knew you</u>: depart from Me, ye that work iniquity.**

What is the will of the Father regarding salvation?

John 6:40

40. **And <u>this is the will</u> of Him that sent Me, that every one which seeth the Son, and <u>believeth on Him</u>, may have everlasting life: and I will raise him up at the last day.**

The will of the Father is for us to have a personal relationship with Jesus His Son. The will of the Father is for us to know Jesus as our personal Savior and Friend. Ritual, religious activity and good works cannot replace this.

1 John 5:11-12

11. And this is the record, that <u>God hath given to us eternal life</u>, and this life is in His Son.

12. <u>He that hath the Son hath life; and he that hath not the Son of God hath not life</u>.

We begin this relationship by asking the Holy Spirit of Jesus into our life.

Hebrews 4:16

16. Let us therefore come boldly unto the throne of grace, that we may <u>obtain mercy</u>, and <u>find grace</u> to help in time of need.

I would like to share a little more of my testimony to illustrate how life-changing Hebrews 4:16 is. In the third grade I learned salvation was more than just being saved from Hell. I learned that Jesus could also change my life in the here and now. I attended a one-room country schoolhouse called Lyons School through the second grade, and then I was bused to town. It was the beginning of a new school year, and I just turned eight years old. After I got off the bus at Cedar Springs Elementary, a little girl told me to beat up another little kid. I did, but the problem was that this kid had a big friend. He was older and much bigger than I was. He was a bully and especially liked hitting me. Talk about attending the school of hard knocks! It was rough, but I was too embarrassed to tell anyone. A friend of mine once told the bully to leave me alone. The bully responded by slamming my friend's head against the school building wall, so he ran off crying. I didn't have many friends, but there was one true Friend that sticketh closer than a brother. That friend is God. One morning near the end of the school year, I told God I had learned my lesson. I would never be a bully or pick fights again and prayed for God to please take this person out of my life. When I got off the bus, a friend told me that the bully had been kicked out of school. I never saw him again. I was amazed and learned some important lessons that day. It became clear to me that God can change my circumstance once I've learned the lesson and ask for His help in faith. Since that day, there have been countless times God has delivered me from the enemy or blessed me with answered prayers. It all began with that little light. I wanted to know the truth about creation and destiny. God responded with more light and made it clear to me that I needed a deliverer. God also made clear that the choice was entirely mine. I could ask Him in or shut Him out. In faith, I choose to ask Him in.

Luke 11:13

13. If ye then, being evil, know how to give good gifts unto your children: how much more shall your Heavenly Father <u>give the Holy Spirit to them that ask Him</u>?

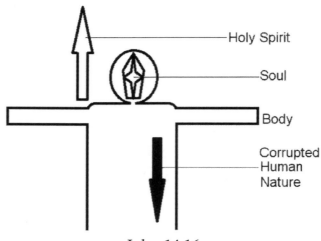

John 14:16

16. And I will pray the Father, and <u>He shall give you </u>another Comforter, that He may <u>abide with you for ever</u>;

Comforter is another name for the Holy Spirit. Once the Holy Spirit comes in, He will never leave. He will be with us forever.

He gives us a new identity. He is the key to eternal life. He is available to you for the asking.

John 10:28

28. And <u>I give</u> unto them <u>eternal life</u>; and they shall <u>never perish</u>, neither shall any man pluck them out of My hand.

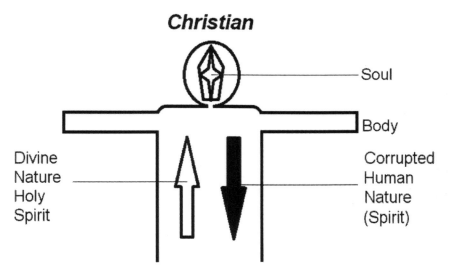

The Holy Spirit is the key to Heaven.

John 14:17

17. Even the <u>Spirit of truth</u>; whom the world cannot receive, because it seeth him not, neither knoweth him: but ye know him; for he dwelleth with you, and <u>shall be in you</u>.

The Holy Spirit is also the Key to unlock mysteries and give us wisdom in our daily life.

John 14:26

26. But the <u>Comforter, which is the Holy Ghost, whom the Father will send in My name</u>, He shall teach you all things, and bring all things to your remembrance, whatsoever I have said unto you.

CHAPTER 13

WHAT GOOD IS GOOD WORKS?

James 2:18-20

^{18.} **Yea, a man may say, thou hast faith, and I have works: shew me thy faith without thy works, and I will shew thee my faith by my works.**

^{19.} **Thou believest that there is one God; thou doest well: the <u>devils also believe, and tremble</u>.**

^{20.} **But wilt thou know, O vain man, that <u>faith without works is dead?</u>**

This passage seems to contradict the previous chapter. In this chapter we will get into how our works reflect our faith. To clear up the confusion and apparent contradiction let's properly define the word "works." Works can refer to a job you do for which you expect to be paid. However, when it appears in the Bible, works is better defined as actions. Using the proper definitions will soon clear up the confusion. As a result, verse 18 would read, "I will show thee my faith by my actions." We will get back to how that makes a difference in a moment, but first let's look at verse 19 which clarifies that true faith is more than believing. The devils have no doubt that God is real, but belief alone does not qualify them for Heaven. The problem for the devils is that they have no capacity to receive the life-transforming Holy Spirit, which is the key to redemption. You have to be born of water (have a natural mortal birth) before you can be born-again of the Spirit.

John 3:5-7

^{5.} **Jesus answered, Verily, verily, I say unto thee, Except a man be <u>born of water and of the Spirit</u>, he cannot enter into the kingdom of God.**

6. That which is <u>born of the flesh</u> is flesh; and that which is <u>born of the Spirit</u> is spirit.

7. Marvel not that I said unto thee, Ye must be born again.

As a man, I could believe to the point of having no doubt that God is real and still go to Hell. This statement does not belittle believing, because I can't go to Heaven unless I believe.

Hebrews 11:6

6. But <u>without faith it is impossible to please Him</u>: for he that cometh to God must believe that He is, and that He is a rewarder of them that diligently seek Him.

Believing is the first step toward salvation, but it is incomplete without action. Faith without action is dead.

James 2:26

26. For as the body without the spirit is dead, so faith without works is dead also.

Our faith is revealed by our works. There are different applications or types of faith. There is saving faith, which has a similar but different action than the faith that produces spiritual growth. *Selah.* If I have faith that the Bible is true and can improve my life, I will read the Bible to grow spiritually. If I believe this and do not read the Bible then my faith is dead resulting in a useless belief that has no real affect on my life. If you read the second chapter of James you will notice that it is predominantly referring to how we treat others not how we become part of God's family. James is elaborating on ministering faith which involves reaching out to others. *Selah.* What dose the Bible say the proper action (or work) is for life changing saving faith?

Romans 8:15

15. For ye have not received the spirit of bondage again to fear; but ye <u>have received the Spirit of adoption</u>, whereby we cry, Abba, Father.

The key is whether or not you have received the Holy Spirit. Can I earn the Holy Spirit by my good works? No, my action (works) was to receive the Holy Spirit. After I believe in God and what Jesus has done, I ask the Spirit of Jesus into my heart (core of my life). The only action here was to stop avoiding and receive the Holy Spirit. This is called repentance because we turn to God and welcome the Holy Spirit of Jesus into our life. He comes to us as a free gift that Jesus paid for on the cross.

Galatians 3:2-3

2. This only would I learn of you, <u>received ye the Spirit by the works of the law, or by the hearing of faith?</u>

3. Are ye so foolish? Having begun in the Spirit, are ye now made perfect by the flesh?

Becoming more religious or legalistic does not produce salvation or spiritual growth. Spiritual growth does involve avoiding things that will drown out the voice of God. We are born-again by responding to God's voice in our heart and receiving the Holy Spirit. Spending time with the Holy Spirit perfects us. We allow Him to connect us with Jesus. This results in the fruit of the Spirit being manifested in our life.

Galatians 5:22-23 (NAS)

22. But the <u>fruit of the Spirit</u> is love, joy, peace, patience, kindness, goodness, faithfulness,

23. gentleness, self-control; against such things there is no law.

John 15:4-5

^{4.} <u>Abide in Me, and I in you</u>. **As the branch cannot bear fruit of itself, except it abide in the vine; no more can ye, except ye <u>abide in Me</u>.**

^{5.} **I am the vine, ye are the branches: He that <u>abideth in Me, and I in him</u>, the same <u>bringeth forth much fruit</u>: for without Me ye can do nothing.**

Consistently enjoying and producing the pure fruit of the Spirit in spite of our circumstances is the evidence of spiritual growth. *Selah.* The Holy Spirit patiently speaks to everyone. He speaks to the lost, directing them away from Satan's plans. The Holy Spirit knocks on the door of our hearts hoping we will respond by letting Him in. If we constantly resist Him, He will eventually quit knocking and speaking to us, unless someone is praying for us (Exodus 32:9-14, Exodus 33:13-17). On the other hand if we ask the Holy Spirit into our hearts, He will adopt us into the family of God and become our closest friend and partner. The Bible says that He will never leave us after He comes into our heart (John 14:16). Therefore we are not to fear loosing our salvation. Even if I backslide and become a disobedient and rebellious child, I will still be a child. As a child in need of discipline, I can expect chastisement, not abandonment.

Proverbs 3:11-12

^{11.} **My son, despise not the chastening of the LORD; neither be weary of His correction:**

^{12.} **For whom the LORD loveth He correcteth; even as a father the son in whom he delighteth.**

Hebrews 12:6-7

6. **For whom the Lord loveth He chasteneth, and scourgeth every son whom He receiveth.**

7. **If ye endure chastening, God dealeth with you as with sons; for what son is he whom the father chasteneth not?**

Philippians 1:6

6. **Being confident of this very thing, that He which hath begun a good work in you will perform it until the day of Jesus Christ:**

Hebrews 12:8

8. **But if ye be without chastisement, whereof all are partakers, then are ye bastards, and not sons.**

Discipline is not always immediate. God hopes we will choose to repent from sin. God encourages us to be self-disciplined. By self-discipline I am referring to self-control, which is one of the fruit of the Spirit.

1 Corinthians 11:31

31. **For if we would judge ourselves, we should not be judged.**

Self-discipline cannot earn us salvation but it is a sign of maturity. *Selah.* If salvation is paid for and I can't earn it, then why bother doing good works? Why not be free of self-discipline and do what comes natural? Good works affect our quality of life both here and in eternity. To be clear, our home in Heaven is a gift from God to us. It's better than receiving an oceanfront mansion; but if I did receive the gift of a mansion, my good works would be my personal touch such as decorating, landscaping, and furnishing the mansion.

Galatians 6:7-10

7. **Be not deceived; God is not mocked: for <u>whatsoever a man soweth, that shall he also reap</u>.**

8. **For he that soweth to his flesh shall of the flesh reap corruption; but he that soweth to the Spirit shall of the Spirit reap life everlasting.**

9. **And let us not be weary in well doing: for <u>in due season we shall reap, if we faint not</u>.**

10. **As we have therefore opportunity, let us do good unto all men, especially unto them who are of the household of faith.**

Once we receive the Holy Spirit, the Spirit will enable us to sow good deed seeds that will develop into everlasting rewards and treasures in Heaven. If I refuse to do good works here then God will deny us eternal rewards when we get to Heaven. That is what Jesus was telling His disciples in Mathew 10:33. If we read the context of Mathew chapter 10, Jesus is telling His followers of the power, persecution, and price of becoming His disciples. Jesus ends the chapter by pointing out the rewards to those that do not deny Him. It is our rewards in Heaven that we have to work for not our home in Heaven. *Selah.* Sowing and reaping will also affect our quality of life here on Earth. There is usually a period of time between seedtime and harvest, but make no mistake, they are connected. What we consistently sow we will eventually reap. The type of seed, the environment and the quality of the ground will determine the kind of harvest we will see. The principle of sowing and reaping is a powerful truth that applies to everyone, saved and unsaved. It can be either positive or negative. It applies to many areas of our lives and is the key to the abundant life. *Selah.*

John 10:10

10. **The thief cometh** not, but for to <u>steal,</u> and to <u>kill,</u> and to <u>destroy</u>: I am come that they might have life, and that they might have it more abundantly.

This verse reveals the contrasting objectives of Christ and Satan (the thief). Satan's job description is to kill, steal, and destroy. Either directly or indirectly, the suffering in this world comes from previous seeds that matured in satanic gardens, sometimes three or more generations earlier, sometimes yesterday. Indirectly God takes responsibility for Satan's actions because God has the power to restrict or bind Satan. God allows Satan a limited amount of time in order to provide the environment that gives us the freedom to choose between good and evil. When we sow seeds (actions) contrary to God's Word (even in ignorance), we open the door to experience satanic harvests of corruption, destruction, and misery. God is merciful and He loves us. It is God's desire to spare us unnecessary sorrow and provide a way to enjoy a constructive rewarding environment. Jesus stated that His job description is to give us life and abundance, supplying everything that is needed for our fulfillment. If we apply God's principles consistently to our lives, then sooner or later we will experience the abundant blessings of God. This applies to a nation, a family, and an individual. *Selah.* The principle of sowing and reaping is also called the law of multiplication because you normally reap far more than you sow. When Christians want to apply the principle of sowing and reaping to their finances in order to see an increase, the first thing they should know is that they cannot sow what is not theirs. For example, if I borrow money from someone and promise to pay it back at $100 a month, that $100 every month does not belong to me until the debt is paid off. It belongs to the lender. I can't just decide to take the lender's $100 and give it to God.

Psalm 37:21

21. **The** <u>**wicked borroweth, and payeth not again**</u>**: but the righteous sheweth mercy, and giveth.**

However, there are exceptions. There may be times when we find ourselves drowning in debt and poverty. Maybe it wasn't even our fault. God is merciful and didn't cause our problem – that's the Devil's domain. If you cannot pay your obligations without a miracle, God may give you special instruction about what to do and where to sow. Then, by faith we receive deliverance as seen in 2Kings 4:1-7. Sowing in obedience to the Word of God also applies if we are suffering in poverty and starvation as seen in 1Kings 17:8-16. If we consistently and properly apply the principles of the Bible, including Biblical sowing and reaping, then we will avoid drowning in debt or deficiency. If a financial storm does come our way (from the Devil), it will simply be a test of our faith and will soon pass, as we see in the book of Job. *Selah.* Setting the exceptions aside, the principles remain true. It is not right for me to take your money and give it to God for a blessing, just as it's not right for me to take God's money and invest it, expecting a blessing. While it's true that everything is God's by right of creation, God doesn't claim 90% of it. As a Christian, 90% of what I earn is my after-tithe pay, and I'm free to do what I want with it. As a Christian, a citizen of the kingdom of God, 10% of my income is for supporting the work of God at my church. This is not legalism. Tithes and offerings started way back in Genesis, before the Law of Moses.

Genesis 4:4

4. **And Abel, he also brought of the firstlings of his flock and of the fat thereof. And** <u>**the Lord had respect unto Abel and to his offering**</u>**:**

Genesis 14:18-20

18. And Melchizedek king of Salem brought forth bread and wine: and he was the priest of the Most High God.

19. And he blessed him, and said, blessed be Abram of the Most High God, possessor of Heaven and Earth:

20. And blessed be the Most High God, which hath delivered thine enemies into thy hand. And he gave him tithes of all.

Genesis 28:22

22. And this stone, which I have set for a pillar, shall be God's house: and of all that Thou shalt give me I will surely give the tenth unto Thee.

Malachi 3:8

8. Will a man rob God? Yet ye have robbed Me. But ye say, wherein have we robbed Thee? In tithes and offerings.

I was about twenty years old when God gave me a dream regarding money. In my dream, I was walking through a sand dune desert. Then I saw a couple of dollars in the sand, and then a few more. I picked up the bills and followed the money trail. As I topped one of the dunes, I looked down into a large sand crater. There was money blowing around all over the place. Then I saw a wallet full of money there on the ground, and my heart sank. After a few moments, I said okay, if I find out who owns the money, I would give it back. I opened the wallet, and to my surprise, the identification inside belonged to Jesus Christ. I became excited and then heard a voice saying, just give Me what's in My wallet. You can keep the rest. I woke up encouraged, with a fresh understanding of how our giving represents our honesty. After we are honest citizens of the kingdom of God and give Jesus our King back His wallet (the 10% tithe), the remaining 90% is ours with

God's blessing. We can sow seeds with our 90% and have faith for a harvest. I like the way the NIV Bible makes this clear.

2 Corinthians 9:6-12 (NIV)

6. Remember this: <u>whoever sows sparingly will also reap sparingly, and whoever sows generously will also reap generously</u>.

7. Each man should give what he has decided in his heart to give, not reluctantly or under compulsion, for <u>God loves a cheerful giver</u>.

8. And God is able to make all grace abound to you, so that in all things at all times, having all that you need, you will abound in every good work.

9. As it is written: "He has scattered abroad His gifts to the poor; His righteousness endures forever."

10. Now He who supplies seed to the sower and bread for food will also supply and increase your store of seed and will enlarge the harvest of your righteousness.

11. You will be made rich in every way so that you can be generous on every occasion, and through us <u>your generosity will result in thanksgiving to God</u>.

12. This service that you perform is not only supplying the needs of God's people but is also overflowing in many expressions of thanks to God.

The true sower knows that you can't out give God.

Philippians 4:19

19. But my God shall supply all your need according to His riches in glory by Christ Jesus.

I have seen some seed bring quick harvest. That can be a real faith builder, but the best harvest comes much later.

Matthew 6:19-21

19. **Lay not up for yourselves treasures upon Earth, where moth and rust doth corrupt, and where thieves break through and steal:**

20. **But <u>lay up for yourselves treasures in Heaven,</u> where neither moth nor rust doth corrupt, and where thieves do not break through nor steal:**

21. **For where your treasure is, there will your heart be also.**

God does not want us to be heartbroken by lost treasures, so He encourages us to have eternal treasures that are out of Satan's reach. *Selah.* God is not against us having nice things here on Earth but He does not want things to have us. God has blessed me with many nice things. Some I worked hard for and others were unexpected gifts. Some things were the result of answered prayers. For instance, growing up I had prayed that God would provide a nice house to live in when I got married. I was 30 years old when Marsha and I planed our wedding. We did not have a lot of money but decided to buy a house and have the wedding at home. We gave financially to God's work and prayed that God would direct us to the right house. We decided we would each choose two things that we wanted in our house. Marsha chose a swimming pool and a kitchen that was unseen from the living room. I jokingly said, it would be nice if our house had a lighthouse but my choice was a waterfront back yard and a nice view through glass doors. Some said it's unlikely to find a house like that in our price range. We looked at several houses in the Fort Lauderdale area but none of them had all 4 things. It was around Thanksgiving 1986 that we opened the door to the only house that qualified as an answer to our prayer. Immediately we knew this house on 30th court was our home. As we looked in from the living room door, we could clearly see all 4 things at once. 1) The easy access galley kitchen was unseen from the living room. 2) It had ten-foot glass doors and six-foot glass doors separated by a 33-inch wall. 3) They opened up to the screened in pool and deck aria. 4) Most of the house had a great view of a 200-foot wide section of the Middle River. It even had another set of glass doors in the bedroom with the same southern view of the pool, river and the island across the river. This river connects the Everglades to the Atlantic Ocean and surrounds the "island city" which is in the northeast section of Fort Lauderdale. This house just came on the marked at $94,000. It was in good condition and in a convenient location, yet it was the cheapest house that we had looked at. They accepted our offer of $90,000 and we began the process of getting a mortgage and planning the wedding. To make a long story short, a week before the wedding, out-of-state relatives began to arrive. The problem was we did not have the house yet. Finally on Marsha's birthday February 10 we were told the FHA mortgage was approved and we would receive our house the next day. It was on Wednesday that the house became ours and we had three days to decorate for the wedding. God's fingerprints were all over the timing. On Saturday February 14 1987 we enjoyed our wedding in the back yard with our family and friends, just as God would have it. A few weeks later we were just getting settled in when Marsha called me out to the patio and pointed to the 33-inch poolside wall between the glass doors. There was a lighthouse painted on that wall. Marsha reminded me of my lighthouse comment and said God even gave you a lighthouse. God enabled us to pay off the mortgage on our tenth anniversary. Our debt free home is the result of prayer and following God's direction. We are far from perfect and have our struggles but more than three decades later we are still enjoying God's blessings in our home. I am grateful for my home but I know that this is nothing compared to our eternal home which God is preparing for us in Heaven. I'm exited about what God is preparing. I plan on savoring that first day in paradise. *Selah.* There is much more to good works than sowing and reaping money or tangible things. Good works also applies to our relationships. Jesus is your friend even if you don't realize it. Jesus is also a friend to the lost (Zechariah 13:6) and to those that betray Him (Matthew 26:47-50). These kind of one-sided friendships break Jesus' heart. Although some do not realize it, the Devil is not their friend; he is their enemy. The Devil has an active campaign to destroy us, but Jesus has an active campaign to save us. If we allow the seed of covenant friendship (Holy Spirit) to be planted in our heart, then we have the opportunity to see it grow into becoming a friend to God. This is a mutual friendship. Being a "friend of God" is a friendship where we are identified with God and God with us. This goes beyond "Jesus loves me," to actively demonstrating that I love and trust Jesus. As an example, lets look at how Abraham's relationship with God developed. Before Abraham came to the Promised Land he became a child of God by believing God's Word and responded to God's call.

Genesis 12:1

1. **Now the LORD had said unto Abram, Get thee out of thy country, and from thy kindred, and from thy father's house, unto a land that I will shew thee:**

Genesis 15:6-7

6. **And <u>he believed in the LORD</u>; and He counted it to him for righteousness.**

7. **And He said unto him, I am the LORD that brought thee out of Ur of the Chaldees, to give thee this land to inherit it.**

In faith Abraham began to follow God as His child but was not fully committed to following God as His disciple. Because of the circumstances Abraham headed for Egypt and then began a lying lifestyle until he got caught (Genesis 12:9-19). Ten years later he demonstrated his lack of trust in God's Word and timing, which produced Ishmael (Genesis 16:1-16). Abraham still did not fully trust God and continued to backslide into lies and ½ trues until Isaac was born (Genesis 20:1-18). Abraham learned from his failures. His faith and trust had developed by the time Isaac became a teenager.

James 2:21-23 (NKJV)

21. **Was not Abraham our father justified by works when he offered Isaac his son on the altar?**

22. **Do you see that faith was working together with his works, and by works faith was made perfect?**

23. **And the Scripture was fulfilled which says, "Abraham believed God, and it was accounted to him for righteousness." And <u>he was called the friend of God</u>.**

God wanted Abraham's trust and obedience not his supreme sacrifice or religious works of self-righteousness.

Romans 4:3

3. **For what saith the Scripture? <u>Abraham believed God</u>, and it was counted unto him for righteousness.**

Both Abraham and Isaac acted in complete obedience before seeing the provision of God. As a result they both left the mountain of sacrifice rejoicing (Genesis 22:15-18). Making God's Word more valuable than Abraham's treasured son had nothing to do with Abraham's salvation experience, but it greatly deepened his unwavering commitment to God as his friend. By obedience and trusting God with his most treasured gifts and possessions, Abraham strengthened his mutual friendship with God. Satan's ability to use earthly treasure, such as his beloved son, to emotionally distress Abraham was severely limited. Because of his trust and obedience, Abraham experienced peace, and his faith and faithfulness were increased.

John 14:27

27. **Peace I leave with you, <u>My peace I give unto you</u>: not as the world giveth, give I unto you. <u>Let not your heart be troubled, neither let it be afraid</u>.**

God has many children, but not as many friends. To be a friend to God is a high honor. It is based on trust, obedience, and discipline. To be adopted as a child of God is a free gift, but you have to earn the right to be called a "friend of God." Imagine the all-powerful King of kings, Creator of the universe, enjoying your friendship and making Himself known on your behalf. Love rooted in trust is the one key action or work that activates this kind of friendship with God. "Love" is the essential law of God's kingdom.

James 2:8

8. **If ye fulfil the <u>royal law</u> according to the Scripture, thou shalt <u>love</u> thy neighbour as thyself, ye do well:**

The one thing Jesus wants His friends to focus on is love.

John 15:12-14

12. **<u>This is My commandment, that ye love one another</u>, as I have loved you.**

13. **Greater <u>love</u> hath no man than this, that a man lay down his life for his friends.**

14. **<u>Ye are My friends, if ye do whatsoever I command you.</u>**

CHAPTER 14

THE WAR WITHIN

Romans 7:15-20 (NIV)

^{15.} I do not understand what I do. For what I want to do I do not do, but what I hate I do.

^{16.} And If I do what I do not want to do, I agree that the law is good.

^{17.} As it is, it is no longer I myself who do it, but it is sin living in me.

^{18.} I know that nothing good lives in me, that is, in <u>my sinful nature</u>. For I have the desire to do what is good, but I cannot carry it out.

^{19.} For what I do is not the good I want to do; no, the evil I do not want to do – this I keep on doing.

^{20.} Now if I do what I do not want to do, it is no longer I who do it, but it is sin living in me that does it.

I like the way the NIV translation makes this passage obvious. We are not at war with our body. Our body is not the enemy. Our body needs discipline; and by the grace of God, it is brought under control. It's also clear that we are not the enemy, because our soul desires to do good and cries out for help. Our enemy is our "sinful nature," often referred to as the flesh. Just as Satan did not go away when Jesus came to Earth, the old fallen human nature does not go away when we receive the new Divine Nature. If anything, the conflict becomes more apparent. In order to defeat our enemy, we first need to identify, recognize, and distinguish it from our body, soul, and Divine Nature. Our soul needs to become skillful at discerning the source of our motivation and information.

Hebrews 5:13-14

13. **For every one that useth milk is unskilful in the Word of righteousness: for he is a babe.**

14. **But strong meat belongeth to them that are of full age, even those who <u>by reason of use have their senses exercised to discern both good and evil</u>.**

Some of the contrasting identities, definitions, and symbols of the two natures within a Christian are shown in this chapter. Once we recognize and understand the difference between them, we can better identify the source of the voices or thoughts in our head. For example, if a voice generally condemns us without encouraging us to do right, it is probably the Accuser. However, if it points out a specific sin, indicating the need to repent and do something else, it is probably our friend the Counselor. These diagrams reflect how the two natures are in opposition to one another.

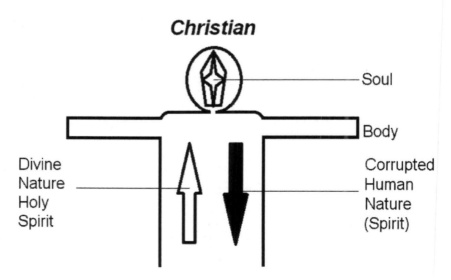

Christian

A Christian's 2 Natures

The Holy Spirit	The Human Spirit
Identity of Christ	Identity of Self
Spirit	Flesh
Divine Nature	Fallen Nature
Holy-Pure-Good	Carnal-Worldly-Sinful
New Man	Old Man
Fresh Water	Salt Water

Flowing Well of Living Water------------------------Bitter Fountain

New Heart --Wicked Heart

Good Tree--Corrupt Tree

Source of Good Fruit----------------------------Source of Evil Fruit

Comforter---Judgmental

Counselor--Accuser

Reconciler ---Condemner

Source of Love and Respect---------------Source of Lust and Pride

Servant of Christ------------------------------------Servant of Satan

Light-Illuminating----------------------------Darkness-Blinding

Full of Truth--Deceiver

Child of God--------------------------------------Child of the Devil

Source of Empowering Faith----------Source of Debilitating Fear

The two natures are the antitheses of each other. Let's look at what the Bible has to say about these two natures within a Christian.

John 7:38-39

38. He that believeth on Me, as the Scripture hath said, <u>out of his belly shall flow rivers of living water.</u>

39. (But <u>this spake He of the Spirit</u>, which they that believe on Him should receive: for the <u>Holy Ghost</u> was not yet given; because that Jesus was not yet glorified.)

John 4:14

14. **But whosoever drinketh of the water that I shall give him shall never thirst; but the water that I shall give him <u>shall be in him a well of water springing up</u> into everlasting life.**

When we receive the Holy Ghost at salvation, we receive a new nature. As we just read in John, the Divine Nature is symbolized by a river or well of Living Water. The Divine Nature is not only a refreshing fountain, but He also satisfies our core desire, providing eternal life. We have a choice, whether to let the Living Water of the Holy Spirit cleanse us and refresh others or not. Make no mistake something is going to flow from us to others.

James 3:9-12

9. **Therewith bless we God, even the Father; and therewith curse we men, which are made after the similitude of God.**

10. **Out of the same mouth proceedeth blessing and cursing. My brethren, these things ought not so to be.**

11. **Doth a fountain send forth <u>at the same place sweet water and bitter?</u>**

12. **Can the fig tree, My brethren, bear olive berries? Either a vine, figs? So can <u>no fountain both yield salt water and fresh</u>.**

Every Christian has two natures or fountains of water. One is sweet Living Water, while the other is bitter polluted water. The Bible has much to say about what comes out of our mouth. Our soul can flavor, filter, and suppress what comes out of our mouth. Our soul also has a voice and can independently cry out with emotion for help. However, there is a spiritual force that influences the direction of our lives. It produces the inspiration for our actions and words. The source of this inspiration is either the Divine Nature producing a new loving heart, or the human nature manifesting our old selfish heart.

Matthew 15:18-19

18. But those things which proceed out of the mouth come forth <u>from the heart</u>; and they defile the man.

19. For out of the heart proceed evil thoughts, murders, adulteries, fornications, thefts, false witness, blasphemies:

The word heart can refer to our emotions, which can be good or bad. However, here God is referring to our core problem, the corrupted heart. The natural heart is corrupted because it is filled with the polluted water of the old nature. *Selah.* The Bible is clear that a Christian has two natures. One nature is corrupt, the other is the Divine Nature. They are symbolized in many ways; two fountains, two hearts and also two trees. These two natures are symbolized by trees because they are rooted by seed and have many branches of thinking. They also bear various fruits.

Luke 6:43-45

43. For <u>a good tree bringeth not forth corrupt fruit; neither doth a corrupt tree bring forth good fruit</u>

44. For every tree is <u>known by his own fruit</u>. For of thorns men do not gather figs, nor of a bramble bush gather they grapes.

45. A good man out of the good treasure of his heart bringeth forth that which is good; and an evil man out of the evil treasure of his heart bringeth forth that which is evil: for <u>of the abundance of the heart his mouth speaketh</u>.

Matthew 7:16-20

16. Ye shall know them by their fruits. Do men gather grapes of thorns, or figs of thistles?

17. **Even so every good tree bringeth forth good fruit; but a corrupt tree bringeth forth evil fruit.**

18. **A good tree cannot bring forth evil fruit, neither can a corrupt tree bring forth good fruit.**

19. **Every tree that bringeth not forth good fruit is hewn down, and cast into the fire.**

20. **Wherefore by their fruits ye shall know them.**

Matthew 12:33-35

33. **Either make the tree good, and his fruit good; or else make the tree corrupt, and his fruit corrupt: for the tree is known by his fruit.**

34. **O generation of vipers, how can ye, being evil, speak good things? For out of the abundance of the heart the mouth speaketh.**

35. **A good man out of the good treasure of the heart bringeth forth good things: and an evil man out of the evil treasure bringeth forth evil things.**

Our words can give us a clue as to which nature we are plugged into and spending time communicating with, thereby allowing it to become our inspiration. *Selah.* We cannot change an evil tree into a good tree or a good tree into a corrupt tree according to verse 18. The trees (our natures) do not change. The change in verse 33 is referring to our time and connection with the tree, the source from which we are feeding and drinking to support our thought life. Our heart and soul will take on the characteristics and bear the fruit of the nature to which we are devoted (John 15:5). Our connection to the root of sin (our fallen human nature) is natural, but to be connected to the Divine Nature requires a decision by our soul to be grafted onto a different root or vine or tree (Romans 11:24). You will find an interesting parallel if you look at the orange tree. The fruit of a natural orange tree is bitter but a grafted orange tree produces good fruit. The characteristics or fruit we bear, whether bitter or sweet, can be suppressed for a small or insignificant crop or enhanced for a great harvest. Whether large or small, the identity of the fruit will come from the nature or root that fathers it. The fruits of the human nature and the Divine Nature are different, consistent, and identifiable.

Galatians 5:19-23 (NKJV)

19. Now the works of the flesh are evident, which are: adultery, fornication, uncleanness, lewdness,

20. idolatry, sorcery, hatred, contentions, jealousies, outbursts of wrath, selfish ambitions, dissensions, heresies,

21. envy, murders, drunkenness, revelries, and the like; of which I tell you beforehand, just as I also told you in time past, that those who practice <u>such things will not inherit the kingdom of God</u>.

22. But the fruit of the Spirit is love, joy, peace, longsuffering, kindness, goodness, faithfulness,

23. gentleness, self-control. Against such there is no law.

While it is possible for any soul to act well behaved and pleasant, such behavior is in spite of our fallen human nature. For that reason, without the Holy Spirit's help, good behavior tends to be superficial and temporary. If you don't believe that, just ask anyone who's been married for a few years. Everyone has bad days and bad patches; but in a good marriage, both spouses will forgive and work toward improvement. *Selah.* The fallen human nature that the Bible refers to as the "Old Man" or the "flesh" is the source of all our bad actions. Therefore, it will "not inherit the kingdom of God." For the Christian, there is coming a time when the influence of the old nature will be completely removed; but for now, we have to deal with it. This is the time of war, for gaining victory or suffering losses. Now is the time for choices that will affect our destiny for eternity.

1 John 4:1

1. Beloved, believe not every spirit, but <u>try the spirits whether they are of God</u>: because many false prophets are gone out into the world.

The question is; will our soul be faithful, true, and devoted to God? If not, we will be drawn to and seduced by God's enemies.

Luke 11:23

23. <u>He that is not with Me is against Me</u>: and he that gathereth not with Me scattereth.

James 1:13-15

13. Let no man say when he is tempted, I am tempted of God: for God cannot be tempted with evil, neither tempteth He any man:

14. But <u>every man is tempted, when he is drawn away of his own lust</u>, and enticed.

15. Then <u>when lust hath conceived, it bringeth forth sin</u>: and sin, when it is <u>finished, bringeth forth death</u>.

I like the way the Amplified Bible makes our problem with the Old Man so clear and easy to understand. Before we read this passage I want to give you a quick note on the difference between our jealousy and God's jealousy. Our jealousy is generally rooted in lust and insecurity. God is not insecure. God's love is pure and unselfish. It is far beyond the way a good father would love his teenage daughter and want to protect her. God's jealousy is not focused on what He can get, but instead it is focused on keeping us from being hurt. If God sees an unhealthy attraction develop, He is emotionally concerned (jealous) and desires to save us from unnecessary pain.

James 4:1-8 (AMP)

1. **What leads to strife (discord and feuds) and how do conflicts (quarrels and fightings) originate among you? Do they not arise from your sensual desires that are ever warring in your bodily members?**

2. **You are jealous and covet what others have and your desires go unfulfilled; so you become murderers. To hate is to murder as far as your hearts are concerned. You burn with envy and anger and are not able to obtain the gratification, the contentment, and the happiness that you seek, so you fight and war. You do not have, because you do not ask.**

3. **Or you do ask God for them and yet fail to receive, because you ask with wrong purpose and evil, selfish motives. Your intention is when you get what you desire to spend it in sensual pleasures.**

4. **You are like <u>unfaithful wives having illicit love affairs with the world and breaking your marriage vow to God</u>! Do you not know that being the world's friend is being God's enemy? So whoever chooses to be a friend of the world takes his stand as an enemy of God.**

5. **Or do you suppose that the Scripture is speaking to no purpose that says, <u>the Spirit whom He has caused to dwell in</u>**

us yearns over us and He yearns for the Spirit to be welcome with a jealous love?

6. But He gives us more and more grace (power of the Holy Spirit, to meet this evil tendency and all others fully). That is why He says, God sets Himself against the proud and haughty, but gives grace continually to the lowly (those who are humble enough to receive it).

7. So be subject to God. Resist the Devil. Stand firm against him, and he will flee from you.

8. Come close to God and He will come close to you. Recognize that you are sinners, get your soiled hands clean; realize that you have been disloyal wavering individuals with divided interests, and purify your hearts of your spiritual adultery.

Christians are Christ-ones – children of the Father, partners with Jesus Christ and in covenant union with the Holy Spirit. Metaphorically speaking, a Christian soul becomes the bride of the Holy Spirit of Jesus Christ. The problem is that our background is not pure, so we struggle to be faithful. Our fallen nature is an enemy to God and dangerous to us, because it is a seductive door that leads to corruption and destruction. For our soul to be faithful to God, it must resist flirting with the old nature's thought patterns.

1 Corinthians 10:13-14

13. There hath no temptation taken you but such as is common to man: but God is faithful, who will not suffer you to be tempted above that ye are able; but will with the temptation also make a way to escape, that ye may be able to bear it.

14. Wherefore, my dearly beloved, flee from idolatry.

God said to resist the Devil and deny our sinful self, but He never said to resist temptation. God dose not want us to fight with temptation because we will probably loose. Instead of entangling ourselves in a fight with temptation, God wants us to turn and walk away. Matter of fact, don't just walk, RUN! God said to flee from temptation (1 Timothy 6:11, 2 Timothy 2:22, 1 Corinthians 6:18). Sometimes the way to escape temptation is obvious. However, how do we escape our self, the source of most of our temptations? How can we become dead to self and yet live? Being born again is like a marriage covenant between our soul and the Holy Spirit. Spiritually speaking, the Holy Spirit becomes our husband, soul mate, and new partner. Because of that union, we become part of the family of God. There is no longer the phrase "until death do us part," because the Holy Spirit has provided eternal life. The death applies to our soul's old vile husband, the human nature, which died in the Garden of Eden. Even though it died, it's still actively spreading decay and corruption. I don't know if Paul realized it or not, but I believe the Holy Spirit had these things in mind as a secondary application when He inspired Paul to record the following:

Romans 7:1-4

1. Know ye not, brethren, (for I speak to them that know the law,) how that the law hath dominion over a man as long as he liveth?

2. For the woman which hath an husband is bound by the law to her husband so long as he liveth; but <u>if the husband be dead, she is loosed</u> from the law of her husband.

3. So then if, while her husband liveth, she be married to another man, she shall be called an adulteress: but <u>if her husband be dead, she is free</u> from that law; so that she is no adulteress, though she be married to another man.

4. **Wherefore, my brethren, ye also are become dead to the law by the body of Christ; that <u>ye should be married to another</u>, even to Him who is raised from the dead, <u>that we should bring forth fruit unto God.</u>**

Because of the Holy Spirit, we are given eternal life and a new identity. I am a new creation in Christ. I need to crucify and bury the rotting corpse of the "Old Man" of death and corruption. I need to separate and quarantine him away from me so he doesn't infect me. The problem is that I can't actually bury him yet. I can't remove him from my house (my body). Although with the help of the Holy Spirit, I can prepare a place for this leprous rotting trash. That is where my personal cross comes in. The Apostle Paul was quite familiar with the crosses of Roman crucifixions. Once a man is put on a cross, he has no control. He may yell and scream for a while, but is powerless to take action to change his crucifixion and eventual burial. Now is the time we will either experience nature-crucifixion or soul-contamination. Later, there will be a burial ceremony at Judgment Day. *Selah.* However you want to picture it, a restraining confinement has to be prepared for the Old Man. The problem is the Old Man is a spirit. Therefore, the nails that bind him must be spiritually powerful and remain active in order to continue to restrain and contain him. The following three "nails" are needed to keep the Old Man on the cross.

<u>Nail 1</u>: Dedicate the body. (This is applied to our physical environment and activities)

We need to clean house inside and outside, purifying our environment. Remove all the Old Man's trash from our living area. This is personal. I need not be concerned about anyone else's trash. Commit your body to Jesus Christ in prayer and ask Him for strength, daily wisdom, and direction. It is more powerful to pray these things out loud and repeat them often. As you hear yourself consistently repeating these declarations, by God's grace, your thoughts will focus and your faith will grow. This will influence the direction of your actions and the quality of your environment.

Romans 12:1-2

1. **I beseech you therefore, brethren, by the mercies of God, that ye <u>present your bodies a living sacrifice</u>, holy, acceptable unto God, which is your reasonable service.**

2. **And <u>be not conformed to this world</u>: but be ye <u>transformed by the renewing of your mind</u>, that ye may prove what is that good, and acceptable, and perfect, will of God.**

<u>Nail 2</u>: Purify the mind. (This is applied to our soul, which is the decision maker)

We need a new mindset. Start thinking of yourself as a new person, a child of God. Realize that the old person is dead; so get rid of his corrupt stinking thinking. Declare aloud that you have the mind of Christ. Get to know the mind of Christ by meditating on the Word of God.

Philippians 2:3-7

3. **<u>Let nothing be done through strife or vainglory; but in lowliness of mind let each esteem other better than themselves.</u>**

4. **Look not every man on his own things, but every man also on the things of others.**

5. **<u>Let this mind be in you, which was also in Christ Jesus:</u>**

6. **Who, being in the form of God, thought it not robbery to be equal with God:**

7. **But made Himself of no reputation, and took upon Him the form of a servant, and was made in the likeness of men:**

Humbly pray for illumination, wisdom, and direction.

Philippians 4:6-7

6. **Be careful for nothing; but in every thing by prayer and supplication with <u>thanksgiving</u> let your requests be made known unto God.**

7. **And the <u>peace of God</u>, which passeth all understanding, shall <u>keep your hearts and minds</u> through Christ Jesus.**

2 Timothy 1:7

7. **<u>For God hath not given us the spirit of fear</u>; but of power, and of love, and of a <u>sound mind</u>.**

Reject thoughts of fear and anxiety by claiming faith in God's love for you and God's power to conquer evil. God knows how to turn bad things around and use them for our good (Romans 8:28). In the middle of conflict God will direct us to victory through His Word and by His Spirit. If gilt is a problem, realize the Old Man is always guilty, but we are not the Old Man. We are a new creation. *Selah.* We can choose to improve our life and thoughts by considering what the Bible says to think on.

Philippians 4:8

8. **Finally, brethren, whatsoever things are <u>true</u>, whatsoever things are <u>honest</u>, whatsoever things are <u>just</u>, whatsoever things are <u>pure</u>, whatsoever things are <u>lovely</u>, whatsoever things are of <u>good report</u>; if there be any <u>virtue</u>, and if there be any <u>praise</u>, <u>think on these things</u>.**

<u>Nail 3</u>: Fellowship. (This is applied to our heart, which is our communication connection)

Pray and participate in God's Word. Spend time reading, learning, meditating, and talking to God about the principles in His Bible. Regardless of how we feel, we should begin each day by personalizing the Bible. For instance declare Psalm 118:24 – **This is the day the Lord has made.** *"I"* **will rejoice and be glad in it.** Then add a phrase like, because something good is going to happen to me today in Jesus' name, thank you, Jesus. As God blesses you, allow God to bless others through you. Reach out to others and get involved with your local church.

Hebrews 10:25

25. Not forsaking the assembling of ourselves together, as the manner of some is; but exhorting one another: and so much the more, as ye see the day approaching.

We need fellowship with other Christians. We are all broken people. A church that focuses on the Holy Bible is a place for us broken people to participate in the restoration of others as well as ourselves. *Selah.* If I am struggling with repentance from sin, it may be best to reverse the order and start with the foundational third nail. Make sure this nail is secure by dedicating myself to a Bible based church. Read the Bible on a daily basis and recognize its power. Start with prayer, focus on God, and spend time in God's Word and with God's people. Then we will be able to identify and connect to the Divine Nature for help. Dedication is a personal thing. Nobody can do it for me, not even God. God has given us a freewill to choose his ways or not. Only I can dedicate myself to the Divine Nature and His Word. If I do, then God will empower me for true victory.

2 Peter 1:3-4

3. According as His Divine power hath given unto us all things that pertain unto life and godliness, through the knowledge of Him that hath called us to glory and virtue:

4. **Whereby are given unto us exceeding great and <u>precious promises</u>: that <u>by these ye might be partakers of the Divine Nature</u>, having escaped the corruption that is in the world through lust.**

The key to connecting to the Divine Nature is learning God's Word, so that we can recognize God's voice, know God's ways, and claim our new identity. If you have received the Holy Ghost, you are a new creation, a child of God. Do not let the old identity of the past dictate your future.

Romans 6:13, 16-22

13. **Neither yield ye your members as instruments of unrighteousness unto sin: but yield yourselves unto God, as those that are alive from the dead, and your members as instruments of righteousness unto God.**

16. **Know ye not, that to whom ye yield yourselves servants to obey, <u>his servants ye are to whom ye obey</u>; whether of sin unto death, or of obedience unto righteousness?**

17. **But God be thanked, that ye were the servants of sin, but ye have obeyed from the heart that form of doctrine which was delivered you.**

18. **Being then made free from sin, ye became the servants of righteousness.**

19. **I speak after the manner of men because of the infirmity of your flesh: for as ye have yielded your members servants to uncleanness and to iniquity unto iniquity; <u>even so now</u> yield your members servants to righteousness unto holiness.**

20. **For when ye were the servants of sin, ye were free from righteousness.**

21. **What fruit had ye then in those things whereof ye are now ashamed? For the end of those things is death.**

22. **But now being made free from sin, and become servants to God, ye have your fruit unto holiness, and the end everlasting life.**

All the shameful fruit of the Old Man, ends up in Heaven's graveyard which is called the Lake of Fire. All shame as well as our old identity is removed from the children of God.

Romans 8:1

1. **There is therefore now no condemnation to them which are in Christ Jesus, who walk not after the flesh, but after the Spirit.**

It takes all three spiritual spikes to hold the Old Man on the cross and liberate our lifestyle. The less you feed or listen to the Old Man, the less noise he will make. God has a great plan for your life. It starts with knowing His precious promises.

Joshua 1:8

8. **This book of the law shall not depart out of thy mouth; but thou shalt meditate therein day and night, that thou mayest observe to do according to all that is written therein: for then thou shalt make thy way prosperous, and then thou shalt have good success.**

Hebrews 12:1-2

1. **Wherefore seeing we also are compassed about with so great a cloud of witnesses, let us lay aside every weight, and the sin which doth so easily beset us, and let us run with patience the race that is set before us,**

2. **Looking unto Jesus the author and finisher of our faith; who for the joy that was set before Him endured the cross, despising**

the shame, and is set down at the right hand of the throne of God.

If we crucify our selfish corrupting nature by dedicating our bodies, purifying our minds, fellowshipping with God and His people, then blessings will overtake us.

Psalm 1:1-3

1. Blessed is the man that <u>walketh</u> not in the counsel of the ungodly, nor <u>standeth</u> in the way of sinners, nor <u>sitteth</u> in the seat of the scornful.

2. But his delight is in the law of the Lord; and in His law doth he <u>meditate day and night</u>.

3. And he shall be <u>like a tree</u> planted by the rivers of water, that bringeth forth <u>his fruit in his season</u>; his leaf also shall not wither; and whatsoever he doeth shall prosper.

Deuteronomy 28:3

3. Blessed shalt thou be in the city, and blessed shalt thou be in the field.

Deuteronomy 28:2

2. And all these blessings shall come on thee, and <u>overtake</u> thee, <u>if</u> thou shalt hearken unto the voice of the LORD thy God.

CHAPTER 15

WALKING IN THE LIGHT

Colossians 3:8-10

8. But now ye also put off all these; anger, wrath, malice, blasphemy, filthy communication out of your mouth.

9. Lie not one to another, seeing that ye have <u>put off the Old Man with his deeds;</u>

10. And have <u>put on the New Man, which is renewed in knowledge</u> after the image of Him that created him:

Putting off the Old Man (old nature's identity) and putting on the New Man (new nature's identity) is a choice done by faith. In the military the clothing identifies the person wearing them. In a similar way, the Old Man and the New Man are like spiritual clothing that identifies us. We are naturally born into the family of Adam and inherit his covering of sin and corruption. When we are born-again into God's family we inherit a robe of righteousness because of what Jesus has done for us.

Isaiah 61:10

10. I will greatly rejoice in the LORD, my soul shall be joyful in my God; for He hath clothed me with the garments of salvation, He hath covered me with the robe of righteousness, as a bridegroom decketh himself with ornaments, and as a bride adorneth herself with her jewels.

God has provided a way for us to take off the carnal identity of this world, which the Bible refers to as filthy rags (grave clothes). In exchange I can put on the shining armor of God, reflecting my new identity as an eternal child of God. That is how we become a powerful representative of Christ, and God's kingdom is advanced. However, breaking the addiction and association to

313

the Old Man is much easier said than done. To do so we need to crush the walls around our heart, which are built of anger, rebellion, selfishness and pride. We do this by letting God's love and light in. We start this process by trusting God and opining our heart up to correction, which leads to verbal confession. True confession is not making excuses. True confession comes only after we see the reality of our shortcomings, are grieved by our sins, and desire is to turn away from them. Biblical confession is not just admitting a mistake or bad attitude. Life-changing confession involves a desire to repent, or at least a willingness to let God start the process in you. The mindset of repentance means that we desire to turn from the deeds of our old nature and be conformed to the image of Christ. Our confession may involve other people.

Matthew 5:23-24

23. Therefore if thou bring thy gift to the altar, and there rememberest that thy brother hath ought against thee;

24. Leave there thy gift before the altar, and go thy way; first be reconciled to thy brother, and then come and offer thy gift.

The confession should be focused in the realm of the violation. If it's between you and another person, go to that person if possible. If it's a group, go to them and acknowledge the change of heart. If the violation is just between you and God, spend enough time with God to see yourself forgiven. Then move on with a clean conscience. *Selah.* After we reject the Old Man (fallen nature) from connecting to and enslaving our soul through confession and active repentance, we need to put on the New Man (the new identity). There are basically two steps to putting on this new identity.

Step 1: Activate faith. See yourself in God and God in you. Know that the true reflection of God is Christ.

Step 2: Surrender all your personal rights and release God's Spirit to flow through you and from you. It's a cleansing force that will bear refreshing fruit.

1 Peter 1:22

22. **Seeing <u>ye have purified your souls in obeying the truth through the Spirit unto unfeigned love</u> of the brethren, see that ye love one another with a pure heart fervently:**

Philippians 2:13

13. **For <u>it is God which worketh in you</u> both <u>to will</u> and <u>to do</u> of His good pleasure.**

The process is simple, but not easy, because we so often want to hang on to some of our old identity and the rights we want to exercise for ourselves. Phrases like I have a right to feel this way, I have a right to that, or you have no right to do that to me, come from the Old Man. It's a struggle to fight for my personal rights and walk in love at the same time. Jesus continually acknowledged the truth with love, but typically avoided getting involved in self-defense.

Mark 15:2-5

2. **And Pilate <u>asked Him</u>, art Thou the king of the Jews? And <u>He answering said unto him</u>, thou sayest it.**

3. **And the chief priests <u>accused Him of many things: but He answered nothing</u>.**

4. **And Pilate asked Him again, saying, answerest Thou nothing? Behold how many things they witness against Thee.**

5. **But Jesus yet answered nothing; so that Pilate marvelled.**

Allow God to be your defender as you defend others (because of love for them). We do not need to become sidetracked answering our critics or responding to the many accusations authored by Satan. However, there are times when we need to explain ourselves in order to clear up confusion or remove ourselves from an unnecessary abuse (Matthew 5:9-16). The Holy Spirit will make these exceptions clear. He will empower us with peace regarding the action we need to take, so that we can maintain an attitude of love. Our focus needs to be on love not self-defense. Maintaining love for God and His creation is our highest priority. Creation has been damaged by sin. The restoration process has begun because of love. Remember one of God's highest creations are people.

Matthew 22:35-40

35. **Then one of them, which was a lawyer, asked Him a question, tempting Him, and saying,**

36. **Master, which is the great commandment in the law?**

37. **Jesus said unto him, thou shalt <u>love the Lord thy God</u> with all thy heart, and with all thy soul, and with all thy mind.**

38. **This is the first and great commandment.**

39. **And the second is like unto it, thou shalt <u>love thy neighbour</u> as thyself.**

40. **<u>On these two commandments hang all</u> the law and the prophets.**

How important is love?

1 Corinthians 13:1-3

1. **Though I speak with the tongues of men and of angels, and have not charity, I am become as sounding brass, or a tinkling cymbal.**

2. **And though I have the gift of prophecy, and understand all mysteries, and all knowledge; and though I have all faith, so that I could remove mountains, and have not charity, I am nothing.**

3. **And though I bestow all my goods to feed the poor, and though I give my body to be burned, and have not charity, it profiteth me nothing.**

How do I show love?

1 Corinthians 13:4-6

4. **Charity suffereth long, and is kind; charity envieth not; charity vaunteth not itself, is not puffed up,**

5. **Doth not behave itself unseemly, seeketh not her own, is not easily provoked, thinketh no evil;**

6. **Rejoiceth not in iniquity, but rejoiceth in the truth;**

The word "charity" here is a selfless giving love. Out of the four Greek words for love, the one used here for this special form of love is "Agape." It is the highest form of love. It is a selfless sacrificial love, God's love. Love is our key indicator that the Holy Spirit of God is in control of us and that we have His identity. Love is the main fruit of the Holy Spirit. Without love, the gifts of the Spirit become contaminated and will not operate correctly. Love is like the fuel that propels a car to its destination. If we are low on fuel, we have a choice – either fill up or fall short. Even if I have the most beautiful, powerful, expensive auto of my dreams, it will leave me stranded and be of little use if I don't continually refuel. God gives us the spiritual gifts and talents (our vehicle). However, it is up to us to keep our vehicle clean and refueled for service. *Selah.*

1 John 2:9-11

[9] **He that saith he is in the light, and hateth his brother, is in darkness even until now.**

[10] **He that loveth his brother abideth in the light, and there is none occasion of stumbling in him.**

[11] **But he that hateth his brother is in darkness, and walketh in darkness, and knoweth not whither he goeth, because that darkness hath blinded his eyes.**

If we dam up the flow of the river of love, we end up in a flood of darkness. Things will get out of perspective, and our priorities will change. Without love, we cannot walk in the light of God or be in harmony with the Holy Spirit. As a Christian I can be out of fellowship with God but I won't loose my salvation because the Bible says the Spirit of God will never leave me.

Hebrews 13:5

[5] **Let your conversation be without covetousness; and be content with such things as ye have: for He hath said, I will never leave thee, nor forsake thee.**

The Spirit of God will always be within me because Jesus gave me His Spirit as a free gift when I asked Him to save me.

1 John 4:13-17

[13] **Hereby know we that we dwell in Him, and He in us, because He hath given us of His Spirit.**

^{14.} **And we have seen and do testify that the Father sent the Son to be the Saviour of the world.**

^{15.} **<u>Whosoever shall confess</u> that Jesus is the Son of God, <u>God dwelleth in him, and he in God</u>.**

^{16.} **And we have known and <u>believed the love that God hath to us. God is love</u>; and He that dwelleth in love dwelleth in God, and God in him.**

^{17.} **Herein is our love made perfect, that we may have boldness in the day of judgment: because <u>as He is, so are we in this world</u>.**

God doesn't love us because of our good works. God loves us because of who He is. God is love and much more. Jesus came to Earth to demonstrate God's love by suffering for us, then freely giving us eternal life in Heaven. Now He has commissioned us to pick up where He left off.

2 Corinthians 5:19-20

^{19.} **To wit, that <u>God was in Christ, reconciling the world unto Himself, not imputing their trespasses unto them</u>; and hath committed unto us the word of reconciliation.**

^{20.} **Now then we <u>are ambassadors for Christ</u>, as though God did beseech you by us: we pray you in Christ's stead, be ye reconciled to God.**

I could sum up the whole Bible and God's plan for my life in one word. That word is a commandment I must always follow. You guessed it. That all-important word is LOVE.

1 John 4:21

^{21.} **And this <u>commandment</u> have we from Him, that he who loveth God <u>love</u> his brother also.**

We are not just to love our brethren, family, and friends. We are instructed to love everyone.

Luke 6:31-33

^{31.} **And as ye would that men should do to you, do ye also to them likewise.**

^{32.} **For if <u>ye love them which love you, what thank have ye? For sinners also love those that love them.</u>**

^{33.} **And if ye do good to them which do good to you, what thank have ye? For sinners also do even the same.**

Matthew 5:43-44

^{43.} **Ye have heard that it hath been said, thou shalt love thy neighbour, and hate thine enemy.**

^{44.} **But I say unto you, <u>love your enemies</u>, bless them that curse you, do good to them that hate you, and <u>pray for them</u> which despitefully use you, and persecute you;**

Persecution was a reality to the early Christians, yet they were instructed to love and pray for their persecutors. I believe "Andronicus and Junia" were lovingly praying for their persecutors. They were Christians who stood out and were noted among the Apostles. As a matter of fact, their close relative was one of the worst persecutors of the early church. His name was Saul.

Romans 16:7

7. **Salute Andronicus and Junia, my kinsmen, and my fellow prisoners, who are of <u>note among the apostles</u>, who also were <u>in Christ before me</u>.**

Do you think Andronicus and Junia believed that God answered their prayers when Saul was converted on the road to Damascus and became the Apostle Paul? That is the kind of love we need to have. A desire to see our worst enemy delivered from Satan's grasp and converted to Christ. That is being "more than conquerors" of our enemy (Romans 8:37). Rather than destroying our enemy, our enemy becomes our greatest ally. This is far more beneficial to both parties. We are to love, hope, and pray that everyone's soul will be set free from Satan and his deceptions, even our worst enemies. *Selah.* If God opens the door for it, love sometimes needs to correct, discipline, or even rebuke in order to avoid further danger or destruction. This is tough love, which when applied with the right spirit is true love. If we are the ones being disciplined or corrected, we need to respond in love, even if the punishment seems misguided. Tough love may seem harsh to the casual observer. God was demonstrating a lot of tough love in the Old Testament as He dealt with satanic influences and actions. God was preparing and preserving a nation (Genesis 22:18, Genesis 28:14-17) that would provide all mankind with the Holy Bible and the Savior of the world. This resulted in ground zero in the spiritual war of the ages. Satan did everything he could to infiltrate, defile and destroy the people and bloodline of Jesus. Whether it is removing bad influences or reproving bad actions, the motivation of the disciplinary actions of love are to preserve and promote good.

Proverbs 3:11-12

11. My son, despise not the chastening of the Lord; neither be weary of his correction:

12. For whom the Lord <u>loveth He correcteth</u>; even as a father the son in whom he delighteth.

If God is correcting us, we must consider it a learning experience. When we learn the lesson, we will develop spiritually and enjoy a blessing.

Proverbs 1:23

23. <u>Turn</u> you at My reproof: behold, I will pour out <u>My Spirit</u> unto you, I will <u>make known</u> My Words unto you.

After Jesus arose from the dead, He appeared to Saul. Saul was a zealous supporter of his religion, but his zeal was misguided. Saul was spiritually blind and living in deception.

Acts 9:1-2

1. And Saul, yet breathing out threatenings and slaughter against the disciples of the Lord, went unto the high priest,

2. And desired of him letters to Damascus to the synagogues, that if he found any of this way, whether they were men or women, he might bring them bound unto Jerusalem.

Saul was fighting against his Redeemer, when suddenly the "Light of the World" (Jesus) appeared to him. It temporarily blinded him physically, but opened his eyes spiritually.

Acts 9:3-9

3. And as he journeyed, he came near Damascus: and suddenly there shined round about him a light from Heaven:

4. And he fell to the earth, and heard a voice saying unto him, Saul, Saul, why persecutest thou Me?

5. And he said, who art thou, Lord? And the Lord said, I am Jesus whom thou persecutest: it is hard for thee to kick against the pricks.

6. And he trembling and astonished said, Lord, what wilt thou have me to do? And the Lord said unto him, arise, and go into the city, and it shall be told thee what thou must do.

7. And the men which journeyed with him stood speechless, <u>hearing a voice, but seeing no man</u>.

8. And Saul arose from the earth; and when his eyes were opened, he saw no man: but they led him by the hand, and brought him into Damascus.

9. And he was three days without sight, and neither did eat nor drink.

At that time, Saul gave his life to Christ and received a new identity. He was no longer a lost soul. Saul was born again and came to be known as the Apostle Paul, a man of God. His new identity came with new conflicts. It was not easy. Symbolically speaking, Paul came out of the bondage of Egypt and found himself in the wilderness. In the wilderness the cares of this world can really seem to close in on you. The wilderness is a place between Egypt (the satanic world system) and the Promised Land (a place of victory, leading to peace). The wilderness is a struggle. Paul left Egypt (his old identity as Saul). Now as Paul, he was seeing God's leading and provision and was destined for Heaven, but he wanted more. He wasn't satisfied with just being a child of God. He wanted to develop and grow in grace. He didn't want to stop in the wilderness or go back to

Egypt (metaphorically speaking). His desire was to live in the Promised Land. *Selah.* Writing down our goals helps us to achieve them. Paul recorded in wiring his goal was to occupy the Promised Land.

Philippians 3:12-14

12. Not as though I had already attained, either were already perfect: but I follow after, if that I may apprehend that for which also I am apprehended of Christ Jesus.

13. Brethren, <u>I count not myself to have apprehended: but this one thing I do, forgetting those things which are behind, and reaching forth unto those things which are before,</u>

14. <u>I press toward the mark for the prize of the high calling</u> of God in Christ Jesus.

Just like the early Israelites, many Christians turn back after they first see the Promised Land (their "high calling"). They see the obstacles and consider the fruit unattainable, or they attempt to attain the Promised Land by their own willpower instead of submitting to God's Word and depending on God's help. The problem most Christians face is that every day is a new day, and we tend to wake up in the wilderness. Every day we need to decide to cross over to the Promised Land. In fact, every hour can be a challenge to remain in this special place and not be lured back to the stresses and selfishness of the wilderness.

Hebrews 4:9-11

9. There remaineth therefore a rest to the people of God.

10. For <u>he that is entered into his rest, he also hath ceased from his own works,</u> as God did from His.

^{11.} **Let us labour therefore to enter into that rest, lest any man fall after the same example of unbelief.**

Paul was ready to rest from his own personal agenda. He chose to take his position in the armed forces of God and fight the good fight of faith.

2 Timothy 2:4

^{4.} **No man that warreth <u>entangleth himself with the affairs of this life</u>; that he may please Him who hath chosen him to <u>be a soldier</u>.**

Paul had received the key to the Promised Land of victory over the circumstances. The key was in his next new identity, being establish "in Christ" instead of in Paul. This new identity has a different perspective, a different value system regarding the temporary and the eternal things in this life. The "in Christ" identity has a different mindset. It sets us free from the self-absorbed identity and attitude of our old nature. By visualizing what it means to be "in Christ" and then acting as an extension of Him, we serve as His representatives in this place and moment of time. Spirit-filled Christians are able to maintain an attitude of love, peace, and joy, in spite of any negative circumstances (Acts 16:9-30). They may not be happy because happiness is based on what is happening. Happiness is not appropriate if it is a time to mourn (John 11:33-35).

Romans 12:15

^{15.} **Rejoice with them that do rejoice, and weep with them that weep.**

Joy is different than happiness because joy is based on knowing God holds my future and He loves me and can work all things out for my good. Spirit-filled Christians have learned the Joy of the Lord is their strength.

Nehemiah 8:10b

10b. ...for this day is holy unto our Lord: neither be ye sorry; for <u>the joy of the LORD is your strength</u>.

A Spirit-filled Christian's words and actions tend to be wise, yet humble. This is not achieved casually or naturally. The transformation happens by meditation and recognition of what it means to be conformed to the image of Christ. *Selah.*

Romans 13:12-14

12. The night is far spent, the day is at hand: let us therefore cast off the works of darkness, and let us <u>put on the armour of light</u>.

13. Let us walk honestly, as in the day; not in rioting and drunkenness, not in chambering and wantonness, not in strife and envying.

14. <u>But put ye on the Lord Jesus Christ</u>, and make not provision for the flesh, to fulfil the lusts thereof.

Like many people, I usually get dressed in the morning. It has become a routine, but that is all right. Routines can be good. There is another good routine that I try to be consistent about – getting dressed spiritually. As part of my morning prayers, I put on the armor of light. There are some variations in the wording but I follow the same basic pattern for the process. I usually begin at my head by praying for the helmet of salvation so that I will have the mind of Christ to think His thoughts, see through His eyes and hear His instructions. Then I put on the breastplate of righteousness so that I will reflect God's ways. This involves asking God to cleanse my heart from all anger and unrighteousness and fill it with His love. I also ask God to protect my wife's heart from the evil one as well as mine. Then I fasten the belt of truth around my waist so that I can see clearly the path that I should take today. I pray for the light of God's truth and wisdom to surround me and dispel all darkness and deception. Next I pray for God to continually apply the gospel of peace to my feet, so that I can walk in peace, love, and joy, and all the fruit of the Spirit. Then I ask God to activate the force-field of faith around me, my family, friends, possessions, and whatever I put my hands to today. I pray the surrounding hedge of faith (Job 1:10) would quench all the fiery darts of Satan. I pray for aggressive faith (Matthew 11:12) that will tear down satanic strongholds. I also pray that God would sharpen the sword of the Spirit in my mouth so that I will only speak God's Word and God's will. Then the "I" becomes "we" (in Christ). We ask God's angels to go with us, before us, and after us to minister on our behalf and give us favor with mankind. My prayer, desire and expectations are to see the Holy Spirit manifest His presents and expand Jesus' kingdom. My hope is to be a part of the next Great Awakening in spite of my flaws. Therefore I need to be supernaturally equipped for war. I need to be faithfully learning from the Father how to handle the sword of truth.

Ephesians 6:11-18

11. **Put on the whole armour of God, that ye may be able to stand against the wiles of the Devil.**

12. **For we wrestle not against flesh and blood, but against principalities, against powers, against the rulers of the darkness of this world, against spiritual wickedness in high places.**

13. **Wherefore take unto you the whole armour of God, that ye may be able to withstand in the evil day, and having done all, to stand.**

^{14.} **Stand therefore, having your loins girt about with truth, and having on the breastplate of righteousness;**

^{15.} **And your feet shod with the preparation of the gospel of peace;**

^{16.} **Above all, taking the shield of faith, wherewith ye shall <u>be able to quench all the fiery darts of the wicked.</u>**

^{17.} **And take the helmet of salvation, and the s<u>word</u> of the Spirit, which is the <u>Word</u> of God:**

^{18.} **Praying always with all <u>prayer and supplication in the Spirit</u>, and watching thereunto with all perseverance and supplication for all saints;**

There is a spiritual battle going on all around us. This war affects us whether we realize it or not. It is the conflict between good and evil. The kingdom of God is in opposition to the realm of darkness. On one side there is love and truth, on the other, deception and corruption. Have you noticed the attempts in the United States to remove all positive public references to God and His help and influence in our history? The motivation for this antichrist activity obviously comes from Satan working through the corrupt human nature. As Christians, we are called to be God's ambassadors to the souls of this world. We are to love them and open the doors of freedom to them. Many of them are enslaved and deceived by the power of darkness. It doesn't mater how evil a soul may act; souls (people or persons) are not our enemy. They are the prizes. We are ambassadors of God to express His love and truth to every individual, without exception. We are also Christ's soldiers fighting against corruption. We are to fight against corruption and depravity, whether it comes from the fallen nature or the fallen angels. Our weapons are rooted in the attitude of love and the proclamation of truth. To set a soul free we have to deal with their heart. There is a constant battle for the heart. The heart is the key to the redemption of a person and revival of a nation. The heart is transformed by the seed of God's Word taking root in it. It is our job to plant the seeds of truth and water them with love. Not every seed will bear fruit but do not be discouraged. We are not responsible for other people's good or bad decisions. Although, we are called to sow good seed and pray for a harvest. *Selah.* Jesus told a parable in Matthew 13:3-8 and later explained it to His disciples. In this parable the different types of ground are the different conditions of the hearts of mankind. God's Word is the good seed. The parable reveals the enemy's tactics. Satan uses a variety of methods to prevent God's Word from bearing fruit in the hearts of mankind.

Matthew 13:18-23

18. Hear ye therefore the parable of the sower.

19. When any one heareth the Word of the kingdom, and <u>understandeth it not, then cometh the wicked one, and catcheth away that which was sown in his heart</u>. This is he which received seed by the way side

20. But he that received the seed into stony places, the same is he that heareth the Word, and anon with joy receiveth it;

21. Yet <u>hath he not root in himself</u>, but dureth for a while: for when <u>tribulation or persecution</u> ariseth because of the Word, by and by he is offended.

22. He also that received seed among the thorns is he that heareth the Word; and the <u>care of this world</u>, and the

deceitfulness of riches, choke the Word, and he becometh unfruitful.

23. **But he that received seed into the <u>good ground is he that heareth the Word, and understandeth it; which also beareth fruit</u>, and bringeth forth, some a hundredfold, some sixty, some thirty.**

In this parable, the first three types of ground represent the hearts of unsaved souls. Some of them may look religious for a while, but the seed never took root or became a part of them. Outwardly, they were just going through the motions until it either wasn't popular anymore or they were lured away by the stresses of life and worldly values. The "good ground" is the one where the seed took root and represents the redeemed. Our relationship to the seed of God's Word will make a big difference at the end. *Selah*. This parable can also be applied to a Christians' spiritual growth and the obstacles to bearing fruit. As a Christian, if we don't understand or misunderstand the Bible we will lack a good spiritual foundation. Without a good foundation we will not have the ability to resist opposition when it confronts us. If our dedication to learn the Bible becomes chocked out by circumstances and distractions we will become vulnerable to the enemy. If we yield to the corrupt old nature (Satan's spy) within us, we will become a POW (prisoner of war). Surrendering to corruption limits our ability to fight or resist corruption. To be free, we need to repent and apply God's helmet of salvation so that we can start accessing the mind, power, and Spirit of Christ. Then we need to take large doses of the Word of God to cleanse our heart (Ephesians 5:26).

Ephesians 4:17-32

17. This I say therefore, and testify in the Lord, that ye henceforth walk not as other Gentiles walk, in the vanity of their mind,

18. Having the understanding darkened, being alienated from the life of God through the ignorance that is in them, because of the blindness of their heart:

19. Who being past feeling have given themselves over unto lasciviousness, to work all uncleanness with greediness.

20. But ye have not so learned Christ;

21. If so be that ye have heard Him, and have been taught by Him, as the truth is in Jesus:

22. That ye put off concerning the former conversation the Old Man, which is corrupt according to the deceitful lusts;

23. And be renewed in the spirit of your mind;

24. And that ye put on the New Man, which after God is created in righteousness and true holiness.

25. Wherefore putting away lying, speak every man truth with his neighbour: for we are members one of another.

26. Be ye angry, and sin not: let not the sun go down upon your wrath:

27. Neither give place to the Devil.

28. Let him that stole steal no more: but rather let him labour, working with his hands the thing which is good, that he may have to give to him that needeth.

29. <u>Let no corrupt communication proceed out of your mouth, but that which is good to the use of edifying, that it may minister grace unto the hearers.</u>

30. And <u>grieve not the Holy Spirit of God</u>, whereby ye are sealed unto the day of redemption.

31. <u>Let all bitterness, and wrath, and anger, and clamour, and evil speaking, be put away from you</u>, with all malice:

32. And <u>be ye kind one to another, tenderhearted, forgiving one another, even as God for Christ's sake hath forgiven you</u>.

In this culture war, there are heroes and casualties, battles won and battles lost; but in the end, Satan loses, Christians win. In fact, Jesus already won the war by laying down His mortal life on the cross, resulting in His victorious resurrection. Now what we need to learn is how to apply Christ's ultimate victory to our current battle. *Selah.* Paul was a hero of the faith, but he did not start out that way. Paul experienced three stages in his spiritual journey. First, he realized he was lost and fighting for the wrong side. Second he became born-again by receiving the Divine Nature, and he changed his name from Saul to Paul. In the third stage, he considered the corrupted human nature powerless over him, dedicated himself to the Divine Nature, and changed his identity and authority from Paul to "in Christ."

Colossians 3:2-3

2. <u>Set your affection on things above, not on things on the Earth</u>.

3. For ye are dead, and your life is hid with Christ in God.

To consider yourself dead means you give up your right to complain, be angry, or refuse to love. You give up your right to be in charge of your fame, fortune, and lifestyle. You trust God with all these areas of your life.

Galatians 2:20

20. **I am crucified with Christ: nevertheless I live; yet <u>not I, but Christ</u> liveth in me: and the life which I now live in the flesh I live by the faith of the Son of God, who loved me, and gave Himself for me.**

Paul's new identity was to be a powerful instrument to reveal and release God's love. In doing so, he was in perfect harmony with God's power. He humbly became not Saul, not Paul, but Christ's voice, hands, feet, and actions.

Matthew 16:24-25

24. **Then said Jesus unto his disciples, if any man will come after Me, let him <u>deny himself</u>, and take up his cross, and follow Me.**

25. **For whosoever will save his life shall lose it: and whosoever will lose his life for My sake shall find it.**

Things done in the flesh for personal glory will fade away in time, but the things God does through you will become incredibly rewarding. Whoever puts themselves first will be considered last or least in the kingdom of God. On the other hand, whoever puts God first and themselves last will be the first or the greatest in God's kingdom. Before we focus on others, we should evaluate our priorities. In Luke 6:41-42 and Matthew 7:3-5, Jesus said, "First cast the beam out of thine own eye; and then shalt thou see clearly" to help others; more specifically to allow God to shine through you (Matthew 6:22-24, Ephesians 5:8-11, Matthew 5:14-16). The beam in the eye represents seeing things through the filthy, distorted, dark glasses of the old nature.

CHAPTER 15

Deep Foundations

Luke 14:28-30, 33

28. For which of you, intending to build a tower, sitteth not down first, and counteth the cost, whether he have sufficient to finish it?

29. Lest haply, after he hath laid the foundation, and is not able to finish it, all that behold it begin to mock him,

30. Saying, this man began to build, and was not able to finish.

33. So likewise, whosoever he be of you that forsaketh not all that he hath, he cannot <u>be My disciple</u>.

Jesus is not saying that we must take a vow of poverty, but rather that we need to give up all our rights and ownership and replace them with instruction and stewardship. Basically, we give all our possessions to God. This is a completely different perspective on the same stuff. It tends to free us from the stress and struggle of building our own kingdom in the wilderness. Instead, we become managers of the King of kings' things. As we take care of the King's things here where the Devil is constantly trying to corrupt, steal, and destroy, our King is preparing our personal possessions in a place where the Devil can't touch them. *Selah.* Living in the Promised Land means that we daily crucify our selfish ambitions of promoting our own kingdom. We become spiritual warriors under our Supreme Commander and are His representatives under His authority. We put on the armor of light, our new "in Christ" identity which contains our authority and responsibility. Then we monitor and adjust our attitude to trust God in every situation.

Philippians 4:11-13

11. Not that I speak in respect of want: for I have learned, in whatsoever state I am, therewith to be content.

334

12. **I know both how to be abased, and I know how to abound: every where and <u>in all things I am instructed</u> both to be full and to be hungry, both to abound and to suffer need.**

13. **<u>I can do all things through Christ which strengtheneth me.</u>**

It is not always easy; but in order to walk in the light, we must surrender our right to complain. We surrender our right not to love. By God's grace, we demonstrate love, hope, peace, joy, patience, gentleness, self-control, faithfulness, and goodness in all circumstances. God is looking for people to represent Him in every area and situation of life.

Philippians 3:7
7. **But what <u>things were gain to me, those I counted loss for Christ</u>.**

It was Paul's desire to be hidden in the identity of Christ. Jim Elliott, a famous missionary and martyr, wisely stated, "It is no fool to give up what he cannot keep to gain what he cannot lose."

Philippians 1:21
21. **For to me to <u>live is Christ</u>, and to <u>die is gain</u>.**

Section 4

Transformation

CHAPTER 16

FROM CORRUPTION TO PERFECTION

Ephesians 5:5-11

5. **For this ye know, that no whoremonger, nor unclean person, nor covetous man, who is an idolater, hath any inheritance in the kingdom of Christ and of God.**

6. **Let no man deceive you with vain words: for because of these things cometh the wrath of God upon the children of disobedience.**

7. **Be not ye therefore partakers with them.**

8. **For <u>ye were sometimes darkness, but now are ye light in the Lord: walk as children of light</u>:**

9. **(For the fruit of the Spirit is in all goodness and righteousness and truth;)**

10. **<u>Proving what is acceptable unto the Lord.</u>**

11. **<u>And have no fellowship with the unfruitful works of darkness</u>, but rather reprove them.**

The works of darkness will not be allowed in Heaven. The works of darkness will have no rewards or "inheritance" in Heaven. In Verses 7, 8, and 11, we are encouraged not to spend time making memories with the works of darkness, but instead to "walk (live, make memories) as children of light." Let our identity be as children of light, not children of disobedience and darkness.

Revelation 21:8

8. **But the fearful, and unbelieving, and the abominable, and murderers, and whoremongers, and sorcerers, and idolaters,**

337

and all liars, shall have their part in the lake which burneth with fire and brimstone: which is the second death.

Who will not be perfected? Who will be cast into Hell Fire instead of going to Heaven? What is their identity? In these two passages, we have a partial list that includes the fearful and liars, along with covetous and unclean persons. Some have misunderstood these verses, believing that bad people go to Hell and good people go to Heaven. The problem with that idea is it's based on either an assumption or a misinterpretation, instead of the facts. There are many Biblical references that give specific details concerning salvation. They make it clear that our redemption is not based on our good works. The process of salvation is the most important foundational truth we need to understand in order to enjoy everlasting life in Paradise. It is one of the first doctrines recorded by John, Jesus' closest disciple.

John 3:16-18

16. **For God so loved the world, that He gave His only begotten Son, that <u>whosoever believeth in Him should not perish, but have everlasting life.</u>**

17. **For God sent not his Son into the world to condemn the world, but that the world <u>through Him might be saved.</u>**

18. **<u>He that believeth on Him is not condemned</u>: but he that believeth not is condemned already, because he hath not believed in the name of the only begotten Son of God.**

John 1:12

12. **But <u>as many as received Him,</u> to them gave He power to become the sons of God, even to <u>them that believe</u> on His name:**

Another problem with believing that good people go to Heaven and bad people go to Hell is that we are not perfect. We cannot be good people 100% of the time.

Isaiah 64:6

6. But <u>we are all</u> as an unclean thing, and all our righteousness are as filthy rags; and we all do fade as a leaf; and our iniquities, like the wind, have taken us away.

Romans 3:12

12. They are <u>all gone out of the way</u>, they are together become unprofitable; <u>there is none that doeth good</u>, <u>no, not one</u>.

Romans 3:23

23. For <u>all have sinned</u>, and come short of the glory of God.

Therefore, none of us can qualify by our own actions to become part of a perfect Heaven, because we are not perfect.

Matthew 5:48

48. Be ye therefore perfect, even as your Father which is in <u>Heaven is perfect</u>.

The standard in Heaven is perfection. There is absolutely no lying, no deception, no fearful worrying, no lusting, no steeling, and no defilement in Heaven. God does not grade us on a curve or scale of how we compare to others. If we've ever lied, been fearful, been unclean morally or ethically, desired to take something that belonged to another (coveted), committed idolatry by valuing anything above God and His Word, then we have dark spots. All of us have identified with the works of darkness at some time, and may even be "partakers with them" again. Therefore, in our natural condition, we would contaminate God's spotless perfect Heaven. The following is another Bible passage that is easily misunderstood:

1 Corinthians 3:16-17

16. **Know ye not that <u>ye are the temple of God, and that the Spirit of God dwelleth in you</u>?**

17. **If any man defile the temple of God, <u>him shall God destroy</u>; for the temple of God is holy, which temple ye are.**

Because of Verse 17, some have even thought that anyone, even a Christian, who commits suicide, will end up in Hell. According to the Bible, this is simply not true. This passage is not talking about a man who smokes, overeats, gets drunk, or commits suicide. It is talking about the root of all those things – the Old Man. It is the Old Man (the old human nature) who defiles the temple. The Old Man is the source of our bad attitudes and actions. We will not find any bad attitudes or actions in Paradise. Therefore, something has to be done about the Old Man who defiles us and defiles our environment.

Ephesians 4:22

22. **That ye put off concerning the former conversation <u>the Old Man, which is corrupt</u> according to the deceitful lusts;**

Colossians 3:8-9

8. **But <u>now ye also put off all these</u>; anger, wrath, malice, blasphemy, filthy communication out of your mouth.**

9. **Lie not one to another, seeing that ye have put off <u>the Old Man with his deeds</u>;**

Our temple is our body. When we ask the Holy Spirit of Jesus into our body as our Savior, our body becomes His body. The New Nature is the undefiled identity of our future perfected body. The old nature has lost its authority. The old nature is the Old Man who defiles the temple of God, and "him shall God destroy." Jesus told a parable regarding a wedding feast. At the end of this parable, Jesus spoke of a specific man. I believe that man is the Old Man who was not covered by the garment of righteousness provided by the king. The parable implies that judgment will fall on the Old Man at this special time, and he will be removed. His presence and activity will never again be related to us who are truly born-again Christians. Jesus is not saying by this parable that we might loose our salvation. Instead Jesus is saying we will be set free and loose the Old Man. Lets focus on this parable with this in mind to see what Jesus is describing.

Matthew 22:10-13

10. So those servants went out into the highways, and <u>gathered together all as many as they found, both bad and good</u>: and the wedding was furnished with guests.

11. And when the king came in to see the guests, he saw there <u>a man</u> which had not on a wedding garment:

12. And he saith unto him, friend, how camest thou in hither <u>not having a wedding garment</u>? And he was speechless.

13. Then said the king to the servants, bind him hand and foot, and <u>take him away</u>, and cast him into outer darkness; there shall be weeping and gnashing of teeth.

The Bible is very clear that once we have possession of the Holy Spirit, He has possession of us. Once we have asked Him in, He will never leave us. When we are born again into the family of God, we are placed in the spiritual body of Christ, whether we act like it or not. Notice the phrase in verse 10 "both bad and good." We are not the lost, but we will be judged and may suffer losses.

1 Corinthians 3:11-15

11. For other foundation can no man lay than that is laid, which is Jesus Christ.

12. Now if any man build upon this foundation gold, silver, precious stones, wood, hay, stubble;

13. <u>Every man's work shall be made manifest</u>: for the day shall declare it, because <u>it shall be revealed</u> by fire; and the fire shall try every man's work of what sort it is.

14. If any man's work abide which he hath built thereupon, he shall receive a reward.

15. <u>If any man's work shall be burned, he shall suffer loss: but he himself shall be saved</u>; yet so as by fire.

This passage is not talking about the lost at Judgment Day. Instead, it's referring to the saved at the time of rewards or loss of benefits. This is often referred to as the Judgment Seat of Christ or the Bema Seat Judgment. This occurs well before the Great White Throne Judgment. Notice in verse 15 that a Christian may suffer losses for bad behavior, but "he himself shall be saved." This applies to all Christians, men and women, slave and free, Jew and Gentile.

Galatians 3:28

28. There is neither Jew nor Greek, there is neither bond nor free, there is neither male nor female: for <u>ye are all one in Christ Jesus</u>.

There will be many wonderful rewards at the Judgment Seat of Christ, but this is also a time of exposing and purifying. It's kind of like opening a festering wound to release the poison. It is a time of clearing the air of misunderstandings and clearly seeing the whole picture of life's activity.

Luke 12:2-3

2. For **there is nothing covered, that shall not be revealed; neither hid, that shall not be known.**

3. Therefore whatsoever ye have spoken in darkness shall be heard in the light; and that which ye have spoken in the ear in closets shall be proclaimed upon the housetops.

Proverbs 1:10, 15-17 (NIV)

10. My son, **if sinners entice you, do not give in to them.**

15. My son, **do not go along with them, do not set foot on their paths;**

16. For their feet rush into sin, they are swift to shed blood.

17. How useless to spread a net **in full view of all** the birds!

Matthew 10:26

26. Fear them not therefore: for **there is nothing covered, that shall not be revealed; and hid, that shall not be known.**

Everything will be seen clearly, even the motives, influences, misunderstandings, and hidden things.

1 Corinthians 4:5

5. Therefore judge nothing before the time, until the **Lord come, who both will bring to light the hidden things of darkness,** and will **make manifest the counsels of the hearts:** and then shall every man have praise of God.

God does not ignore or hide our sins. King David can testify to that. In the Bible, we find David's worst sins in 2Samuel 11:1

through 12:14, leading to Psalm 32. Christ's blood paid the debt and covers every sin a Christian commits, without exception. Furthermore, by confessing and repenting of our sins, we receive instant forgiveness and restored fellowship with God. However, I believe that the separating of our sin and all its consequences from us, "as far as the east is from the west" (Psalm 103:12) does not actually and fully happen until the Judgment Seat of Christ.

2 Corinthians 5:10

10. For <u>we must all appear before the Judgment Seat of Christ</u>; that every one may receive the <u>things done</u> in his body, according to that he hath done, whether it be <u>good or bad</u>.

At that time, we will see everything, the good and the bad. We will not be proud. We will instead be humbly and eternally grateful to Jesus Christ for removing the sinful identity and making us a new creation. We will fully understand each other and ourselves. We will see and understand the root of division and conflict. Two Christians that were at war with each other will see the true enemy and unit against the Old Man. This is how they will be liberated from hate and united in love and restoration (1Corinthians 13:12). We will know and fully understand what Christ liberated us from. We will fully recognize the root of sin, the Old Man in us and others, the problems he has caused, and the need for him to go.

Luke 3:9

9. And now also the axe is laid unto the <u>root of the trees: every tree therefore which bringeth not forth good fruit is hewn down, and cast into the fire</u>.

This is done for us so that we may be one in love and unity, yet individual in personality and rewards. We will not have true and consistent unity, love, respect, or peace until this happens. *Selah.*

Jesus told many parables illustrating His kingdom. The religious leaders of that time were looking for anything they could use against Jesus (Luke 20:19-26). Parables were nonthreatening to Roman authority, but more importantly they were memorable and visually insightful. Lets examine one of Jesus' kingdom parables and see what is being said.

Matthew 13:24-30

24. **Another parable put He forth unto them, saying, the kingdom of Heaven is likened unto <u>a man which sowed good seed in his field</u>:**

25. **But while men slept, <u>his enemy came and sowed tares among the wheat</u>, and went his way.**

26. **But when the blade was sprung up, and brought forth fruit, then appeared the tares also.**

27. **So the servants of the householder came and said unto him, Sir, didst not thou sow good seed in thy field? From whence then hath it tares?**

28. **He said unto them, an enemy hath done this. The servants said unto him, wilt thou then that we go and gather them up?**

29. **But he said, nay; lest while ye gather up the tares, ye root up also the wheat with them.**

30. **<u>Let both grow together until the harvest</u>: and in the time of harvest I will say to the reapers, gather ye together first the tares, and bind them in bundles to burn them: but gather the wheat into my barn.**

There are many applications of this parable. The plight of humanity may not be an obvious application but lets take a moment and look at the historical parallels. The first man and woman started out good (seen in verse 24 as good seed). Then Adam and Eve received the corrupting seed of sin, which the enemy came and planted (seen in verse 25). Their first descendants (their fruit) were Cain and Abel. In these first two male descendants we can see the conflict between the tares and the wheat. Abel the second born son represented the wheat as well as the second birth. He was the good seed and Cain the bad seed. The Bible reveals that the sin in Cain killed Abel. This was the first demonstration that sin kills, even the righteous (Hebrews 11:4). The death of Abel was not the end of the good seed because Seth was born and raised up to replace Abel (Genesis 4:25-26). Seth was the forefather of Enoch, Noah, Shem, Abraham, David, Mary and Jesus. Our world is full of death and corruption, which reveals that sin is still active in our world. Therefore we have to learn to deal with it. *Selah.* I have heard a good illustration that this life is like a railroad track. On one track are good things and on the other bad things. We are riding on both tracks at the same time. Everyone experiences both good and bad. Often both good and bad are impacting us at the same time. Life in this world will remain a mixture of good and evil until it has fully matured and come to its final destination. The good and the bad will dwell together until the end. Then there will be a separation as illustrated in verse 30 of the previous Scripture. *Selah.* Most people know that there is good and bad in this world but fail to understand why. Let's focus on the two key applications of the previous parable to help us understand the times in which we live and the opportunities we have to magnify the good.

The First and primary Application of the parable (the saved and the lost): Jesus used this parable to identify our destiny. There are only two classes of people in this world, the saved and the lost. Jesus Himself gave the disciples the core meaning of the parable.

Matthew 13:36-43

36. Then Jesus sent the multitude away, and went into the house: and His disciples came unto Him, saying, declare unto us the parable of the tares of the field.

37. He answered and said unto them, He that soweth the good seed is the Son of man;

38. The field is the world; the <u>good seed are the children of the kingdom</u>; but the <u>tares are the children of the wicked one</u>;

39. The <u>enemy that sowed them is the Devil</u>; the harvest is the end of the world; and the reapers are the angels.

40. As therefore the tares are gathered and burned in the fire; so shall it be in the end of this world.

41. The Son of man shall send forth His angels, and they <u>shall gather out of His kingdom all things that offend, and them which do iniquity</u>;

42. And <u>shall cast them into a furnace of fire</u>: there shall be wailing and gnashing of teeth.

43. Then shall the righteous shine forth as the sun in the kingdom of their Father. <u>Who hath ears to hear, let him hear</u>.

This separation is literally performed at the end of this world (Revelation 20:9 through Revelation 21:4). There are only two eternal destinations. The saved and the lost will dwell together for now but every person will go to one of two places – either Heaven or the Lake of Fire. Even in our churches, there is a mixture of seed sown by God and seed sown by the Devil. The Bible tells us there was even a tare (Judas) among Jesus' twelve disciples. Jesus recognized and used Judas as an example for us of how we are to live with the tares. We are not to condemn and uproot, but rather love and provide for them. We are not to follow the tares, but allow them to follow us and possibly be transformed. Anyone can be transformed by letting the seed of God in their heart. If you choose to harden your heart and reject God's seed of transformation you are doomed.

<u>The Second Application addresses the root produced by the seeds</u> (the human nature and the Divine Nature): I believe we can see a deeper hidden spiritual truth illustrated in this parable. The entity that makes us "children of the kingdom" or "children of the Wicked One" is our nature. In the wheat and tares parable, these two natures are identified as two different seeds that develop a different root system. The identity of the tares would be that which the Devil planted or what the Devil fathered. The Devil doesn't actually have children, but as shared in Chapter 3 of this book, he is the father of our corrupt fallen human nature. The tares (our fallen human natures) will remain throughout this life, but will be separated at the end and cast into the Lake of Fire. *Selah.* God so loved all the people of the world that even before the creation of the world, He prepared a way for them to become children of God, or as in this parable, be identified as wheat. The transformation comes from the combination of good ground and good seed. Wheat and tares look similar at first, but they mature differently. Only one has a true salvation experience.

1 Peter 1:18-20

[18.] **Forasmuch as ye know that ye were not redeemed with corruptible things, as silver and gold, from your vain conversation received by tradition from your fathers;**

[19.] **But with the precious blood of Christ, as of a lamb without blemish and without spot:**

20. **Who verily was <u>foreordained before the foundation of the world, but was manifest in these last times for you</u>,**

Redemption is not an afterthought to fix a problem. The seed of redemption was prepared to come forth before we had a problem (before the tares appeared). Redemption is receiving the Divine Nature of Jesus, which the "Word" of God (John 1:1) has made available to us. This implantation was foreordained to redeem our soul and make us a new creation. The soul has an option to allow transformation or resist it. It can go from the identity of a field of weeds choking out God's blessings to "good ground" for God's seed to bear precious fruit. The seed gives the field its identity, just as the nature gives the soul its identity.

2 Corinthians 5:17
17. **Therefore <u>if any man be in Christ, he is a new creature</u>: old things are passed away; behold, all things are become new.**

At the moment of conversion our name is written in the Lambs book of life. We are positionally sanctified (set apart) and identified as "in Christ." It doesn't matter how things look or feel our identity and destiny has changed.

Ephesians 2:13
13. **But now <u>in Christ Jesus</u> ye who sometimes were far off are made nigh by the blood of Christ.**

When we receive Christ, God no longer sees us the same way. From God's point of view, everything changes. Our identity is His child, and our destiny is perfection.

Ephesians 2:6
6. **And hath raised us up together, and made us sit together in heavenly places <u>in Christ Jesus</u>:**

From the moment of our conversion, God recognizes and knows us as "in Christ Jesus." This kind of knowing is an intimate experiential knowledge like in Genesis 4:1 and 4:25. The people God knows in this way are predestinated to be conformed to the image of Christ. This means that we will be without corruption after we die. Our destiny is predetermined and prearranged to be without corruption. We are predestinated to perfection.

Romans 8:29-30

29. **For whom He did foreknow, He also did <u>predestinate to be conformed to the image of His Son</u>, that He might be the firstborn among many brethren.**

30. **Moreover whom He did predestinate, them He also called: and whom He called, them He also justified: and whom He justified, <u>them He also glorified</u>.**

These two verses reveal the progression to glorification. It starts with a relationship to Jesus that changes our destiny and positions us to be identified as God's children. This will lead to our transformation from corruption to perfection. There is some confusion about this passage in Romans, so let's examine the five key words carefully one at a time.

1: <u>Foreknow</u>: means to know before. Before what? The Father knows the future as well as He knows the past. God's foreknowledge is beyond our comprehension, but we can understand what His Word tells us in this verse. This verse is referring to an intimate knowledge. God knows us intimately as family members before the end of this life. This results in our final destination being changed to Heaven because we are identified and known as God's children. If God dose not know us intimately our destiny is not Heaven (Matthew 7:23).

2: <u>Predestinate</u>: has two parts:

- First – there would be a predetermined path of redemption. Our predetermined path according to Jesus is **"Ye must be born again"** (John 3:3,7). When we are born again we are then identified "in Christ," as member of God's family.
- Second – there would be a predesigned destination. Our predesigned destination is to be perfect like Christ and have a special place in Heaven prepared specifically for us.

3: <u>Called:</u> One day God will call us home and we will be separated from our sin nature resulting in us being "Justified"

4: <u>Justified</u>: Just-as-if-I'd-Never-Sinned. We will be completely free of all sin and shame because we will be a new creation with a new pedigree of "in Christ" instead of "in Adam." We will leave behind all association to fallen humanity just as eagles leave behind the eggshells that they were hatch from.

5: <u>Glorified:</u> Once we are completely justified we will be "<u>Glorified</u>" in our new immortal sinless bodies. *Selah.*

1 Corinthians 15:22

22. **For as <u>in Adam all die</u>, even so <u>in Christ shall all be made alive</u>.**

God sees our future as clearly as if it were our present. He sees us as the new creation we will be, as if it has already happened. In God's mind, it's as good as done.

Isaiah 46:9-13

9. **Remember the former things of old: for I am God, and there is none else; I am God, and there is none like Me,**

10. **Declaring the end from the beginning, and from ancient times the things that are not yet done, saying, <u>My counsel shall stand</u>, and <u>I will do all my pleasure</u>:**

11. **Calling a ravenous bird from the east, the man that executeth my counsel from a far country: yea, <u>I have spoken it, I will also bring it to pass; I have purposed it, I will also do it.</u>**

12. **Hearken unto Me, ye stouthearted, that are far from righteousness:**

13. **I bring near My righteousness; it shall not be far off, and My salvation shall not tarry: and I will place salvation in Zion for Israel my glory.**

God predestinated Israel to be the birthplace of Jesus our Savior. God demonstrated His glorious thinking, foresight and ability regarding predestination when He spoke to Abraham. Abraham followed God while he was elderly and childless, yet God saw him as the father of many nations.

Romans 4:17

17. **(As it is written, I have made thee a father of many nations,) before him whom he believed, even God, who quickeneth the dead, and <u>calleth those things which be not as though they were</u>.**

Abraham is the father of the Jewish nation through Isaac. He is also the father of the Muslim nations through Ismael. Many do not realize it, but later Abraham had many other children as well (Genesis 24:67-25:6). The fourth chapter of Romans refers to Abraham as the father of the believing nations. This makes Abraham also a patriarch of Christianity because Jesus is the seed of Abraham. Abraham has been called the father of faith but in reality he did not always walk in faith. He took a step of faith and then stumbled over fear. He got up and took another step of faith and stumbled over circumstances. He learned to take God at his Word. Abraham learned God could be trusted no mater what the situation looks like. *Selah.* God demonstrated this same foresight "and calleth those things which be not as though they were" (Romans 7:14) when He sent His Word to Gideon, who at the time was poor, both in means and attitude.

Judges 6:15

15. **And he said unto Him, Oh my Lord, wherewith shall I save Israel? Behold, <u>my family is poor</u> in Manasseh, and <u>I am the least in my father's house</u>.**

Nevertheless, God saw Gideon's destiny as a great deliverer, bold and courageous.

Judges 6:12

12. **And the angel of the Lord appeared unto him, and said unto him, <u>the Lord is with thee, thou mighty man of valour</u>.**

Gideon believed God (as God knew he would with a little convincing) and fulfilled his destiny. Which destiny will we fulfill? Will it be our destiny from God as wheat (as illustrate in the kingdom of Heaven parable), or will we suffer loss through unbelief? God has a great plan for our life, but it is rooted in our response to His Word. What makes us the wheat is the Divine Nature that identifies us with Christ. There is a constant battle for ground raging in our mortal life between the old and new natures. In the end, the old nature and its fruit will be uprooted, separated, and burned; but those things attached to the new nature will be preserved for enjoyment.

Ezekiel 11:19-20

19. And I will give them one heart, and <u>I will put a new Spirit within you; and I will take the stony heart</u> out of their flesh, and will give them an heart of flesh:

20. That they may walk in My statutes, and keep Mine ordinances, and do them: and <u>they shall be My people, and I will be their God.</u>

Ezekiel 36:26-27

26. A new heart also will I give you, and <u>a new Spirit will I put within you: and I will take away the stony heart</u> out of your flesh, and I will give you an heart of flesh.

27. And I will put My Spirit within you, and cause you to walk in My statutes, and ye shall keep My judgments, and do them.

While these two passages look the same, one illustrates that God's offer of redemption goes out to all, while the other makes it personal. God is talking to you directly. The new identity starts here and makes us eligible for the final transforming heart transplant.

Romans 2:29 *(with a clarifying note)*

29. But he is a Jew, *(part of the family of Jesus)* which is one inwardly; and <u>circumcision is that of the heart, in the spirit,</u> and not in the letter; whose praise is not of men, but of God.

At the Judgment seat of Christ our heart connection to sin will be cut off and completely removed. The removal of the dark human spirit results in a new transformed heart. We will have a heart of love with no room for hate. The source of corruption will be removed and replaced by the source of perfection, the Divine Nature.

Colossians 2:11

11. In whom also ye are <u>circumcised with the circumcision made without hands, in putting off</u> the body of the sins of <u>the flesh</u> by the circumcision of Christ:

Our sin and even our connection to sin will be completely removed. We will no longer be sinners. Never again will we be tempted to defile ourselves. *Selah.* There are three major separations (or circumcisions) coming in the future.

<u>Separation 1</u>: Separating the truth from the deceptions. All the darkness and gray areas will be enlightened and dispelled by the light of truth. God's Word will be proven true, wise, and forever glorified. All the lies and deceptions planted by Satan will be uprooted and exposed. Deception will never again be able to choke out the truth. In the end everyone will know and understand "what is truth" (John 18:38).

<u>Separation 2</u>: Separating the saved from the lost. All those who reject God's redemption, thereby continuing in their corruption and rebellion, will be removed and quarantined in the Lake of Fire. They will forever be an example of the result of sin. Before Satan fell he did not realize the power and destructive ability of sin and rebellion. Adam and Eve were ignorant as well. The Lake of Fire will dispel this ignorant. *Selah.* The saved will experience another major separation.

<u>Separation 3</u>: Cutting away the Old Man, the identity of corruption. The fallen human nature, which produces a hard "stony heart," will be separated and removed. The living heart and Nature of God will fill the void that was once corrupt. No longer will it be said that we act like mere men.

1 Corinthians 3:3

³· **For ye are yet carnal: for whereas there is among you envying, and strife, and divisions, are ye not carnal, and <u>walk as men</u>?**

We will no longer be part of the human race, but will instead be part of the Divine family of God. The transformation will be more remarkable than when a caterpillar becomes a butterfly. The caterpillar must die so the butterfly can fly. Our soul will experience the refreshing removal of our core problem, the human nature. Then we will consistently act like our new identity, the children of God.

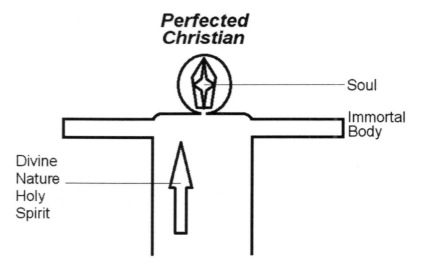

Now is the time to choose your identity by faith. There is nothing more important than this decision. I pray that you choose wisely.

Romans 8:18-19

¹⁸· **For I reckon that the sufferings of this present time are not worthy to be compared with the glory which shall be revealed in us.**

¹⁹· **For the earnest expectation of the creature waiteth for the <u>manifestation of the sons of God</u>.**

CHAPTER 17

THE DEVIL'S FINAL DESTINY

Luke 10:18

18. And He said unto them, **I beheld Satan as lightning fall from Heaven.**

Jesus is referring to events that happened before the creation of Adam. Satan's revolt and fall is the origin of evil.

Isaiah 14:12-15

12. **How art thou fallen from Heaven, O Lucifer, son of the morning!** How art thou cut down to the ground, which didst weaken the nations!

13. For thou hast said in thine heart, **I will** ascend into Heaven, **I will** exalt my throne above the stars of God: **I will** sit also upon the mount of the congregation, in the sides of the north:

14. **I will** ascend above the heights of the clouds; **I will be like the Most High.**

15. Yet thou **shalt be brought down to Hell,** to the sides of **the pit.**

The definition of "Lucifer" is light-bearer. Lucifer is another name for "Satan," the "Devil," or the fallen "Angel of Light." God created him as a powerful good angel, an "Anointed Cherub." I believe that Lucifer was one of the first, if not the first, of the angels created at the dawn of angelic creation. He was probably in charge of praise and worship to God and had tremendous musical ability. He was a powerful influence in Heaven, but he also had a mind of his own. Eventually he became proud of himself and coveted the power and position Jesus his creator rightfully possessed.

Ezekiel 28:14-17

14. **Thou art the anointed cherub** that covereth; and I have set thee so: thou wast upon the holy mountain of God; thou hast walked up and down in the midst of the stones of fire.

15. **Thou wast perfect in thy ways from the day that thou wast created, till iniquity was found in thee.**

16. By the multitude of thy merchandise they have filled the midst of thee with violence, and thou hast sinned: **therefore I will cast thee as profane out of the mountain of God**: and I will destroy thee, o covering cherub, from the midst of the stones of fire.

17. **Thine heart was lifted up because of thy beauty, thou hast corrupted thy wisdom by reason of thy brightness**: I will cast thee to the ground, I will lay thee before kings, that they may behold thee.

Lucifer's pride and envy of Jesus brought strife to Heaven. He started to speak out and act upon his selfish ambitions (Matthew 12:34). This led to a division in Heaven. Ultimately, a third of the angels followed Satan as their new ruler and were cast out of Heaven. Those who followed Satan became fallen angels, demons, and evil principalities.

Revelation 12:3-4

3. And there appeared another **wonder in Heaven; and behold a great red dragon,** having seven heads and ten horns, and seven crowns upon his heads.

4. And **his tail drew the third part of the stars of Heaven, and did cast them to the Earth**: and the dragon stood before the woman which was ready to be delivered, for to devour her child as soon as it was born.

This is symbolic language, but it offers us a peek at Satan the great dragon and the third part of the nations of Heaven that followed him. They became corrupted angels and were exiled to our galaxy. They now influence the part of creation we know as Earth (Ephesians 6:12). *Selah.* There are some that believe Satan's fall happened in the Garden of Eden after Adam was created. They say; it was jealousy of man that caused Satan to fall. They say; God would not put His newly created man in a place where satanic evil might "devour" him. What dose the Bible say about these three presumptions? Would God put Adam in a place where God knew evil was present? The fact is, God told Adam about the tree of good and evil. When God created Adam and Eve He knew that they would be confronted and fall to Satan's deceptions. That is why God prepared a deliverer before the foundation of the world (1Peter 1:18-20). Yes, God knew that Satan (John 8:44) was in the Garden of Eden (Ezekiel 28:13). God knew that Satan would tempt Eve to eat of the tree of knowledge of good and evil. God also knew that Satan would use Eve to seduce Adam to sin. God warned Adam not to eat of the fruit of the forbidden tree. Adam and Eve could choose to obey God and remain perfect, or sin. Satan once had a choice to obey God and remain perfect or rebel. The ability to choose is essential to having the ability to show love. God knows how to handle bad actions and even use them to promote something good. Therefore, would God put His newly created man where he would be confronted by evil? Would God put His newborn son in a place ruled by an evil tyrant? God did these things for the eventual greater good that would result. Question two; does the Bible say where Satan was when he became corrupted? Isaiah 14:12 tells us that Satan was in Heaven not the Garden of Eden at the time of his fall. Ezekiel 28:16 gets even more specific and reveals that Satan was in the capital city of Heaven at the time of his fall. Question three; does the Bible say what caused Satan to be corrupted? Was it Adam? The Bible indicates Satan was focused on himself and became proud (Ezekiel 28:16-17). This caused him to be self-centered (greedy and vehement) instead of God-centered (loving and kind). Because of this he was cast out of the capital of Heaven resulting in all the prideful "I will" declarations recorded in Isaiah 14:13-14. I believe God created mankind after this rebellion took place. I believe the new creation of mankind, which enabled the new creation of the children of God, was an act of Heavenly restoration to replace the corrupted removed angels. *Selah.* It is logical and Biblical to believe that after Satan became corrupted, he then saw his replacement and considered how he could defile it. Although Satan did succeed in defiling mankind, he will ultimately be defeated and God will have a family. Now, many years later, Satan is still the corrupting force that "weakens the nations." Satan's fall began when he tried to usurp God's place and authority in Heaven, but his fall is not over yet. He is still trying to usurp God's place and authority with mankind. However, Satan has an expiration date. There is coming a time when he will be permanently "brought down to Hell," but that time is not yet. In the meantime, he is still useful in allowing us to see the differences between the fruits of good and evil, as well as the danger and destruction that result from rebelling against perfection.

1 Peter 5:8-10

8. **Be sober, be vigilant; because your adversary the Devil, as a roaring lion, walketh about, <u>seeking whom he may devour</u>:**

9. **Whom <u>resist stedfast in the faith</u>, knowing that the same afflictions are accomplished in your brethren that are in the world.**

10. **But the God of all grace, who hath called us unto his eternal glory by Christ Jesus, <u>after that ye have suffered a while, make you perfect</u>, stablish, strengthen, settle you.**

The Devil is real and active in the world today. There is coming a day when the Devil will be removed.

Revelation 20:1-3

1. **And I saw an angel come down from Heaven, having the key of the bottomless pit and a great chain in his hand.**

2. **And he laid hold on <u>the dragon, that old serpent, which is the Devil</u>, and Satan, and <u>bound him a thousand years,</u>**

3. **And cast him into the bottomless pit, and shut him up, and set a seal upon him, that he <u>should deceive the nations no more, till the thousand years should be fulfilled</u>: and after that he must be loosed a <u>little season</u>.**

Before Satan is permanently eliminated, he will be temporarily eliminated during the Millennial Reign of Christ. Satan will be removed, and Jesus will rule as King over the Earth for a thousand years. At the end of the thousand years, Satan will be released to make his last stand and final rebellion. Before the Millennial Reign of Christ begins, Satan is allowed to bring about what we refer to as the Great Tribulation. *Selah.* There are many opinions about the end of the world and the events leading up to that final day. Even among Bible scholars, there are many contrasting interpretations about the end times and the book of Revelation. There are basically three sections to the book of Revelation. The church age is addressed in Revelation chapters 1 through 3. Then John is caught up to Heaven and God gives him a variety of spiritual visions. In chapters 4 through 19, there is a lot of symbolism mixed in with John's literal observations. I believe that in these chapters, the Bible reveals several points of view on at least three subjects: the Great Tribulation, Jesus and Satan's activities, and the end of ungodly government. However, they are not necessarily in order. Whenever you read something along the lines of "and I saw," "and I beheld" or "after this I beheld," it is beginning a new point of view. If you read the center section of the book Revelation with this in mind instead of trying to put everything together chronologically it will make more sense. Chapter 19 is a transitional chapter. It contains a lot of symbolism but it also begins the chronological portion of the book. Revelation 19 through 22 describes the progression from this creation to God's next grand creation and reveals our future home. *Selah.* Let's examine the prophetic Scriptures and see if we can find a logical outline and reasonable sequence of events that is in harmony with the totality of Scripture. The Bible contains the interpretation of its symbolism and concepts. Lets start by understanding what the Bible is referring to as the "first resurrection." This is mentioned in the chronological part of the book of Revelation.

Revelation 20:4-6

4. **And I saw thrones, and they sat upon them, and judgment was given unto them: and I saw the souls of them that were beheaded for the witness of Jesus, and for the Word of God, and which had not worshipped the beast, neither his image, neither had received his mark upon their foreheads, or In their hands; and <u>they lived and reigned with Christ a thousand years</u>.**

5. **But the rest of the dead lived not again until the thousand years were finished. This is the <u>first resurrection</u>.**

6. **Blessed and holy is he that hath part in the <u>first resurrection</u>: on such the second death hath no power, but they shall be**

priests of God and of Christ, and <u>shall reign with him a thousand years</u>.

The "first resurrection" refers to the redeemed (both living and dead) that take part in the rapture. Rapture means physically or bodily removing people from the earth. There are different thoughts on whether the rapture is before, in the middle of, or at the end of the Great Tribulation, or only at the end of the world. I believe that there are many raptures. Enoch was the first one raptured (Genesis 5:24), and then Elijah (2Kings 2:11). The day of Jesus' resurrection, there was a "first fruits" rapture of saints who first gave witness to people living in Jerusalem before going to Heaven (Matthew 27:52-53), and there was Jesus' rapture (Acts 1:9). I believe that God empowers the Church (Christ's Body) to hold back Satan's plans (2Thessalonians 2:6-8). After the rapture of the Church, Satan will empower his final Antichrist, and tribulation will take place like the world has never known.

Revelation 3:10

10. **Because thou hast kept the word of my patience, I also will <u>keep thee from the hour of temptation, which shall come upon all the world</u>, to try them that dwell upon the Earth.**

Luke 21:35-36

35. **For as a snare <u>shall it come on all them that dwell on the face of the whole Earth</u>.**

36. **Watch ye therefore, and pray always, that <u>ye may be accounted worthy to escape all these things that shall come to pass, and to stand before the Son of man</u>.**

At the end of the Church Age and before the Great Tribulation, the true Church (the Body of Christ) will be raptured.

1 Thessalonians 4:16-17

16. **For the Lord himself shall descend from heaven with a shout, with the voice of the archangel, and with the trump of God: and the dead in Christ shall rise first:**

17. **Then we which are alive and remain shall be caught up together with them in the clouds, to meet the Lord in the air: and so shall we ever be with the Lord.**

The rapture of the Church will begin with a sudden earthshaking shout of joy. The born-again children of God will meet Jesus Christ in the clouds and go with Him to the third Heaven to begin a special celebration. *Selah.* By the way, time will operate at a different rate in Heaven. It will seem limitless, yet orderly. We will no longer be subject to time. Instead, time will be subject to us, the family of God (Joshua 10:12-14, 2Kings 20:8-11). At the conclusion of the Church Age, the Father will send His Son to bring home the Church and prepare for the "Marriage Supper of the Lamb" (Revelation 19:7-9). Following the rapture of the Church will be what is referred to as Daniel's 70th Week for the Jewish Nation. This is the seven-year tribulation period called "Jacobs Trouble." It is not the Church's Tribulation. I believe that Jacob's Tribulation begins at the end of the Church Age. This is not to say that we don't have tribulation now, because Jesus stated, "In the world ye shall have tribulation" (John 16:33); but at the end, the tribulation will be significantly greater.

Matthew 24:21

21. **For then shall be <u>great tribulation, such as was not since the beginning</u> of the world to this time, no, <u>nor ever shall be.</u>**

Even after the rapture of the Church, there will be other raptures. During the Great Tribulation we see the rapture of the "two

364

witnesses." They were killed in the street of Jerusalem and televised for the entire world to see (Revelation 11:3-10).

Revelation 11:11-12

11. **And after three days and an half the Spirit of life from God entered into them, and they stood upon their feet; and great fear fell upon them which saw them.**

12. **And they heard a great voice from heaven saying unto them, Come up hither. And <u>they ascended up to heaven in a cloud;</u> and their enemies beheld them.**

We know that one of these witnesses is Elijah (Elias). Many assume the other prophet may be Moses because he appeared with Elijah and talked with Jesus on the mount of transfiguration.

Matthew 17:2-3

2. **And was transfigured before them: and <u>His face did shine as the sun</u>, and His raiment was white as the light.**

3. **And, behold, there appeared unto them Moses and Elias talking with Him.**

I believe that 40 years before Moses died, he appeared with Jesus for this important summit meeting. How is that possible, since Moses died centuries earlier? God is not subject to time. I believe that God took Moses from Mount Sinai to see Jesus the redeeming Lamb of God. After Moses spoke face to face with Jesus, the glory lingered. As he came down from Mount Sinai, Moses' face was literally beaming.

Exodus 34:29-30

29. **And it came to pass, when Moses came down from Mount Sinai with the two tables of testimony in Moses' hand, when he**

came down from the mount, that Moses wist not that the <u>skin of his face shone</u> while he talked with him.

30. And when Aaron and all the children of Israel saw Moses, behold, the <u>skin of his face shone; and they were afraid to come nigh him</u>.

Moses may be with Elijah prophesying and doing miracles during the Great Tribulation. Some of their miracles remind us of Moses. Nevertheless, I believe the weight of Scripture is pointing to someone else. I do not believe the other prophet is Moses because (unlike Elijah) Moses died thousands of years ago.

Deuteronomy. 34:5-7

5. So Moses the servant of the LORD <u>died there in the land of Moab, according to the Word of the LORD</u>.

6. And <u>He buried him</u> in a valley in the land of Moab, over against Bethpeor: but no man knoweth of <u>his sepulchre</u> unto this day.

7. And <u>Moses was an hundred and twenty years old when he died</u>: his eye was not dim, nor his natural force abated.

Moses' grave is not a memorial for some to go and worship at, but Moses has a grave according to the Bible. If it is Moses appearing in the future, then his body must be revived from the dead not resurrected. God does revive the dead. For instance Jesus revived his friend Lazarus after he was dead four days. Later Lazarus died again. Jesus was resurrected from the dead and will never die again. If the mystery prophet is Moses, he must be mortal in order to lay his life down as a martyr and 3 ½ days latter be resurrected and raptured. *Selah.* I believe Enoch may be a better fit.

Hebrews 11:5

5. By faith Enoch was translated that he should not see death; and was not found, because <u>God had translated him</u>: for before his translation he had this testimony, that he pleased God.

This sounds a very similar to what happened to Philip in Acts 8:39-40. Philip vanished from one place then appeared in another and continued his evangelistic ministry. Elijah and Enoch were both prophets who haven't died yet and retain their mortality. There is nobody like them. Therefore they can be placed in a future ministry as mortals. Because they are mortals they can die as martyrs and be resurrected to immortality. The New Testament quotes Enoch describing Jesus' second coming.

Jude 14

14. And <u>Enoch also, the seventh from Adam, prophesied</u> of these, saying, behold, <u>the Lord cometh</u> with ten thousands of His saints,

Jude 15 (NKJV)

15. "<u>to execute judgment</u> on all, to convict all who are ungodly among them of all their ungodly deeds which they have committed in an ungodly way, and of all the harsh things which ungodly sinners have spoken against Him."

Enoch has a special destiny and he is mentioned in both the Old and New Testaments of the Bible. We are all descendants of Enoch, and he may have a word of warning for all his children, both Jew and Gentile. Whoever is with Elijah as an end-time prophet, both he and Elijah will be killed. After three and a half days, they are resurrected and are then raptured (Revelation 11:11-12). *Selah.* The tribulation saints who are killed will also be raptured (Revelation 7:9,13-14, Revelation 20:4). At the end of the world, everyone else will be raised from the earth to be judged.

Revelation 20:13

13. And the sea gave up the dead which were in it; and death and Hell delivered up the dead which were in them: and <u>they were judged every man according to their works</u>.

The Bible records many raptures from the beginning of Genesis to the end of Revelation. Except for the last one, they are all part of what is referred to as the "first resurrection." They are the redeemed that appear at the Judgment seat of Christ. At the end the lost will be raptured to stand before God and receive judgment and penalty. The first resurrection is not a particular rapture, but it's all the redeemed who receive immortal bodies like Christ. They will be the saints from which God chooses His government and establishes the kingdom of God on Earth.

Revelation 20:5b-6

5b. This is the <u>first resurrection</u>.

6. Blessed and holy is he that hath part in the <u>first resurrection</u>: on such the <u>second death hath no power</u>, but they shall be priests of God and of Christ, and <u>shall reign with Him a thousand years</u>.

Those of us who are a part of the first resurrection will see life on Earth without Satan. The immortal children of God will rule under Jesus the glorified King of kings. There will also be mortal people who live through the Great Tribulation and do not receive Satan's mark. It will not be easy to live through the Great Tribulation because of all the satanic activity.

Revelation 13:16-17

16. And he causeth all, both small and great, rich and poor, free and bond, to <u>receive a mark</u> in their <u>right hand</u>, or in their <u>foreheads</u>:

17. **And that <u>no man might buy or sell, save he that had the</u> <u>mark</u>, or the <u>name of the beast</u>, or the <u>number</u> of his name.**

The Satanic implant (mark) is mandatory in all countries under the Antichrist control. With supernatural ability the (Beast) satanic government will dominant the world. The Antichrist will be completely possessed by Satan himself.

2 Thessalonians 2:9-10

9. **Even him, whose coming is after the working of Satan with all <u>power</u> and <u>signs</u> and <u>lying wonders</u>,**

10. **And with all deceivableness of unrighteousness in them that perish; <u>because they received not the love of the truth</u>, that they might be saved.**

I believe God will allow technology to increase to a point that the Antichrist will use it in a mind control chip. The mark of the beast will put the receivers under a "strong delusion" (2Thessalonians 2:11-12) and not allow them to turn to Jesus. That is why the Bible says that everyone that receives the mark of the beast is doomed.

Revelation 14:11

11. **And the smoke of their torment ascendeth up for <u>ever and</u> <u>ever</u>: and they have no rest day nor night, who worship the beast and his image, and <u>whosoever receiveth the mark</u> of his name.**

All those who resist the mark of the beast to the end will avoid the satanic brainwashing of his mark of allegiance. They will have their names written in the Lamb's Book of Life. This means they have been in the book of (mortal) life; and instead of being blotted out, they will be moved to the book of (eternal) life, referred to as "the Book of Life of the Lamb." Most people will not resist the mark of the beast to the end. They will be blotted out of the book of life and be eternally lost. *Selah.* The Antichrist will have great military (hard) power symbolized by iron, as well as diplomatic (soft) power symbolized by potters' clay (Daniel 2:41-43). In spite of the Antichrist's charisma, his demonic kingdom will be full of strife, fear, deception, and division. It will promote satanic worship with a vengeance toward any resistance.

Revelation 13:4-8

4. And <u>they worshipped the dragon</u> which gave power unto the beast: and they worshipped the beast, saying, who is like unto the beast? <u>Who is able to make war with him</u>?

5. And there was given unto him a <u>mouth speaking great things</u> and blasphemies; and power was given unto him to continue forty and two months.

6. And he opened his mouth in blasphemy against God, to blaspheme His name, and His tabernacle, and them that dwell in Heaven.

7. And <u>it was given unto him to make war with the saints,</u> and to overcome them: and power was given him over all kindreds, and tongues, and nations.

8. And all that dwell upon the Earth shall worship him, <u>whose names are not written in the book of life of the Lamb</u> slain from the foundation of the world.

This is a key passage to unlock the mysteries of the Great Tribulation. During the Great Tribulation the Antichrist is empowered by Satan (the dragon) to be the final head and mouthpiece of the beast (Daniel 7:19-25). Daniel identifies the Antichrist as the last horn on the beast (Daniel 7:7-8) with a legacy that goes back to the Roman Empire and before that to the Grecian Empire and the days of Alexander the Great (Daniel 8:19-25). He will dominate the world more than any nation or man before him. The Bible tells us that there are a few exceptions. There are nations that will resist and escape this satanic government.

Daniel 11:41

41. **He shall enter also into the glorious land, and many countries shall be overthrown: but <u>these shall escape out of his hand</u>, even Edom, and Moab, and the chief of the children of Ammon.**

There is also symbolic language that the Jews have a way to escape the Antichrist when he takes over their land. The Jewish nation is referred to as the woman that that bore the man-child (Jesus).

Revelation 12:5-6

5. **And she brought forth a man child, who was to rule all nations with a rod of iron: and her Child was caught up unto God, and to His throne.**

6. **And the <u>woman fled into the wilderness</u>, where she hath a <u>place prepared of God</u>, that they should feed her there a thousand two hundred and threescore days.**

Revelation 12:14

14. **And to the woman were given two wings of a <u>great eagle</u>, that she might fly into the wilderness, into her place, where she is nourished for a time, and times, and half a time, from the face of the serpent.**

Is the "great eagle" a reference to the United States helping Israel in this time of crises? If this is the United States then it has turned from Satan's delusions and experienced a wide spread revival. This particular great awakening would have happened after the rapture of the church. If the U.S.A. truly becomes a Christian nation, then is Satan (the serpent/dragon) at war with the United States?

Revelation 12:17

17. And the dragon was wroth with the woman, and went to make war with the <u>remnant of her seed, which keep the commandments of God</u>, and have the <u>testimony of Jesus Christ</u>.

Satan is at war against the United States and our Godly heritage even now. Many know that Satan's war-strategy is to invade and divide the people with delusions and corruptions. He doses this by removing Christianity from the public and government places. Where he can't hide the church, he attempts to divide the church with false traditions and things that do not add up. I believe Satan will be defeated before the rapture of the church and the USA will experience a widespread transforming Great Awakening of Biblical truth.

Ephesians 5:26-27

26. That He might sanctify and cleanse it with the washing of water <u>by the Word,</u>

27. <u>That He might present it to Himself a glorious church</u>, not having spot, or wrinkle, or any such thing; but that it should be holy and without blemish.

Then the triumphal church will be raptured leaving behind a Godly legacy that will begin the Tribulation Church. As a transition to the last 3½ years of the Great Tribulation, it looks like the United States may go though massive nuclear destruction (Revelation 8:7-13?). We know the few nations that resist the

Antichrist are able to do so because they have truly become God-fearing nations (Revelation 13:7-8). Nevertheless, the Antichrist and his government will dominate the entire world with a reign of terror and deception that has never been seen before. This reign of terror will be short-lived because Jesus the King of kings will come back to this very same Earth and set up His kingdom (Daniel 2:34-35). *Selah.*

Matthew 25:31-34

31. **When the Son of man shall come in His glory, and all the holy angels with Him, then shall He sit upon the throne of His glory:**

32. **And before Him shall be gathered all nations: and He shall separate them one from another, as a shepherd divideth his sheep from the goats:**

33. **And He shall set the sheep on His right hand, but the goats on the left.**

34. **Then shall the King say unto them on His right hand, come, ye blessed of My Father, inherit the kingdom prepared for you from the foundation of the world:**

Those who resist the Antichrist and survive will be repopulating the Earth, working and living their normal lives blessed by God. On the other hand, the reign of terror is over for those nations and people that were part of the Antichrist's world domination. All those who received and promoted the mark of the beast will be separated and removed.

Matthew 25:41-46

41. **Then shall He say also unto them on the left hand, depart from Me, ye cursed, into everlasting fire, prepared for the Devil and his angels:**

42. For I was an hungred, and ye gave Me no meat: I was thirsty, and ye gave Me no Drink:

43. I was a stranger, and ye took Me not in: naked, and ye clothed Me not: sick, and in prison, and ye visited Me not.

44. Then shall <u>they also answer Him, saying, Lord</u>, when saw we Thee an hungred, or athirst, or a stranger, or naked, or sick, or in prison, and did not minister unto Thee?

45. Then shall He answer them, saying, verily I say unto you, inasmuch as <u>ye did it not to one of the least of these, ye did it not to Me</u>.

46. And <u>these shall go away into everlasting punishment</u>: but the righteous into life eternal.

The lost will recognize Christ's authority and call Him "Lord" before they "go away into everlasting punishment."

Philippians 2:9-11

9. Wherefore God also hath highly exalted Him, and given Him a name which is above every name:

10. That at the name of Jesus <u>every knee should bow</u>, of things in <u>Heaven</u>, and things in <u>earth</u>, and things <u>under the earth</u>;

11. And that <u>every tongue should confess that Jesus Christ is Lord</u>, to the glory of God the Father.

Everyone will call Jesus Lord, but not everyone will call Jesus Savior. For the people and nations that remain, Jesus will be both Savior and King. In this special last millennium of this Earth, Satan and his influence will be removed.

Revelation 20:1-3

1. And I saw an angel come down from heaven, having the key of the bottomless pit and a great chain in his hand.

2. And he laid hold on the <u>dragon, that old serpent, which is the Devil, and Satan, and bound him a thousand years,</u>

3. And cast him into the bottomless pit, and shut him up, and set a seal upon him, that he should deceive the nations no more, till the thousand years should be fulfilled: and after that he must be loosed a little season.

Jesus will personally establish His kingdom and authority on our planet.

Daniel 7:14

14. And there was given Him dominion, and glory, and a kingdom, that all people, nations, and languages, should serve Him: <u>His dominion is an everlasting dominion, which shall not pass away, and His kingdom that which shall not be destroyed.</u>

When Jesus comes back there will be sweeping changes at every level. The human lifespan will be greatly increased. People will be able to live even longer than Methuselah, who died the year of the Great Flood at 969 years old. The survivors of the Great Tribulation will be similar to Noah's family because they will repopulate the Earth. They will still be mortal and will have mortal children, like Adam and Eve did. At 100 years old, you will still be considered a child, not that you haven't matured, but rather that you have only experienced a small portion of your potential lifespan. The only reason your life may be cut short is for crimes you commit that make you accused and result in your execution.

Isaiah 65:20-25

20. There shall be no more thence an infant of days, nor an old man that hath not filled his days: for the child shall <u>die an hundred years old; but the sinner being an hundred years old shall be accursed</u>.

21. And they shall build houses, and inhabit them; and they shall plant vineyards, and eat the fruit of them.

22. They shall not build, and another inhabit; they shall not plant, and another eat: for as the days of a tree are the days of My people, and Mine elect shall <u>long enjoy the work of their hands</u>.

23. They shall not labour in vain, nor bring forth for trouble; <u>for they are the seed</u> of the blessed of the Lord, and <u>their offspring with them</u>.

24. And it shall come to pass, that before they call, I will answer; and <u>while they are yet speaking, I will hear</u>.

25. The wolf and the lamb shall feed together, and the lion shall eat straw like the bullock: and dust shall be the serpent's meat. They shall not hurt nor destroy in all My holy mountain, saith the Lord.

The example set forth by swift and righteous capital punishment will result in the majority of the population keeping themselves under control. Crime will be rare, and if committed, God would bring justice quickly. Mortal people will still have their old natures. They will not be perfect. However, instead of spending time spreading corruption, they will be spending time developing their homes, enjoying their families, and enjoying the fruits of their labor. They will be enjoying creation and getting to know God their Creator.

Isaiah 11:6-9

6. **The wolf also shall dwell with the lamb, and the leopard shall lie down with the kid; and the calf and the young lion and the fatling together; and a little child shall lead them.**

7. **And the cow and the bear shall feed; their young ones shall lie down together: and the <u>lion shall eat straw</u> like the ox.**

8. **And the sucking child shall play on the hole of the asp, and the weaned child shall put his hand on the cockatrice den.**

9. **<u>They shall not hurt nor destroy</u> in all My holy mountain: for the Earth shall be full of the knowledge of the Lord, as the waters cover the sea.**

This will be the most wonderful time on Earth. Crime will be at an all-time low and prosperity at an all time high. At the end of this special millennium will come an opportunity to choose for all those who have not made their choice between Satan and Jesus. There are no exceptions; sooner or later everyone has an opportunity to choose between Jesus and Satan. All the angels have already chosen. All mankind that lived before this seventh millennium have already made their choice, except those who died before the age of accountability. Therefore, there are two types of people who haven't made the choice to reject Satan by personally receiving Jesus as their spiritual authority.

<u>First</u>: Children who were born during this last millennium who multiplied and replenished the Earth. By the end of the millennium everyone, without exception, will have known Jesus for many years and will have decision-making ability. Therefore, there will be no children born near the end of this millennium (Isaiah 65:20).

Second: Babies who died and people who were too mentally immature to know right from wrong. They will have developed during the millennium (2Samual 12:23) and will have the opportunity to make their personal choice. They do not get a free pass, but they will be encouraged to make the right choice.

Sad to say, of these two groups, many will not make the right choice.

Revelation 20:7-8

7. **And when the thousand years are expired, Satan shall be loosed out of his prison,**

8. **And shall go out to deceive the nations which are in the four quarters of the Earth, God and Magog, to gather them together to battle: the number of whom is as the sand of the sea.**

At the end of this millennium, Earth's population will probably be at an all-time high; yet everyone will enjoy their own personal property, abundant food, and opportunity for trade and prosperity. However, even the best environment cannot fix mankind's heart of corruption or tendency for rebellion. It does not matter if everyone else is rebelling against God's Word; it is never wise to join that crowd. It is never wise to follow and promote a popular lie, especially if you know the truth (Mathew 12:40-45). If we do not walk in the light of Biblical truth it is inevitable we will inter into the darkness of deception. At the end of this world, the sheer number of those in rebellion because of satanic deception will be vast. The Bible often uses the terms "as the sand of the sea" or "as the stars of heaven" as visual references to a large number that is hard to comprehend (Hebrews 11:12). A number we could not count to in a lifetime (Genesis 15:5). *Selah.* Why would anyone want to join Satan and fight against the Creator of Paradise? The reason is deception.

Satan deceived one-third of God's angels and the majority of our human race. At the end of this last millennium Satan again denies God's Word and no doubt promises to set people free from God's rules. However, the rebellion will be short-lived. Once everyone has made his or her decision to commit to Jesus or against Him, judgment will fall. Jesus makes a statement in Luke that applies to both the present and the end.

Luke 11:23

23. **He that is not with Me is against Me: and he that gathereth not with Me scattereth.**

There is no middle ground. Even now you are either saved or lost. You are either in harmony with Jesus or out of harmony. However, now the lost can become saved and be united with Jesus. At the end you are locked into being either saved or lost. At the end the lost will be permanently separated from the saved. Your eternal destiny will be either with Satan or with Jesus. Your destiny is based on your decision of faith before your time is spent. Don't let the Devil deceive you into wasting all your time chasing his tempting attractions. Don't let the Devil or any preacher tell you there is no Judgment Day or eternal Lake of Fire.

Revelation 20:10-12

10. **And the Devil that deceived them was cast into the Lake of Fire and brimstone, where the beast and the false prophet are, and shall be tormented day and night for ever and ever.**

11. **And I saw a great white throne, and Him that sat on it, from whose face the Earth and the Heaven fled away; and there was found no place for them.**

12. And I saw the dead, small and great, stand before God; and the <u>books</u> were opened: and <u>another book was opened, which is the book of life</u>: and <u>the dead were judged out of those things which were written in the books, according to their works</u>.

The Devil and his deceptions will be permanently removed. The Devil joins his religious and political leaders who have already been in the Lake of Fire for at least 365,000 days (Revelation 19:20). Nowhere in the Bible, Satan or anyone else ever comes out of the Lake of Fire. At the Great White Throne Judgment, there will be no distractions. Everyone will clearly see the errors of their ways. This is the final judgment that will permanently separate the lost from the saved.

Matthew 13:49-50

49. So shall it be <u>at the end of the world</u>: the angels shall come forth, and <u>sever the wicked from among the just,</u>

50. And <u>shall cast them into the furnace of fire</u>: there shall be wailing and gnashing of teeth.

Revelation 20:13-15

13. And the sea gave up the dead which were in it; and death and Hell delivered up the dead which were in them: and they were judged every man according to their works.

14. And <u>death and Hell were cast into the Lake of Fire</u>. This is the <u>second death</u>.

15. And <u>whosoever was not found written in the book of life was cast into the Lake of Fire</u>.

Hell will be literally removed from the Earth and cast into the Lake of Fire. The Lake of Fire will be the permanent monument and symbol of the result of sin and rebellion. It reveals the contrast between good and evil (John 1:1-17, John 3:14-21). There you can plainly see what happens if God removals His light and blessing. What remains and takes over is darkness and torment. In this life we often don't recognize God's many blessings and opportunities. Torment is the natural effect of God removing His blessing just as darkness is the natural effect of removing the light. The Lake of Fire is the antithesis of God. *Selah.* Some may say this is extreme, but they don't realize how devastating and contagious sin is. There are five important points to consider before you criticize God's solution for sin and rebellion.

First: We will not cease to exist. Our spirits are immortal and will continue "for ever and ever." If our soul did not last forever there would be no need for an eternal destination for the lost. They would just leave a legacy and then disintegrate. Since spirits are eternal they need an eternal destination. The Bible states that after Judgment Day there are only two destinations for an immortal spirit – Heaven (see the next chapter) or the Lake of Fire (Revelation 20:10-15). Angels are also immortal spirits. Judgment day will reveal the restricted destiny for both fallen humanity and fallen angels. Demons are not in charge of Hell or the Lake of Fire. They are confined by Hell Fire and have lost all authority and ability to deceive and destroy. Hell fire was created for the Devil and his demons (Matthew 25:41). It is the demonic influences and actions that have destroyed our once perfect world. Some fallen angels became so vile they had to be confined early. They have been in Hell for thousands of years and are still in Hell today awaiting their judgment and destiny in the Lake of Fire.

2 Peter 2:4

4. For if God spared not the angels that sinned, but cast them down to Hell, and delivered them into chains of darkness, to be reserved unto judgment;

Jude 6

6. And the angels which kept not their first estate, but left their own habitation, He hath reserved in everlasting chains under darkness unto the judgment of the great day.

All the fallen angels as well as Adams rebellious descendants will face Judgment Day. Judgment Day will reveal why God will no longer be merciful to them and why they cannot be aloud in Heaven but instead will be quarantined in the Lake of Fire. God will no longer tolerate people killing, defiling, torturing or deceiving and stealing from each other. Nor will God tolerate anyone trashing and destroying His magnificent creation after Judgment Day. *Selah.* Jesus often used extremely graphic language to warn us about the devastation of the "eternal fire" (Mathew 5:29-30, Mathew 13:41-42, Mathew 13:49-50, Mathew 18:8-9).

Mark 9:43-48

43. And if thy hand offend thee, cut it off: it is better for thee to enter into life maimed, than having two hands to go into Hell, into the fire that never shall be quenched:

44. Where their worm dieth not, and the fire is not quenched.

45. And if thy foot offend thee, cut it off: it is better for thee to enter halt into life, than having two feet to be cast into Hell, into the fire that never shall be quenched:

46. Where their worm dieth not, and the fire is not quenched.

47. **And if thine eye offend thee, pluck it out: <u>it is better for thee to enter into the kingdom of God</u> with one eye, <u>than</u> having two eyes to be <u>cast into Hell fire</u>:**

48. **Where their worm <u>dieth not</u>, and the <u>fire is not quenched</u>.**

<u>Second</u>: All of Heaven is pure and perfect, because the cancer of corruption will be in the Lake of Fire, which is designed to contain corruption. God created us as free moral agents with the ability to love or rebel and hate. The Lake of Fire is not for redemption; it is a necessity to quarantine the satanic and rebellious from corrupting the Godly. God will not allow corruption to take over Heaven as it has the Earth. The Earth is an example of what happens to a perfect world after a small seed of corruption is planted and allowed to grow. *Selah.* God gives us a choice of either transformation or separation. Separation from the wicked is taught in both Old and New Testaments.

Exodus 23:32-33

32. **Thou shalt make no covenant with them, nor with their gods.**

33. **<u>They shall not dwell in thy land, lest they make thee sin against Me</u>: for if thou serve their gods, it will surely be a snare unto thee.**

Some think they know better than God on these matters and preach unity and compromise. Unity and compromise may be appropriate for those already married, in order to walk in love with their spouse. It may also be appropriate in a few other arias but it is a bad policy when it comes to spiritual issues. If you unite or compromise to please Satan, you will regret it. History continually reveals that God is correct in our need to be separated from the satanic and avoid spiritual poisoning.

Deuteronomy 7:2-5

2. **And when the LORD thy God shall deliver them before thee; thou shalt smite them, and utterly destroy them; thou shalt make no covenant with them, nor shew mercy unto them:**

3. **Neither shalt thou make marriages with them; thy daughter thou shalt not give unto his son, nor his daughter shalt thou take unto thy son.**

4. **For <u>they will turn away thy son from following Me, that they may serve other gods</u>: so will the anger of the LORD be kindled against you, and destroy thee suddenly.**

5. **But thus shall ye deal with them; ye shall <u>destroy</u> their altars, and <u>break down</u> their images, and <u>cut down</u> their groves, and <u>burn</u> their graven images <u>with fire</u>.**

This may be hard for many to understand but God was uprooting a people who were engulfed in satanic unity. They were committed to torturous human sacrifices and immorality. For more than 470 years, God had been patently watching these people get worse and increasingly vile before judgment fell on them (Genesis 15:16). At that time God was purifying and preparing a small part of the word (Israel) to bring forth His unpolluted Word and His uncontaminated Son. Jesus and the Bible would become a transforming blessing to the whole world (Psalm 107:20). *Selah.* Both, history and the Bible verify that Israel joined in pagan practices and suffered greatly for it. Secular Humanism is a popular form of rebellion today. The result is the same as any other form of rejecting God our Creator. It connects us to Satan and his plans to poison us. Satanic poison is like a radioactive plague; it is both corrupting and contagious. God knows that separation from contamination is the only way to preserve perfection in Heaven.

2 Corinthians 6:14-18

^{14.} **Be ye not unequally yoked together with unbelievers: for what fellowship hath righteousness with unrighteousness?** and what communion hath light with darkness?

^{15.} And what concord hath Christ with Belial? or what part hath he that believeth with an infidel?

^{16.} **And what agreement hath the temple of God with idols?** for ye are the temple of the living God; as God hath said, I will dwell in them, and walk in them; and I will be their God, and they shall be my people.

^{17.} Wherefore **come out from among them,** and **be ye separate,** saith the Lord, and touch not the unclean thing; and I will receive you,

^{18.} And will be a Father unto you, and **ye shall be My sons and daughters,** saith the Lord Almighty.

Third: You may not agree, but the reality is that Judgment Day will be a fair process. Accountability is necessary because God has endowed us with a free will. Some say you can't categorize sin and no sin is better or worse than the other. It's true that none of us has a position of being a self-righteous judge (Luke 18:9-14) but God does categorize sin (John 19:11) and we can agree with God. No sin is good, but some sins are more devastating to individuals and to the societies in which they live. Just as there are different rewards in Heaven there are degrees of suffering in the Lake of Fire. The individual's level of knowledge, rebellion and corruption will determine the amount of condemnation they will receive. Much of the degree of torment is self-inflicted. For instance, an alcoholic will have an endless strong desire for a drink without it ever being fulfilled.

Proverbs 5:22

22. His own iniquities shall take the wicked himself, and he shall be holden with the cords of his sins.

Sowing and reaping applies to this life but it is magnified in eternity. The unbeliever's judgment will be according to their sins. The seeds of sin sown in this short life will eventually engulf the unbelievers with an overwhelming harvest of eternal regret. The Lake of Fire is full of torment, despair, and unfulfilled desires. Jesus is called the savior because He suffered and died for us to take our place and penalty. Jesus has made a way that we can be set free from sin and Hell Fire, if we will trust Him. Jesus invites you to joining His family but He will not make you join His family. Everyone will be judged first on his or her choice regarding Jesus' invitation. Everyone will be judged second on his or her chosen lifestyle. *Selah.* Jesus told this parable about the judgment of the lost. The servant in this parable is a religious opportunist, like Judas. He is never called a son.

Luke 12:45-48

45. But and if that servant say in his heart, My lord delayeth his coming; and shall begin to beat the menservants and maidens, and to eat and drink, and to be drunken;

46. The lord of that servant will come in a day when he looketh not for him, and at an hour when he is not aware, and will cut him in sunder, and <u>will appoint him his portion with the unbelievers</u>.

47. And that servant, which <u>knew his lord's will</u>, and <u>prepared not himself, neither did according to his will</u>, shall be beaten with <u>many stripes</u>.

48. **But <u>he that knew not, and did commit things worthy of stripes, shall be beaten with few stripes</u>. For unto whomsoever much is given, of him shall be much required: and to whom men have committed much, of him they will ask the more.**

The striping is a symbol of layers of punishment. Some religious people who believe in God, but reject the Holy Spirit will see more punishment than some ignorant pagans will. All sin brings various amounts of penalties. The penalty is based on the extent of rejecting God's ways, balanced with the knowledge the individual possesses, resulting in the amount of blame for the transgression. Everyone at the Great White Throne Judgment has some level of knowledge regarding "good and evil" (right and wrong). Therefore, they are responsible for their sin and are held accountable. Ignorance only reduces the penalty; it does not eliminate the consequences for sin.

Matthew 11:22-24

22. **But I say unto you, it shall be <u>more tolerable</u> for Tyre and Sidon <u>at the day of judgment</u>, than for you.**

23. **And thou, Capernaum, which art exalted unto Heaven, shalt be brought down to Hell: for if the mighty works, which have been done in thee, had been done in Sodom, it would have remained until this day.**

24. **But I say unto you, that <u>it shall be more tolerable</u> for the land of Sodom in the day of judgment, <u>than for thee</u>.**

<u>Fourth</u>: There will never be a need for future creations to experiment with corruption and rebellion, because they can see a complete history lesson at the Lake of Fire.

Jude 7

7. **Even as Sodom and Gomorrha, and the cities about them in like manner, giving themselves over to fornication, and going after strange flesh, are <u>set forth for an example</u>, suffering the vengeance of <u>eternal fire</u>.**

Nothing will be hidden. There will be no mystery. All of the knowledge of good and evil will be revealed (1Corinthians 10:5-11).

1 Corinthians 10:11

11. **Now all these things happened unto them for en<u>samples</u>: and they are written for our admonition, <u>upon whom the ends of the world are come.</u>**

Mark 4:22

22. **For there is <u>nothing hid</u>, which shall not be manifested; neither was any thing kept secret, but that it should come abroad.**

Luke 12:2

2. **For there is <u>nothing covered, that shall not be revealed;</u> neither hid, that shall not be known.**

Mathew 10:26

26. **Fear them not therefore: for there is <u>nothing</u> covered, that shall not be revealed; and <u>hid, that shall not be known.</u>**

Instead of deception, there will be perception. It will be obvious how a seed of sin can grow and destroy a perfect world, resulting in endless suffering. This will allow everyone to make an undeceived and wise choice to obey our loving Creator and remain perfect, rather than being ushered into the world of corruption (Hebrews 10:26-27, Hebrews 6:4-6).

Psalm 19:9

9. **The fear of the LORD is <u>clean,</u> <u>enduring for ever: the</u> <u>judgments of the LORD are true</u> and righteous altogether.**

Isaiah 66:24

24. **And they shall go forth, and look upon the carcases of the <u>men that have transgressed against Me</u>: for their worm <u>shall not die, neither shall their fire be quenched;</u> and they shall be an abhorring unto all flesh.**

The Lake of Fire is a sobering fact. There is no doubt about it, and eventually everyone will know all about the Lake of Fire. *Selah.* I would like to share my opinion of what Isaiah 66:24 is describing. You may recall the sacrifice that Elijah made on top of Mount Carmel. There was a circle of water around the sacrifice. Fire fell from Heaven and engulfed the sacrifice in flame. It also consumed the manmade river around the altar.

1 Kings 18:38

38. **Then the <u>fire of the Lord fell, and consumed the burnt sacrifice,</u> and the wood, and the stones, and the dust, and <u>licked up the water</u> that was in the trench.**

It would not surprise me if the Lake of Fire looks similar to that sacrifice, but on a much larger scale. The water around the burning sacrifice would symbolize the layers of time on Earth. In this "river of time" or "circle of life," you could see everything that happened, all the levels and progressions of mankind. You would be able to see the demonic influences behind the violence and corruption. Also reveled would be the redemptive acts of God and His followers. The Bible tells us that we are being observed.

Hebrews 12:1

1. **Wherefore <u>seeing we also are compassed about with so great a cloud of witnesses</u>, let us lay aside every weight, and the sin which doth so easily beset us, and let us run with patience the race that is set before us,**

When we step out of time and this life is permanently over, we will be on the side of Hell Fire or on the side of open endless freedom and blessing. There is no crossing over once you are out of time. You are either with Christ or with the Antichrist. Even if this is not a literal picture of the Lake of Fire, the monument to corruption, it's an interesting allegory of truth. I pray that you check out of this life on the right side – with Jesus Christ.

<u>Fifth</u>: If we choose to reject Jesus, He has made a way that we can be completely and eternally separated from Him. To be completely separated from Jesus is to be completely separated from His light of life, provisions for construction and endowments of joy.

John 8:12

12. **Then Jesus spoke to them again, saying, "<u>I am the light</u> of the world. He who follows Me shall not walk in darkness, but have <u>the light of life</u>."**

The Bible states the Lake of Fire was prepared for the Devil and his demons. Yet, it is capable of containing all those who embrace the curse of rejecting their Creator.

Matthew 25:41

41. **Then shall He say also unto them on the left hand, Depart from Me, ye cursed, into <u>everlasting fire, prepared for the Devil and his angels</u>:**

Jesus has prepared a better place for you.

CHAPTER 17
The Devil's Final Destiny

John 14:2
2. **In My Father's house are many mansions: if it were not so, I would have told you. <u>I go to prepare a place for you</u>.**

The choice is ours, whether we end up in Hell Fire or perfected for Heaven. No one is predestinated to go to Hell (2Peter 3:9). The Great Physician Jesus not only suffered to pay for the sins of the whole world, but also provided the inoculation, so we would not have to be quarantined in Hell. However, by design, He needs our consent to give us the antidote. Our consent is an act of faith and trust in God's free gift. Faith has an expiration date (Hebrews 11:1). If we could be purified by fire or consent to salvation in the Lake of Fire (as I have heard some say), then why would the False Prophet wait and suffer for a 1000+ years and still not repent?

Revelation 20:10
10. **And <u>the Devil that deceived them was cast into the Lake of Fire</u> and brimstone, <u>where the beast and the false prophet are</u>, and shall be <u>tormented day and night for ever and ever</u>.**

When Jesus judged the False Prophet it was too late for him to be saved. He went to the Lake of Fire early to show that no one, not even a religious man, will ever get out of the Lake of Fire. At Judgment Day, it is too late to implement faith or trust because we will be confronted with our activity resulting in our destiny. At that time we will see everything clearly. We will see our chosen path in life and the destination at the end. Any statement made by the lost at judgment time would not be an act of faith, trust, or love. Instead, it would be a desperate act of self-defense. If God ignored sin and let the rebellious go free (to be a repeat offender) at Judgment Day, He would deny the value of His own Son and Word. It would also be a bad precedent for the vast number of future creations. Also there would be no history lesson

391

or lasting monument to warn the many future creations about the danger and result of sin. Therefore another Great Tribulation would be possible without a visual understanding and reminder of the consequences of sin and rebellion. By design the new Heaven and Earth will always be full of peace, love and joy. God said there would never be another Great Tribulation.

Matthew 24:21

21. **For then shall be <u>great tribulation,</u> such as was not since the beginning of the world to this time, <u>no, nor ever shall be</u>.**

The Great Tribulation will never be repeated because all of Heaven will be aware of the Lake of Fire and what it contains and how it came to be. We will be perfected free moral agents and retain our free will to choose God's ways or rebel. Nevertheless, no one will be tempted lose their perfection and join that satanic rebellion or start their own. *Selah.* The Bible says now is the time of salvation. Now you have an opportunity to choose to be prepared for Heaven by receiving Jesus as your savior. All you have to do is ask Jesus' Holy Spirit into your heart.

2 Corinthians 6:2 (NKJV)

2. **For He says: "In an acceptable time I have heard you, And in the day of salvation I have helped you." Behold, <u>now is the accepted time; behold, now is the day of salvation</u>.**

The truth is that God is "Holy, Holy, Holy," to the third degree and He loves His creation (Revelation 4:8-11). God is the personification of wisdom. He will judge according to the laws He established. He will put an eternal end to sin's attraction and contagious corruption. God loves us and has made a way for us to be separated and cleansed from sin making us fit for Heaven. It is found in our personal relationship to Jesus Christ and His

Holy Spirit. *Selah.* In review, here are five of the many reasons the Lake of Fire is a wise and just creation of God.

1. We are eternal beings and need an eternal home. God provided a choice of one of two places. You can be with Christ or with the Antichrist.

2. All of Heaven is pure and perfect; because the cancer of sin that corrupted the Earth will be isolated in the Lake of Fire.

3. Judgment day will be severe but just. We will clearly see how devastating sin is. We will also understand sowing and reaping and the consequents of our decisions.

4. There will never be a temptation for future creations to experiment with corruption and rebellion, because they can see a complete history lesson at the Lake of Fire.

5. The choice is ours whether we end up in the Lake of Fire or are perfected for Heaven. We have no one to blame but ourselves if we end up in the Lake of Fire. That will be clearly seen and understood at Judgment Day.

1 Peter 3:18

[18.] **For <u>Christ also hath once suffered for sins, the just for the unjust, that He might bring us to God</u>, being put to death in the flesh, but quickened by the Spirit:**

Joshua 24:15

[15.] **And if it seem evil unto you to serve the LORD, <u>choose</u> you this day whom ye will serve; whether the gods which your fathers served that were on the other side of the flood, or the gods of the Amorites, in whose land ye dwell: but <u>as for me and my house, we will serve the LORD</u>.**

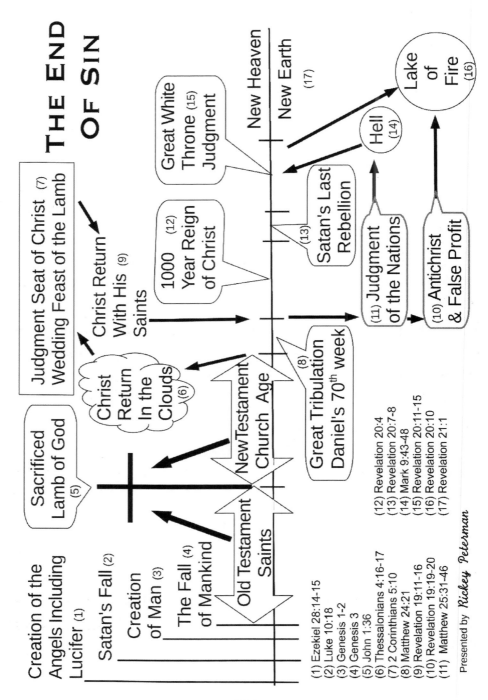

THE END OF SIN

Creation of the Angels Including Lucifer (1)

Satan's Fall (2)

Creation of Man (3)

The Fall (4) of Mankind

Old Testament Saints

Sacrificed Lamb of God (5)

Christ Return In the Clouds (6)

New Testament Church Age

Judgment Seat of Christ (7) Wedding Feast of the Lamb

Christ Return With His (9) Saints

Great Tribulation Daniel's 70th week (8)

1000 Year Reign of Christ (12)

Great White Throne (15) Judgment

Satan's Last Rebellion (13)

New Heaven

New Earth (17)

Hell (14)

Judgment (11) of the Nations

Antichrist (10) & False Profit

Lake of Fire (16)

(1) Ezekiel 28:14-15
(2) Luke 10:18
(3) Genesis 1-2
(4) Genesis 3
(5) John 1:36
(6) Thessalonians 4:16-17
(7) 2 Corinthians 5:10
(8) Matthew 24:21
(9) Revelation 19:11-16
(10) Revelation 19:19-20
(11) Matthew 25:31-46
(12) Revelation 20:4
(13) Revelation 20:7-8
(14) Mark 9:43-48
(15) Revelation 20:11-15
(16) Revelation 20:10
(17) Revelation 21:1

Presented by *Rickey Peterman*

CHAPTER 18

HEAVEN

2 Corinthians 12:2

2. I knew a man in Christ above fourteen years ago, (whether in the body, I cannot tell; or whether out of the body, I cannot tell: God knoweth;) such an one caught up to the <u>Third Heaven</u>.

The mention of the "Third Heaven" lets us know that, at the present time, there are three levels that are referred to as heaven. The first heaven is our atmosphere around the Earth, our sky where the clouds drift by and the birds fly.

Genesis 1:20

20. And God said, Let the waters bring forth abundantly the moving creature that hath life, and <u>fowl that may fly above the earth in the open firmament of heaven</u>.

Some people picture eternity in Heaven as sitting on a cloud and singing forevermore. According to the Bible, that's not quite accurate. The second heaven is the great outer space, full of darkness, doted with countless stars.

Genesis 1:14-18

14. And God said, let there be <u>lights in the firmament of the heaven</u> to divide the day from the night; and let them be for signs, and for seasons, and for days, and years:

15. And let them be for lights in the firmament of the heaven to give light upon the Earth: and it was so.

16. And God made two great lights; the <u>greater light to rule the day</u>, and the <u>lesser light to rule the night</u>: He made the <u>stars also</u>.

17. And <u>God set them in the firmament of the heaven to give light upon the Earth,</u>

18. And to rule over the day and over the night, and to divide the light from the darkness: and God saw that it was good.

We are just beginning to realize how big this second heaven is. I once heard someone refer to Heaven as a distant planet, but like sitting on a cloud, sitting on a planet is not accurate either. The first heaven surrounds the Earth, and the second heaven surrounds the first heaven. The third Heaven (where God was when He created the first two heavens) surrounds outer space (the second heaven). The third Heaven has a Capital City where the throne of God is located. We cannot measure the second or third heavens, but we do know enough to get some perspective of them. To get some idea of Heaven's size, we could look at the dot at the end of this sentence. Imagine that this dot represents the first heaven that surrounds the Earth. The second heaven would be the Earth on which the dot is located. From that viewpoint, everything surrounding the scope of the Earth would be the endless third Heaven. I believe that the third Heaven surrounds the first two heavens physically as well as spiritually. By spiritually, I am talking about dimensions beyond our three-dimensional universe. Therefore, there is plenty of room for expansion. Heaven will never be over populated, and there will always be new places to explore and things to do. In this life we cannot reach the third Heaven by natural means, but Jesus and His angels can cross that distance in less than the blink of an eye. For Jesus and His angels to come from Heaven to Earth is no harder than opening a door and stepping into our dimension. They can appear out of nowhere, or they can (humorously speaking) take the stairs as in Jacob's dream.

Genesis 28:12

12. And he dreamed, and behold a ladder set up on the earth, and the top of it reached to Heaven: and behold the angels of God ascending and descending on it.

God opened the door of His elevator to John.

Revelation 4:1-2

1. After this I looked, and, behold, a door was opened in Heaven: and the first voice which I heard was as it were of a trumpet talking with me; which said, come up hither, and I will shew thee things which must be hereafter.

2. And immediately I was in the spirit: and, behold, a throne was set in Heaven, and One sat on the throne.

God can use a dream or vision to show us spiritual things, but He can also use a supernatural event. For instance, look at Enoch, who (humorously speaking) God beamed up with His supernatural transporter.

Genesis 5:22-24

22. And Enoch walked with God after he begat Methuselah three hundred years, and begat sons and daughters:

23. And all the days of Enoch were three hundred sixty and five years:

24. And Enoch walked with God: and he was not; for God took him.

God sent His chariot for Elijah.

2 Kings 2:11

11. And it came to pass, as they still went on, and talked, that, behold, there appeared a chariot of fire, and horses of fire, and

parted them both asunder; and Elijah went up by a whirlwind into Heaven.

Here is a thought about God's chariots and horses (2Kings 6:17), pillar (Exodus 13:21) and tongues of fire (Acts 2:3-4) that are mentioned in the Bible. Most of us have seen a returning space capsule or meteor. They look like balls of fire as they inter our atmosphere (1st heaven). Although they look like fire they are not made of fire. Maybe sometimes the chariots, horses and other Heavenly things also looked like they were surrounded by fire as they entered our dimension. Here is another example described by Ezekiel of Heavenly beings entering our atmosphere surrounded by fire.

Ezekiel 1:4-5

4. **And I looked, and, behold, a whirlwind came <u>out of the north</u>, a great cloud, and a <u>fire infolding itself</u>, and a brightness was about it, and out of the midst thereof as the colour of amber, <u>out of the midst of the fire</u>.**

5. **Also out of the midst thereof came the likeness of four living creatures. And this was their appearance; they had the likeness of a man.**

Ezekiel also sees Jesus revealed in the midst of Heavenly fire in Ezekiel chapter 8. In Heaven we may have a whole new perspective of the fire barrier between Heaven and corruption.

1 Corinthians 3:13

13. **Every man's work shall be made manifest: for the day shall declare it, because it shall be revealed by fire; and the fire shall try every man's work of what sort it is.**

Humor and speculation aside, the fact is that Jesus and the angels are not bound by time or space, and they can open doors for us that we would never even see on our own. Some of the details are a little fuzzy, but the Bible is very clear that Heaven is a real place. It is tangible and full of good things for our enjoyment. It will never end. It is eternal. *Selah.* The Bible gives us a vague idea of some parts of Heaven. The glorious details will be filled in later.

1 Corinthians 13:12

¹². For <u>now we see through a glass, darkly; but then</u> face to face: <u>now I know in part; but then shall I know</u> even as also I am known.

I believe this verse is referring to the coming perfected Heavens and Earth and not the completion of the Bible as some have said. The Bible was completed long ago, but we still "know in part; but then" when we are perfected in Heaven we shall know like never before. Now we just see a vague incomplete outline of our future home. Now we can get a taste of the good things to come but latter we will be feasting at the banquet in Heaven. Bible is full of insights to Heaven and how it will be different from this life. The Bible also opens doors to allow us to experience a hint of God's glory. In Heaven we will be engulfed in it. Following God's Word is the key to experiencing God's glory. A wise person should be in a process of continually learning and applying Biblical truths (John 13:17) and discarding false assumptions.

1 Corinthians 13:10

¹⁰. But when that which is perfect is come, then that which is in part shall be done away.

There is a big difference between our limited knowledge and occasional misunderstandings "now" and experiencing the completion of the "perfect" kingdom of God on Earth (Revelation 21:1-7). I look forward to that time with great expectation.

Matthew 6:10

10. Thy kingdom come. Thy will be done in Earth, as it is in Heaven.

To give us some idea of what we can expect, let's look at what the Bible says about Heaven and Earth. First of all, at the end of the 1000-year Reign of Christ, there will be a radical change. The Earth will be completely renovated by fire removing all contamination and then remade.

Ecclesiastes 1:4

4. One generation passeth away, and another generation cometh: but the <u>Earth abideth for ever</u>.

Earth will be an eternal part of Heaven. The Earth as we know it will be destroyed. The last time Earth was destroyed was during Noah's Great Flood. There was a transparent H_2O layer in the atmosphere (the first heaven) to shield the people from the harmful radiation of the sun. It was a much better filter than our present ozone layer. The Earth was like a greenhouse, and people lived longer in a healthier environment. The water surrounding the Earth came down, and the floods came up from under the ground (earth). The world we know now is much different than the world before Noah's flood.

2 Peter 3:5-7

5. For this they willingly are ignorant of, that by the Word of God the heavens were of old, and the <u>earth standing out of the water and in the water</u>:

6. Whereby <u>the world that then was, being overflowed with water, perished</u>:

^{7.} **But the heavens and the Earth, which are now, by the same Word are kept in store, reserved unto fire against the day of judgment and perdition of ungodly men.**

The cleansing renovation by water was minor compared to the destruction and purifying renovation that is coming by fire.

Hebrews 1:10-12

^{10.} **And, Thou, Lord, in the beginning hast laid the foundation of <u>the earth</u>; and <u>the heavens</u> are the works of Thine hands:**

^{11.} **They shall perish; but Thou remainest; and <u>they all shall wax old as doth a garment</u>;**

^{12.} **<u>And as a vesture shalt Thou fold them up, and they shall be changed</u>: but Thou art the same, and Thy years shall not fail.**

There is coming a day when the aging heavens and our planet Earth will need to be purified and renewed. "Heavens" are plural in the preceding verses, so it is probably talking about our ozone atmosphere as well as our galaxy and possibly the entire second heaven. *Selah*. On God's calendar there are events that precede the new Heavens and Earth. There will be a Great Tribulation. Following that there is an initial wave of judgment upon Jesus' return to Earth (Revelation 19:15), followed by a period of peace (Isaiah 11:4-9). This is the "Day of the Lord" which will last a thousand years.

2 Peter 3:8

^{8.} **But, beloved, be not ignorant of this one thing, that <u>one day</u> is with the Lord <u>as a thousand years</u>, and a <u>thousand years as one day</u>.**

Jesus will judge and govern this Earth for a thousand years (Revelation 20:6). The many references to the "Day of the Lord" focus on the beginning judgment and the concluding Great White Throne Judgment (Revelation 20:11). In the final wave of judgment we see heaven and Earth departing (Revelation 6:14-17, Revelation 20:11-12). *Selah.* Remember events recorded in Revelation are not necessarily in order. Whenever you read something along the lines of "and I saw," "and I beheld" or "after this I beheld" or "after these things I saw" it is beginning a new point of view. For example, Revelation 6:12-17 looks like the arrival of the final Judgment Day.

Revelation 6:12-17

12. **And I beheld when He had opened the sixth seal, and, lo, there was a great earthquake; and the sun became black as sackcloth of hair, and the moon became as blood;**

13. **And the stars of heaven fell unto the earth, even as a fig tree casteth her untimely figs, when she is shaken of a mighty wind.**

14. **And the heaven departed as a scroll when it is rolled together; and every mountain and island were moved out of their places.**

15. **And the kings of the Earth, and the great men, and the rich men, and the chief captains, and the mighty men, and every bondman, and every free man, hid themselves in the dens and in the rocks of the mountains;**

16. **And said to the mountains and rocks, fall on us, and hide us from the face of Him that sitteth on the throne, and from the wrath of the Lamb:**

17. **For the great day of His wrath is come; and who shall be able to stand?**

The Great White Throne Judgment will be both traumatic and dramatic as Hell explodes out of the center of the Earth, delivering the lost souls to judgment. Then it is cast into the Lake of Fire. *Selah.* Fire will come up and crash down on the Earth, much like the water did in the Great Flood. At the last judgment, the very earth the unsaved are trying to hide behind will vanish, and they will enter a new dimension of time and space. All will stand naked before God.

Revelation 20:11-15

11. And I saw <u>a great white throne, and Him that sat on it, from whose face the Earth and the heaven fled away;</u> and there was found no place for them.

12. And <u>I saw the dead, small and great, stand before God;</u> and the books were opened: and another book was opened, which is the book of life: and <u>the dead were judged</u> out of those things which were written in the books, according to their works.

13. And the sea gave up the dead which were in it; and death and Hell delivered up the dead which were in them: and they were judged every man according to their works.

14. And death and Hell were cast into the Lake of Fire. <u>This is the second death.</u>

15. And whosoever was not found written in the book of life was cast into the Lake of Fire.

The Lake of Fire is Hell's final home. There are many references to this traumatic time of purification and renovation. Here are just a couple.

Isaiah 64:1-4

1. Oh that Thou wouldest <u>rend the heavens</u>, that Thou wouldest <u>come down, that the mountains might flow down at Thy presence,</u>

2. <u>As when the melting fire burneth, the fire causeth the waters to boil,</u> to make Thy name known to Thine adversaries, that the nations may tremble at Thy presence!

3. When Thou didst terrible things which we looked not for, Thou camest down, the mountains flowed down at Thy presence.

4. For since the beginning of the world men have not heard, nor perceived by the ear, neither hath the eye seen, O God, beside Thee, what He hath prepared for him that waiteth for Him.

2 Peter 3:9-13

9. The Lord is not slack concerning His promise, as some men count slackness; but is longsuffering to us-ward, <u>not willing that any should perish, but that all should come to repentance.</u>

10. <u>But the day of the Lord will come as a thief in the night;</u> in the which the <u>heavens shall pass away with a great noise,</u> and the <u>elements shall melt with fervent heat, the Earth also and the works that are therein shall be burned up.</u>

11. Seeing then that <u>all these things shall be dissolved,</u> what manner of persons ought ye to be in all holy conversation and godliness,

12. Looking for and hasting unto <u>the coming of the day of God, wherein the heavens being on fire shall be dissolved, and the elements shall melt with fervent heat?</u>

13. **Nevertheless we, <u>according to His promise, look for new Heavens and a new Earth</u>, wherein dwelleth righteousness.**

The process of separating the wheat (saved) from the tares (lost) is probably more traumatic than we can imagine.

Psalm 21:9-11

9. **Thou shalt make them as a <u>fiery oven</u> in the time of Thine anger: the LORD shall swallow them up in His wrath, and the <u>fire shall devour them</u>.**

10. <u>**Their fruit shalt Thou destroy from the Earth, and their seed**</u> **from among the children of men.**

11. <u>**For they intended evil**</u> **against Thee: they imagined a mischievous device, which they are not able to perform.**

The purification process has to be done in order to stop the plague of corruption and destruction caused by sin and rebellion. Those who choose not to rebel against God's perfect plan will be able to enjoy God's perfect plan. The time of mourning will pass and will never return.

Revelation 21:4

4. **And God shall <u>wipe away all tears</u> from their eyes; and there shall be <u>no more death</u>, neither <u>sorrow</u>, nor <u>crying</u>, neither shall there be any more <u>pain</u>: for the former things are passed away.**

Hell will be literally removed from the Earth. What remains will be a fresh new Paradise, free of all corruption and contamination. In this new Earth and Heavens, there won't even be a hint of the former corruptions or problems unless you visit the Lake of Fire. Even there, you won't be contaminated, but instead educated. Everything in Paradise will be beneficial to the population of Paradise.

Isaiah 65:17

17. For, behold, I create new Heavens and a new Earth: and the former shall not be remembered, nor come into mind.

I don't believe this means that God is going to give us amnesia, making us naive. Then we would have no understanding of history, redemption, or the holes in Jesus' hands and feet. I believe these things will be clearly seen and better understood than ever before. When God says, "The former shall not be remembered or come to mind," I believe He is referring to the former wicked thoughts and activities of our old nature. Our eyes will be opened and we will have the perfect mind of Christ. We will not be blinded by deception and misplaced affections ever again. Our losses and "former troubles" will fade away and pale over time, in light of the glorious place in which we find ourselves. It's good to have a time of grieving, tears, and remorse for the lost; but eventually we refocus on the future and move on. We won't see our relationship to the lost the same way after we are perfected. We won't blame God for the lost because we will see all that God went through for our redemption. We will understand how evil and deceitful Satan was and how he was steeling and corrupting what was precious to God and us. We will also understand how devastating sin is and why God will not allow it to contaminate Heaven. As free moral agents we will be free from all sin and have no desire to become contaminated with it ever again. *Selah.* Terrifying attacks of insecurity or corrupting sinful temptations will not come to mind in Heaven. When we are perfected and glorified, we will see everything clearly. We will understand good and evil and will never confuse the two again, because we will not be naive like Adam and Eve. I believe we will always remember that Jesus died for our sins and be grateful to Him for our redemption. We will be looking ahead to our developing relationship with the King of kings so much that it will obscure the past. *Selah.* There will be books in Heaven, and one of them is the eternal Holy Bible, full of history, both good and bad. The difference will be that in Heaven we will see things through God's eyes without the contamination of the corrupt human nature. Thoughts of the Old Man will never again come to mind. The Old Man has deceived me at times and contaminated my life, but I am not the Old Man. I am a "new creature" (2Corinthian 5:17). Our shortcomings and identity of corruption will not be remembered against us. Sin will not be identified with us, because it and everything attached to the Old Man will be permanently separated from us. We will truly be a new creation in Christ.

Romans 8:1

1. **There is therefore now <u>no condemnation to them which are in Christ Jesus</u>, who walk not after the flesh, but after the Spirit.**

We are born-again into a new family with a new heritage. We will no longer be sinners associated with shame, but instead we will be seen as stars in the family of God. When we are glorified, no shame or hint of darkness will linger. We will be perfected and surrounded by the Joy of the Lord. *Selah.* So, what does God reveal in His Word about Heaven, our future home?

Revelation 21:1

1. **And I saw a <u>new Heaven</u> and a <u>new Earth</u>: for the first heaven and the first earth were passed away; and there was <u>no more sea</u>.**

The new Earth will have rivers and lakes, but no vast saltwater oceans. Without the oceans, which now cover most of our planet, the new Earth will have more land to populate.

Hebrews 11:16

16. **But now they desire a <u>better country</u>, that is, an heavenly: wherefore God is not ashamed to be called their God: for He hath <u>prepared for them a city</u>.**

No doubt, there will be plenty of nature and countryside, but there is also a special city being prepared for us. It is the capital city of the kingdom of God. Now Heaven's capital city is probably somewhere to the north of us (Psalm 48:1-3, Ezekiel 1:3-4, Isaiah 14:12-14). An old fashion compass, which we use for navigation, will point out the general direction of Heaven's capital city. It is located in the third Heaven. After Jesus (the King of kings) has finished remodeling it, this city will be moved from the third Heaven so that it can be seen from the new Earth. Let's take a close look at this city's description in the Bible and see what it will look like. The first thing we see is that it will be descending to the Earth. Its appearance is like a radiant crystal-clear jasper gemstone.

Revelation 21:10-11

10. **And he carried me away in the spirit to <u>a great and high mountain</u>, and shewed me that great city, the holy Jerusalem, <u>descending out of Heaven</u> from God,**

11. **Having the glory of God: and her <u>light</u> was like unto a <u>stone most precious</u>, even like a <u>jasper stone, clear as crystal</u>;**

I once thought of the capital city as a cube, but the Bible seems to describe it as more of a mountain. In the Bible, a mountain is often a large hill but sometimes a mountain refers to an earthly or heavenly kingdom. The "Mountain of the Lord" and "Mount Zion" are references to God's capital city. God will give us eternal roots inside His capital city.

Exodus 15: 17-18

17. Thou shalt bring them in, and <u>plant them in the mountain of thine inheritance</u>, in the place, O Lord, which <u>Thou hast made for Thee to dwell in</u>, in the <u>sanctuary, O Lord, which Thy hands have established</u>.

18. The Lord shall reign <u>for ever</u> and ever.

God's everlasting capital city will become our eternal home. It glows with God's Shekinah Glory. There is always light shining out of it. Therefore, darkness has no place in it. There are no shadows or dark alleys in it.

Isaiah 60:19-20

19. The sun shall be no more thy light by day; neither for brightness shall the moon give light unto thee: but the Lord shall be unto thee an everlasting light, and thy God thy glory.

20. Thy sun shall no more go down; neither shall thy moon withdraw itself: for the Lord shall be thine everlasting light, and <u>the days of thy mourning shall be ended</u>.

Revelation 21:23-25

23. And the city had no need of the sun, neither of the moon, to shine in it: for the <u>glory of God did lighten it</u>, and the Lamb is the light thereof.

24. And the <u>nations</u> of them which are saved shall <u>walk in the light of it</u>: and the kings of the Earth do bring their glory and honour into it.

25. And the gates of it shall not be shut at all by day: for there shall be <u>no night there</u>.

Who are these "nations of them which are saved" and earthily kings? I believe the Bible tells us who they are, but before we look at the nations of the new Earth let's take a closer look at the city that the "kings of the Earth" are visiting. This city's light shines down on the Earth, sort of like the sun does now. Because it is able to shine on all the Earth, I believe that the city is like a satellite and does not sit on the ground. If it sat on the Earth, the opposite side of the planet would never see its light because the Earth would eclipse it. The Earth and its satellite city of God will probably have patterns of rotation and orbit for it to be able to light the whole planet at some point. In addition, I am sure that God would arrange for us to see some awesome views of the new Earth being illuminated from this glorious city as they do their cosmic dance.

Revelation 22:5

5. **And there shall be <u>no night there</u>; and they need no candle, neither light of the sun; for the Lord God giveth them light: and they <u>shall reign for ever and ever</u>.**

There is no night in the city, but could there be night on the Earth? One thing for sure is that we will get to enjoy it forever. It will never be corrupted. It's not going to wear out or go away. *Selah.* Let's see what we can determine about the size of this eternal capital city.

Revelation 21:16

16. **And the city <u>lieth four square</u>, and the <u>length is as large as the breadth</u>: and he measured the city with the reed, twelve thousand furlongs. The <u>length and the breadth and the height of it are equal</u>.**

Another reason the capital city of Heaven would not rest on the Earth (besides the illumination and visual advantages) is because its size would probably throw the Earth out of balance. These measurements are not symbolic. God gives us the shape and measurements in the previous verse. The foundation is square. It "lieth four square." Today we use different terms of measurement, but a "furlong" is an old English word for approximately ⅛ of a mile. Therefore the bottom of the first foundation would be about 1400 to 1500 miles long and 1400 to 1500 miles wide. The city would be roughly half the size of the United States. It would also be 1400 to 1500 miles tall. Our moon is roughly 2150 miles across, so this city would be almost ¾ the size of the moon. I have read that the sun is 400 times bigger than the moon and about 400 times further away. That is why the sun and moon can look the same size from the Earth. If this capital city of Heaven were 100,000 miles above the Earth, it would look noticeably larger than the sun or moon, because the moon's orbit varies between 225,000 and 252,000 miles away from the Earth; and this city is almost ¾ the diameter of the moon. One thing is for sure, it's a mighty big city that will be seen in the sky coming toward the Earth and positioning itself in the perfect location.

Revelation 21:17

¹⁷· **And he measured the wall thereof, <u>an hundred and forty and four cubits</u>, according to the measure of a man, that is, of the angel.**

The length of a "cubit" is the length from the average man's elbow to the end of the middle finger, about a foot and a half more or less. So, the thickness of the walls would be well over half the length of a football field. The walls and first foundation will look like a polished jasper gemstone, except that they will be "clear as crystal." They will be transparent so that you would see both the golden streets and the colorful interior light shining out, probably much like a cut diamond or crystal prism.

Revelation 21:18

18. And the building of the <u>wall</u> of it was of <u>jasper</u>: and the city was pure gold, <u>like unto clear glass</u>.

Each of the four walls has three gates or entrances. Because of the walls thickness these entrances will be like tunnels.

Revelation 21:13-14

13. On the <u>east three gates</u>; on the <u>north three gates</u>; on the <u>south three gates</u>; and on the <u>west three gates</u>.

14. And the wall of the city had <u>twelve foundations</u>, and in them the names of the twelve apostles of the Lamb.

The walls have 12 foundations, not piled on top of one another, which would be one foundation comprised of 12 materials. It would make a lot of sense that if you had a 1500-mile tall city, there would be levels or, in this case, 12 floors or foundations. There could be more than 100 miles between one floor and the next level up. That's higher than our atmosphere, our first heaven. Although there is no exact line of demarcation, the most common measurement for the end of our atmosphere and the beginning of outer space is 62 miles above sea level. The current space station is only about 220 miles up. Therefore, the distance from Earth to the space station would be comparable to going up a large hill on the third floor, and there would be nine floors above that! If I could get in my car and drive straight up at 60 mph, it would take me about an hour and forty minutes to get to the next floor, thus leaving plenty of room for mountains and sky. Each floor has one gate to enter and leave the city (John 10:9).

Revelation 21:19-21

19. And the <u>foundations</u> of the wall of the city were <u>garnished</u> with all manner of precious stones. The <u>first foundation</u> was <u>jasper</u>; the second, <u>sapphire</u>; the third, a <u>chalcedony</u>; the fourth, an <u>emerald</u>;

20. The fifth, <u>sardonyx</u>; the sixth, <u>sardius</u>; the seventh, <u>chrysolite</u>; the eighth, <u>beryl</u>; the ninth, a <u>topaz</u>; the tenth, a <u>chrysoprasus</u>; the eleventh, a <u>jacinth</u>; the twelfth, <u>an amethyst</u>.

21. And the twelve <u>gates</u> were twelve <u>pearls</u>; every several gate was of one pearl: and the street of the city was pure gold, as it were transparent glass.

Each floor is different and "garnished" or decorated with all kinds of jewels. From the pearly gates to the streets of translucent gold, the city will be full of shimmering twinkling color. The walls and the bottom floor will look like jasper that is "clear as crystal." Jasper is not naturally clear and is hard to describe exactly because it can be found in any and every color, including black and white. It is often multiple colors with differing designs or patterns. Jasper can appear spotted or have a linear pattern. On one side, a jasper stone can look like a beautiful sunset over a mountain range, while the other side might be completely different. This is why jasper is such a good gem to describe the exterior of the Capital City. The sidewalls of the city will no doubt have lines where the 12 foundations (levels) connect or protrude as balconies. The bottom would be more spotted with an array of shapes, lines, and colors because of the roads, rivers, landscapes, and mansions above it. The base and the walls are transparent, "clear as crystal" and "like unto clear glass," similar to a diamond. However, unlike a diamond, there will be a collage of colors and patterns under the surface resembling a polished jasper stone. Inside the city, each level will be special. The floor above the first foundation will be sapphire blue. Each floor above that will be a different color, yellow, red, blue or green. The top floor will be purple amethyst. The Bible gives a detailed outline of the city and materials at different areas. So, what color will the roof be? What material will be used for the roof? The Bible only describes the 12 square foundations and the 4 walls. It makes sense to me that if you measured from the center of the first foundation straight up 1500 miles and then joined the 4 walls together at an apex, there would be no roof; and the whole city would look like a mountain or gemstone cut to reflect multiple colors of light, like a prism. On the top floor we would find God's throne with a cathedral ceiling reflecting a rainbow of color.

Revelation 4:2-3

2. **And immediately I was in the spirit: and, behold, a throne was set in Heaven, and One sat on the throne.**

3. **And He that sat was to look upon like a jasper and a sardine stone: and there was <u>a rainbow round about the throne</u>, in sight like unto an emerald.**

Revelation 22:1

1. **And he shewed me a <u>pure river</u> of water of life, clear as crystal, proceeding out of the throne of God and of the Lamb.**

The city will also have running water. No doubt, the river would run all through the city and would probably have majestic waterfalls as it drops to the next floor. Jesus enjoyed gardens; so His home city would probably have many aspects of a garden with trees, flowers, and colorful fruits. There will be a special tree that we first saw in the Garden of Eden (Genesis 3:22-24). It appears this tree will grow in multiple locations along the riverbank and in the middle of the divided highway.

Revelation 22:2

2. **In the midst of the street of it, and on either side of the river, was there the tree of life, which bare twelve manner of fruits, and yielded her fruit every month: and the leaves of the tree were for the healing of the nations.**

I was asked what the healing of the nations meant, but at the time I did not have a good answer. Although I believed this is more than just symbolism, I didn't have the key to unlock that mystery. There seamed to be a missing piece of the puzzle, so I could not see how these words were connected to the big picture presented in the Holy Bible. I was praying and nearing the end of the rewrite of this book when I read a familiar verse shared earlier in this chapter.

Revelation 21:24

24. **And the nations of them which are saved shall walk in the light of it: and the kings of the Earth do bring their glory and honour into it.**

As I pondered the ramifications of what God was saying here and where the people of the new Earth came from, I began to see something that I had not seen before. For the next couple of mornings as I was walking and talking with God, I ask Him if what I was beginning to see was true or are there Bible passages that deny it. The Holy Spirit began bringing to mind and linking up several Bible passages supporting the revelation. I began to wonder if I could remember the combination of diverse passages in the way that they came to me. Therefore when I got home I started writing them down as I remembered them. Although this is a fresh insight and not tested by time or debate, I thought I would take a few pages and share it with you for your consideration. I believe you will find it interesting. It has changed my perception of Heaven by adding a new dimension to what I already knew. Here is some Biblical background and a glimpse at what I was beginning to see. To start with, we need to realize that additions to the 1st resurrection conclude at the beginning of the last millennium. One reason for this is because the Judgment Seat of Christ (where those of the 1st resurrection will be judged) concludes before Jesus comes back to Earth.

Revelation 20:6

6. **Blessed and holy is he that hath part in the <u>first resurrection</u>: on such the second death hath no power, but <u>they</u> shall be priests of God and of Christ, and <u>shall reign with Him a thousand years</u>.**

Mortals that come out of the Great Tribulation and inter the last millennium will have an increased lifespan, but are not part of Christ's prefect government. The mortal people living during Christ's 1000-year reign are not a part of the 1st resurrection. They are in God's kingdom but not part of God's immortal ruling family. They are not part of God's purified priesthood. Remember, this Millennium begins after the Marriage Supper of the Lamb and Judgment Seat of Christ. The Judgment seat of Christ is where my life will be examined. I will be judged for the decisions I've made and receive rewards or losses. Then Christ and those of the 1st resurrection will come back to Earth to overthrow the Antichrist and rule for a thousand years. At the end of this last Millennium is Satan's final season of rebellion. Satan's final rebellion ends with devastating results. All mortals die. Everyone that was not judged at the judgment seat of Christ will face a different judgment. They will stand before the Great White Throne Judgment. Most believe that everyone standing at this Judgment is lost. The Bible does not say that. Although it does indicate that most of them are lost. Everyone that rejected

Jesus' gift of salvation, as well as all humanity that lived trough the millennial reign of Christ will be judged at this judgment.

Revelation 20:12

12. **And I saw the dead, small and great, stand before God; and the books were opened: and <u>another book was opened, which is the book of life</u>: and the dead were <u>judged out of those things which were written in the books</u>, according to their works.**

At the end of this world, I believe there are some that (like in the Great Tribulation) reject Satan and have committed themselves to Jesus. Therefore they have their names written in the book of eternal life. Details about the survivors of the Great Tribulation are found in chapter 16 of this book. Bible is clear that all those that came out of the Great Tribulation and entered the last millennium as mortals already have their names in the "book of life of the Lamb" (Revelation 13:8).

Revelation 20:15

15. **And <u>whosoever was not found</u> written in the book of life was cast into the Lake of Fire.**

The phrase "whosoever was not found written in the book of life" implies there are some that were found in the book of life. Therefore some people at the Great White Throne Judgment may hear the same words Jesus announced to the redeemed when He came back to the Earth.

Matthew 25:34

34. **Then shall the King say unto them on his right hand, Come, ye blessed of my Father, inherit the kingdom prepared for you from the foundation of the world:**

This time they will have to be transformed since their bodies died at the end of the old world. There will be no flesh, as we know it in Heaven. No fallen human natures. No corrupted human bodies producing waste. *Selah.* What I am about to share is the part of the puzzle that I did not see before. I began to realize how well it fit the entire Biblical picture and answers the question from Revelation 22:2 regarding why "the leaves of the tree were for the healing of the nations." I don't think you can dismiss it if you see it. These redeemed mortals will receive non-ageing bodies like Adam and Eve were originally created with. Remember it wasn't until Adam and Eve sinned that corruption entered their bodies, which eventually produced the death of their bodies. Yet even then, God had to removed the healing tree of life that would sustain their defiled bodies.

Genesis 3:22-24

22. **And the LORD God said, Behold, the man is become as one of Us, to know good and evil: and now, <u>lest he put forth his hand, and take also of the tree of life, and eat, and live for ever</u>:**

23. **<u>Therefore the LORD God sent him forth from the garden of Eden,</u> to till the ground from whence he was taken.**

24. **<u>So He drove out the man;</u> and He placed at the east of the garden of Eden Cherubims, and a flaming sword which turned every way, <u>to keep the way of the tree of life</u>.**

This is open to debate and disagreement because the Bible says no flesh (as we know it) will enter Heaven. What I am beginning to realize is that the mortals of the last millennium that have their names in the book of eternal life will receive a new type of glorified human body after the Great White Throne Judgment.

1 Corinthians 15:35-40 (NLT)

35. But someone may ask, "How will the dead be raised? What kind of bodies will they have?"

36. What a foolish question! When you put a seed into the ground, it doesn't grow into a plant unless it dies first.

37. And what you put in the ground is not the plant that will grow, but only a bare seed of wheat or whatever you are planting.

38. Then <u>God gives it the new body He wants it to have. A different plant grows from each kind of seed.</u>

39. Similarly there are different kinds of flesh – one kind for humans, another for animals, another for birds, and another for fish.

40. <u>There are also bodies in the heavens and bodies on the Earth.</u> The glory of the heavenly bodies is <u>different</u> from the glory of the earthly bodies.

This chapter goes on to focus on the transformation of the "1st resurrection." The transformation of the "1st resurrection" will happen after the rapture of the church and before Jesus' second coming to Earth. The children of God are included in the diversity of heavenly bodies. *Selah.* The Bible states in a variety of places that there are different kinds of angels with various types of bodies. There is a difference between angels and God's family (1Corinthians 6:2-3). What I did not realize is that there is also a difference between the "1st resurrection" (God's family) and "the nations of them which are saved." *Selah.* Christians living today will have a body like Jesus now has. We will look at our new bodies later in this chapter, but first lets see what kind of bodies the people of the new Earth will have. Thankfully, they will be different from our present bodies in many ways. The human bodies of the new Earth will have an improved anatomy. For instance, they will be able to fully digest food. There is no waste or corruption in Heaven. Nor are there any foul odors, except probably and appropriately at the Lake of Fire. Deuteronomy 23:12-14 will not be necessary in Heaven's capital city or the new Earth. Actually, the place outside the camp that was set-aside for waist and corruption (Deuteronomy 23:12) was used throughout the Bible as a visual metaphor of Hell, which will be in the Lake of Fire. *Selah*. Beside a perfected, non-polluting human body, this new human-race will also have a clean circumcised heart and receive a new purified human nature. It will be similar to the pure nature that mankind was originally created with.

Ezekiel 11:19

19. **And I will give them one heart, and I will put a <u>new spirit within you; and I will take the stony heart out of their flesh, and will give them an heart of flesh</u>:**

God is able to give these redeemed mortals a new pure human nature, which enables their souls to be part of the new Earth. *Selah*. No doubt some of these souls will be descendants of Abraham. Throughout eternity they will continue to reproduce until they are as countless as the stars. No-doubt, God will continue to expand this population throughout the new heavens and their leaders will visit Heaven's capital satellite city (Revelation 21:24). Abraham's seed will truly be just as God told Abraham.

Genesis 15:5

5. **Then He brought him outside and said, "Look now toward heaven, and count the stars if you are able to number them." And He said to him, "<u>So shall your descendants be</u>."**

Throughout eternity new people can be born and grow up to peak maturity. They will not get sick, die or even look old or feeble. This is because Jesus delivered them from sickness, death and corruption. *Selah.* Now considering the earlier question regarding what does the Healing of the nations mean? Why would anyone need the tree of life to heal him or her in a prefect place like Heaven? Well, apparently although there is no pain in Heaven, a human being may be able to do things (such as participate in some sport or adventure) that might damage some part of their body. The leaves from the tree of life will provide healing and restoration. That could be one of the many reasons the kings of the Earth are coming and going from God's capital city, the New Jerusalem. You may say that you can't have a damaged body in a perfect Heaven. Let's not forget that there is already one damaged body in Heaven. Jesus' resurrected body still has nail holes in it (John 20:27, Revelation 5:12). These scars are a reminder of what Jesus went through for you and me (Isaiah 53:5). The Bible clearly indicates that there will be no corruption in Heaven. The Bible also indicates in the perfected world there will be more diversity than we can envision (1Corinthians 2:9, 2Corinthians 4:18). The millennial reign of Christ may reflect what Heaven is like more than we realize (Daniel 2:44). There are many types of angels of which the Bible mentions a few. God created mankind with the ability to reproduce and fill the Earth. I believe the Bible indicates God has made a way for them to be in Heaven in their distinct but purified forms. It is fine if you disagree, but I believe these are the nations of the redeemed (Matthew 25:31-34). The survivors of the Great Tribulation are not part of the 1st resurrection but because their names are in the Lamb's Book of Life, they will have an eternal home in paradise. *Selah.* God also has a royal family that will rule with Him throughout eternity (1Corinthians 6:3). They are referred to as the 1st resurrection. They are a new creation. They are the "children of God" (Romans 8:14-23). This is the time in which God is building His family and preparing a place for them to live. Lets take another look at this glorious city, which is the capital of Heaven and our future home. If it is shaped like a mountain then the top floor would be smaller than the bottom floor. If there were a 100-mile gap between the floors, the amethyst (purple quartz) floor would be about 400 miles across. The walls would be nearly 300 miles tall and angled so they come together at the top forming a triangle. The Throne of God would be at the center of this floor and probably elevated above the floor (Ezekiel 1:25-26). There would be plenty of room for God's governors (Revelation 4:4) and guest (Revelation 19:4-6). Although for grand celebrations such as mentioned in Revelation 5:11, the walls would need to be covered with large balconies to contain the number mentioned there. This "most holy place" in Heaven would also have dimensions beyond our three-dimensional understanding, making God's throne aria limitless (Revelation 7:9-12). Looking down through the floors, we would find many mansions, including yours and mine.

John 14:2

2. **In My Father's house are many <u>mansions</u>: if it were not so, I would have told you. <u>I go to prepare a place for you</u>.**

Notice that God is the one who prepares our mansion and location in His house (His city). There are some that like to interpret this verse as rooms in the Fathers house. Although that may be an accurate interpretation of the words, I believe it sends the wrong message. It sounds like I have a room or a condo in a big building. Having a room in a house may sound like communal living. Having a room in someone else's house limits the satisfaction of property ownership. The lack of ownership, responsibility and reward is the problem with socialism. God is not a socialist. He is a King with a kingdom. When I think of a glorious kingdom it brings to mind castles. Great kingdoms have multiple royal mansions surrounded with beautiful landscapes. I believe our inheritance in Heaven will far exceed anything we have ever seen in this life. Its type of government is a kingdom with ownership of lands and mansions. In the Bible, a royal family is often referred to as the house of a king (2Samuel 3:1, 2Samuel 9:1, Luke 1:27). We can thank Jesus for preparing for us a place in the Father's royal family. We can also thank Jesus for preparing for each individual in God's family a personal residence that is fitting for royalty. There is a popular saying that "God builds our heavenly home, but we send up the building materials." If that were true, then what about deathbed conversions? The thief on the cross who turned to Jesus only lived a few more hours before going to Paradise. Much like the converted thief, some people do little, if any good works and therefore send up almost nothing. Does God prepare them a mansion, even without their good works? Yes, but their mansions will be poorly furnished because they did not lay up treasures in Heaven through their good works. Shortly before Jesus was crucified, He mentioned that there would always be the (relatively) poor.

Mark 14:7

⁷· **For <u>ye have the poor with you always</u>, and whensoever ye will <u>ye may do them good</u>: but Me ye have not always.**

There will be those who have less treasure, but there will be no homeless people in Heaven. Everyone will have their own beautiful home in Paradise as a gift, specially prepared for them by Jesus their King. Everyone's mansion will be glorious because Jesus paid the price to give us our dream homes. We can't earn our heavenly place. We will not compete with each other for our place in this capital city. I'm not trying to take your place, and trying to take my place won't fulfill or benefit you. There are simply no bad neighborhoods or shabby shacks in Heaven (Matthew 20:1-15) *Selah*. The perception of location, position, and government is quite different in Heaven. Jesus' disciples struggled a little with these concepts. When the disciples attempted to apply worldly standers to their view of Heaven, Jesus had to correct them.

Mark 9:33-34

33. And He came to Capernaum: and being in the house He asked them, what was it that ye disputed among yourselves by the way?

34. But they held their peace: for by the way <u>they had disputed among themselves, who should be the greatest</u>.

Later James and John conferred with their mother who, as a good mother often does, probably encouraged them to greatness.

Matthew 20:20-21

20. Then came to Him the mother of Zebedee's children <u>with her sons, worshipping Him</u>, and desiring a certain thing of Him.

21. And He said unto her, what wilt thou? She saith unto Him, grant that <u>these my two sons may sit, the one on Thy right hand, and the other on the left, in Thy kingdom</u>.

James and John agreed that their mother would spearhead the campaign for their places in glory. They may have been hoping to be the first to name and claim their positions in Heaven. After their mother finished her request, they came forward to confirm their desire.

Mark 10:35-37

35. **And James and John, the sons of Zebedee, come unto Him, saying, Master, we would that Thou shouldest do for us whatsoever we shall desire.**

36. **And He said unto them, what would ye that I should do for you?**

37. **They said unto Him, <u>grant unto us that we may sit, one on Thy right hand, and the other on Thy left hand, in Thy glory</u>.**

Jesus responded insightfully to their request.

Mark 10:40

40. **But to sit on My right hand and on My left hand is not Mine to give; but it shall be <u>given to them for whom it is prepared</u>.**

Let's look closely at the motivation and the consequences of this request. First, what was the motivation? We may not know someone's true motivation until judgment day. We may not even recognize some of our own motivations until judgment day. This is because motivations can be deeply rooted and complicated by various emotions and perceptions. Nonetheless, at judgment day I think we will see that James and John's motivation at that moment was vainglory. Vainglory is the desire to get ahead of, or be greater than, someone else. It comes from the prideful old nature. It wants to be recognized as superior, even if it means going behind someone's back or tearing someone else down. It is an attitude of self-promotion. Don't confuse self-promotion with volunteering. They are motivated by two different spirits. It is good to offer our help and talents when we see a need. We should live with an attitude of pleasing God, irrespective of popular opinion. The crowd is fickle. They may praise you right before they crucify you. Competition for the crowd's attention and approval is fierce. Prideful self-promotion is not good because it tends to promote disrespect, manipulation, and an attitude of a bitter rivalry. In the extreme, it results in hating your enemy (any person opposing you). Self-promotion lacks the mutual respect of being on the same team or in the same activity. This prideful attitude of superiority and entitlement breeds an environment of envy, slander, anger, and bitter fighting. We often see this played out in sports today. Challenging one another to greatness is good, and sports are good; but in God's eyes, it's not who wins or loses, but rather how you play the game. Did you prepare? Did you do your best? Did you face the challenge with the right attitude? If we disrespect anyone, we will find that our actions are rooted in pride, not consideration and mutual respect. Love is a much better source of renewable energy than arrogant anger. Nelson Mandela learned this and it transformed his life and his nation. He started with legalism then tried terrorism, which led to bondage. He learned the transforming power of love and respect. Then he applied it, setting him and his nation free. This attitude formed the foundation for South Africa to win the 1995 Rugby World Cup. To respect others is not necessarily to honor them, because some people are just not honorable (Proverbs 26:1). However, to disrespect others is to (among other things) underestimate their potential. Mutual respect is very important to God. He desires wisdom and respect to be part of our daily lifestyle, even in competitive sports. That is why it is good to see competitors shake hands after an intense sporting event as a gesture of mutual respect. *Selah*. When it comes to our eternal destiny, Jesus made it clear that we cannot win or earn our place in His city by being better or smarter than someone else. Instead, our place in the city is solely based on God's choosing. Just as there is assigned seating in God's throne room (Mark 10:40, Revelation 4:4), God will joyfully prepare a place especially for you and me because He loves us. In a sense, it already belongs to us (Matthew 20:23) and we will love our heavenly homes. Everyone in Heaven will be grateful to God and respectful of their neighbors. *Selah.* James and John's idea of trying to overrule and get ahead of the other disciples by manipulation and self-promotion caused some friction when the other disciples found out what the brothers had done.

Matthew 20:24-28

24. **And when the ten heard it, they were moved with indignation against the two brethren.**

25. **But Jesus called them unto Him, and said, ye know that the princes of the Gentiles exercise <u>dominion</u> over them, and they that are great exercise authority upon them.**

26. **But it shall <u>not be so</u> among you: but <u>whosoever will be great among you, let him be your minister;</u>**

27. **And <u>whosoever will be chief among you, let him be your servant</u>:**

28. **Even as the Son of man came not to be ministered unto, but to minister, and to give His life a ransom for many.**

In Heaven, the leadership does not rule over others as kings do now. It's more like a respectful and considerate family. Loving parents are in charge and take care of the children. The greatest in Heaven will be those who have the greatest ability to serve and will love doing so. The least in Heaven will have the least ability to serve. *Selah.* What I'm about to point out may sound contrary to what I previously stated, but it is not. All of us have personal opportunities for improvement. Development is not based on being better than our peers. In fact, it has nothing to do with our peers. Instead it is rooted in our personal maturity and our developed abilities. Everyone in Heaven will be perfect. Everyone in Heaven will be 100% sinless. Everyone will also be unique with different rewards and abilities. To illustrate this principal; I remember when I was young and looking forward to having the privilege of driving a car. When I finally matured to my mid-teens, I passed the driving test and was granted my drivers license. I was not in competition with anyone else to get my drivers license. All I had to do was qualify. Qualifying and obtaining that license has opened up many opportunities to enjoy "dream come true" road trips, both solo on a chopper motorcycle and with my wife Marsha in a custom van. Even now, many years later, because I received my license to drive, I can enjoy my 1970 Corvette Stingray and motor home to an even greater degree. Some people prefer not to drive and enjoy being chauffeured around. That is fine because I enjoy being the chauffeur. It is rewarding to increase our ability to serve others and enjoy God's extraordinary blessings. Nonetheless, Jesus chooses and prepares our place in His city (John 14:2-3). He has reserved a special place just for you. His free gift to you is wonderful and eternal.

1 Peter 1:4

4. **To an <u>inheritance incorruptible</u>, and <u>undefiled</u>, and that <u>fadeth not</u> away, <u>reserved in Heaven for you</u>,**

Although I'm not competing for your place in the city, I can and should improve mine. I'm not in competition with you to get closer to Jesus. My relationship to Jesus is based on my time spent with Him in prayer, study, and activity. *Selah.* God desires all His children to mature and find joy in working with Him to bless others. Jesus sees the varying degrees of dedication to helping others, and rewards us accordingly (1Corinthians 9:18-25). Our dedication may set us apart and make us eligible for greater service and rewards. Each of us has our own race to run, our own circle of influence.

Hebrews 12:1

1. **Wherefore seeing we also are compassed about with so great a cloud of witnesses, let us lay aside every weight, and the sin which doth so easily beset us, and let us <u>run with patience the race that is set before us</u>,**

In God's eyes I do not win by making others losers. Paul learned this after he became a Christian. In spite of his own confinement he wanted to see others set free.

Philippians 1:14-18

14. **And many of the brethren in the Lord, waxing confident by my bonds, are much more bold to speak the Word without fear.**

15. **Some indeed preach Christ even of envy and strife; and some also of good will:**

16. **The one preach Christ of contention, not sincerely, <u>supposing to add affliction to my bonds</u>:**

17. **<u>But the other of love</u>, knowing that I am set for the defence of the gospel.**

18. **What then? notwithstanding, every way, whether in pretence, or in truth, Christ is preached; and I therein do rejoice, yea, and will rejoice.**

We win by making others winners. Our race is not against each other, but against the clock. One day our time will run out, and we will cross the finish line.

Acts 20:24

24. But none of these things move me, neither count I my life dear unto myself, so that I might <u>finish my course with joy</u>, and the ministry, which I have received of the Lord Jesus, to testify the gospel of the grace of God.

When this life is finished, we will not be finished, but our struggle will be over. Every child of God will stand before the Judgment Seat of Christ and see how God multiplied the fruits of our labors and offerings (John 6:9-12).

2 Timothy 4:6-8

6. For I am now ready to be offered, and the time of my departure is at hand.

7. I have fought a good fight, I have finished my course, I have kept the faith:

8. Henceforth there is laid up for me a crown of righteousness, which the Lord, the righteous judge, shall give me at that day: and <u>not to me only, but unto all them also that love his appearing</u>.

There are very real and permanent treasures we can earn with our good works.

Matthew 6:20

20. But <u>lay up for yourselves treasures</u> in Heaven, where neither moth nor rust doth corrupt, and where thieves do not break through nor steal:

One good work we can all do is helping others to get their rewards and not suffer losses, especially the greatest loss of all – the loss of their eternal home in Heaven. Friendships are the most rewarding thing we can make here on Earth and bring to Heaven.

Selah. We will appreciate the mansion God has prepared for us in the capital city. We will enjoy sharing our treasures, relaxing and spending time entertaining friends in our mansions. It is also possible that there will be other places we can go outside the city that will become exceedingly special to us. We cannot earn our home in Heaven or loose our home once we become part of the family of God, although we can loose rewards and awards. If a Christian denies Jesus or His Word, God may deny them opportunities to experience new adventures with Him (2Timothy 2:12). Jesus told this following parable in Luke about how He will choose His government to rule over the Earth during the last millennium. The money given to the servants represents the opportunities they were given to multiply the kingdom.

Luke 19:15-19

15. **And it came to pass, that when he was returned, having received the kingdom, then he commanded these servants to be called unto him, to whom he had given the money, that he might know how much every man had gained by trading.**

16. **Then came the first, saying, <u>lord, thy pound hath gained ten pounds</u>.**

17. **And he said unto him, well, thou good servant: <u>because thou hast been faithful in a very little, have thou authority over ten cities</u>.**

18. **And the second came, saying, <u>lord, thy pound hath gained five pounds</u>.**

19. **And <u>he said likewise to him, be thou also over five cities</u>.**

I believe this principle may also apply to the new Heaven and new Earth. God the Creator is not finished creating and expanding His kingdom. He will continue to create, and we may be given our own cities and planets to develop. The possibilities in Heaven are endless. *Selah.* On a little smaller scale, what are some of the rewards and treasures revealed in God's Word? As a youngster, I wanted a horse like the Lone Ranger's; a white stallion that would rear up tall on its hind legs before galloping off.

Revelation 19:11, 14

11. **And <u>I saw Heaven opened, and behold a white horse</u>; and He that sat upon him was called faithful and true, and in righteousness He doth judge and make war.**

14. **And the armies which were in Heaven followed Him upon <u>white horses</u>, clothed in fine linen, white and clean.**

There will be horses in Heaven. I don't know if they have wings like Pegasus, but at least some of them can fly. It would be nice to have one of these horses come when I called. It would also be nice to have a stable or big garage connected to my mansion where I could keep my horse. Do you think it would be possible to put together a 1970-style Corvette and a few other muscle cars in my garage? Are there any car enthusiasts out there who enjoy the timeless designs of these unique chariots? Can you imagine what it will be like riding around the streets of Heaven's capital city on a horse or in a custom chariot?

Ezekiel 10:19

19. **And the cherubims lifted up their wings, and mounted up from the earth in my sight: when they went out, the wheels also were beside them, and every one stood at the door of the east gate of the LORD'S house; and the glory of the God of Israel was over them above.**

I believe Heaven and Earth will have many kinds of angels, animals and vehicles. Nevertheless the most significant to us will be the people, the family of God.

Genesis 49:33

33. **And when Jacob had made an end of commanding his sons, he gathered up his feet into the bed, and yielded up the ghost, and <u>was gathered unto his people</u>.**

Everyone in Heaven will be popular and have abundant true friends. Heaven's level of love and respect far exceeds anything on this Earth. Every individual will consistently express love and respect for each other. Imagine the joy of visiting loved ones in their mansions and enjoying God's blessings together. You never have to say good-bye, but instead "see you later."

1 Corinthians 15:41-44

41. **There is one <u>glory</u> of the sun, and another glory of the moon, and another <u>glory</u> of the stars: for one star <u>differeth</u> from another star in <u>glory</u>.**

42. **<u>So also is the resurrection of the dead</u>. It is sown in corruption; it is raised in incorruption:**

43. **It is sown in dishonour; it is <u>raised in glory</u>: it is sown in weakness; it is <u>raised in power</u>:**

44. **It is sown a natural body; it is <u>raised a spiritual body</u>. <u>There is a natural body</u>, and <u>there is a spiritual body</u>.**

1 Corinthians 15:49

49. **And as <u>we have borne the image of the earthy, we shall also bear the image of the heavenly</u>.**

1 Corinthians 15:53-54

53. **For this corruptible must <u>put on incorruption</u>, and this mortal must <u>put on immortality</u>.**

54. **So when this corruptible shall have put on incorruption, and this mortal shall have put on immortality, then shall be brought to pass the saying that is written, death is swallowed up in victory.**

Everyone in Heaven will be friendly to talk to, perfect to walk with, and glorious to be around. Our spiritual bodies will be immortal, but not spirit bodies like a ghost. Your heavenly body will be eternal, tangible, and touchable, like Christ's body after His resurrection.

Philippians 3:21

21. **Who <u>shall change our vile body, that it may be fashioned like unto His glorious body</u>, according to the working whereby He is able even to subdue all things unto Himself.**

The Bible gives us a few hints of the abilities of the glorious resurrection body.

Luke 24:36-43

36. **And as they thus spake, <u>Jesus Himself stood in the midst</u> of them, and saith unto them, peace be unto you.**

37. **But they were terrified and affrighted, and <u>supposed</u> that they had <u>seen a spirit</u>.**

38. **And He said unto them, why are ye troubled? And why do thoughts arise in your hearts?**

39. **Behold My hands and My feet, that it is I Myself: handle Me, and see; for a spirit hath not flesh and bones, as ye see Me have.**

40. And when He had thus spoken, He shewed them His hands and His feet.

41. And while they yet believed not for joy, and wondered, He said unto them, have ye here any meat?

42. And they gave Him a piece of a broiled fish, and of an honeycomb.

43. And <u>**He took it, and did eat before them**</u>.

The disciples thought they had seen a ghost. They knew that Jesus had died and that the doors to the Upper Room were locked. Yet Jesus entered the room just by stepping into their dimension. He seemed to appear out of nowhere.

John 20:26

26. And after eight days again his disciples were within, and Thomas with them: then came Jesus, the doors being shut, and stood in the midst, and said, peace be unto you.

Our supernatural bodies will have the same ability as Jesus and the angels. We will be able to appear and disappear from any dimension or place and see into multiple dimensions. In fact, there could be angels (or demons for that matter) just a few feet from you right now. They are in what some may refer to as the fourth or fifth dimension. Call it what you will, but the important point to recognize is that there are spiritual dimensions. They are a real element of our environment. Just because we rarely see angels in our three-dimensional world doesn't mean they are not here. Even though we can't see them, they can see us and have influence on the things we can see. We see this illustrated when a foreign king wanted to capture Elisha. Lets look again at this revealing event. This foreign king decided to send his massive army to seize Elisha.

CHAPTER 18
Deep Foundations

2 Kings 6:14-15

14. **Therefore sent he thither horses, and chariots, and a great host: and they came by night, and compassed the city about.**

15. **And when the servant of the man of God was risen early, and gone forth, behold, an host compassed the city both with horses and chariots. And his servant said unto him, alas, my master! How shall we do?**

Then Elisha asked God to open his servant's eyes to see into that spiritual dimension where the angels were waiting for his command.

2 Kings 6:16-18

16. **And he answered, fear not: for they that be with us are more than they that be with them.**

17. **And Elisha prayed, and said, Lord, <u>I pray thee, open his eyes, that he may see. And the Lord opened the eyes of the young man; and he saw</u>: and, behold, the mountain was <u>full of horses and chariots of fire</u> round about Elisha.**

18. **And when they came down to him, Elisha prayed unto the Lord, and said, smite this people, I pray thee, with blindness. And He smote them with blindness according to the word of Elisha.**

The angels were already there, but the servant couldn't see them. The angels were not only there, but they were also able to supernaturally transform the situation. Instead of the army capturing Elisha, Elisha captured the army and led them to Elisha's king. *Selah*. Like the angels, our new bodies will have powers and abilities far beyond anything in this world. Also like God's angels, those of the glorified family of God will not be able to reproduce and make their own families.

Matthew 22:30

^{30.} **For in the resurrection they neither marry, nor are given in marriage, but are as the angels of God in Heaven.**

Our memories of earthly relationships regarding husbands, wives and children will be surpassed by our glorious loving relationships with our Father God and His family. We will have brothers and sisters, not husbands and wives. In Heaven the family of God will be uniquely glorious and exclusive. What I mean by exclusive is that once the Judgment seat of Christ has concluded there will be no additions to God's family (Matthew 25:10-12). There well always be new creations and perfected humanity will multiply but there will be no additions to the royal family of God. God is still adding to His family at this time.

Luke 14:23

^{23.} **And the Lord said unto the servant, Go out into the highways and hedges, and compel them to come in, <u>that My house may be filled</u>.**

Not long from now the last person will be added and we will participate in the wedding feast of the Lamb. Then there will be a type of honeymoon for a thousand years before we take up residence in our new eternal home. Every mansion in God's glorious City will be occupied and no more will be built. Although Heaven is endless, the size of Heaven's capital city will not be expanded beyond the Bible's outlines. God's family will not expand once completed; therefore the city will never be overpopulated. There will always be plenty of room for spacious mansions, beautiful parks and gardens and special places to take guests. It is an honor beyond comprehension to be at home in God's capital city. We can enjoy the expansion of the human family of Earth just as Jesus enjoys it. We can come and go from our city to the Earth or anywhere else we want to go without restrictions or limitations. Just like Jesus, we will be able to travel unlimited distances. It will be no harder than the simple decision to make the trip. I would be able to sit with Jesus in His palace, and decide to go and be tangibly on a far away planet to discuss current events and then come back again on the same day. Jesus demonstrated this very thing on Resurrection Day. Before Jesus went to the throne of God in Heaven He talked with Mary (John 20:17). Then after that He appeared in Heaven (Revelation 5:5-9?). Then Jesus came back to Earth and appeared to His disciples on the road (Luke 24:12-31). He departed from them by vanishing before their eyes. Later that day He appeared in the upper room seemingly out of nowhere (Luke 24:35-39). He was not and is not bound by time or space. Yet He is touchable. He has substance. He demonstrated that he could still enjoy food (Luke 24:41-43). When He disappeared, the food that He ate was not left behind. *Selah.* We will eat and celebrate with Jesus and our other friends on many occasions in the future. We will enjoy perfectly prepared food in an astonishing environment full of love, laughter and gratitude.

Exodus 12:14

14. And this day shall be unto you for a memorial; and ye shall keep it a feast to the Lord throughout your generations; ye <u>shall keep it a feast by an ordinance for ever</u>.

This verse is referring to the Passover Feast. The Nation of Israel was to remember their deliverance from bondage every year by coming together for the Passover Feast. This was to be done throughout their generations. In 30 AD, a day before the Jewish Passover, Jesus instituted the Christian Passover. We call it the Lord's Supper (it is described in detail in Chapter 9). The Jewish Passover was, in a sense, the wrapper that concealed the Lord's Supper. When the time was right, the wrapper was torn open to reveal the precious seed of redemption, the true Passover Lamb. Out of the Passover events came the Lord's Supper, the celebration of the true redeeming Lamb of God and our atonement. I believe it is the Lord's Supper that we will be keeping as a memorial celebration feast forever, not the Jewish Passover, because there will be no killing of lambs or anything else in Heaven. The Lord's Supper is a combination two symbolic Jewish feasts: the first feast Passover and the last feast Atonement (Revelation 22:13).

Matthew 26:29

29. **But I say unto you, I will not drink henceforth of this <u>fruit of the vine</u>, until <u>that day</u> when <u>I drink it new with you in My Father's kingdom</u>.**

Revelation 19:1, 6-9

1. **And after these things I heard a great voice of much people in Heaven, saying, alleluia; salvation, and glory, and honour, and power, unto the Lord our God:**

6. **And I heard as it were the voice of a great multitude, and as the voice of many waters, and as the voice of mighty thunderings, saying, alleluia: for the Lord God omnipotent reigneth.**

7. **Let us be glad and rejoice, and give honour to Him: for <u>the marriage of the Lamb is come</u>, and His wife hath made herself ready.**

8. **And to her was granted that she should be arrayed in fine linen, clean and white: for the fine linen is the righteousness of saints.**

^{9.} **And he saith unto me, write, <u>blessed are they which are called unto the marriage supper of the Lamb</u>. And he saith unto me, these are the true sayings of God.**

In this passage, the lamb is symbolic for Jesus Christ the Lamb of God, and the wife represents the redeemed taking their place at His side in the family of God. In Heaven there will be many celebrations and family reunions. Heaven will be full of joy and endless good times. In Heaven there will be no waste, repulsive pollution, or anything vile; but there will be plenty of eating, drinking, and celebrating with glorified loved-ones.

1 John 3:1-2

^{1.} **Behold, what manner of love the Father hath bestowed upon us, that <u>we should be called the sons of God</u>: therefore the world knoweth us not, because it knew Him not.**

^{2.} **Beloved, <u>now are we the sons of God, and it doth not yet appear what we shall be</u>: but we know that, when He shall appear, <u>we shall be like Him</u>; for we shall see Him as He is.**

Section 5

Illumination

CHAPTER 19

RECONCILING APPARENT CONTRADICTIONS

Proverbs 25:2

2. It is the **glory of God to conceal a thing** but the **honor of kings is to search out a matter**.

There are verses in the Bible that seem to contradict each other. When some people come across them and fail to properly search out the matter, they may lose faith or zeal and question the Bible's accuracy. The Bible contains life-changing facts that a child can understand, as well as some complex mysteries that are hard for anyone to understand. If we want to go deeper than John 3:16 then we need the Holy Spirit to open our eyes to see what God is saying. Without the Holy Spirit we won't even truly comprehend John 3:16. The Holy Spirit will deliver us from deceptions and false assumptions. The Holy Spirit will open our ears so we can hear God speak to us through the Scriptures. The Holy Spirit will put the Bible in the proper perspective and accurately teach us the deep and complex things from God.

John 14:26

26. But the Comforter, which is **the Holy Ghost**, whom the Father will send in My name, He **shall teach you** all things, and bring all things to your remembrance, whatsoever I have said unto you.

Things we do not understand should not sidetrack us, but instead help us to realize there are things the Holy Spirit has yet to reveal to us.

John 16:12-13

12. **I have yet many things to say unto you**, but ye cannot bear them now.

13. Howbeit when He, the Spirit of truth, is come, <u>He will guide you into all truth</u>: for He shall not speak of Himself; but whatsoever He shall hear, that shall He speak: and He will shew you things to come.

We should primarily focus on connecting to the Holy Spirit and consider what God is clearly showing us. By reflecting on what God has shown us, the Holy Spirit will illuminate our next step and expand our comprehension of our situation. *Selah.* If we are God's children because of the New Covenant, we should concentrate on following the way of life that God clearly reveals to us in the New Testament. However, we should not completely ignore puzzling Bible verses because they may be the key to our greatest revelations. The best thing to do with puzzling passages is to keep them in our heart and pray for wisdom to see how they fit the big Biblical picture (Psalm 119:18). Jesus' mother Mary had a hard time understanding the things she was seeing and hearing but she continued to reflect on them.

Luke 2:50-51

50. And <u>they understood not the saying which He spake unto them</u>.

51. And He went down with them, and came to Nazareth, and was subject unto them: but His mother <u>kept all these sayings in her heart</u>.

Luke 2:19

19. But Mary <u>kept all these things, and pondered them in her heart</u>.

After Jesus died, Mary and Jesus' disciple John became very close (John 19:25-27). I'm sure that John enjoyed Mary talking about her life with Jesus. We don't need to get theological to share our testimony. Every Christian should be able to share what God has done for them. Every Christian should continue to grow in faith and Biblical knowledge in order to teach and disciple others. We should continue to pray for wisdom and share what God makes clear to us. If God points out something we are teaching or doing that is not consistent with His Word then we are responsible to make the correction. If we resist correction and continue teaching and doing things that are not in harmony with the Bible we will do more harm than good (Mathew 12:30). The problem with teaching things we do not properly understand is that it causes confusion. Biblical confusion results in unbalanced church doctrines, which divide the body of Christ. We are free to have diversity in style but we should be unified in truth (Luke 9:49-50). Conflicting Biblical doctrines are a lot like the old story of three blind men describing an elephant. One is at the foot and claims an elephant is firm like an oak tree. Another is at the tail and says no an elephant is flexible like a rope. The third blind man is at the head and says you are both wrong it is Simi rigid like a large water hose. It is easy to get confused if you don't see the big picture. Even if we see most of the big picture there may be a couple of Bible verses that appear irreconcilable. They are like trying to put a triangle in a circular hole of a jigsaw puzzle. Critics of the Bible say it cannot be done; but they are stuck in two-dimensional thinking. If the triangle is actually a cone then it can be turned correctly to fit the circle and solve the riddle. It will also add another dimension to the puzzle. It will add depth to the mountain of God's Word. *Selah.* Sometimes our confusion is not from a lack of information or lack of perspective but instead it is from false information. The Devil was not born yesterday. Satan has a long history of planting false information then later using it to deceive people. All scientist, archaeologist and historians that come against the Bible will one day be proved wrong. Many have already been proven wrong but Satan continues to use them or replace them with new deceptions. For instance you cannot reconcile Darwin's theory of evolution with the Bible's account of creation. Who do you trust? The choice is yours (Joshua 24:15). If you say you're an intellectual and trust the evidence, then note the weight of evidence is increasingly on the side of intelligent creation. *Selah*. Our faith in God's Word is tested the most when we are confronted with superficial contradictions. In the light of Proverbs 25:2, let's look at God's Word regarding some concealed, less obvious, and hard to understand truths in the Bible. There are some tools and perspectives that can help us unlock these Biblical mysteries. Doctrine should be the total of what the Bible has to say on a particular matter. Most doctrines have a contrary verse that seems to see things differently. It may be hard to explain how that verse fits the big picture. This is where much of the Christian confusion and many divisions often originate. For instance, the doctrine regarding the process of redemption is very clear in the Bible (as we see in Chapter 11). Yet, Mark, a convert of Peter (1Peter 5:13), seems to add baptism to the doctrine of redemption.

Mark 16:16

16. **He that believeth <u>and is baptized</u> shall be saved: but he that believeth not shall be damned.**

I have heard it said, "You must be baptized to be saved. The Bible says so." For that reason, let's take a closer look at this verse and try to understand how we should approach these cryptic scriptures. There are three points to understand and connect in order to see what is actually stated here.

<u>First</u>: A clue for proper interpretation is actually contained in the verse itself. The verse concludes with, "He that believeth not shall

Deep Foundations

be damned." Therefore, the damned are all those who do not believe.

Second: The Bible teaches that water baptism is not necessary for salvation. The most famous verse in the Bible, doesn't mention any need for water baptism to qualify for salvation.

John 3:16

16. For God so loved the world, that He gave His only begotten Son, that <u>whosoever believeth in Him should not perish, but have everlasting life</u>.

If you read the context of this verse you will see it clarifies that the condemned are the unbelievers, not the unbaptized. The Bible also clarifies that the kind of belief mentioned in John 3:16 is a reference to faith not just head knowledge. Saving faith means you not only believe Jesus exists but you believe you can have a personal relationship with Him. We see this demonstrated when Jesus was on the cross. There where two sinner on crosses next to Him. Both believed that Jesus existed. One turned to Jesus in faith and said, "Remember me when you enter your kingdom." Jesus replied, "Today you will be with me in Paradise." Jesus responded to the one that turned to Him in faith and said he was saved. Also notice that Jesus did not mention any need to be baptized for salvation. Instead Jesus said salvation belongs to all those that come to Him (John 6:37-40).

John 6:47

47. Verily, verily, I say unto you, <u>He that believeth</u> on Me <u>hath everlasting life</u>.

Romans 10:13

13. For <u>whosoever</u> shall call upon the name of the Lord shall be saved.

Reconciling Apparent Contradictions

Once again the belief that Jesus is referring to is saving faith. Both sinners crucified next to Jesus believed that Jesus existed, but one demonstrated saving faith because he believed he could have a relationship with Jesus. That sinner was saved because he acted on his desire to know Jesus by calling out to Him. *Selah.* We will not get very deeply into the doctrine of baptisms here, but as seen in chapter 7, true Christian water baptism happens after we are born again. It is an action of obedience and discipleship. Some people are baptized shortly after they become believers, and that is good. I had been saved for more than a decade when I was baptized at the age of 20. I already enjoyed a personal relationship with Christ and had witnessed many prayers dramatically answered. My baptism was an act of discipleship and commitment to Christ, not salvation by Christ. Baptism is a choice we make to yield to Jesus as Lord of our lives after we have received him as Savior of our souls. Baptism is a meaningful and glorious ceremony we go through to identify with the death, burial, and resurrection of Jesus. Thus, going beneath the water and rising out of it is a symbol and testimony of our death and burial to self in order to enjoy our resurrection life in Christ.

Romans 6:3-4

3. **Know ye not, that so many of us as were baptized into Jesus Christ were <u>baptized into His death</u>?**

4. **Therefore we are <u>buried with Him by baptism</u> into death: that <u>like as Christ was raised up from the dead</u> by the glory of the Father, even so we also should <u>walk in newness of life</u>.**

The Christian baptism is a baptism of discipleship. The process of discipleship starts with recognizing there is a need to change. Then believing God has a plan for salvation. Then, personally submitting to God's plan by receiving the Holy Ghost. Then

Deep Foundations

becoming a disciple of Jesus by being baptized in His name. The time it takes to start and complete this initial conversion experience with the evidence of a changed life depends on the individual. The Christian baptism of discipleship is different from John the Baptist's baptism of repentance. John's baptism of repentance was a statement that from that moment the individual was going to attempt to change the direction of their life. The Christian baptism is a statement that Jesus has already changed our life by giving us the Holy Spirit.

Acts 19:2-5

2. He said unto them, <u>Have ye received the Holy Ghost</u> since ye believed? And they said unto him, We have not so much as heard whether there be any Holy Ghost.

3. And he said unto them, <u>Unto what then were ye baptized?</u> And they said, Unto John's baptism.

4. Then said Paul, John verily baptized with the baptism of repentance, saying unto the people, that they should believe on him which should come after him, that is, on Christ Jesus.

5. When they heard this, they were baptized in the name of the Lord Jesus.

These men may have believed that Jesus was the Messiah but their good works of repentance was what saved them. Or they may have been born-again but were unaware of their relationship to the Holy Spirit. Both of these situations are common to religious people. You may receive Jesus' Spirit in your heart without any outward manifestations. The lack of Biblical understanding can mislead or limit your faith resulting in confusion and a lack of miraculous manifestations.

Reconciling Apparent Contradictions

Matthew 13:58

58. And He did <u>not many mighty works</u> there <u>because of their unbelief</u>.

Everyone has faith in something but God is looking for people that have faith in His Word.

Romans 10:17

17. So then faith cometh by hearing, and hearing by the Word of God.

Once these twelve men understood the Holy Spirit of Jesus was actually in their heart, they were properly baptized in the name of Jesus. Then Paul laid his hands on them to anoint them for spiritual service and the Holy Spirit "came upon them" with power to witness God's presents and proclaim God's goodness (Acts 19:6). This progression of spiritual growth becomes clearer as we gather all the passages on the subject. *Selah.* Every Christian starts out as a spiritual baby and should focus on what they can digest.

1 Peter 2:2

2. As newborn babes, desire the sincere milk of the Word, that ye may grow thereby:

1 Corinthians 3:2

2. I have fed you with milk, and not with meat: for hitherto ye were not able to bear it, neither yet now are ye able.

Hebrews 5:14

14. But strong meat belongeth to them that are of full age, even those who <u>by reason of use</u> have their senses exercised to discern both good and evil.

CHAPTER 19
Deep Foundations

As we mature we are able to discern what is true and reject all deceptions and distortions. We see this Biblical progression of spiritual growth starts with the Holy Ghost. After we receive Jesus' Spirit in our heart, we can be properly baptized in water in order to identify with Jesus as His disciple. This sequence is clearly stated earlier in the book of Acts.

Acts 10:47

47. **Can any man forbid <u>water</u>, that should not be <u>baptized</u>, which <u>have received the Holy Ghost</u> as well as we?**

Notice that the proper meaning and context of water baptism became clear as the early church matured. First came the Holy Ghost and salvation, and then baptism with water. They did not need to be baptized with water to qualify to receive the Holy Spirit.

John 14:16

16. **And I will pray the Father, and He shall <u>give you</u> another Comforter, that He may <u>abide with you for ever;</u>**

The Holy Ghost (Comforter) is a gift. The Holy Ghost will not leave us once we receive Him into our heart.

John 14:26

26. **But <u>the Comforter, which is the Holy Ghost, whom the Father will send in My name</u>, He shall teach you all things, and bring all things to your remembrance, whatsoever I have said unto you.**

The Holy Ghost comes to us in the name of Jesus. We cannot earn the Holy Ghost by being baptized in water. All we have to do is simply ask.

Reconciling Apparent Contradictions

Luke 11:13

13. If ye then, being evil, know how to give good gifts unto your children: how much more shall your heavenly Father give the Holy Spirit <u>to them that ask Him</u>?

Luke 11:9

9. And <u>I say unto you, Ask</u>, and it shall be given you; seek, and ye shall find; knock, and it shall be opened unto you.

It is the Holy Spirit that transforms us into children of God, not water-baptism.

Romans 8:14-15

14. For as many as are led by the Spirit of God, <u>they are the sons of God</u>.

15. For ye have not received the spirit of bondage again to fear; but ye have received the <u>Spirit of adoption</u>, whereby we cry, Abba, Father.

Our union with Holy Ghost is essential and the only thing necessary to make us children of God. If you are water baptized, but do not receive the Holy Spirit, then you are not a child of God.

Romans 8:9 (NIV)

9. You, however, are not in the realm of the flesh but are in the realm of the Spirit, <u>if</u> indeed the <u>Spirit of God lives in you. And if anyone does not have the Spirit of Christ, they do not belong to Christ.</u>

<u>Third</u>: Since being saved is the result of having the "Spirit of Christ" not water-baptism then why is this verse in the Bible? Why did God the Holy Spirit allow Mark, even move Mark, to state, "And be baptized to be saved"? Mark's statement may

Deep Foundations

seem to be contrary, but it actually adds clarification. Although baptism often refers to baptism by water, in Mark 16:16 it refers to baptism of the Spirit. Mark began his gospel by quoting John the Baptist who was pointing out there is a Spirit baptism.

Mark 1:8

8. **I indeed have baptized you with water: but He shall <u>baptize you with the Holy Ghost.</u>**

Therefore, Mark 16:16 actually confirms the doctrine of salvation, that you must first believe in Jesus' atoning work on the cross and then receive the Holy Spirit as your soul mate and spiritual covering. It is because of the Holy Spirit that you are born-again into the family of God and have a home in Heaven. Simply put, you first need to believe and then receive Jesus' Spirit into your heart, thus beginning the eternal relationship between you and God. So, an amplified Biblical reading of Mark 16:16 would be, "believeth and is baptized (with the Holy Ghost) shall be saved." In baseball terms, believing is like getting on base. It doesn't matter if you are on first, second, or third base, you need to get to home-plate (receive the Holy Spirit of Jesus) before the inning is over, to make it count on the scoreboard. It is after we believe: 1st base God is the creator, 2nd base Jesus is God and became a sinless man, 3rd base Jesus died for my sins and offers me salvation as a free gift, then I can get to home-plate receive salvation and make it count. It is after I believe and receive Jesus' Holy Spirit into my heart that I can be properly water baptized to celebrate and demonstrate my dedication to Jesus. *Selah.* Following Christ qualifies us to receive water baptism as well as a baptism of power. This is the anointing and supernatural ability to accomplish the work of God and expand the kingdom of God. *Selah.*

Reconciling Apparent Contradictions

The process of becoming a Christian is easy to explain once you understand the progression. However, it is a bit harder to explain why Christians hold worship services on Sunday, an apparent violation of the Fourth Commandment.

Exodus 20:8-11

8. **Remember the Sabbath day, to keep it holy.**

9. **Six days shalt thou labour, and do all thy work:**

10. **But the <u>seventh day is the Sabbath</u> of the Lord thy God: in it thou shalt not do any work, thou, nor thy son, nor thy daughter, thy manservant, nor thy maidservant, nor thy cattle, nor thy stranger that is within thy gates:**

11. **For in six days the Lord made Heaven and Earth, the sea, and all that in them is, and rested the seventh day: wherefore the Lord blessed the Sabbath day, and hallowed it.**

In the Ten Commandments, the Sabbath is Saturday, the last day of the week. It was a day to be dedicated to thanking God for His blessings, a day to enjoy the fruits of our labors, a day to relax, refresh, and refocus on our relationship with God. However, the Law provides an exception to this commandment for the priests of the temple.

Matthew 12:5

5. **Or have ye not read in the law, how that on the Sabbath days <u>the priests in the temple profane the Sabbath, and are blameless?</u>**

Hebrews 4:14

14. **Seeing then that we have a great <u>High Priest</u>, that is passed into heavens, <u>Jesus the Son of God</u>, let us hold fast our profession.**

Jesus' duties as our priest supersede the Law of the Sabbath. This does not mean that the law is void. Rather, it means that there are certain duties that take priority over and are exempted from this law. For perspective consider the law of gravity. Gravity is good; it holds us to the earth. We are subject to the law of gravity until we get onboard an airplane, and the law of aerodynamics takes over. Gravity still exists but when we are in a plane flying, we are enjoying a higher law. *Selah.* So how does this principle apply to us as believers?

Romans 12:5

5. **So we, being many, are one body <u>in Christ</u>, and every one members one of another.**

Romans 8:1-2

1. **There is therefore now <u>no condemnation to them which are in Christ Jesus</u>, who walk not after the flesh, but after the Spirit.**

2. **For the law of the Spirit of <u>life in Christ Jesus hath made me free</u> from the law of sin and death.**

Colossians 2:16

16. **Let no man therefore judge you in meat, or in drink, or in respect to an holyday, or of the new moon, or of the <u>Sabbath days</u>:**

Because Jesus Christ holds the office of priest, He is free to work on the Sabbath; and if I am "in Christ," then that same freedom applies to me. *Selah.* The principle of having a day of rest remains a blessing that we should enjoy.

Mark 2:27

27. **And He said unto them, The Sabbath was made for man, and not man for the Sabbath:**

CHAPTER 19
Reconciling Apparent Contradictions

The Bible acknowledges that in order to enjoy good health, we need our rest. We need a brake from the stresses of this life. We should also apply the Biblical information concerning what to eat and what not to eat. For example, our Creator points out in the Old Testament that it is not healthy to eat shellfish or pork products. This is not because they didn't have refrigerators to store their food. Most health food experts can explain the various problems with these foods. However, do not offend or insult anyone serving them to you. Just pray and enjoy their hospitality (1Corinthians 10:27). The Bible even tells us how to prepare and grow healthy food. For instance, don't eat the fat, drain the blood, and always cook the meat. The land should have a Sabbath year every seven years to rejuvenate nutrients for the crops. However, we do not have to be legalistic about these things, because they are addressing the temporary physical world more than the eternal spiritual world. In Heaven, none of these laws will apply to us. We will live by higher laws and principles. We will not need a Sabbath day to rest, because we will "run and not get weary" (Isaiah 40:28-31). In a sense, Heaven is a perpetual Sabbath. We will enjoy endless stress-free leisure time with God and no longer be subject to the stresses of this world that pull us down. *Selah.* Before we get to Heaven, we have special privileges and responsibilities. God has appointed us as ambassadors of His kingdom. We have received a pardon for our sins and have become part of a new royal priesthood.

1 Peter 2:9-10

⁹· **But ye are a <u>chosen generation, a royal priesthood</u>, an holy nation, a peculiar people; that ye should shew forth the praises of Him who hath called you out of darkness into His marvellous light:**

455

^{10.} **Which in time past were not a people, but are now the people of God: which had not obtained mercy, but now have obtained mercy.**

Because we are in the royal priesthood of Christ, we are free and not bound by the Sabbath law.

2 Corinthians 5:17-18, 20

^{17.} **Therefore <u>if any man be in Christ, he is a new creature</u>: old things are passed away; behold, all things are become new.**

^{18.} **And all things are of God, who hath reconciled us to Himself by Jesus Christ, and <u>hath given to us the ministry of reconciliation;</u>**

^{20.} **<u>Now then we are ambassadors for Christ</u>, as though God did beseech you by us: we pray you in Christ's stead, be ye reconciled to God.**

Since we are legally free, it is good for us to gather on Sundays to worship God. Sunday is a unique day of the week with special significance to our redemption. Sunday is the day of Jesus Christ's Resurrection. The first disciples came together on Sunday.

John 20:19

^{19.} **Then the same day at evening, being the <u>first day of the week</u>, when the doors were shut where <u>the disciples were assembled</u> for fear of the Jews, <u>came Jesus and stood in the midst, and saith unto them, Peace</u> be unto you.**

This was Resurrection Sunday, the same day as the first fruits wave offering according to Leviticus 23:10-12. There were special events in the Jewish year that only happened on Sunday. Starting

Reconciling Apparent Contradictions

at this first fruits Sunday as day one, the 50th day was the Sunday of Pentecost (which the Jews call the Feast of Weeks).

Leviticus 23:15-16

15. **And ye shall count unto you from the <u>morrow after the Sabbath</u>, from the day that ye brought the sheaf of the wave offering; seven Sabbaths shall be complete:**

16. **Even unto the <u>morrow after the seventh Sabbath</u> shall ye number fifty days; and ye shall offer a new meat offering unto the Lord.**

The definition of Pentecost is fifty. It was the day the Holy Spirit empowered the disciples for evangelism (Acts 2:1-11). Pentecost was on Sunday, the day "after the seventh Sabbath," the "first day of the week." Sunday is a spiritually significant day for the followers of Christ. You could say the birth of the church happened on Sunday. Sunday remained a day for first fruits offerings and for collections to help the saints in need.

1 Corinthians 16:1-2

1. **<u>Now concerning the collection for the saints</u>, as I have given order to the churches of Galatia, even so do ye.**

2. **<u>Upon the first day of the week</u> let every one of you lay by him in store, as God hath prospered him, that there be no gatherings when I come.**

Acts 20:7

7. **And <u>upon the first day of the week, when the disciples came together to break bread, Paul preached unto them</u>, ready to depart on the morrow; and continues his speech unto midnight.**

Christians gathered on Sundays to celebrate the rising of the Son, not the sun. The reason the early disciples habitually gathered on

457

CHAPTER 19
Deep Foundations

Resurrection Day was to praise God and remember Jesus with the Lord's Supper. They also honored God's Word and examined ways to apply it. They encouraged each other and gave offerings. We should continue to do the same. Any day people come together to do these things is a good day. *Selah.*

Keeping in mind everything we have seen up to this point, let's look at a verse that seems to contradict the doctrine concerning our fallen human nature presented previously in this book.

1 Thessalonians 5:23

23. **And the very God of peace <u>sanctify</u> you wholly: and I pray God your <u>whole spirit</u> and soul and body be preserved <u>blameless</u> unto the coming of our Lord Jesus Christ.**

My pastor from 1983 to 1990 went by the name of Pastor Rick. I shared my Biblical concepts regarding our human nature with him. Then Pastor Rick brought 1Thessalonians 5:23 to my attention. Because of this verse, I thought I was mistaken in my beliefs about our fallen human spirit and our need for it to be replaced. However, the Holy Spirit kept bringing to mind all the many references shared earlier until I knew for certain that the doctrine about our fallen human nature and its eventual removal was solid and true. One verse dose not completely redefine or disregard dozens of other verses on the same subject. This is where many become confused and go astray. Either their theology becomes out of balance creating the common divisions and heresies of our day or confusion sets in, robbing our zeal for the truth. Some have gone as far as becoming cynical about God and the Bible. God has all the answers but He is looking for true disciples that won't go astray as soon as they are confronted with a puzzling verse or perplexing Biblical concept.

CHAPTER 19
Reconciling Apparent Contradictions

John 6:66-67
66. From that time many of his disciples went back, and walked no more with him.

67. Then said Jesus unto the twelve, Will ye also go away?

God will communicate truth to the devoted.

Habakkuk 2:2-3
2. And the Lord answered me, and said, write the vision, and make it plain upon tables, that he may run that readeth it.

3. For the vision is yet for an appointed time, but at the end it shall speak and not lie: though it tarry, wait for it: because it will surely come, it will not tarry.

Habakkuk 2:2 became my pastor's favorite verse to quote for a while back in the 1980's but I was more focused on Habakkuk 2:3. *Selah.* Knowing the doctrine was strong, true, and balanced, I waited on God for years to help me understand this apparent contradiction. I still did not fully understand this contrary verse when God called me to start writing this book. I remember it was on a Thursday morning and I was sitting by the pool having my morning coffee talking with God. In my heart I heard Him say "Start the book today." I was a bit overwhelmed for a moment then I asked God to confirm His word to me. Latter that day, I came home for lunch and turned on the news as usual. As soon as the TV came on, it said, "Don't die without writing that book." I was a bit surprised, it was not the news but instead it was Pastor Rick on TBN. That day I got some 3X5 index cards and started writing down many of the Bible verses shared in this book. God continued to encourage and help me. I was on a major learning curve regarding book writing and publishing. A few years later, even though the manuscript was not quite ready, I printed 2500 hardcover books titled *Revelation Illumination*. It was the end of November 2012 when I took my car trailer from Florida to Ohio to pick up the books and start distributing them. On 4/27/2014 I started a YouTube video series on the book called *Deep Foundations*. I was nervous in front of the camera but confident in the information God gave me to present. I was also disappointed in the lack of interest in the classes. In spite of the lack of interest I was determined to finish the classes. God taught me a couple of things during that time. One of them had to do with this part of this chapter. 1Thessalonians 5:23 was still a little fuzzy to me and seemed unsettled. I studied the original language and could reconcile the verse, but it seamed to lac resolution. At the end of 2014 it was time to do a class video on the book's lasts chapter containing this puzzling verse. That is when God revealed to me a clear understanding of 1Thessalonians 5:23. It opened up insights to me I had never seen before. It was like being in a dark room with a penlight and someone suddenly turned on the floodlights. Everything became clear with the proper perspective. I saw a new dimension of truth, which inspired me to add chapter 4 to this edition of the book. I share this to illustrate that we may not have all the pieces of the puzzle and may feel unqualified when God calls us to do something. If we are faithful to God's Word, then eventually we will find it rewarding and transforming. We see this played out in the ten lepers Jesus cured.

Luke 17:14

14. **And when He saw them, He said unto them, Go shew yourselves unto the priests. And it came to pass, that, <u>as they went</u>, they were cleansed.**

God is looking for those that will trust Him and respond to His Word in spite of our limited knowledge and undesirable

Reconciling Apparent Contradictions

circumstances. *Selah.* Let's examine 1Thessalonians 5:23 and see if we can understand what God was saying though the Apostle Paul. Paul's statement is actually consistent with the mountain of God's Word, in spite of its contrasting appearance. The key confusing words are "whole spirit," especially when used in a phrase "spirit and soul and body." Remember from Chapter 2 that the definition of spirit is an "unseen motivator." This definition is always appropriate every place the word spirit is used. That alone clears up the other seemingly conflicting verses. Here the context appears to imply that the unseen motivator would be our human nature, because it is connected to the soul and body in this sentence. However, we know from many verses in the Bible that the human nature is corrupt and is to blame for most our bad actions. Therefore, it cannot be blameless. It is "desperately wicked" and will never be sanctified. Consequently, the depraved human spirit that corrupts the soul needs to be removed and replaced by the Divine Nature that we inherit by receiving the Holy Spirit. We closely examined the many scriptures pointing out these things earlier in this book. If we look again at 1Thessalonians 5:23 with that in mind, the verse states that your whole unseen motivator and "soul and body be preserved blameless..." Since the potentially blameless unseen motivator (spirit) is not our human nature, then what is it? Why is this verse in the Bible? Here is what the Holy Spirit pointed out to me before making the December 28 2014 YouTube video on this chapter. The first thing to realize is this is a concluding statement in a letter from Paul to the church at Thessalonica. It is sort of like the doxology hymn or word of blessing some churches end their Sunday service with. As a young man Paul was a Pharisee. He knew the Old Testament Scriptures very well. We can see what Paul is saying by looking at the Old Testament. Moses makes a parallel statement. Moses also addresses three separate areas we have that are capable of demonstrating love for God.

Deuteronomy 6:5

5. And thou shalt love the LORD thy God with all thine <u>heart</u>, and with all thy <u>soul</u>, and with all thy <u>might</u>.

This was a concluding summery of the 10 commandments given in the previous chapter of Deuteronomy. Every Jew was familiar with this statement in Deuteronomy 6:5. We see in the next several verses that they were told to pass it on to the next generation.

Deuteronomy 6:6-9

6. And these words, which I command thee this day, <u>shall be in thine heart</u>:

7. And thou shalt <u>teach them diligently unto thy children</u>, and shalt <u>talk of them</u> when thou sittest in thine house, and when thou walkest by the way, and when thou liest down, and when thou risest up.

8. And thou shalt bind them for a sign upon thine hand, and they shall be as frontlets between thine eyes.

9. And thou shalt <u>write them</u> upon the posts of thy house, and on thy gates.

Some Jews would literally bind these scriptures on their head or arm in a little box called a phylactery and many posted them on the doorpost of their home. *Selah.* Let's look at the similarities between Deuteronomy 6:5 and 1Thessalonians 5:23. When we fit them together they reveal what Paul was actually saying. Notice that the whole spirit is a reference to the whole heart not the human nature.

462

Reconciling Apparent Contradictions

Deuteronomy 6:5 *overlaid with* 1 Thessalonians 5:23

5. **And thou shalt love the LORD thy God with <u>all thine heart</u> (*whole spirit*), and with all thy <u>soul</u>, and with all thy (*body's*) might.**

1 Thessalonians 5:23 *overlaid with* Deuteronomy 6:5

23. **And the very God of peace <u>sanctify</u> you wholly: and I pray God your <u>whole spirit</u> (*heart*) and <u>soul</u> and (*strength or might of*) <u>body</u> be preserved <u>blameless</u> unto the coming of our Lord Jesus Christ.**

The three-fold cord of devotion starts with the heart illuminating the soul and finally leads to the body's actions of love and devotion. *Selah.* In this light it makes perfect sense and is in harmony with the all of God's Word. We could stop here knowing that there is no contradiction but lets go deeper to see the important truth reveled here which I shared in the original edition of this book. Using the *Strong's Exhaustive Concordance* we can look up the word "whole." Every verse containing that word will be listed. You can compare verses using that word, although this time we will look at the Greek word for "whole" located in 1Thessalonians. The *Strong's* Greek Concordance number for this word will be found at the end of the phrase. It is #3648. We then turn to the Greek dictionary in the back and see that the word #3648 is taken from two root words: #3650 which means "complete;" and #2819 which means "an acquisition, heritage, inheritance." Therefore, this phrase could read, "your whole acquired motivation." Where did this motivation come from? It's acquired. It's not natural, and we are not born with it. This particular motivation comes from our connection to the Divine Nature (the Holy Spirit). We receive the Divine Nature as an inheritance and heritage from Jesus. It is our choice to let God

Deep Foundations

motivate us completely and consistently or not. So, what is really being said in this verse? To get a clearer look at the truth revealed here and its relevance, let's step back and look at the big picture. It is important to remember that the Divine Nature is always good, and in God's eyes, the fallen human nature is always bad. They never change, but our connection to them is constantly changing. The connection is our conscious or subconscious choice to draw from a source that will become our inspiration or get us motivated. This connection is similar to the fuel hose we pull off the gas pump and insert into our car. The hose (representing our heart) is not the fuel, but it can transfer the fuel of our choice and refuel our car, or in this case, reenergize our soul's attitudes and body's actions. We can be naturally motivated, but we can also choose to circumcise the connection to the Old Man, refocus on our relationship with God and change our motivation. If we choose to change our motivation even in the middle of an action, it will spiritually alter the event. *Selah.* In an attempt to illustrate this potentially blameless motivating connection and how it works, I would like to share another more detailed metaphor. Let's imagine that the Divine Nature is a great spotlight and the fallen human nature a short-wave UV black-light. When unfiltered and activated, this black-light's illumination can damage our eyes and potentially cause blindness. Its UV rays can also cause cancer. Cancer is defined as rebellious cells clustering together. The short-wave UV black-light can also cause other mutations and damage our immune system as well. On the other hand, the spotlight is known for dispelling darkness and allowing us to see things more clearly. So, here we have two lights, a spotlight and a black-light. One is from Jesus, the wisdom of God, the "True Light" (John 1:1-9, John 3:19-21).

CHAPTER 19
Reconciling Apparent Contradictions

1 John 1:5

5. This then is the message which we have heard of Him, and declare unto you, that <u>God is light, and in him is no darkness at all</u>.

John 8:12

12. Then spake Jesus again unto them, saying, <u>I am the light of the world</u>: <u>he that followeth Me shall not walk in darkness</u>, but shall have the light of life.

John 12:46

46. I am come a light into the world, that <u>whosoever believeth on Me should not abide in darkness</u>.

Matthew 5:16

16. <u>Let your light so shine</u> before men, that they may see your good works, and glorify your Father which is in Heaven.

Ephesians 5:8

8. For ye were sometimes darkness, but now are ye light in the Lord: <u>walk as children of light</u>:

Acts 26:18

18. To open their eyes, and <u>to turn them from darkness to light</u>, and <u>from the power of Satan unto God</u>, that they may receive forgiveness of sins, and inheritance among them which are sanctified by faith that is in Me.

The Spirit of God is like a spotlight allowing us to see things more clearly. The black light is emanating from Lucifer the dark angel of light. Lucifer is the author of the "wisdom of this world" system. He attempts to replace the light of God with his distorted tainted light and is very deceptive in doing so.

Deep Foundations

2 Corinthians 11:14
14. **And no marvel; for Satan himself is transformed into an angel of light.**

In the following two translations of Isaiah 14:12 notice the subtle difference in the wording. They are both translating the same verse but use a different name in referring to Satan.

Isaiah 14:12 (King James Version)
12. **How art thou fallen from Heaven, O <u>Lucifer,</u> son of the morning! how art thou cut down to the ground, which didst weaken the nations!**

Isaiah 14:12 (New International Version)
12. **How you have fallen from heaven, <u>morning star,</u> son of the dawn! You have been cast down to the earth, you who once laid low the nations!**

The name Lucifer means light bearer and is a well-recognized name for Satan. The new MEV Bible uses the name Lucifer but some translations call Lucifer a bright star or morning star. The problem with calling Lucifer the "Morning Star" is that in every translation Jesus said He was the "Morning Star."

Revelation 22:16
16. **<u>I Jesus</u> have sent mine angel to testify unto you these things in the churches. <u>I am</u> the root and the offspring of David, and the bright and <u>morning star.</u>**

Satan would like us to believe he is the star and guiding light. Satan would like to confuse us, as to who is the Morning Star.

Revelation 2:28
28. **And I will give him the <u>morning star.</u>**

Reconciling Apparent Contradictions

Don't be confused about who's light God wants to give us. Don't allow Satan to brainwash and blind you.

2 Corinthians 4:4

4. **In whom the <u>god of this world hath blinded the minds of them which believe not</u>, lest the light of the glorious gospel of Christ, who is the image of God, should shine unto them.**

Ephesians 6:12

12. **For we wrestle not against flesh and blood, but against principalities, against powers, <u>against the rulers of the darkness of this world</u>, against <u>spiritual wickedness</u> in high places.**

The intensity of both types of lights can be adjusted brighter or dimmer, but they are what they are. They do not change their true identity or function. Our ability to be influenced by them comes from our connection to them. It is like a fiber optic bridge that comes into our soul and illuminates us with information. This fiber optic bridge is not the light source, but its appearance changes according to the light source to which it is connected. The true light from the Divine Nature or the black distorting light from the fallen nature identifies us and colors everything we see and do. It is this motivating light that comes to us from our nature, through the (heart) bridge, that brings the seed into the soul, identifying what kind of fruit we will bear; light or darkness.

Luke 11:35

35. **Take heed therefore that the light which is in thee be not darkness.**

Deep Foundations

Christian

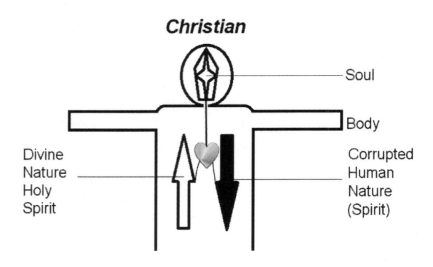

Our soul has a choice to receive or reject the thought seed. If we receive consistent seed, it will certainly bear fruit and come through our soul in the form of expressed ideas, actions, and attitudes. Sometimes it takes just one seed. *Selah.* We will be held accountable for what we permit to cross the bridge and bear fruit in our soul. We can attempt to stop or reduce the flow of traffic coming from our corrupted nature; although it is best to change the source of the thought traffic to the new identity (our new nature) and open up lanes for greater traffic flow. We do this by first getting to know God's Word. I enjoy listening to narrated Bibles to get the flow and context of the Scriptures. It is not a bad idea to play an audio Bible as you go to sleep or possibly even through the night. Try to open the Bible and prayerfully read something every day. Spend time casually taking with God throughout the day. Express to God your feelings and questions, as well as your hopes and concerns. Keep the lines of communication with God open.

1 Thessalonians 5:17

[17.] **Pray** without ceasing.

Reconciling Apparent Contradictions

In addition to spending time with God, we need to fellowship with God's people. We do this by attending a Bible believing church and getting involved there.

Hebrews 10:25

25. **Not forsaking the assembling of ourselves together, as the manner of some is; but exhorting one another: and so much the more, as ye see the day approaching.**

There is no perfect church. At this time, each and every one of us still has that trouble-making nature. It will show up at some point, causing friction and strife. This adversity gives us opportunity to encourage others and be encouraged to become stronger and walk in the light of *agape* love and forgiveness. *Selah.* We have the choice to be motivated and energized by God and walk in His light, or not. There are two internal sources for a Christian's inspiration and motivation which affect our attitudes and actions. In 1Thessalonians 5:23, Paul simply states that our motives are as important as our attitudes and actions in determining whether we will be held blameless and receive praise and rewards. These are the three categories God is looking at – motives, attitudes, and actions. This verse refers to these three areas as "spirit and soul and body." The potentially blameless "spirit" is speaking of our heart-felt motivations, not our species (nature). The "soul" in this verse represents our chosen attitude more than our given personality. Then there are our physical actions, both private and public, which are represented by the word "body." This verse gives us a standard by which to examine whether we will be "blameless" and eligible for wonderful everlasting rewards. We need to look at the action coming from our body that our soul is so exited about doing and see if our motivation is love and obedience to God or something

Deep Foundations

else. An interpretative reading of 1Thessalonians 5:23 could look like this:

AND THE VERY GOD OF PEACE: the source of satisfaction and fulfillment

SANCTIFY: sets us apart for special use and relationship

YOU WHOLLY: every part that should be dedicated unto God is reflecting Christ

AND I PRAY GOD: and in conclusion, my empowering request to our Creator for you is that

YOUR WHOLE SPIRIT: your acquired mind of Christ becomes your complete and consistent source for inspiration and heart-felt motivation

AND SOUL: your reputation for purity, fruitfulness, and a good attitude

AND BODY: your generosity, and wise actions of self-discipline

BE PRESERVED BLAMELESS: that you did what you were able to do in these three areas (Heart, Soul and Body) and received instruction and correction positively

UNTO: from now until you are completely delivered from sin and mortality

THE COMING OF OUR LORD: when the King of kings comes to establish His perfect kingdom and reward His people

JESUS CHRIST: our Redeemer and our Completer, our God and our Brother, our Friend and our Lord.

CHAPTER 19

Reconciling Apparent Contradictions

With the proper perspective and correct interpretation, there is no contradiction. But beware; we need to be cautious that an explanation is not actually a rationalization. That is why even with a good explanation of a puzzling verse it's still important to find a second witness or a back-up verse that states the same or similar thing. We found that in Deuteronomy 6:5 which we examined earlier. The Bible often calls for two or three witnesses to establish a matter. Are there other passages that support the use of the word "spirit" in 1Thessalonians 5:23 as a reference to our heart motivation? Paul, who God used to bring us 1Thessalonians 5:23, also gave us 1Corinthians 4:3-5, which focuses on the heart at judgment time. In verses 3 and 4 Paul reserves true judgment to God who knows us better than we know ourselves. In verse 5 he addresses Christ bringing everything into the light, even our thoughts and motivations.

1 Corinthians 4:5

5. **Therefore judge nothing before the time, until the Lord come, who both will <u>bring to light the hidden things</u> of darkness and will make manifest the <u>counsels of the hearts</u>: and then shall every man have praise of God.**

God sees these "counsels" that inspire and influence our actions as being connected to one of two types of hearts. One heart speaks with the selfish wisdom of this world and is in unity with the Deceiver himself. The other heart is connected to the heavenly Counselor, offering eternal wisdom rooted in love. We hear both of these counsels. The question is, which one do we plug into and consider, thereby receiving inspiration and motivation? It is our choice. God is looking at the hearts of mankind to see who He can use and rewarded with good fruit for their labor. We need to consider who is motivating us to see whether we will have true praise at judgment time and receive our eternal rewards. Or we may find that our motives polluted our actions and some of our rewards are history.

Matthew 6:1-6

1. **Take heed that ye do not your alms before men, to be seen of them: otherwise ye have no reward of your Father which is in Heaven.**

2. Therefore when thou doest thine alms, do not sound a trumpet before thee, as the hypocrites do in the synagogues and in the streets, that **they may have glory of men. Verily I say unto you, they have their reward.**

3. But when thou doest alms, let not thy left hand know what thy right hand doeth:

4. That thine alms may be in secret: and thy **Father which seeth in secret Himself shall reward thee openly.**

5. And when thou prayest, thou shalt not be as the hypocrites are: for they love to pray standing in the synagogues and in the corners of the streets, that **they may be seen of men. Verily I say unto you, they have their reward.**

6. But thou, when thou prayest, enter into thy closet, and when thou hast shut thy door, pray to thy Father which is in secret; and **thy Father which seeth in secret shall reward thee openly.**

We have covered a lot of complex subjects in this book. We need God's light to see things clearly. I believe that the more times you read this book in its entirety, including looking up all the Bible references, the more you will get out of it. The bottom line is that the Bible is true. Everything will make sense sooner or later as we read, meditate, and pray about what God has revealed to us in His Word.

CHAPTER 19
Reconciling Apparent Contradictions

1 Corinthians 2:12-14

12. Now we have received, not the spirit of the world, but the <u>Spirit which is of God; that we might know the things that are freely given to us of God</u>.

13. Which things also we speak, not in the words which man's wisdom teacheth, but which the <u>Holy Ghost teacheth; comparing spiritual things with spiritual</u>.

14. But the natural man receiveth not the things of the Spirit of God; for they are foolishness unto him: neither can he know them because they are spiritually discerned.

Proverbs 3:5-6

5. <u>Trust in the Lord</u> with all thine heart: and lean not unto thine own understanding.

6. In all thy ways acknowledge Him, and <u>He shall direct thy paths</u>.

Ephesians 1:17-18

17. That the God of our Lord Jesus Christ, the <u>Father of glory, may give unto you the spirit of wisdom and revelation in the knowledge of Him</u>.

18. The <u>eyes of your understanding being enlightened</u>; that ye may know what is the hope of His calling, and what the riches of the glory of His inheritance in the saints.

I believe that God would like to use this book to challenge all of us to know and trust the Bible as well as experience life at the highest standard. If the information in this book was helpful to you, I would like to ask you to tell your friends about Deep Foundations and post a comment to encourage others to read it. You may want to get a copy for your Pastor or Sunday-School teacher and discuss the contents of this book with them. I believe that if we expose and reject the deceiver's distortions of the truth by embracing and promoting God's Word, we will see victory and the kingdom of God will be expanded. Our dark world needs to see the light of truth. There are many that are discouraged and tired of the direction this world has been going. They are ready for revival. Please don't surrender to the deceiver or procrastinate in following what God is asking you to do today.

John 4:35

35. **Say not ye, There are yet four months, and then cometh harvest? behold, I say unto you, Lift up your eyes, and look on the fields; for they are white already to harvest.**

Satan wants to hide and divide us so he can continue to deceive and corrupt our communities. Satan wants us to fear correcting our commonly accepted unbiblical traditions and doctrines. Satan also wants us to pass his distortions of the truth onto the new believers as well as the next generation. God has a stern warning in Mark 7:7-9 for those that continue to do this. *Selah.* God wants us to unify and become one in revealing the Light of Truth. This does not mean we lose our individuality. God does not want us to become a clone of our neighbor or become hypocrites just ignorantly parroting each other. To illustrate what I'm saying, imagine that I have a guitar with only one string properly tuned. When I strum all the strings together it would sound terrible, even though one string is properly tuned. Now realize that if the world looks at the church and sees divisive competition, conflicting doctrines and traditions, and self-righteous attitudes, then it looks a lot like that guitar sounds, not very attractive. Jesus is the one string that is in tune with the Father. He is the Cornerstone that we need to find our place beside. As each individual comes into harmony with Jesus' Word and attitude,

Reconciling Apparent Contradictions

the tone becomes unified and amplified. When two strings get in the pocket of perfect pitch they become louder and take on a fuller sound than they could make separately. All of us need occasional tuning but imagine if, for a special period of time every string became tuned and more instruments joined the symphony of truth and love. Then we would see a Great Awakening of supernatural joy and celebration on a scale that is rare in this world. Many have heard the song "The Touch of the Master's Hand." It is about an old violin seemingly worthless because it was so badly out of tune. After the master tuned it, it became priceless. I want Jesus to tune me. Do you want Jesus to tune you? Jesus wants to tune the whole church, in order to empower it to ignite the next Great Awakening. Notice that near the end of Jesus' mortal life, how many times He prayed that we would be one in the truth.

John 17:17-23

17. **Sanctify them through Thy <u>truth</u>: Thy Word is <u>truth</u>.**

18. **As Thou hast sent Me into the world, even so have I also sent them into the world.**

19. **And for their sakes I sanctify Myself, that they also might be sanctified through the <u>truth</u>.**

20. **Neither pray I for these alone, but for them also which shall believe on Me through their word;**

21. **That they <u>all may be one</u>; as Thou, Father, art in Me, and I in Thee, that they also may be <u>one</u> in Us: <u>that the world may believe</u> that Thou hast sent Me.**

22. **And the glory which Thou gavest Me I have given them; that they may be <u>one</u>, even as We are <u>one</u>:**

Deep Foundations

23. I in them, and Thou in Me, that they may be made perfect in one; and that the world may know that Thou hast sent Me, and hast loved them, as Thou hast loved Me.

Jesus' prayer to the Father will be answered. The question is, will it be answered in our generation or will Jesus have to wait. If you understood chapter 6 of this book you know we have plenty of time for revivals and even another Great Awakening before the end of the world. *Selah.* The synergy of unity in Biblical truth has enormous power. The multiple points of light will drive back the promoters of evil darkness, which has blinded our world.

John 3:20-21 (NKJV)

20. For everyone practicing evil hates the light and does not come to the light, lest his deeds should be exposed.

21. But he who does the truth comes to the light, that his deeds may be clearly seen, that they have been done in God.

I believe the next Great Awakening starts with prayer and us being in harmony with God's Word in order to see God's extraordinary power manifested.

I humbly thank you for sharing your review of Deep Foundations with Amazon as well your friends, pastors, teachers and others.

May God empower and bless you.

John 8:32

32. And ye shall know the truth, and the truth shall make you free.

69486981R00269

Made in the USA
Middletown, DE
11 April 2018